The Economics of Europe and the European Union

This distinctive textbook combines comprehensive coverage of the key policy areas of the European Union with analysis of individual countries, including the recent accession countries and Turkey. Part I analyzes the economic bases for the rise of the European Union from its origins in the post-World War II recovery to its historic enlargement in 2004. Part II takes up the different nation state perspectives on the EU's economic policies by looking in turn at all European countries, whether members of the EU or not. The book is unique in providing both an EU perspective and European nation-state perspective on the major policy issues which have arisen since the end of World War II, as well as putting the economic analysis into a historical narrative which emphasizes the responses of policy-makers to external shocks such as the Cold War, oil shocks, German reunification, and the collapse of the Soviet Union.

Larry Neal is a Research Associate at NBER and Professor Emeritus of Economics at the University of Illinois at Urbana-Champaign, where he was Founding Director of the European Union Centre.

The Economics of Europe and the European Union

Larry Neal

CAMBRIDGE
UNIVERSITY PRESS

CAMBRIDGE UNIVERSITY PRESS
Cambridge, New York, Melbourne, Madrid, Cape Town, Singapore, São Paulo, Delhi

Cambridge University Press
The Edinburgh Building, Cambridge CB2 8RU, UK

Published in the United States of America by Cambridge University Press, New York

www.cambridge.org
Information on this title: www.cambridge.org/9780521683012

© Larry Neal 2007

First published 2007
Reprinted 2008

Printed in the United Kingdom at the University Press, Cambridge

A catalogue record for this publication is available from the British Library

ISBN 978-0-521-86451-0 hardback
ISBN 978-0-521-68301-2 paperback

Contents

Part I   The economics of the European Union

Part II   The economies of Europe

Figures

Tables

Boxes

Part I

The economics of the European Union

Old Europe, new Europe: the role of the European Union

In Athens, Greece, origin of the Western ideals of democracy and human rights, the heads of government of twenty-five European nation states gathered to sign the Treaty of Accession into the European Union on April 16, 2003. Fifteen nations were already member states of the European Union and they had unanimously agreed to accept all ten of the accession states into their club, out of the thirteen candidate countries that had applied. But the agreement was conditional on each of the ten applicants agreeing to accept all the existing rules of the club as explained to them and interpreted by the fifteen incumbents (the so-called *acquis communautaire* of the European Union). Further, each of the ten applicants had to demonstrate to the satisfaction of the incumbents not only that they accepted all the *acquis* but that they were capable of putting it into practice on their own, without extensive subsidies or technical assistance from the existing members. Throughout the rest of the year each accession state put the treaty to a referendum of their voters, and in May 2004 the European Union expanded its size to twenty-five member states, with a population of 454.5 million and an estimated gross domestic product (GDP) of $10.3 trillion, making it the largest economy in the world, surpassing the United States of America, with its fifty states, 280.5 million people, and GDP of $10.1 trillion.[1]

The terms on which the ten new members entered the European Union were extensive: 80,000 pages of existing rules, regulations, directives, and laws that the fifteen existing members had accumulated over the previous forty-five years were divided up into thirty-one separate chapters that each applicant had to transpose into its own legal and political system. The terms were also rigorous: the new members had to take on the obligations of full membership immediately but were forced to phase in gradually the benefits of access to the agricultural supports, regional funds, and the single market in goods, services, labor, and capital. Even before being considered as candidates for membership, the accession countries had to meet the so-called "Copenhagen criteria," criteria agreed on by the fifteen incumbents at the European Council meeting at Copenhagen in 1993. This meant that each applicant had to demonstrate to the satisfaction of the existing members of the European Union that:

(1) it had a functioning democracy, with the rule of law and respect for human rights;

(2) it had a functioning market economy capable of withstanding the competition from the more advanced market economies of the European Union without recourse to extensive subsidies or protective measures; and

(3) it had the administrative capability to implement and enforce the *acquis* of the European Union with its own civil servants.

Meanwhile, all twenty-five nations, incumbent and the accession states alike, were participating in a Constitutional Convention with the goal of replacing the existing institutional structure and operating procedures with a simpler, more coherent system that would enable the twenty-five to accomplish their common goals expeditiously and efficiently. The Constitutional Convention recognized that, with the major expansion of 2004, the European Union had outgrown its operational framework. Its set of institutions and procedures had been put together, piece by piece, over the past forty-five years on the basis of the shared goals of a much smaller number of countries, each led by a generation of politicians determined never to let something as terrible as World War II occur again on their land or with their people. With the collapse of the Soviet Union and the strong reaction of the central and eastern European countries against centrally planned economies and monolithic political control by the Communist Party, the division of Europe created after World War II could be undone at last. Once again, the vision of a united Europe, at peace within itself and with its neighbors, enjoying economic prosperity and unleashing the creative potential of its population, seemed within reach. But how could this be accomplished in a lasting way, not to be undone by provoking military responses from a threatened Russia or the Islamic world? The Constitutional Convention of the European Union was a concerted effort to build upon the proven accomplishments of the past half-century of recovery from World War II among the nation states of western Europe.

Unfortunately for the good intentions of the Convention delegates, both the French and Dutch voters rejected ratification of the proposed constitution in successive referendums held in May 2005. What this means for the future reforms of the European Union's institutions is unclear, but what is clear is that the failure of the referendums in two countries at the heart of Europe stemmed more from citizens' concerns about their economic future than from concerns about the effective operation of the European Union. The interplay of the economic policies of the European Union, operating as a supranational organization, with the economic policies of the individual member states, responding as sovereign nation states to the demands of their respective electorates, therefore, will determine the future of the political organization of Europe. Hence the structure of the present work, which analyzes first the economic policies of the European Union and then the economic results for the individual European economies.

This volume attempts to frame these economic issues in a coherent analytical framework found useful by economists, but especially by economic historians, in their efforts to understand the continuing interplay between economics and politics. The New Institutional Economics, first developed by economic historians Douglass North and Lance Davis, takes for granted that political institutions, which set the "rules of the game" for economic activity, are designed to protect and sustain the economic welfare of the governing classes. Institutions change only slowly in response to economic forces over time, but are forced to make more drastic changes the longer they delay in reform or the more troublesome their results are in the face of economic changes. At the heart of Europe's economic difficulties today are the desires of citizens in both the fifteen incumbent nation states and the ten accession nation states to maintain and improve their economic welfare in the face of rapid technological changes and the expansion of global economic markets for capital, labor, goods, and services. Moreover, globalization creates more frequent and more severe shocks economically than Europe has experienced since World War II. It is precisely the ability of Europe's economic institutions to respond effectively to the shocks of globalization that concerns European policy-makers and citizens.

The Constitutional Convention

The Constitutional Convention was motivated by a concern that building the enlarged European Union on the basis of the existing *acquis* will create institutional rigidities that will fail under the duress of future shocks, whether they arise from technological changes, military threats, natural disasters, or terrorist attacks. To date, the creation of the *acquis* has been cumulative; an institutional ratchet effect has been deliberately installed so that no reversals of course are possible. For example, there has never been an "exit clause" in any of the treaties forming the basis of the European Union, so that no country has the legal option of withdrawing from the European Union once it has entered. Moreover, there is no provision for expelling a member country even when its absence is heartily desired by the other members! The proposed constitution made explicit both that a member could withdraw and that a member could be expelled. It may well be that the vision of a united Europe, prosperous and peaceful, would be better served by a complementary process of *debarras communal* – regular removals of practices and policies that are no longer useful for Europe as a whole, even if particular interest groups have come to rely on them.

For political scientists, the fascination of the exercise of trying to formulate a written and durable constitution for the European Union is considerable; will these twenty-five sovereign nation states, each with a proud national identity and a history of frequent warfare with its neighbors, be able to devise a workable arrangement? The current organization is a set of ad hoc arrangements that have arisen to meet various challenges realistically, while maintaining the possibility that the ideal of a pan-European superstate might some day be achieved. Idealists characterize the existing structure as resting on three pillars.

Pillar 1, the European Community, which deals with the Common External Tariff and all trade issues with the rest of the world, the Common Agricultural Policy, structural funds, the single market, the common currency – in short, with all the matters that are discussed and analyzed in detail in part I of this book.

Pillar 2, the Common Foreign and Security Policy, which deals with European initiatives to develop a common stance on foreign policy issues, as well the creation of the military apparatus necessary to achieve the agreed policy goals.

Pillar 3, Justice and Home Affairs, which deals with maintaining a common border policy with respect to refugees, and creating a common European police force with common domestic security objectives, such as coping with drug traffic and terrorists.

The European Union considers that it is a *supranational organization* to date only with respect to Pillar 1, because it is only in these matters that the member states have formally ceded some of their sovereignty to the decision-making bodies of the European Union. Under Pillars 2 and 3, by contrast, each member state must agree if it is willing to cooperate with the others on any of the initiatives undertaken, which makes the European Union an inter-governmental organization in these matters, at least to date. To deal with all the issues that arise under each of the three pillars, the fifteen member states, as of 2003, had developed six basic institutions, each with unique characteristics that – in combination – make the European Union such a fascinating object of study for political scientists. They can be roughly thought of as comprising the executive (or administrative), legislative, and judicial branches of government.

The *executive branch*, charged with initiating legislation and then administering the operation of the European Union's activities, is the European Commission, headquartered in Brussels, divided into twenty directorates and overseen by the President of the Commission. The directors are allocated among the member states, each state being entitled to one director, with the largest five states entitled to two each. The President is nominated by the European Council and approved by the European Parliament. The Commission, while charged with drafting legislation and then managing and administering the competences of the European Union, has only limited enforcement powers, as it must call upon the police authorities of the member states to enforce its decisions. In case of continued non-compliance, it is confined to levying fines upon member states. Real power, however, can be and is exercised by the European Council, the heads of government of each member state. They have full police powers at their disposal within their respective countries, so if they agree upon a course of action it will usually be made effective. Because all member states are parliamentary democracies, in which the head of government is determined by the legislative majority in the parliament, the necessary legislation will also be enacted to carry out the consensus policy of the European Council.

The *legislative branch* has two components: the Council of Ministers, with real power vested in it by the governments of the member states as each country is represented by the relevant minister from its governing Cabinet; and the European Parliament, which has mainly symbolic power, based on popular elections of its members throughout the European Union's member states. The Council of Ministers is usually composed of the foreign ministers from each member state, but if the matter to be decided is agricultural policy, for example, the agriculture ministers will comprise the Council for agricultural legislation. Increasingly, over time, the European Parliament has taken a more substantive role in forcing modifications, or at least delay, in legislation passed by the Council. With the Treaty of Amsterdam, signed in 1997, the Parliament became a more powerful legislative partner, taking on co-decision authority over most of the EU's legislation. The power of the purse, which historically has determined the power of parliaments in the evolution of Western democracies, is kept by the Council, however, and each successive treaty has insisted that the European Union operate annually on a balanced budget. The constitution would, however, give the European Union legal personality, meaning that it could issue debt in its own name in the future. In the meantime, the European Council must decide the funding provided over a seven-year period,

2000–2006 and 2007–2013. The Parliament can, however, reject, the entire budget proposals of the Commission, even when approved by the Council of Ministers. As this would also mean cutting off the substantial salaries and expense accounts of Members of the European Parliament (MEPs) until the Council of Ministers came to terms, however, it is doubtful that this power would ever be exercised.

The *judicial branch* also has two components: the European Court of Justice, with a judge appointed from each member state and a Chief Justice elected among them; and the Court of First Instance. The Court of Justice is charged with ruling on matters of dispute between the European Union and any of its member states or citizens, including corporations and other non-governmental organizations, as well as interpreting the accumulated treaty provisions as they apply to the external relations of the European Union with non-member states. The Court of First Instance is devoted to dealing with an increasingly important aspect of European Union enforcement powers: competition policy. It has final say over disputes between individual firms or governments and the Commission over interpretation of the single market's directives and can levy fines as well as force divestitures by firms. An economist might want to add as well the Court of Auditors, which is charged with auditing the accounts of the Commission to ensure that balanced budgets are maintained and that expenditures are in accord with the legislative decisions of the Council and the European Parliament. It, too, can levy fines or require repayment of EU funds judged to have been ill-spent by the recipients.

To these basic political institutions, which can readily be divided into those that correspond to an intergovernmental organization (the European Council, the Council of Ministers, and the Court of Auditors) and those that correspond to a supranational organization (the Commission, the Parliament, and the Courts of Justice and First Instance), the European Union created the European Central Bank in 1999, charged with the creation of the common currency, the euro, the unit of account for all financial operations of the European Union and the national unit of account for initially eleven of its fifteen incumbent members, and then twelve, when it was adopted by Greece in 2001.

For economists the European Central Bank (ECB), the most recent institutional innovation of the European Union, is the most interesting, precisely because it has been made as independent as possible from the political institutions of the European Union (just described above) and, moreover, from the political institutions of the individual nation states. Not only is the European Central Bank located in Frankfurt, Germany, away from Brussels, Luxembourg, and Strasbourg, where the political institutions of the European Union are located, but its President is appointed for a fixed term of eight years by the heads of government in the European Council. Note that all heads of government of member states are elected, not appointed, and their term of office is always less than eight years, so the President of the European Central Bank has real political independence, as do the Vice-President and the four other members of the Executive Board, all of whom are appointed for fixed terms. While the Executive Board is responsible for the daily operation of the ECB, the strategic decisions are taken by the Governing Council, which consists of the six members of the Executive Board plus the governors of the national central banks that have adopted the euro. But each governor of a participating national central bank is also required to be independent of his or her government.

For economists enamored of the virtuous performance historically of politically independent central banks, the unprecedented degree of political independence of the European Central Bank augurs well for the future of the euro and the monetary policy of the eurozone. For historians, noting that monetary policy has always been driven in the past by political considerations, the lack of political support for the ECB other than international treaty is bothersome. How will the ECB be able to withstand popular discontent if its pursuit of price stability is seen as damaging to the achievement of other goals, such as full employment, or economic growth? By treaty, the European Central Bank is charged with maintaining price stability within the European Union and has been given complete control over the supply of the common currency. To date, however, it has not been given regulatory authority over the financial sectors of the member states, which means that financial innovations may occur that will disrupt the relationship between the rate of growth of the money supply and the rate of inflation within the EU.

Adventurous as this innovation in monetary policy is, economists also find the efforts to wrest control of fiscal policy from the hands of political authorities even more interesting, even bizarre. Prior to adopting the common currency and ceding control of monetary policy to the European Central Bank, each participating government was required to meet the so-called Maastricht criteria. There were five criteria:

(1) maintain inflation rates within one percentage point of the average of the three lowest rates of inflation within the European Union;
(2) maintain interest rates within one percentage point of the average of the lowest rates of interest on long-term government bonds within the European Union;
(3) maintain the exchange rate of the national currency within 2% of parity with the euro (known as the European Currency Unit, or ECU, prior to 1999) for at least two years;

(4) maintain a government deficit equivalent to less than 3% of gross domestic product; and

(5) maintain a ratio of government debt to GDP of less than 60%.

The Maastricht criteria were designed to ensure that each participating country was already committed to, and capable of, achieving price stability on its own. The first three criteria are really three different, and redundant, ways of measuring price stability. If the third criterion was achieved – maintaining a stable exchange rate with respect to the common currency – then the inflation targets and interest rate targets should follow as a matter of course. To the extent that long-term interest rates reflect inflation risk, they should fall as inflation is controlled within a country. Only if a country's inflation rate is close to that of its trading partners will its exchange rate be stable as well. The three criteria were presumably intended to protect against a country using special interventions for a limited period of time to maintain exchange rate stability or low inflation rates, or reduced interest rates, while letting one or more of the other measures of price stability absorb the pressures of inflation.

The final two measures, however, went a step further, and were presumably designed to ensure that a country did not build up pressures to increase the quantity of money in order to finance excessive government expenditures. Inflationary potential would then be indicated by persistent large deficits on the part of the government and by a mounting size of government debt relative to gross domestic product. Weak governments faced with such situations have typically resorted to forcing the central bank to supply it with fresh money, leading to inflationary spirals. In the event, any number of governments exceeded the debt limit when the deadline for monetary union approached in 1999, but if they had succeeded in meeting the monetary goals (the first three Maastricht criteria) it turned out that they met the deficit criterion as well and therefore could show progress toward meeting the debt, and final, criterion. Was this a temporary effect, created mainly by refinancing existing debt with lower interest-bearing debt, or a permanent result of institutional reform? Just to make sure that there would be no backsliding by new governments, a supplementary agreement was signed, called the Stability and Growth Pact.

The *Stability and Growth Pact* has less authority than a treaty, but pledges each member state of the eurozone to keep future government deficits below 3% of gross domestic product, with a penalty assessed on any country that violated this limit. Rightly labeled by Romano Prodi, President of the European Commission, as one of the dumbest economic arrangements ever made, the Stability and Growth Pact has been violated persistently by France and

Germany, precisely the two countries most insistent on creating the pact in the first place. After both countries had violated the 3% limit of government deficits for three years running, with no end in sight, the Council of Ministers in 2005 worked out a "reinterpretation" of the Stability and Growth Pact, designed to make it more workable without shelving it entirely.

In the future, governments violating the 3% limit due to special circumstances that made unusual funding demands upon the government could exclude those expenditures from the calculation of the deficit. Germany was especially successful in arguing that the reunification expenses required to bring the infrastructure of the former East Germany up to West Germany's standards should not be included when calculating its deficits. These have continued for fifteen years, however, so a cynic might argue that Germany was able to define away a self-imposed expenditure. Other countries, seeing the opportunity to make similar self-serving definitions of parts of their expenditures, such as disaster relief, construction of large infrastructure projects (e.g. the Olympic facilities constructed by Greece for the 2004 games), went along. Essentially, this compromise solution eliminated the Stability and Growth Pact as a commitment mechanism to keep the budgets of member states in line.

The budget of the European Union

The fastidious concern of the EU over the possibility that some sovereign nation states might abuse their access to a common pool of resources, the supply of money in the case of the eurozone, is the outcome of experience with financing the European Union itself. By treaty, the European Union is required to operate on a balanced budget from year to year, and it is not allowed to issue bonds of any kind. For the first twelve years of its existence the European Union, then known as the European Economic Community (EEC), with the European Coal and Steel Community (ECSC) and Euratom affiliated with it, subsisted on annual grants from the member states, although the ECSC had its own source of revenue from a commission on sales of coal and steel.

The original six founding members agreed that the EEC should have its "own resources," derived from the tariff revenues it collected under the Common External Tariff (CET) agreed upon by all member countries of the EU, plus – later – the levies imposed on agricultural imports under the Common Agricultural Policy (CAP). For reasons explored in detail in chapter 4, these own resources proved increasingly inadequate to finance the expenditures required by the price support programs of the CAP, so they were expanded to include a

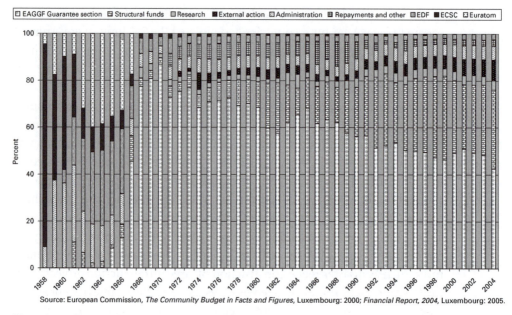

Source: European Commission, *The Community Budget in Facts and Figures,* Luxembourg: 2000; *Financial Report, 2004,* Luxembourg: 2005.

Figure 1.1 EU expenditures by category, 1958–2004

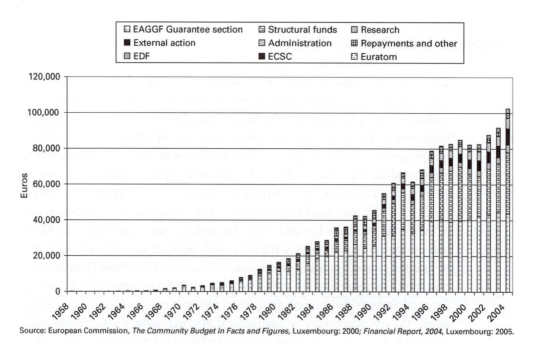

Source: European Commission, *The Community Budget in Facts and Figures,* Luxembourg: 2000; *Financial Report, 2004,* Luxembourg: 2005.

Figure 1.2 Growth of the EU budget by category, 1958–2004

small fraction of the value added taxes collected by each member state government (the Luxembourg Agreement, 1970). While each government entering the European Union had to adopt a value added tax as its main form of indirect tax on the sales of goods and services, it remained the sovereign decision of each country to determine both the tax base (the range of goods and services that would be subject to the tax) and the tax rate (the rate of taxation on each good or service subject to the tax). Consequently, the share of "own resources" of the EU in this form varied widely from member to member, with the poorer members finally realizing that what they were paying was more, as a share of their gross domestic product, than the richer members were paying.

Realization of the inequity created by using the value added tax as a base for assessment of the member states led to the creation of the fourth "own resource" of the EU. This is a fixed (and tiny) share of each country's GDP, to be contributed annually, as well as a fixed share of the value added tax (the Delors Agreement, 1987). Figure 1.3 shows the relative share of each of the four main sources of revenue for the operations of the EU from 1971 through 2005. For the period 2000 through 2006 the EU's "financial perspective" limited the total of all sources of revenue to an upper limit of 1.27% of the combined GDP of the fifteen member states, and then limited expenditures on all categories to no more than 1.13% to 1.18% of total GDP. The initial discussions over the next seven-year period, 2007–2013, began with agreement among the incumbent member states that all sources of revenue would be kept under an upper limit of 1% of the combined GDP of the twenty-five member states.

What all this means is that the financing of the EU is limited by the willingness of the member states to release part of their revenues to the common pool of resources. From an economist's perspective, then, the EU is clearly an intergovernmental organization. As the governments of the members pay the bills in agreed proportions, they clearly feel justified in determining the policies of the EU, especially as to where the money is spent within the EU. The history of the EU's budget, therefore, can be seen as a continuing effort by political idealists to release the EU from the constraints on activities implied by the intergovernmental character of its financing. The ideal of achieving a supranational European Union has always been confronted by the resistance of the individual governments, concerned that they get a good return nationally on the dues they have paid to the EU.

These concerns have, naturally, led to a close examination by each country of how much it pays in compared to how much it receives in money benefits. For many years, this kind of exercise was rejected by the Commission, as it was clearly antithetical to the mission of the EU, which the Commission felt

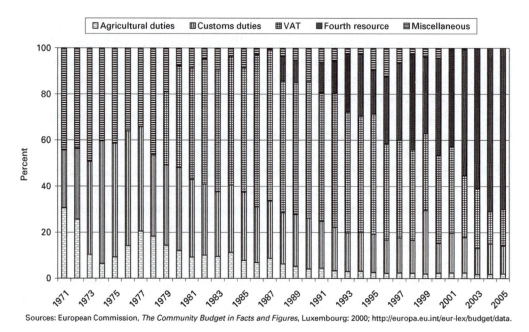

Sources: European Commission, *The Community Budget in Facts and Figures*, Luxembourg: 2000; http://europa.eu.int/eur-lex/budget/data.

Figure 1.3   Composition of EU revenues, 1971–2005

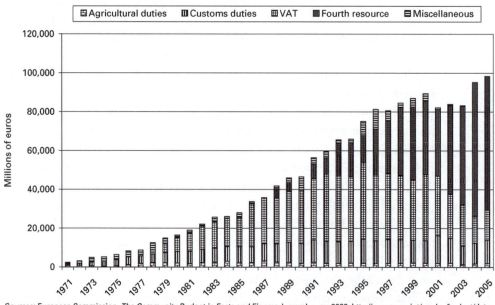

Sources: European Commission, *The Community Budget in Facts and Figures*, Luxembourg: 2000; http://europa.eu.int/eur-lex/budget/data.

Figure 1.4   Growth of the EUs "own resources," 1971–2005

was to gain increases in output for all in a common market, not to redistribute resources among the member states. Nevertheless, British economists in particular found this a useful exercise after Britain joined in 1973. By then, the Common Agricultural Policy was in full swing, based on price supports pegged above world market levels in order to encourage self-sufficiency in food. The United Kingdom, by contrast, had abandoned price supports after World War II in order to give its industrial, urban population the benefit of the lowest prices available on world markets. By adopting the CAP, the United Kingdom ended up raising food prices to its consumers, but turned the excess over world prices back to the European Economic Community in the form of agricultural levies. With by far the smallest share of its labor force in agriculture among the members of the EEC at the time, Britain received little in the form of agricultural subsidies for its few farmers.

Putting up with paying in much more than it was receiving from the EEC for a number of years, Britain finally received a rebate on its payments in 1984. The *British rebate* has continued through the financial perspective of 2000–2006. Given the implications that a rebate might well be in order for other member states, the Commission began to keep track itself of the way each member state paid toward the budget of the EU and how much benefit each member state received from each of the EU's programs. Moreover, as the listing of EU agencies and their headquarters in http://europa.eu/agencies/community_agencies/index_en.htm shows, the EU has diligently spread the offices for its various community activities among all the member states. This gives the citizens of each member state a visible sign of the benefits they receive from the EU in return for the resources they have committed to Brussels.

For example, figure 1.5 compares the level of EU spending in each member with the resources taken by the EU from each in 1998, whatever the form of spending or the category of resource turned over. Clearly, in that year, as in most, Germany and the United Kingdom were net contributors on a large scale to the EU, and the United Kingdom's net contribution remained after receiving a substantial rebate of nearly €3.2 billion. Small wonder that Germany then began to make noises that it, too, deserved a rebate! Instead, Germany and France cooperated to set the limits on both the total revenues of the EU and as a percentage of the EU gross domestic product. Further, they set limits on the proportion of total expenditures that could be taken by the price support programs of the CAP. What figure 1.5 does show as well is that the richer countries within the EU were all net contributors, while the poorer countries – Spain, Greece, Ireland, and Portugal – were all net beneficiaries. Looked at this

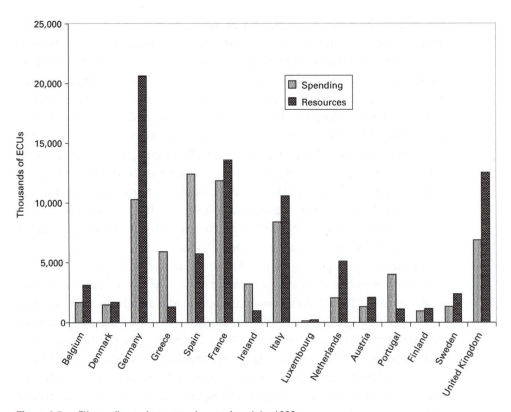

Figure 1.5   EU spending and resources by member state, 1998

way, the EU over time has become, in fact, a redistributive agency, taking from the wealthier, larger members and giving to the poorer, smaller members.

The seven-year perspective had been introduced in 1988 by Jacques Delors, then President of the Commission, so that the annual wrangles over how to deal with the frequent budget overruns (caused by the unpredictable outlays committed under the Common Agricultural Policy) were eliminated. Now the budget has to be balanced over a seven-year period, which could allow some latitude for budget deficits in any given year. Even these, however, are forestalled by limiting the total expenditure allowed in a year for agricultural subsidies and structural funds, which account for the bulk of the EU expenditures. The proposed constitution that was rejected in 2005 included provisions that were intended to ameliorate some of the problems of the budget, which has strayed greatly from the ideals laid out by the founding fathers of the EU. With the rejection of the constitution, the EU budget will continue to be a contentious issue, especially because the voting power of the richer countries remains less than it would have been had the constitution been adopted. In the financial perspective of 2000–2006, explicit provision was made for helping the accession countries adapt to the *acquis* of the EU by providing increasing amounts to them from 2002 through 2006. Since their accession in 2004, however, the ten new members have a voice in determining EU policies and a common cause to extract maximum benefits from their wealthier neighbors to the west.

An important aspect of the constitution is that it would have, for the first time, given legal personality to the EU. Legal personality means that the EU, on its own recognizance, could have entered into treaties and contracts with other legal persons – including other nation states, but also corporations, households, and individual citizens of whatever country. Legal personality also means that the EU would have been able to issue debt in its own name, something explicitly forbidden to it to date. Explicit provision was also made that the EU could, had the constitution been adopted, levy taxes in its own name to fund its activities, including, presumably, the servicing of its own debt instruments. As it is, the EU is confined to acting as a coordinating agent for raising funds from the member states to carry out activities for which it is responsible – for example, the reconstruction of Kosovo.

Another provision suggested in the constitution would allow the EU to have its "own resources," which could be limited to the existing set of revenue sources, but would open the door to levying some kind of tax or user fee. That would be necessary to give credible backing to any debt it might issue in the future. Of course, all this is speculation, because it is certain that the EU constitution will constrain it to have a balanced budget annually. But the ability to issue the equivalent of tax anticipation notes (something any local school district in America can do) would allow the EU to be much more effective in carrying out the policies assigned to it, whatever they may be in the future.

The Nice Treaty

The Nice Treaty of December 2000 was finally ratified by all fifteen member states by February 2003. Its importance lay in determining the representation of all twenty-seven potential members in the two legislative branches of the European Union – the Council of Ministers and the European Parliament. As only the twenty-five member states have been subject to the terms of the Nice Treaty since May 2004, figure 1.7 shows the relative weights of each

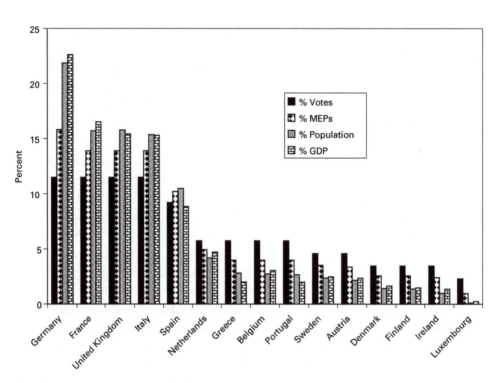

Figure 1.6 EU-15, pre-2004 arrangements

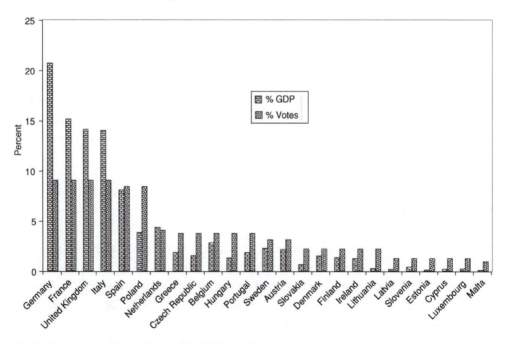

Figure 1.7 Weights of votes in Council and GDP for EU-25

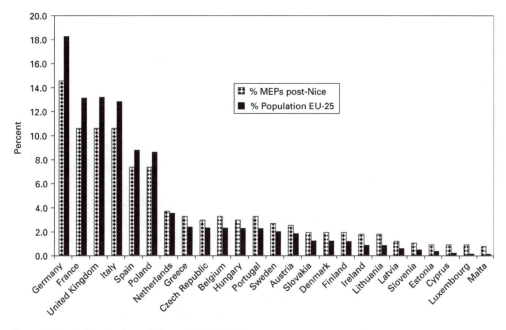

Figure 1.8   Political and population weights, EU-25

in the Council of Ministers, which remains the dominant legislative branch, compared with the weights of each country in the total GDP of the expanded European Union. It is evident that voting strength is deliberately "degressive," to use the word inserted into the May draft of the constitution. In other words, the political structure of the EU is intended to continue to give the smaller countries sufficient influence that they can defend their national interests against the exercise of economic power by their larger neighbors. In particular, the accession countries will be well over-represented within the deliberations over future EU policies.

Figure 1.8 compares the relative weights of each of the twenty-five countries in the European Parliament with the relative size of each country's population in the expanded European Union. The number of Members of the European Parliament allotted to each country more nearly represents the relative size of each country – in particular, Germany now has more MEPs than any other country, although its votes in the Council of Ministers are the same as for France, Italy, and the United Kingdom. Nevertheless, the political intent is again clearly to favor the smaller countries over the larger countries. It seems evident that redistribution of EU resources in favor of smaller, poorer countries will continue to be the economic outcome in the future, as it has been in the past. This is especially the case since the constitution, which would have modified the voting structure agreed upon in the Nice Treaty more in favor of the large, rich countries, was rejected in 2005.

Conclusion

This brief overview of the current and projected state of the finances of the European Union and the political arrangements that determine them should have convinced the reader that the EU is, as its publicists proclaim, a unique experiment. In many respects, it appears to be internally contradictory among its stated goals, as well as in the means chosen to achieve them. While trying to be innovative in order to avoid the tragedies of Europe's past, the architects of the EU have insisted on maintaining as long as possible each program that has been developed, simply adding new ones to the existing panoply of competences as needed. The Constitutional Convention of 2003 was responsible for drafting a constitution that would simplify and rationalize the *acquis communautaire* that the previous fifteen member states have accumulated, and have insisted upon encumbering the accession states with all of it. But the ten accession states will have a major voice – indeed, an over-represented voice – in the ratification, and amendment, of the proposed constitution now that they are full voting members. It is ironic, therefore, that rejection of the constitution came from popular votes within two of the original founding member states of the EU – France and the Netherlands.

In sorting out which of the programs have proven their long-run value and which have long outgrown their usefulness, all twenty-five member states will have to consider, first, how these programs evolved into their current state and, second, how their own national economic self-interest might best be served. The non-member states will also have to consider whether they wish to join on the terms dictated by the existing members, or whether their interests are best served by negotiating special arrangements. The rest of the world has a great stake in the final outcome, as European failures to achieve peaceful solutions to their problems in the past have inflicted grievous harm to the rest of the world, as well as to the inhabitants of Europe. The remainder of this book is intended as a helpful guide for all concerned, first, to the historical development of the economic policies of the European Union and, second, to the economic issues confronting the various economies of Europe, both the members and non-members of the European Union. The European Union epitomizes what impatient Americans have dismissively termed "old

Europe." The accession countries, and not a few of the current members who have joined in previous enlargements, may prefigure a "new Europe." Such sweeping generalizations, however, always founder when confronted with the details of the real world, always more complicated than one would like. It's to these details of the "economics of Europe" at the outset of the twenty-first century that we must now turn.

NOTE

1. Source: Central Intelligence Agency, *World Factbook 2002*, available at http://www.cia.gov/cia/publications/factbook/. Population and GDP figures are estimates for 2002, and GDP is measured in terms of 1999 purchasing power parity (PPP) dollars, to make international comparisons possible.

2 A dispute over origins: the European view versus the American perspective

Today the leaders of both the European Union and the United States proclaim the strength of their ties and mutual support for each other's policies and values. It is certainly the case that economic relationships are deeply embedded, given the extent of trade and investment between the two economic superpowers. But conflicts arise repeatedly, sometimes leading to economic sanctions imposed as temporary surtaxes on the imports from the trading partner found guilty of violating international agreements according to the World Trade Organization (WTO). Each party feels especially aggrieved when the other does not appear to share its concern to maintain a particular policy that has been taken for granted as part of the shared heritage of the Atlantic community. Such misunderstandings and mutual exasperations date back to the origins of the European Union in the immediate aftermath of World War II. It's useful for understanding the sources of continued tension in EU–US relations to take a fresh look at the period before the creation of the European Economic Community in 1958. Over this formative period, 1945–58, both European leaders and American policy-makers laid down the foundations that set the course of development for the European Union and the individual nations that emerged from Nazi domination. On both sides of the Atlantic, key decision-makers were determined to avoid the mistakes made after the conclusion of World War I – mistakes that had led to World War II, in the opinion of most. Institutions that had failed, therefore, were set aside and replaced with new institutions that might be better; better at least for the new governments trying to re-establish their legitimacy as postwar recovery began.

Money was the key to recovery, as manufacturing and distribution facilities had to be rebuilt, inventories of consumer goods replenished, and the entire apparatus of a civilian economy restored. Meanwhile, armies had to be demobilized, prisoners released and returned to their homes (if they still existed), refugees housed and fed until they could be settled permanently. All this went on while the two mightiest military forces in the history of the world remained poised on European soil, ready to initiate conflict again if needed.

How recovery was set in motion and then sustained is a story in which both Europeans and Americans can take justifiable pride.

The American institutional innovations: dealing with the dollar shortage

Perhaps the greatest influence of the war on postwar European economies was to alter their trading relationships, both with each other and with the rest of the world. The lack of a multilateral trading system saddled Europe with a serious balance of payments disequilibrium. Europe's commercial problems stemmed from several different sources. The war had witnessed the liquidation or destruction of foreign property holdings. In 1950/1 earnings from this source were, in real terms, less than a quarter what they had been in 1938, and that in itself was a substantial improvement over the previous years. Besides this, countries were rapidly incurring new debts to finance reconstruction. For example, the United Kingdom incurred debts to the United States and Canada of $1 billion at the end of the war, and in 1947 borrowed $4.4 billion from the United States and $1.25 billion from Canada. France borrowed $1.9 billion the same year.

Unable to increase earnings from services to foreigners (e.g. tourism, shipping, insurance, or finance), the European countries were forced to expand their commodity exports. But they could not sell to just any foreign customer. The absence of domestic supplies or of imports from traditional European sources, especially eastern Europe and West Germany, increased their dependence on the dollar area. The dollar deficit increased enormously compared with their prewar experience and it could not be offset by export earnings to colonies or to eastern Europe. The scarcity of earnings in hard (convertible to dollar) currencies forced the European countries to restrict imports and to control trade through bilateral agreements, augmented with quantitative restrictions and exchange controls.

The dollar shortage can be understood most clearly in terms of a standard supply–demand portrayal of the foreign exchange market. The European need for imports from the United States translates then into a demand curve for dollars in the foreign exchange market, where dollars are bought and sold. The demand curve had been shifted out for every country in Europe thanks to the wartime destruction and the military diversion of civilian production facilities. The supply curve of dollars, in turn, is based on the US demand for imports from Europe. Thanks to the high tariffs in the United States and the plentiful supply of domestic products available as substitutes for European goods, not to mention the unavailability of European consumption goods in any case, the supply curve of dollars had been shifted inward. Both situations could be expected to change as conversion occurred on both sides of the Atlantic from a war economy to a civilian economy.

A complication had been added, however, by the Bretton Woods agreement, signed in July 1944. The Bretton Woods system, as it came to be called, was the first of the major institutional changes in the international economy made by the Allies as their victory appeared imminent. The treaty committed all the signatories to fixed exchange rates with the dollar, the value of which, in turn, was defined in terms of gold at $35 per ounce of pure gold. Each country joining the International Monetary Fund (IMF), which was set up by the Bretton Woods agreement, had to pay in its share of the capital stock that gave the IMF its initial supply of operating funds. Part of the share could be paid in terms of the country's own currency, but part had to be paid as well in either gold or dollars. To minimize the cost of acquiring the necessary gold and dollars, each country naturally tended to overvalue its own currency, which it could produce at will, in terms of the dollar. This also had the advantage of decreasing the cost to a country of acquiring dollars in the foreign exchange markets in order to pay for imports from any other country, as the dollar was clearly the currency preferred for payment by any exporter in the world. The fixed exchange rate set at this time acted as a price ceiling that kept the price of dollars in terms of, say, pounds sterling from rising high enough to equilibrate supply and demand. Each European nation, then, was trapped in a situation of continued excess demand for dollars.

The resulting situation is portrayed in figure 2.1, where the solid lines for the supply curve of dollars, the demand curve for dollars, and the price ceiling set for dollars in terms of a European currency depict the situation in 1945. The dotted lines show how the situation could have looked in 1950, after a substantial amount of recovery had taken place in Europe, Marshall Plan aid had been distributed in large quantities, and all the European currencies had devalued, most by the same 30.5% that the British pound had been devalued, and the European Payments Union (EPU) established. Each program – the Marshall Plan, IMF devaluations, and the European Payments Union – was an attack on the problem from one of the three possibilities:
(1) increase the supply of dollars;
(2) remove or at least raise the price ceiling on dollars; or
(3) decrease the demand for dollars.

Any one approach could have solved the problem on its own if pursued vigorously enough. All three were used, in the event, and each approach proved

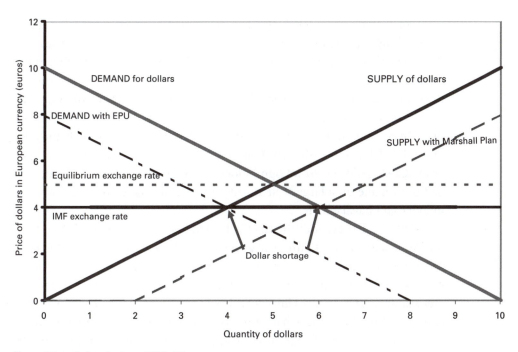

Figure 2.1   Dollar shortage, 1945–50

effective. Figure 2.1 shows that the dollar shortage could have been eliminated by 1950 using any of the strategies. In fact, the opinion more and more of economic historians is that the dollar shortage was eliminated sometime between 1950 and 1952. Policy-makers in both the United States and Europe, however, continued to think a dollar shortage existed until 1958. The shortage rather quickly turned into an increasing dollar surplus, thanks to the continued use of the same strategies to eliminate the dollar shortage that were initiated after 1945. By 1971 the dollar surplus was so overwhelming that the United States abandoned its commitment to convert dollars into gold, and in 1973 all the IMF countries abandoned their commitment to fixed exchange rates as well. Whenever and however the shortage was eliminated, it is useful to think of the programs described below as attacks on the problem of the dollar shortage using one of the three basic approaches.

1 Increase the supply of dollars: the Marshall Plan (1948–52)

First, the United States made major efforts to increase the supply of dollars. Under this heading, one can count the US contribution of nearly $4 billion to the United Nations Relief and Rehabilitation Administration's expenditures in Europe, 1945–7, as well as the expenses of US military occupation forces in Germany and bases established in Italy, France, and Britain, at least to the extent they were spent on local supplies and services. The United States made a loan of $5 billion in 1945 to the United Kingdom to compensate the British for terminating the Lend-Lease program at the end of the war. The major condition for this loan, however, was that the British should restore the convertibility of the pound sterling after two years. When the British did this in July 1947, unfortunately, their reserves of dollars and gold were almost immediately paid out to foreign holders of claims on sterling – claims that had been made on a large scale during the war to finance Britain's overseas military and naval efforts.

All these dollar expenditures by the United States were not enough to fund the immediate needs of European governments to restore law and order, convert military manpower and production to civilian uses, and provide housing and jobs for their returning peoples. In June 1947, in his commencement address at Harvard University, US Secretary of State George Marshall announced to the world what came to be known as the Marshall Plan for Europe. The Marshall Plan transferred about $12.5 billion to Europe in grants, loans, and conditional aid, distributed mainly in the first two years of the program (1948–50). Grants accounted for $9,199.4 million, loans for $1,139.7 million. Conditional aid was awarded as backing the intra-western European payments agreement of 1948 and came to $1,542.9 million.[1] It was administered by the Economic Cooperation Agency (ECA) on the American side and, on the European side, by the Committee for European Economic Cooperation (CEEC) and its successor, the Organisation for European Economic Cooperation (OEEC), which was created to allocate the aid and attempt to solve Europe's problems collectively.

2 Raise the price of the dollar: the devaluations of 1949

While the Marshall Plan was rightly hailed as an unprecedented act of generosity by a victorious military power, it was not sufficient to overcome the dollar shortage overall, and especially not for Britain. In September 1949 the second strategy for solving a dollar shortage was initiated by the British government as it devalued the pound sterling relative to the US dollar by 30.5% (from $4.03 to $2.80). Most European governments followed suit, so that Britain's exchange rates with most of the European currencies remained relatively unchanged. But, overall, the price of the dollar in European currencies was raised, by an average of about 20%. For an economist, it is clear that this was, by itself, the simplest and most effective way to solve the dollar shortage. For a historian, however, it was already evident from the variety of exchange rate changes among the European states that were elicited by the British initiative that political considerations would always make coordinated devaluations difficult to arrange. Consequently, the third strategy was undertaken: helping the Europeans reduce permanently their demand for dollars. The system devised to accomplish this was the European Payments Union. This was mainly a US initiative to help Europeans overcome the problem of a continuing dollar shortage, given that the infusion of Marshall Plan dollars was coming to an end.

3 Reduce the demand for dollars: the European Payments Union (1950–8)

Responding to these problems, and under American pressure, the OEEC members established the European Payments Union on September 19, 1950, applied retroactively to July 1, 1950. Its aim was to facilitate trade and establish a multilateral payments system by helping to clear country imbalances and establishing fully convertible currencies. A country's balance of payments on current account within the EPU was determined by its debts to or from all the other members with respect to trade carried on free of quantitative restrictions or bilateral trade agreements. To participate fully in the clearing system, therefore, a country had to replace its quantitative trade restrictions with tariffs. Tariffs could be high enough to keep trade at the levels pertaining previously at first, but they did allow exporters to increase their exports by cutting prices.

Debits were paid by central banks to the Bank for International Settlements (BIS), which administered the EPU, at first in domestic currency and then increasingly in hard currency, either dollars or gold, up to an initial quota. After the quota was reached, payments had to be entirely in dollars or gold, unless some special arrangement was made. The quotas totaled $3,950 million and were calculated for individual countries on the basis of 15% of the value of their total merchandise trade. Originally the largest quotas were: the United Kingdom, 27% of the total; France, 13%; Belgium and Luxembourg, 9%; the Netherlands, 8%; and West Germany, 8%. The United States provided $350 million, of which some was given to countries with "structural" problems, leaving the initial capital of the EPU at $271.6 million.

According to the original agreement, by the time a country had reached its quota limit, it would have paid 40% in gold and 60% in domestic currency. The system of increasing gold payments improved the incentives from the former agreements: gold or dollar losses would now move countries to cure persistent

Table 2.1 Increasing gold payments with the European Payments Union

		Payments by debtors		Payments to creditor	
Percent of quota		Credit	Gold	Credit	Gold
1st	20	20	0	20	0
2nd	20	16	4	10	10
3rd	20	12	8	10	10
4th	20	8	12	10	10
5th	20	4	16	10	10
	100	60	40	60	40

Source: William Diebold, Jr., *Trade and Payments in Western Europe: A Study in Economic Cooperation 1947–51*, New York: Harper, 1952, p. 95.

deficits, and growing credits would make surplus countries reduce their surpluses. The exact distribution of credit to gold as debt or credit increased is shown in table 2.1.

The 60:40 balance was subsequently altered because it seemed too "soft" on debtors and because the skewed operation of the system (whereby debtors paid in gold at a lower rate than creditors were paid out for the first 80% of the quotas) increased its costs. In mid-1954 the coverage was changed to 50:50, and in 1955 to only 25:75.

Already, by 1953, a number of members permitted multilateral currency arbitrage: currency transactions could be carried out on ordinary foreign exchange markets, not just by central banks, as before. In addition, eight EPU members agreed to standardize the spreads between the official buying and selling limits of their currencies at about 0.75% on either side of parity and to permit banks to deal with each other in any of the eight currencies. These measures, in addition to the increased dollar/gold requirement to settle payments, moved the members closer to convertibility. In 1955 the EPU members further agreed that, when sufficient members so decided (the members so deciding had to hold at least a half of the EPU quotas), they could make their currencies fully convertible. On December 27, 1958, this moment finally arrived. Belgium and Luxembourg, France, Germany, Italy, the Netherlands, and the United Kingdom held more than the required one-half of all EPU quotas and announced that they would make their currencies externally convertible; sixteen non-EPU members announced that they would follow and allow convertibility. The EPU had completed its mission of establishing a working multilateral trade and payments system for Europe and the wider world.

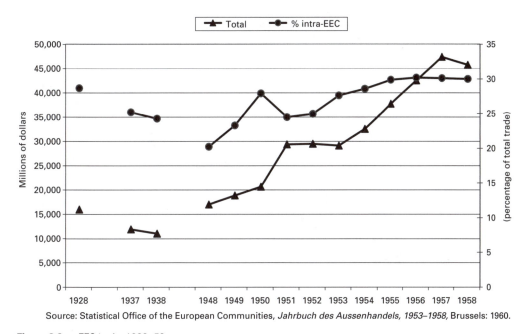

Source: Statistical Office of the European Communities, *Jahrbuch des Aussenhandels, 1953–1958,* Brussels: 1960.

Figure 2.2a   EEC trade, 1928–58

As a temporary scheme to build a sustainable multilateral payments system out of the restrictive bilateral agreements and trade restrictions before 1950, the EPU was a great success. The EPU allowed intra-European trade to expand while maintaining Europe's trade with the dollar and sterling areas. This initiative alone was a historic change, as European nations in the two decades before World War II had tried to redirect their trade toward their respective overseas empires rather than with each other. Figure 2.2a shows the growth of imports worldwide over the period 1928 to 1958. The situation in 1928, the last full year of "normalcy" in the interwar period, was that the future founding members of the EEC accounted for one-fourth of world imports, and of these imports fully three-fourths were from other trading partners outside the future EEC members. In the 1930s, the figures for 1937 and 1938 evoke the collapse of world trade generally, in which the future EEC members shared proportionately. The situation changed dramatically after World War II (the rise in levels for each series is a result of higher price levels after the war and is not important for the changes in trade patterns). The exhausted postwar economies accounted for only about one-sixth of world imports and five-sixths of their imports came from other trading partners. Their recovery in 1948–50 was reflected in their foreign trade mainly by an increase in their imports from one another, a result of the bilateral trade agreements mentioned

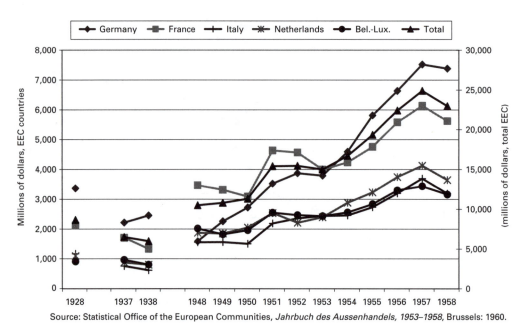

Source: Statistical Office of the European Communities, *Jahrbuch des Aussenhandels, 1953–1958*, Brussels: 1960.

Figure 2.2b   Growth of imports, EEC-6, 1928–58

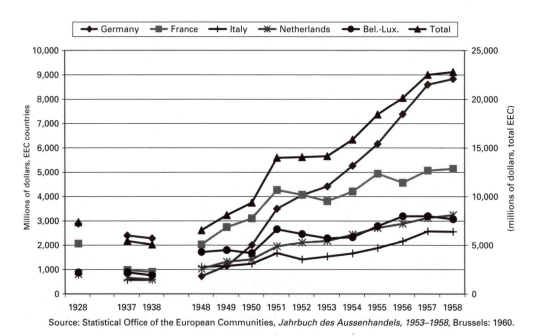

Source: Statistical Office of the European Communities, *Jahrbuch des Aussenhandels, 1953–1958*, Brussels: 1960.

Figure 2.2c   Growth of exports, EEC-6, 1928–58

above. From 1950 on their imports from the rest of the world grew at about the same pace as world imports generally, but their imports from one another continued to grow even more rapidly, a result of the multilateral clearing created by the European Payments Union. By 1958 only 70% of their imports came from the rest of the world, and now the customs union began to work its effect.

It is worthwhile examining figures 2.2b and 2.2c, which show the growth of imports and exports, respectively, for the original six members over the historical period 1928–58. These show the dominant role of Germany in 1928 and the 1930s, then the collapse of the German economy after its defeat in World War II and the partition of a reduced territory into the four occupation zones. The striking thing is the rapid recovery of the reduced German economy to its prewar pre-eminence on the European continent by the mid-1950s. Even more striking is the much more rapid growth of exports than imports for the West German economy. Italy also had a more rapid growth of exports than imports, as did the Netherlands, while Belgium-Luxembourg and France both had slightly higher growth rates of imports than exports prior to the formation of the European Economic Community. A more detailed analysis of the trade patterns[2] shows that, between 1953 and 1958, the percentage of imports for all the EEC members combined fell from every other part of the world, most notably from colonies in Africa and Asia and the sterling area, while rising from North America and eastern Europe. The rise in the share of imports from the latter two areas was almost entirely due to the new trade orientation of West Germany. This, however, was to come to an end in the 1960s.

The final net positions of each member country, along with the cumulative total EPU balance sheet, help explain how the payments actually worked, and to what extent credit was used to ease trade flows by each of the participating nations (table 2.2). From these data it is clear that the major creditors were Belgium and West Germany, with West Germany far and away the most important lender. This dominant financial position of West Germany continued throughout the EEC's development, and is still evident in the relative shares of the member states in the capital of the European Central Bank (see chapter 6). The major deficit countries were France and the United Kingdom, with deficits many times greater than those of any of the other countries. The total position of the cumulative bilateral positions is given in table 2.3.

The total net bilateral transactions were $46.5 billion (the total after all debits and credits were offset). The total commercial transactions, of course, were many times greater. The multilateral compensations were cleared through the EPU at the end of each month and were the amounts by which each country's surpluses with some members were offset against its deficits with others. The

Table 2.2 Cumulative positions of member countries, 1950–8

	Surplus positions*		Deficit positions*
Belgium	+1234	Iceland	−44
Switzerland	+39	Italy	−435
Netherlands	+581	Turkey	−481
West Germany	+4581	Denmark	−272
Sweden	+146	France	−2,953
		United Kingdom	−1,479
		Greece	−317
		Austria	−58
		Norway	−360
		Portugal	−173

* Surplus (+) or deficit (−) in millions of units of account.
Source: BIS, *Annual Report, 1958–59*, Basle: Bank for International Settlements, 1959.

Table 2.3 Total bilateral positions within the EPU, 1950–8

Total (deficits + surpluses)			
of which:	46.5*	100%	
Multilateral compensations	20.0*	43%	
Compensations over time	12.6*	27%	
Special settlements	0.5*	1%	
Balance			
of which settled in:	13.4*	29%	
Gold	10.7*	23%	(80%)
Credit	2.7*	6%	(20%)

* Billions of dollars.
Source: Managing Board of the EPU, *EPU Final Report*, Paris: European Payments Union, 1959, p. 39 (as cited in Jacob Kaplan and Günther Schleiminger, *The European Payments Union Financial Diplomacy in the 1950s*, Oxford: Clarendon Press, 1989, p. 349).

difference between the total clearing and the monthly compensations shows the cumulative total over the whole period of each member's monthly deficits and surpluses with all other members as a group. The payments over time were those consolidated deficits or surpluses that were later – perhaps very many months later – offset by corresponding surpluses or deficits. The total of multilateral trade not cleared each month was some $26.4 billion (1 − 2); of this only $12.6 reversed itself over time. The rest was settled under "special" payments or in direct credit and gold.

The European Payments Union provided the payments mechanism by which intra-European trade expanded rapidly and promoted the economic miracles of growth that began in the 1950s. Moreover, it established a European-based payments mechanism of fixed exchange rates with each other, the result of each country's currency being pegged at a fixed exchange rate to the US dollar. The fault lines that continue to plague European efforts toward ever-closer monetary union appeared as well. Germany acquired a huge surplus; France and Britain accumulated deficits that added up to nearly the German surplus. Turkey and Greece had large deficits, considering the small size of their economies and trade with the rest of Europe. For an economist, how-ever, all this seems in retrospect hardly worth the effort, given the simplicity and effectiveness of concerted devaluations of the European currencies. By adjusting the fixed exchange rate of each currency with respect to the dollar (a procedure explicitly permitted by the IMF) the dollar shortage could have been eliminated with one stroke, or at least with a continuing series of strokes. Then, the dollar glut that emerged at the end of the 1960s could also have been eliminated by revaluations.

The European institutional innovations: solving class conflict

The reason devaluations were not undertaken, according to Barry Eichengreen and Jeffrey Frieden, is that maintaining overvalued currencies, which is what the EPU did, helped European governments establish their political legitimacy with their domestic constituencies in the postwar environment. Overvalued currencies in Europe kept down the domestic price of imported goods, which initially meant foodstuffs and increasingly meant oil (which then had a fixed price in dollars). These factors resulted in nominal wages of workers stretching further, giving them an effective rise in real wages. Overvalued currencies also kept down the prices of raw materials and capital goods imported from dollar areas, which meant most of the rest of the world at the time. These factors reduced manufacturers' costs. Governments then gave industry favorable tax treatment in return for their commitment to maintain high rates of invest-ment and the expansion of employment. Labor unions agreed to restrain demands for higher nominal wages as long as full employment was main-tained by industry. The government committed to a generous social safety net for labor with well-funded pensions and extensive unemployment benefits. Taxes on the high profits of industry and the consumption expenditures of fully employed labor covered the costs of the social welfare commitments by European governments.

In sum, the European Payments Union was a complicated way to solve the dollar shortage, but it was a key factor in helping European governments solve even more complicated problems: how to establish their political legitimacy, maintain full employment, and achieve sustained economic recovery and growth. At the heart of the new institutions established by European governments was their commitment to fixed exchange rates with each other, even if they happened to be overvalued with respect to the rest of the world.

Other European institutional innovations to solve the dollar shortage

While the three-party game analyzed by Eichengreen and Frieden helps one understand how the European governments established their postwar legitimacy after the humiliations and devastation of World War II, more is needed to understand the economic success enjoyed by much of Europe after 1950, and why that success led to the creation of the European Economic Community in 1958. Lurking in the background was a problem that macroeconomic analysts call the "trilemma of open economies." Briefly, while there are advantages for an economy to have (1) fixed exchange rates, (2) monetary independence, and (3) free movement of capital flows with the rest of the world, both history and theory show that it is impossible to maintain all three at the same time.

Currently, the European Union countries participating in the common currency – the euro – have given up monetary independence while keeping fixed exchange rates with each other and allowing free movement of capital with the rest of the world. Those European Union countries not in the euro have given up fixed exchange rates in favor of keeping their monetary independence. In the period from 1945 until well into the 1970s and 1980s, however, all the western European countries maintained capital controls. Giving up the free movement of capital flows with the rest of the world enabled them to keep fixed exchange rates and monetary independence. Capital controls, however, designed to keep foreign reserves from flowing out of a country's central bank, also have the effect of discouraging capital imports by the private sector. Discouraging capital imports, of course, made solving the dollar shortage more difficult. Other initiatives were needed as compensation. All of them helped set the stage for the eventual creation of the European Economic Community.

The first regional trade agreements: 1947–57

The oldest postwar experiment in regional integration in western Europe was the agreement between Belgium and Luxembourg (which had their own economic union, the Belgium–Luxembourg Economic Union [BLEU], dating back to 1921) and the Netherlands – creating what was called Benelux. It was founded on a monetary agreement concluded in 1943 and a customs union treaty signed a year later by the three governments-in-exile in London. Before the war, they had conducted approximately 10% of their trade with each other, although there was an increasing imbalance in favor of the BLEU. The greater wartime damage in the Netherlands served to accentuate the Dutch deficit, which grew by 202% from 1947 to 1951.

Nevertheless, the Benelux customs union for manufactured goods came into force in January 1948, when all tariffs were abolished and a common external tariff was created for the three small, but strategically located, countries. However, trade was still impeded by the widespread imposition of quotas, especially on the side of the Dutch. To remove these, even if only toward the BLEU, threatened merely to aggravate the deficit. Progress was made possible only by two further measures. First, Belgium granted ever-greater credit extensions, which it was willing to do if it meant securing the Dutch market from Germany while the latter's industry was still being kept in check by the occupying powers. Eventually, the problem was subsumed into the European Payments Union when the United States guaranteed that it would make up any shortfall in payments to countries in chronic surplus. Second, the Dutch were able to secure preferential access to the Belgian agricultural market. They had wanted completely free access, as this would have helped remedy the deficit, but they had to make do with a provision that left Belgium's domestic protectionism intact.

The Schuman Plan

If the European Payments Union was the American contribution to the foundation of the European Union, the European Coal and Steel Community was the European contribution. While the EPU included all the Marshall Plan countries, the ECSC included only six countries – France, West Germany, Italy, Belgium, Luxembourg, and the Netherlands. The French proposal came when France was finally convinced that it would not be able to establish some sort of international control of the Ruhr in the postwar settlements and that German reindustrialization was a reality and a major objective for the United States. In this light, the ECSC was an institutional innovation that allowed economic recovery to continue apace in West Germany while maintaining oversight of its strategic industries by France and Italy, enlisting the cooperation of Belgium, Luxembourg, and the Netherlands.

While trade was being liberalized and a multilateral payment system created under the leadership of the United States, the coal and steel sectors of western Europe were slowly recovering from the war. These were key industries that had figured prominently in governmental recovery programs, such as the Monnet Plan in France. They had also played a major role in World War II, when Nazi Germany had commandeered the coal resources of Belgium and the iron ore of Luxembourg into its military production. Further, there was a history of Continental cartels in coal and steel cooperating and competing with each other, starting in the nineteenth century. It was natural, therefore, that the first effort at European cooperation, the European Coal and Steel Community, should focus on these two strategic industries. It was also natural that it focused on the area that economic geographers call the "iron triangle," which includes the iron ore fields of Lorraine and Luxembourg, and the coal fields that stretch from the northwest of France through Belgium to the Ruhr Valley in Germany.

It was not so natural, on these grounds, that the ECSC should include the Netherlands and Italy, which obviously lie outside the iron triangle, in addition to France, Germany, Belgium, and Luxembourg. But the Netherlands was tightly bound to Belgium and Luxembourg in the customs union, while France had intensified its bilateral trade relations with Italy over the preceding five years. As each of the six countries had veto power over strategic decisions, the intergovernmental nature of the ECSC was maintained in reality, even though the organizational structure was designed to make it appear as a supranational organization.

After negotiations beginning in Paris in June 1950, a draft of the Treaty of Paris was initialed on March 19, 1951, by representatives of France, West Germany, Italy, Belgium, the Netherlands, and Luxembourg – the same countries that would sign the Treaty of Rome six years later. The treaty was officially signed and agreed to on April 18, 1951, and the European Coal and Steel Community came into effect in July 1952. The British chose not to join the ECSC. British coal and steel had been nationalized immediately at the end of the war by Britain's Labour government, which intended to manage both sectors for the interests of Britain (and British workers) alone. Moreover, Britain had never participated in the Continental steel cartels before World War II.

The ECSC was created to stabilize prices, ease the distribution of coal during the postwar boom, provide new markets for iron ore and steel, and coordinate competition. To these ends, all import and export duties, subsidies, and other

Table 2.4 Growth of steel trade of ECSC members (millions of dollars)

	Intra-ECSC trade	Crude steel	Steel exports to third countries	Intra-ECSC trade in non-treaty goods
1953	138	95	102	111
1954	200	105	102	125
1955	271	126	121	150
1956	243	136	145	179
1957	271	143	151	193

Source: William Diebold, Jr., *The Schuman Plan: A Study in Economic Cooperation, 1950–1959*, New York: Praeger, 1958, p. 577.

discriminatory measures were immediately abolished on the trade of coal and steel among the six member countries. The overall impact of the ECSC is hard to judge, however. The immediate removal of trade controls differed from the transitional periods common in most European agreements, and thus avoided the indefinite postponement of their removal. However, the actual impact of the tariff removal was minor. In coal there were international agreements and tariffs did not really play a role, except in Italy, which had a 15% rate. For steel, Italian tariffs remained at 11 to 23% *ad valorem* until 1958; France and Germany suspended tariffs before the treaty was signed. Thus, the only tariffs actually removed by the treaty were the already low Benelux tariffs.

The ECSC's impact on pricing was certainly more important. It eliminated dual pricing within the ECSC and created a base-point pricing system. Although price controls and subsidies were not fully abolished, even small progress on this front eased trade. In addition to dual pricing, the discriminatory transport price policies of the ECSC members were eliminated. By volume, coal and steel were two of the most important traded goods, so the reduction of cross-border rates of about 30% had a major impact in reducing transport costs. The opening of the coal and steel trade did expand imports of steel products into France and the Saar, which soared from 27.7 thousand tons in 1952 to 117.6 thousand in 1953. In fact, throughout the 1950s, total intra-community trade grew much more rapidly than production or trade with non-members; intra-ECSC trade in treaty products increased 171% from 1953 to 1957, while production increased only 43% and extra-ECSC trade only 51% (table 2.4). In addition to these concrete effects, the ECSC set the pace and structure of the debate over the next common market for the ECSC six: the European Economic Community.

The Green Pool

Following the implementation of the Schuman Plan and the creation of the European Coal and Steel Community in 1951, negotiations began as well to coordinate intra-European trade in agricultural products. The goal was to create a so-called "Green Pool," in which multilateral settlements of trade in a range of agricultural products would replace the cumbersome bilateral agreements that were covering essential needs. France suggested four categories of agricultural products to be covered: cereals (France as a net exporter would increase markets for its farmers); wine (France was a major exporter, along with Italy); dairy products (the Netherlands was the leading exporter, while others were still rebuilding dairy herds); and fruits and vegetables (Italy could be a major exporter in this category). The idea of expanding the range of products over which trade would be liberalized in order to give everybody involved the chance to win in at least one category has proved to be fruitful time and again in resolving issues within Europe. It just did not work out in this particular case.

As postwar trade developed, the six members of the European Coal and Steel Community found that their needs for imports of foodstuffs in each of the four categories were better satisfied by turning to suppliers outside the ECSC – and, for that matter, outside the OEEC countries that were receiving Marshall Plan aid and benefiting from liberalization within the European Payments Union. Tropical fruits, for example, were in great demand in France, Germany, and the United Kingdom. For all three countries, Spain – excluded from the OEEC and the EPU – was the primary supplier. France and Britain also preferred imports from overseas colonies or ex-colonies to imports from southern Italy. These sources of supply did not require dollars in payment, but were willing to take whatever manufactured goods the importing country could offer in return. Each European government was determined, moreover, to protect its domestic farmers from any threat of cheap competition, whatever the source. As a result, the Green Pool lost all its color and agricultural trade was subsumed under the liberalization procedures of the OEEC. In practice, this meant setting high tariffs on agricultural imports that might be competitive with domestic production, while encouraging local farmers with guarantees of high price supports set in local currencies.

Price support programs now have a bad reputation among policy-makers in all advanced economies. The long-run problems of excess supply and political pressures that were predicted by economists at the time have come to fruition with a vengeance, and are proving quite intractable to solve within the political

Table 2.5 Agricultural products, total export and import values in 1961 at base year (1989–91) prices ($ thousands)

Country	Export values	Import values
Belgium-Luxembourg	925,875	2,268,909
France	4,235,105	6,449,424
Germany	1,625,501	16,006,820
Italy	3,047,674	6,006,376
Netherlands	3,557,255	3,118,051
Denmark	2,073,814	1,330,227
Ireland	2,466,551	726,920
United Kingdom	1,306,974	21,444,320
Greece	274,707	1,449,550
Portugal	294,462	366,583
Spain	1,694,082	1,026,543
Austria	181,252	1,148,252
Finland	81,821	705,182
Sweden	363,718	1,622,584
Czechoslovakia	482,565	2,189,580
Hungary	444,854	454,811
Poland	575,917	1,173,263
Cyprus	98,373	39,768
Malta	30,001	115,298

Source: FAOStat, available at www.fao.org, Economic Commission of Europe trade data.

decision-making processes that have developed over time. Nevertheless, price support programs for the basic foodstuffs that could be produced within western Europe proved very successful in solving the most pressing problem at the time – achieving self-sufficiency in food. By guaranteeing farmers a set price per unit of output achieved at harvest time, government price support programs enabled farmers to invest safely in new equipment, better seed, improved fertilizers, and enlarged acreages. The increased capital stock in agriculture, once in place and financed by borrowed funds, required continued high revenues to be sustained. By 1961 France was close to self-sufficiency overall in agricultural produce, exporting nearly as much in dollar terms as it imported. Germany, by contrast, was still a net importer on a large scale, while Italy and Belgium-Luxembourg were also net importers. Only the Netherlands showed an export surplus in value terms among the original six countries of the Common Market in 1961.

Table 2.5 highlights the trade issues that would envelop the European Union as it expanded membership in the following years. Countries with relatively large agricultural sectors and trade surpluses or balances in agricultural products stood to gain net subsidies from countries with small agricultural sectors and large import deficits. In the case of the Netherlands and Belgium-Luxembourg, it appeared that the Belgian-Luxembourg gains within the European Coal and Steel Community were balanced in principle by the Netherlands' gains within the customs union already established among the three small countries. With West Germany and France, much the same quid pro quo could be foreseen. When it came to the United Kingdom, however, there was no obvious tradeoff possible (nor is there to this day). Happily for the enlargements of the twenty-first century, the countries of central and east Europe were already retreating into relative autarky in agriculture by 1961 as their central planners discouraged trade in general and forced industrialization as much as possible.

Conclusion

Once established, institutional changes that work well for dealing with the immediate problems faced by governments tend to persist. When new problems arise, modifications in existing institutions will be relatively minor unless the problems are especially severe or persist for a long period. The many initiatives taken on both sides of the Atlantic to solve the pressing problem of the "dollar shortage" immediately following World War II created institutions that worked to solve that immediate problem. By 1950, all the evidence is that the dollar shortage was solved; by 1971, in fact, one could argue that a "dollar glut" had arisen that led to the collapse of the Bretton Woods system. But the apparent success of the various initiatives gave credibility to the new arrangements: fixed exchange rates; capital controls; a tripartite agreement among government, capital, and labor; the replacement of quantitative restrictions on trade with transparent and *ad valorem* tariffs; government support for international cartels; and price support programs in agriculture.

NOTES

1. A. S. Milward, *The Reconstruction of Western Europe 1945–51*, London: Metheun, 1984, p. 95.
2. Available in the *Jahrbuch 1953–1958 des Aussenhandels nach Ursprungs- und Bestimmungslandern*, Brussels: Statistical Office of the European Community, 1960.

3 | The customs union and the diversion of trade

The most important aspect of the enlargement of the European Union in 2004 is the expanded market for trade among the member countries that has been created. Further, trade will not be limited to just coal and steel, or manufactured goods, or agricultural goods, as was the case in the European Union as it gradually opened up trading opportunities within western Europe over the decades following the end of World War II. After a reasonably short transition period of adjustment, ranging from five to seven years, depending upon the country and the policy issue, all ten accession countries will be open to, and have opened to them, trade not only in goods but in services, of labor, and of capital, all regardless of nationality. That is the consequence of agreeing to take on the entire *acquis communautaire* of the European Union that has gradually accreted over the past half-century. The economic consequences for the original members and the subsequent entrants have been enormously beneficial; the central and eastern European countries hope that, by leapfrogging over the intermediate stages of institutional adjustments that their western neighbors labored through, they can achieve comparable economic prosperity in a much shorter time. In response to this prospect, the accession countries have already made dramatic structural changes within their economies, expecting that by imitating the economic practices of the western EU countries they will generate rapid economic progress for themselves and their citizens. They might do well to temper their enthusiasm by contemplating how the *acquis* that underpins the single market in goods, services, labor, and capital came into being, and how far short of the ideal it remains.

Background to the Treaty of Rome

By 1957 the export-led economic miracles of West Germany, Italy, and the Netherlands were well recognized, as was the relatively slow growth of France, the United Kingdom, and Belgium. The Belgian economist Alexandre

Lamfalussy explained why the sluggishness of the British and American economies, compared with the successes of the European continent, predated the formation of the European Community.[1] In each case where a European country had achieved the "virtuous circle" of sustained high rates of growth of total output, Lamfalussy found that exports had grown much more rapidly than either imports or total product. This led to large and growing export surpluses that provided the firms in the export sector with the financing they needed to sustain continued high rates of investment. Lamfalussy noted that this worked only if home demand was also strong as a result of governments pursuing full employment policies. As this was universal practice then among all industrial democracies, including the slow-growing economies of the United Kingdom and the United States, the importance of export surpluses was not so much to provide financing for additional investment as to remove balance of payments concerns for governments.

The United Kingdom and France in the 1950s repeatedly ran into balance of payments problems, which led the United Kingdom to restrict home demand, including investment, and led France to devalue or maintain import restrictions and exchange controls. Both strategies reduced investment, reduced export competitiveness, and kept growth slow. The link between high ratios of investment to total output and high rates of growth of total output that Lamfalussy found in his empirical data fitted very nicely with the Keynesian growth theory that dominated economic thinking in the 1950s. According to this view of the economy, the rate of growth of output was determined by the rate of growth of the capital stock, a consequence of a fixed capital–output ratio that was supposed to characterize modern industrial economies. The rate of growth of the capital stock was determined in turn by the share of investment in total national product, which in its turn was limited by the share of savings in total national income.[2] The Harrod–Domar growth model formalized these relationships in the expression $s/k = g$; the warranted rate of growth of total product for a nation, g, was equal to the product of its savings rate, s, and the inverse of its capital–output ratio, k. Export-led growth had the salutary effect of increasing a nation's savings rate by tapping into the funds of foreign customers *and* of decreasing its capital–output ratio by increasing the productivity of its capital stock. The two factors combined to give exporting countries significantly higher rates of growth than importing countries.

Export-led growth appeared to be driving the economic miracles of West Germany and Italy, with the Netherlands benefiting from its preferred position as the gateway for the external trade of a revitalized German economy. Belgium and France lagged noticeably behind, even though they were associated with the export leaders through the European Coal and Steel Community. The idea of a customs union among the members of the ECSC was appealing to the laggards, France and Belgium, so they could imitate the success of the leaders, and it was also appealing to the leaders, West Germany, Italy, and the Netherlands, so they could exploit naturally contiguous markets that they had not yet begun to penetrate and so keep their export booms continuing. Both sets of countries anticipated benefits from trade creation among the member countries. The United States and the United Kingdom were less enthusiastic about the prospects, as were the Scandinavian states. They foresaw dangers of trade diversion because their export markets in Europe would be diminished.

Part I: theory

Creating a customs union is a partial liberalization of trade and should have positive welfare effects for the member countries, although it may have negative welfare effects for non-member countries still facing tariff barriers. Insofar as tariffs are reduced this should create trade and yield a welfare benefit, yet, if a low-cost producer is excluded from the tariff reduction, trade will be *diverted* from the low-cost producer and welfare will be lost. The two phenomena, *trade creation* within a customs union and *trade diversion* from former trading partners now outside the customs union, are most easily analyzed in a comparative statics framework.[3] To give readers a sense of the progress achieved in reality by the Europeans in creating a customs union, we have to understand the historical situation from which they began in 1945. Then, Europeans were not confronted by the choice between autarky and free trade that is presented in a typical international trade textbook; instead, they were forced to work from a situation of autarky, meaning self-sufficiency in all manner of goods. Gradually, they worked forward from autarky to a situation of a customs union. Free trade, the ideal represented in economics textbooks, was never a possibility, because that would have meant importing all manner of consumer goods from the United States, and the "dollar shortage," analyzed in chapter 2, ruled that out. So, the challenge of moving out of autarky was met gradually by finding trading partners that were willing to accept some means of payment other than dollars or gold.

The first step in this direction, building on a wealth of experience that had been accumulated during the 1930s and during World War II under Nazi economic rule, was to arrange *bilateral trade agreements*. These were essentially barter trades, one country agreeing to import a specified quantity of a good

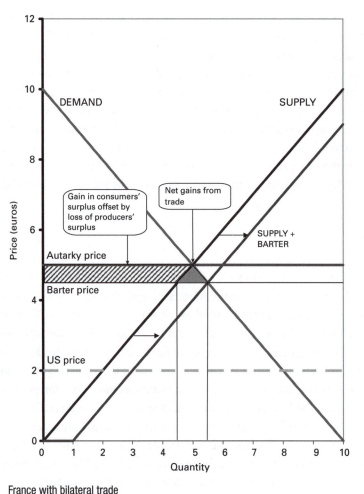

Figure 3.1 France with bilateral trade

from a trading partner, which in turn agreed to import a specified quantity of some other good from the first country. Figure 3.1 represents this situation for France, which excelled in creating bilateral trade agreements, most with Italy, but some even with Spain, as described in chapter 2. The barter for France meant increasing the domestic supply of the good in question by a fixed amount, shown by the rightward shift in the supply curve in figure 3.1. The increase in supply allowed the domestic price of the good to fall, leading to an increase in domestic consumption.

To understand why this was an improvement on the existing situation, one has to take on some analysis of welfare economics. The key concepts are:

- *consumers' surplus*, defined as the area below the demand curve and above the market price of the good;[4] and
- *producers' surplus*, defined as the area above the supply curve and below the market price of the good.[5]

From figure 3.1, it is evident that the increase in supply of the good from a trading partner leads to an increase in consumers' surplus that exceeds the loss in producers' surplus, leaving a triangle of net benefits to France. So even bilateral trade agreements provide a net benefit to a country engaging in them over the situation of autarky. But the costs of negotiating these agreements mounts over time, as the bartered goods are consumed in each country and each country demands changes in the barter terms for the next round of trade. Moreover, there is little opportunity for each government to cover these costs by extracting fees for export licenses and/or import licenses. From a government's point of view, a more efficient method of expanding trade, while avoiding the dollar shortage problem, is to set *quantity restrictions* in the form of import quotas, and then auction off the import licenses to domestic importers. This step in the evolution toward a customs union is depicted in figure 3.2. There, the same amount of the desired good is allowed to be imported, but now the government auctions off the import licenses for that quantity to the highest bidders. In the most efficient case of auctions, the importers will bid up to the market price, less the price they will have to pay to the most efficient exporter of the good. Even if that was not the United States, which in those days it was likely to be, the exporter would most probably demand US dollars in payment. If the French government tried to limit the use of its scarce supply of dollars, say by insisting that the French importers not be allowed to offer dollars to whatever exporter, the government's revenue would fall, as the French importers would have to pay more in French francs to cover the costs of less efficient exporters, say in Germany.

Over the course of the 1950s, as the European Payments Union operated with increasing effectiveness, the constraints of the dollar shortage on French policy were eased considerably. This meant that they could move from the cumbersome, and increasingly complex, array of bilateral trade agreements to a more efficient multilateral trade with all the other European members of the EPU. More importantly, the government could now realize tariff proceeds cheaply by simply imposing a fixed tariff to the price of the desired good when it was imported from whatever country. The incentives then for French importers would be to import from the most efficient supplier, shown as the US price, and the French government would garner the excess revenue in the form of customs duties. This situation is illustrated in figure 3.3, which shows a

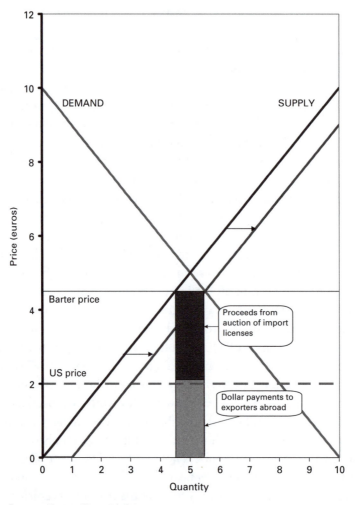

Figure 3.2   France with quantity restrictions

further increase in net gains to the French consumers over the losses incurred by the less efficient French producers. The important point to note is that now the government has a stake in the process of trade liberalization. It gains revenues from the new customs duties while it also reduces costs by eliminating negotiations over bilateral trade agreements and quantitative restrictions, as well as cutting out the extra paperwork required to auction off import licenses.

Efficiency of quota restrictions

French producers benefit from the restriction of imports, but at the expense of French consumers, who are prevented from enjoying the lower prices available

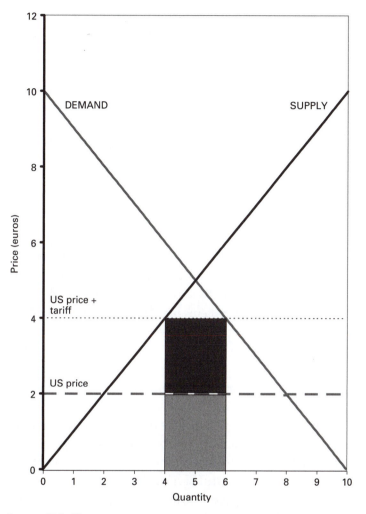

Figure 3.3   France with tariff

from either the West German or US producers. Nevertheless, French consumers enjoy some of the benefits of foreign trade, as the price at which the
market will absorb the US and German imports in addition to French domestic production is lower than the price at which the market will absorb the
supply that can be provided by the high-cost French producers alone (shown
in figure 3.2 again as the "barter price," as the initial import quota will be the
same as under bilateral trade agreements). Moreover, the French government
can extract the difference between the French price and the prices the US
and German producers receive for their exports by auctioning off the import
licenses to French importers. Thus, the government receives the areas shown
as "Proceeds from auction of import licenses."

If France had a free trade policy, it would import from the United States, forcing the domestic price down to the level of the US price. Consumption would rise to the intersection of the US price line and the French demand curve; but French production would be forced down to the intersection of the French supply curve and the US price. While the gain in consumers' surplus outweighs the loss in producers' surplus, giving France a substantial net benefit from opening up trade to all comers, the government would lose a convenient source of revenue. Politically, it is much easier to raise taxes on imported goods than by raising sales taxes on domestic consumption or, worse, raising income taxes on consumers.

Political economy of quota restrictions

Looking at the various differences between free trade and the quota restrictions, one can see why many policy-oriented economists are less than enthusiastic about free trade. Their reluctance to push harder for an improvement in economic efficiency stems mainly from recognizing the political difficulties that policy-makers would confront in displacing so much French production and facilitating the redeployment of French capital, labor, and natural resources into the production of other, diverse, goods, the effects of which are measured in the deadweight loss triangle on the left side of the tariff revenue block in figure 3.3 and the left side of the tariff loss block in figure 3.4. In addition, the government receives revenues from the quota proceeds. Governments are almost always looking for ways to finance projects without having to tax their citizens directly. The argument for moving from quantitative restrictions to tariff barriers, however, is much more compelling. With this policy change, the distribution of gains to consumers and producers does not have to be disturbed and the government itself will end up as the net beneficiary. This is the result of now receiving tariff revenues that should be larger than the proceeds it received from the sale of import licenses.

Tariff barriers: efficiency considerations

Figure 3.3 shows exactly the same demand and supply schedules as in figure 3.2, as well as the same prices for US and German sources of supply.[6] Now a uniform tariff is levied on imports, regardless of their origin, and no restriction is placed on the amount imported. The same deadweight losses occur as before – no surprise – but now the sole foreign source of supply becomes the

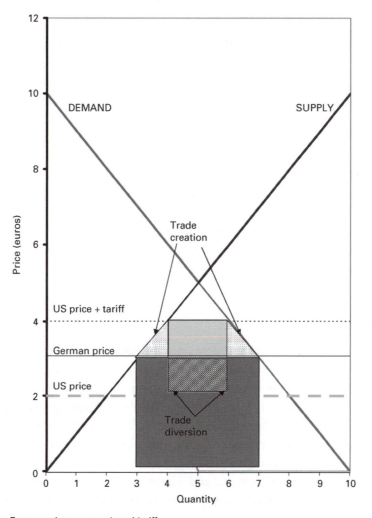

Figure 3.4   France and common external tariff

lowest-cost producer anywhere in the world, in this case the United States. (Remember, we are developing our theory in the context of the international economic situation of the mid-1950s, the golden age for US manufacturing.) As a result, the French government obtains a much larger amount of tariff revenues than it did under the previous regime of quota restrictions. The only losers in this case are the German producers, who now lose their quota on the French market and have to look for alternative buyers for their output either in Germany or in other foreign countries (such as the United States) – or go out of business.

Customs union: comparative statics

It is precisely this situation that a customs union is designed to prevent. Instead of driving German industry further away from cooperation with French industry and looking to increased trade opportunities in Scandinavia and overseas, a customs union would bring German and French industry closer together, albeit at the expense of tariff revenues for the government. Inside a customs union, which erects a common external tariff around the member countries while removing all tariffs on trade among themselves, both French and German firms would enjoy the same level of tariff protection from US and British competition. In the French market, the German producers are given an artificial advantage over the US producers by having no tariff levied against their imports, while the full tariff remains in force against the United States, Britain, Japan, or any potential competitor outside the customs union. French firms receive the same advantage on the German market.

Efficiency analysis

Using the same supply and demand schedules as shown in figures 3.1, 3.2, and 3.3, figure 3.4 illustrates the efficiency effects of such a customs union, which maintains the same tariff as before on US imports, but now eliminates it entirely for imports from Germany. Because German producers are more efficient than their French counterparts in the production of this particular good, total imports increase substantially, while the final price paid by French consumers falls to the level of the German price. Much of the deadweight loss triangles we saw in figures 3.2 and 3.3 are now eliminated. These are counted as net gains to the French economy, but note that they are captured entirely by French consumers. French producers lose, as part of their former production is now taken up by German imports. The French government loses all its tariff revenues that it received previously, because now all the imports are coming from the lowest price source, which has become, thanks to the differential tariff on US goods, Germany. And German imports pay no tariff under the rules of the customs union. Part of the lost tariff revenues are captured, however, by French consumers (and, presumably, can be taxed back by the French government). It is only the amount marked "Trade diversion" that is lost, net, to the French economy.

The three shaded areas in figure 3.4 represent the diverse sources of gains and losses to an importing country that joins a customs union that includes a country with more efficient firms than its own. They are *gains from trade creation* and *losses from trade diversion*.

- *Gains from trade creation.* These are shown as the two right-angled triangles on either side of the lost tariff revenues. The right-hand triangle results from consumption expansion (as a result of more total units of M now being available to French consumers) and the left-hand triangle results from production reduction (as a result of the resources used by less efficient French firms being released to more productive uses in the French economy).

- *Losses from trade diversion.* The patterned rectangle representing the net loss of tariff revenues to the French nation also measures the losses from trade diversion – the cost to the French nation of importing now from a more expensive foreign source than previously. The height of the rectangle is the difference between the German price and the US price for the good, and the length is the amount previously imported from the United States.

The net effect of moving from a tariff situation to a customs union is the sum of the areas of the two triangles representing the gains of trade creation, minus the area of the patterned rectangle representing the loss from trade diversion.[7] In this case, the net outcome is a loss for France for this particular commodity. The outcome, of course, will vary across the many thousands of commodities that can be traded, so it is useful to summarize the key factors that determine whether the outcome will be positive or negative. The area of the right-hand triangle, the gain from expanded consumption, will be larger the more elastic, or price-responsive, the French demand curve for the product. Likewise, the area of the left-hand triangle, the gain from decreased production by the now inefficient firms, will be larger the more elastic or price-responsive the French supply curve for the product. And both will be larger the lower the German price relative to the US price plus the tariff. The area of the patterned rectangle, or net losses of tariff revenues, will be smaller the less was imported in the first place and the closer the German price is to the US price.

Equity evaluation

Now let's examine the distributional effects of the customs union after it has taken full effect while assuming, as is usual in comparative statics analysis, that no changes in the underlying demand and supply curves have occurred in any of the affected countries. Clearly, French consumers have gained over the situation when France imported from the United States with a tariff; consumers' surplus rises by the increased area of the triangle below the demand curve as its base shifts down from the "US price + tariff" to the "German price." In addition to capturing all the trade creation gains analyzed above and taking part of the previous tariff revenues away from the French government (the top half of the rectangle showing customs proceeds in figure 3.3), they have added even more to their total of consumers' surplus at the expense of the French producers, who have now been displaced by the German imports. The French producers have lost a substantial part of their previous market, whether viewed in terms of the absolute quantity produced, in terms of the share of the total domestic consumption, or – as we prefer to do in this kind of evaluation – in terms of the total producers' surplus they enjoy, which has fallen by the area given by the shift of the upper base of the producers' surplus triangle down from the "US price + tariff" to the "German price." The American exporters are nowhere to be seen and are clearly big losers, losing all their previous export earnings shown in figure 3.3. By contrast, German exporters are enormous gainers, with their export earnings exceeding the losses to their American competitors. Germany will clearly become more oriented to the French export market than previously.

It appears on this analysis that the political motivation for a customs union had to be the same as that for the European Coal and Steel Community: to reduce reliance on the United States as a source of supply for vital imports in order to reduce pressure on a recovering nation's tenuous supply of US dollars, while at the same time encouraging the economic integration of a politically weak and physically diminished German nation into western Europe. It also appears on this analysis that it was these political considerations that were dominant, rather than any economic benefits that were foreseen. The efficiency gains were dubious and relatively small at best, whereas the equity implications were obvious and required a substantial reallocation of net benefits, with all the domestic political difficulties such redistributions entail. For these reasons some authors have argued that the creation of a customs union is always welfare-inferior to unilateral tariff reduction. If a country favors a customs union policy it must be due to political constraints that preclude the adoption of free trade.[8]

If policy-makers cannot, for political reasons, create the conditions necessary for maximizing economic efficiency (say, by eliminating all tariff barriers entirely), they can usually improve things nevertheless by creating some of the conditions and settle for "second best" (for example, eliminate all tariff barriers only with some, politically acceptable, countries). The United States accepted the EEC's innovation of a customs union, despite its obvious inconsistency with its long-term goals of promoting multilateral trade under the terms of the General Agreement on Tariffs and Trade (GATT).[9] The basis was the assurance by the EEC that the average tariff rate of the common external tariff would be less, in fact, than the average of the individual countries' tariff schedules before the formation of the customs union. The EEC committed in 1960 to achieving an average 7.4% tariff by 1968, which was significantly lower than the British tariff. In the context of the time, the customs union proposed by the original six was moving in the right direction as far as the United States was concerned, and more rapidly than would be possible otherwise. (The further vicissitudes of tariff negotiations are covered in chapter 7.)

All these analyses are subject to assumptions about the smallness of the country joining the union and the static, one-time welfare effects of the union. In the next sections we relax these assumptions and find that the evaluation of unions is affected.

The dynamics of customs unions

The primary factor in the growth of European production and trade has obviously been technological progress, which has created new goods not even imagined in 1958, reduced the cost of producing other goods that were available in the United States but not yet in Europe, and reduced the business transaction costs, especially the shipping charges and costs of inventory control and marketing. These effects can be captured in our static demand and supply graphs only by showing an outward shift in both demand and supply, but with a larger shift in supply. If the pace of technological progress is the same for all three countries – the importer, the exporter, and the potential customs union partner – then it is clear that trade will expand more rapidly than production, that the importer's consumers and the exporter's producers will reap the largest gains in consumers' surplus and producers' surplus, and that tariff revenues for the importing country's government will increase rapidly as well. All that technological progress does from this perspective is to increase the gains from trade for the winners (the importer's consumers and government, and the exporter's producers) while reducing the size of the losses for the losers (the importer's producers).

But it is clear from the historical record that technological progress has not been evenly distributed across countries, much less among industries within countries. It is also clear that the rapid increases in production typically lead to even more rapid increases in productivity (Verdoorn's Law).[10] This means that the exporting country's productivity will grow more rapidly than productivity in the importing country or in the potential partner country in the customs union; this is often referred to as the polarization effect. Economic historians refer to this phenomenon as another example of path dependency, where chance determines which path an economic activity takes at its beginning, but the path taken by chance then determines the course of the activity ever after. Economic policy-makers have seized upon the idea of path dependency to justify strategic trade policies – policies that use trade barriers and investment incentives to attempt to launch a national industry on a high-productivity path. Economic theorists have tried to analyze its effects in the simplest way possible by building on traditional trade theory, which means using the concept of economies of scale to modify the shape of the supply curves.

The creation of the customs union can have a number of indirect, or dynamic, effects. The elimination of some protection can increase competition and lower transaction costs while allowing firms to benefit either from decreasing cost industries – for example, sectors with high fixed costs – or from scale economies, such as network systems. In addition, any domestic market power is eroded by the increase of competition, which increases domestic welfare by lowering deadweight losses. Thus, the reduction in market barriers can accelerate the process of technological advance referred to above. In fact, the reduction in production costs could, conceivably, move member states' costs closer to world prices, thus lowering any trade diversion effect and increasing the trade creation effect. One of the areas that Europeans point to most frequently is the gains from increasing size, the gains from economies of scale.

Decreasing costs/economies of scale

Economies of scale in production for a particular industry imply that, as inputs are increased, output increases by even a greater amount. Decreasing costs mean that, over an observable range of quantity produced in the industry, its average costs fall. Both imply that, as the amount produced rises, the per-unit costs fall; in other words, the technical efficiency of the firm's production increases. Figure 3.5 shows the effect for our last example of a customs union in which France is the importer, the United States the previous exporter, and Germany the new exporter, thanks to the differential tariff advantage it enjoys inside the customs union of the European Economic Community. As in the case shown in figure 3.4 with constant returns to scale for the United States and Germany, the German exporters and the French consumers gain substantially at the expense of the French producers and government and the US producers.

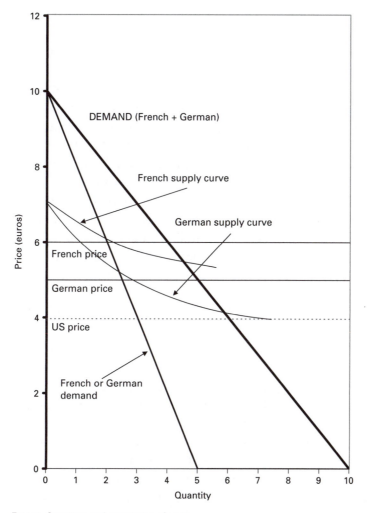

Figure 3.5   France, Germany, and economies of scale

The main differences now with increasing returns to scale are: (1) the difference in gains to the winners and losses to the losers are much greater; (2) the cost advantage of the German producers over the French producers widens enormously, thus wiping out all French production and locking the two economies into this particular trade pattern; and (3) the German producers now obtain a cost advantage over the US producers as well, so that France is now importing, as under the universal tariff regime, from the most efficient supplier in the world – but now that supplier is Germany, not the United States. The reason for these differences from the constant returns to scale scenario shown earlier is that, thanks to economies of scale, both the French producers and the US exporters who are displaced by the German exporters become less efficient, and therefore higher-cost, as they are forced to produce less than before.

Contrasting this result with that shown in figure 3.4, one can see that it predicts the result that has been generated by the formation of the customs union called the European Economic Community. Foreign trade has shifted away from previous partners toward partners within the customs union and trade has increased within the customs union even more than total production, although that has increased as well. The theory of trade creation and diversion by the formation of customs unions under conditions of economies of scale in production leads to many variations on two themes: strategic trade and technological advantage. Before dealing with these policy issues, however, it is best to anchor our analysis in an accurate appreciation of what has happened to trade patterns and technological progress within the EEC since its formation in 1958.

Part II: practice

Given the preceding theory, we would expect the creation of the EEC to increase trade creation more than trade diversion in the member nations. Trade among western European countries has always been relatively high since the end of World War II, and Europe has been a strong industrial area for the whole post-World-War-II period. Indeed, almost all the estimates of trade creation and trade diversion caused by the EEC show that trade creation far exceeded trade diversion. This is true for sectoral studies as well as for economy-wide estimates.[11] For example, Bela Balassa estimated that trade creation for all goods stood at $11.3 billion, while trade diversion was just $0.3 billion.[12] These figures are from a static analysis that ignores the changes through time brought on by the EEC, so they understate the actual gains from trade induced by the formation of the customs union.

The essential feature of a customs union is to change the pattern of trade of the member countries. The EEC has succeeded in doing this to an extent far beyond the wildest expectations of its founding fathers. From having two-thirds of their imports coming from outside the customs union when it was set up in 1958, by 1990 the original six members had over two-thirds of their imports coming from within the customs union, which by then had doubled its membership to twelve countries. And this level of intra-EU trade compared

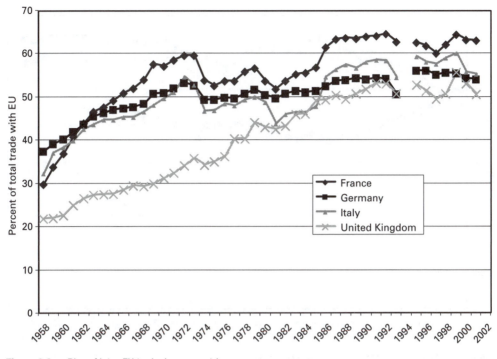

Figure 3.6a Rise of intra-EU trade, large countries

to extra-EU trade has been maintained to the present. The significance of this change in the pattern of imports (which, necessarily, has largely been dupli- cated in the pattern of exports) is often overlooked in view of the even more dramatic increase in the total volume of foreign trade. The rapid growth of west European foreign trade has meant that all trading partners have seen substantial increases in the volume of their exports to the EU. Whether the growth of trade has been primarily because of technological progress or insti- tutional changes, or a felicitous combination of the two processes since World War II, is an open question. But there can be no doubt that the change in the geographical pattern of west European trade has been due to the institutional changes created by the EU.

Figures 3.6a–3.6e illustrate the changing trade orientation of the four major countries, the four high-income countries, the four low-income countries, the last three entrants of the EU-15, and the three remaining outsiders over the entire period 1958–2002. The effect of entry into the customs union is clear for the original six, as the share of their trade with each other rose immediately and strongly. The next six members to join show a similar rise in their share of the trade with the EU-12 when they enter the customs union – the United

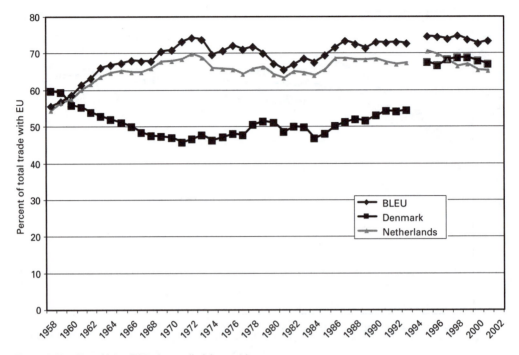

Figure 3.6b Rise of intra-EU trade, small, rich countries

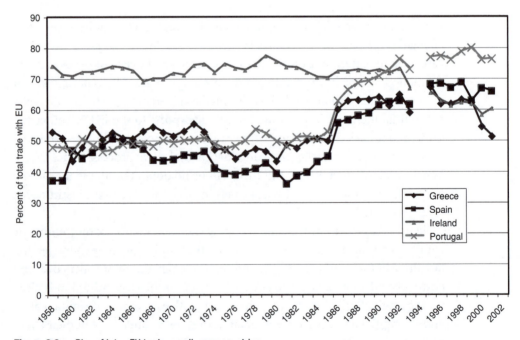

Figure 3.6c Rise of intra-EU trade, small, poor countries

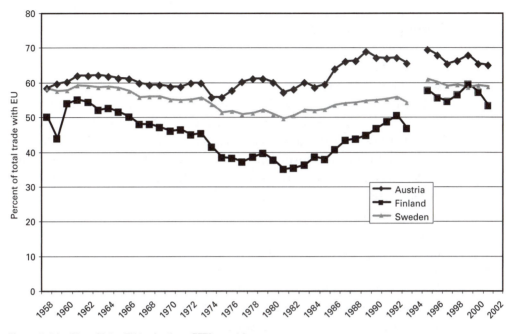

Figure 3.6d Rise of intra-EU trade, three EFTA countries

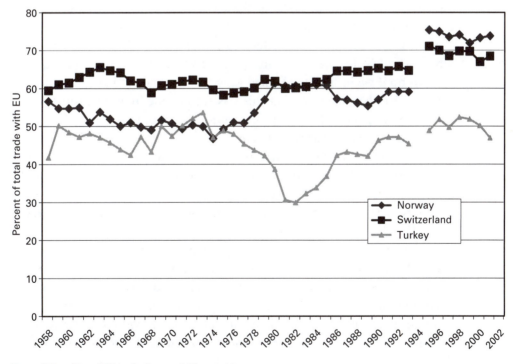

Figure 3.6e Rise of EU trade, three outside countries

Kingdom, Ireland, and Denmark in 1973, Greece in 1980, and Spain and Portugal in 1986. If we anticipate the addition of the North Sea trio in 1973 and calculate what the share of trade with the outside world would have been if they had been included ten years earlier than they were in fact, it also turns out to be around 60%.

In other words, the remaining trade of the original six members with the rest of the world was not focusing on the members-to-be but, rather, on Scandinavia and North America for Germany, Africa for France, the Mediterranean and Latin and North America for Italy. The United Kingdom, meanwhile, concentrated on North America and Oceania. The major countries in Europe were once again targeting different parts of the world for their foreign trade initiatives.

The small countries, by contrast, were committed to focusing their trade on the most aggressively expanding partners, which turned out to be Germany for the Netherlands and Belgium and the United Kingdom for Ireland and Denmark. As might be predicted, the small countries were the first to show the effects of trading preferences created by the EEC and the European Free Trade Association in their trade patterns.

By 1970, the last full year in which the Bretton Woods system of fixed exchange rates with the dollar as the key currency was in effect, the trading pattern of the EEC-6 had dropped its share of imports from the world outside the customs union to 50%, achieving rough equality in their overall trade between EEC members and non-EEC members. Again, the same equality shows up if we include the United Kingdom, Ireland, and Denmark, but by 1970 it had become clear that this was strictly due to an intensification of Irish and Danish trade with the United Kingdom, offsetting their increasing exclusion from the markets of the inner six.[13]

The effects of the customs union on changing the trade pattern of the next three members to join show up clearly in the figures for 1979. This is all the more remarkable due to the temporary increase in the weight of imports from the Organization of Petroleum Exporting Countries, caused by the successive oil price shocks of 1973/4 and 1979. Now the share of imports was greater from within the EEC-9 than from outside. But this was the net result of the small member countries focusing on their trade with large member countries. The large member countries, in turn, were all less focused on trade within the customs union than any of the small member countries were. The four major countries – France, Germany, Italy, and the United Kingdom – differed in the degree to which they concentrated their trade within the Community. France had the greatest trade reliance upon the Community, followed by Germany, Italy, and the United Kingdom.

During the 1980s the drop in the price of oil, especially after 1985, when its fall in terms of dollars was augmented by the fall of the dollar with respect to the European currencies, and the expansion of membership to include first Greece (1980) and then Spain and Portugal (1986) combined to continue the change in trade patterns in favor of imports from within the Common External Tariff area. By 1985 both France and Germany were clearly oriented toward their fellow EEC members in their imports, while only Spain among the large countries was still clearly oriented outside the EEC. All the small countries, with the exception of Portugal, which had not yet formally joined, and Greece, which was still in its transition period of conforming gradually over five years to the CET, were even more committed to trade within the EEC than the large countries. The cases of Ireland and Denmark are especially noteworthy for the progress they had made in reorienting their imports since 1979. But the pace of reorientation was clearly picking up in the 1980s: by 1990 Spain was almost exactly at the EEC-12 average of 59% of imports from within the EEC, and Portugal was close to 70%. Portugal was now one of the most tightly committed countries to trade within the Community, along with the Netherlands and the Belgium–Luxembourg Economic Union. The last three entrants found their trade with the EEC was falling as a share of their total trade until the early 1980s, when more favorable terms were granted to the EFTA countries in general and Finland in particular. This importance of the EU market was maintained after they formally entered the EU on January 1, 1995.

The countries that had lost their relative share in supplying the markets of these rich and growing economies were the Organization of Petroleum Exporting Countries (OPEC) oil exporters, the centrally planned economies of eastern Europe, the ACP countries (African, Caribbean, and Pacific – mainly former colonies of the European powers), and Latin America. Even the United States, with the benefit of sharply lowered prices for its goods in terms of the European currencies, lost some of its small remaining share in the EEC's imports – from 7.9 to 7.5%. Only Japan, the Association of South East Asian Nations, and the EFTA countries increased their share of the EEC-12's imports in the period 1985–90. This continued in an accentuated way the pattern that had begun in the 1950s even before the formation of the European Economic Community. Naturally, these continued and consistent alterations in the pattern of the EEC's trade have raised a variety of policy issues. These will be taken up in chapter 7.

NOTES

1. Alexandre Lamfalussy, *The United Kingdom and the Six: An Essay of Economic Growth in Western Europe*, London: Macmillan, 1963.
2. This view of modern economic growth enjoyed a brief moment of glory as the Harrod–Domar theory. Let K = the capital stock of the economy, Y = the total product (or income) of the economy. The capital–output ratio, K/Y, was assumed to be a constant (around 3.0) denoted as k. If $K/Y = k$, then $\Delta K/\Delta Y = k$, and $\Delta K/K = \Delta Y/Y$ – i.e. the growth rate of K equals the growth rate of Y. The change in capital stock, ΔK, is the same as I, the net investment in the economy. So $I/K = \Delta Y/Y$, the warranted rate of growth, symbolized by g. Multiplying the left-hand side of the equation by Y/Y yields the expression $I/Y * Y/K = \Delta Y/Y$. But the level of I in any year was constrained by the amount of saving available out of current income, S, so $I/Y = S/Y$, or s, the saving ratio of the economy, and $Y/K = 1/k$, yielding the expression in the text, $s/k = g$.
3. "Trade deflection" is another possible result from selectively eliminating tariffs. Imagine two countries creating a free trade area (FTA) – that is, eliminating tariffs between them and retaining separate control of external tariffs. Suppose that the two countries (country 1 and country 2) both import a good from a third country. If the tariff rate for, say, country 1 is higher than for country 2, then both countries before the FTA will import directly from the third country. Once the FTA is created, country 1 will import the third country's good from country 2. The trade from the third country has been "deflected." Once the countries move to a customs union, with a common external tariff, deflection disappears. This sort of problem is most often dealt with by "rules of origin" agreements, which often complicate trade. In a European Free Trade Association (EFTA) report, the rules are shown to be so complex that many EFTA exporters chose to pay the higher non-preferential tariff rather than incur the administrative costs necessary to qualify for zero tariffs! See J. Herin, *Rules of Origin and Differences between Tariff Levels in EFTA and the EC*, Occasional Paper no. 13, Geneva: European Free Trade Association, 1986, quoted in Richard Baldwin, *Towards an Integrated Europe*, London: Centre for Economic Policy Research, 1994.
4. Technically, the demand curve represents the maximum benefit that any set of consumers can derive from consuming the good during the time period implicitly allowed for consumption, expressed in units of currency. The market price shows how many units of currency have to be given up for each unit of good to be consumed. The difference has to be positive for consumers to choose freely to consume the good. The accumulated differences from the origin out to the quantity actually purchased in the market represent the total gain in welfare for consumers.
5. The supply curve represents the cost to all producers of increasing the supply of the good to the market during the time period implicitly assumed in the graph. No producer will be willing to lose money so the amount brought to market has to cost less to produce than the price consumers will pay for it. The accumulated excess of returns gained by all producers supplying the market is producers' surplus.
6. Interested students can reproduce these results, either by hand on graph paper or by using a spreadsheet program on a personal computer. The demand curve is assumed to be $Qd = -3/2\,P + 13.5$; the supply curve is $Qs = P - 1.5$; the US price is $4.00, the German price $4.75, and the French tariff $1.50.

7. For the quantitatively oriented student, the areas so calculated from the assumptions underlying the graphs are:

Left-hand triangle:	$1/2\ (4.0 - 3.25)(.75) = 0.28125$
Right-hand triangle:	$1/2\ (6.375 - 5.25)(.75) = 0.421875$
Rectangle:	$0.75\ (\ 5.25 - 4.0) = 0.9375$
Net gain (loss):	$(0.703125 - 0.9375) = (0.234375)$

8. The generally accepted position has been that, if there are no economies of scale or terms of trade effects, the unilateral tariff reduction is always superior to the customs union. See C. A. Cooper and B. F. Massell, "A new look at customs union theory," *Economic Journal* 75 (300), 1965, pp. 742–7; H. G. Johnson, "An economic theory of protectionism, tariff bargaining and the formation of customs unions," *Journal of Political Economy* 73 (3), 1965, pp. 256–83; and E. Berglas, "Preferential trading theory: the n commodity case," *Journal of Political Economy* 87 (2), 1979, pp. 315–31.

9. Although discriminatory tariffs were not allowed under the GATT per se, they were accepted for the creation of a customs union, and so the EEC was perfectly within the bounds of the GATT.

10. Formulated by the Belgian economist P. J. Verdoorn in "Fattori che regolano lo sviluppo della produttivita del lavoro," *L'industria* 1, 1949, pp. 45–53, and popularized by Nicholas Kaldor in *Causes of the Slow Rate of Economic Growth of the United Kingdom*, Cambridge: Cambridge University Press, 1966.

11. A good overview of these estimates and the effects of the EEC can be found in Michael Davenport's "The economic impact of the EEC," in A. Boltho, *The European Economy: Growth and Crisis*, Oxford: Oxford University Press, 1985, pp. 225–58. A survey of the trade creation/diversion estimation literature is D. G. Mayes, "The effects of economic integration on trade," *Journal of Common Market Studies* 17 (1), 1978, pp. 1–25. Probably the best-known estimates are by Bela Balassa, ed., presented in *European Economic Integration*, Amsterdam: North-Holland, 1975.

12. "Trade creation and trade diversion in the European common market: an appraisal of the evidence," in Bela Balassa, ed., *European Economic Integration*, pp. 79–118.

13. These comments are based on the analysis contained in the publication by the Statistical Office of the European Community, *EC–World Trade: A Statistical Analysis, 1963–1979*, Brussels: 1980.

4 The Common Agricultural Policy and reforms: feeding Europe and then some

At the outset of the customs union, in 1958, agriculture was heavily protected. Recalling that the average tariff on all imports was intended to be 7.4%, it is striking that the average tariff on foodstuffs alone was 14.2%.[1] The high level was not the result of a common consensus that foodstuffs should be protected as much as industrial goods; rather, it was a necessary outcome of considerable divergence in agricultural problems and policies among the member countries. First of all, the relative importance of agriculture ranged from 23% of GDP in Italy to 8.4% in Belgium, where the average farmer earned three times as much as in Italy. The range of prices for basic foodstuffs varied widely. Wheat, for example, was much cheaper in France than in either Italy or Germany. The size of farms varied, although most were too small to make mechanization profitable. Holdings between 0.5 and 5 hectares (1 hectare = 2.471 acres) accounted for 85% of all farms in Italy, 55% of the farms in Germany, and nearly 35% of the farms in France.[2] For the United States, less than 10% of farms were under 5 hectares.[3] Agricultural productivity varied widely as well, with the Dutch using three times as much fertilizer per acre as the French and five times as much as Italian farmers.[4]

To establish a common market in agricultural goods required a common agricultural policy, but to reach agreement on the essential features of such a policy required a willingness by each country to protect not only its own less efficient farmers but also the less efficient farmers in the partner countries as well. The more efficient countries in agricultural production, France and the Netherlands, wanted to speed up the elimination of internal customs barriers on foodstuffs, while the least efficient, Italy and Germany, wanted to slow down the dismantling of internal tariffs in agriculture until a common agricultural policy was agreed on. It was not until 1962 that the Common Agricultural Policy came into practice, despite the urgency for prompt agreement on agricultural policy expressed in Article 40 of the Treaty of Rome. The CAP was supposed to enable the member states to achieve the five objectives for agriculture that they had enunciated in Article 39. These were:

(1) to increase agricultural productivity by promoting technical progress and the optimum use of production factors;

(2) to ensure a fair standard of living to the agricultural community by increasing its per capita income;

(3) to stabilize markets;

(4) to assure the availability of supplies; and

(5) to ensure reasonable consumer prices.

In other words, there was something for everyone, and it was left for future negotiations to determine who could actually get what was promised them. In fact, the overriding priority held in common was to achieve self-sufficiency in agriculture. This had been a goal throughout Europe after World War I, and with the separation of industrial West Germany from agricultural East Germany the urgency of reaching this goal was intensified. The first four objectives are all compatible with the strategic goal of agricultural self-sufficiency, inconsistent though they might be with one another in terms of economic practicality. The last goal was inconsistent with the first four, but was left purposely vague in order to minimize conflict.

During the Stresa Conference, in July 1958, the fundamental principles of the CAP were laid down by the participating farmers' federations and the delegations of the six member states. In June 1960 the Commission submitted its proposals, and in December 1960 the Council adopted three principles.

(1) A single market was to be established, with the free flow of goods and the harmonization of prices and exchange rates.[5]

(2) Community preference was extended to European farmers in the form of price supports and export subsidies, but foreign trade would not be eliminated.

(3) Joint financial responsibility would be accepted by all members through the creation of a common agricultural fund called the European Agricultural Guidance and Guarantee Fund (EAGGF).

It is clear that the goal of agricultural self-sufficiency has been reached. On that criterion, the Common Agricultural Policy must be judged a success. In fact, by 1980 the EEC was exporting more foodstuffs than it was importing, so self-sufficiency in this sense was achieved even before the addition of Greece, Spain, and Portugal to the membership. Over the course of the 1980s the EEC actually increased its net exports, to the extent that traditional exporting nations such as the United States, Canada, and Argentina put considerable pressure on the Community to ease certain features of its policy. Indeed, by the mid-1980s the EEC-10's share of Organisation for Economic Co-operation and Development (OECD) agricultural exports had risen to 56% from 45% in the late 1960s, while its share of OECD agricultural imports had fallen to 55% from 60% over the same period of roughly twenty years. At the same time, the US share of OECD agricultural exports had fallen from 25% to 20%, while its share of imports had remained at about 19%.[6]

Over the course of the 1990s the EU-15's share of world agricultural exports remained around 18%, rising from 16% at the end of the 1980s. Meanwhile, the US share of world agricultural exports fell from 20.7% to 18.6% between 1990 and 1999, so that the EU-15 and the United States were essentially equally important exporters of agricultural products. The EU-15's share of world agricultural imports fell steadily over the 1990s, from 23.1% in the period 1986–99 to 17.9% in 1999, meaning that the EU-15 had become a net exporter as well.[7] The alarming aspect of this development was the EU-15's extravagant use of export subsidies to maintain its rising importance as an exporter of agricultural products. In 1999 the EU spent nearly $6 billion in export subsidies, compared to a mere $80 million spent by the United States. The US total was even less than the $128 million spent by Norway and the $292 million laid out by Switzerland![8]

It is clear that the success of the EU in achieving agricultural self-sufficiency over the years has been due to the price supports and market interventions of the Common Agricultural Policy, not the increased membership to include countries with large agricultural sectors. It was not the addition of Greece, Portugal, and Spain in the 1980s that brought about the export surplus, which had already been achieved even with the addition of the United Kingdom, with its continuing import deficit, in 1973. Moreover, the addition of Austria, Finland, and Sweden in the mid-1990s did nothing to slow down the progress of EU agriculture, despite those three countries reducing the level of support to their agricultural sectors as part of their accession agreements.

The changing composition of the EU membership did, however, change the distribution of subsidies with the agricultural sector. In 1980 dairy products (42.1%), cereals (15.3%), and meat and eggs (14.2%) comprised nearly 72% of guarantee payments. In 1990 these three products made up only 45% of guarantee payments; the rest of the payments were going to new products grown by the new, more agrarian, member countries. By 2001, though, the share of these three categories was back up to 66% of guarantee payments.[9] By this time, however, guarantee payments were a much-reduced share of total CAP expenditures, which in turn were capped at 45% of total EU expenditures for the financial perspective of 2000–2006. The reduction came as the EU succeeded in moving gradually from market interventions to direct payments to farmers based on increasingly restrictive criteria. The resulting proliferation of programs defined for different crops, products, regions, and categories of farmers makes it very difficult to analyze the "common" features of the Common Agricultural Policy. Nevertheless, some simple economic analysis will help clarify how, and why, the CAP has evolved the way it has, and will indicate the way it is likely to evolve within the much enlarged EU.

Price supports versus income supplements

The CAP agreed on by the EEC-6 in 1962 was essentially a price support scheme, in which target prices would be set for each supported commodity that were the same across the entire Community. If the target price was met in each country then there was no impediment to letting the commodity be traded freely among the partner countries. In the early days of the CAP not all agricultural products were included; by 1970 87% were included, and by 1986 91%.

The CAP actually uses three types of market interventions. The first and most prominent is support prices, which cover about two-thirds of all CAP products. The second, covering about a quarter of all products, is simply external protection. Examples of these products are wines, flowers, eggs, poultry, and some fruits and vegetables. The third is special or flat-rate aid for certain products that keeps domestic prices low but supplements farmers' incomes. Examples of these products are olive oil, durum wheat, cotton, and tobacco.

Since the MacSharry reforms, discussed below, and the EU agreement to the Uruguay Round of Agricultural Adjustment (URAA), in 1995, the CAP has moved toward "aid to producers" under a variety of rubrics that reflect the diversity of agricultural interests within the EU of the twenty-first century. For economic analysis, it is easiest to analyze the market interventions, as we can use our standard supply–demand curves and welfare analysis to explore their consequences. The direct aid to producers, however, "decouples" aid payments to farmers from any direct connection to market variables. Moreover, because they are justified for diverse reasons by the member countries (such as protecting the environment from nitrate runoffs, afforestation, the upkeep of rural attractions, compensating for less favored areas, retraining for alternative occupations, and taking early retirement, just to name some of the current categories of aid), member countries are allowed to complement EU expenditures up to certain limits. Thus, direct aid to producers allows the budget problem of the EU to be solved by bringing in national government spending, which raises the possibility of the gradual renationalization of agricultural support programs within the EU.

Market interventions

Because the Community's farmers in the 1960s were still very inefficient relative to those in the United States, Canada, Argentina, and Australia – and the United Kingdom, for that matter – the target prices were typically higher than those in the major exporting countries of the world. To protect EEC agriculture from competition from more efficient farmers in the rest of the world, a variable levy was assessed on imports at each port of entry. The variable levy was set to make up the difference between the target price and the import price at the particular port of entry. In the initial years, when the Community was still a net importer, the variable levy was expected to yield significant revenue that would be allocated directly to the Community as part of its "own resources." Out of these "own resources" the Commission would then be able to finance the purchase of surplus production wherever and whenever it occurred in the Community.

Figure 4.1 illustrates this case. Note that the target price is set sufficiently high to encourage a substantial percentage increase in domestic production, even if the farmers still cannot meet domestic demand for the agricultural good in question. The figure shows only a target price, but in practice a threshold price at the port of entry – for example, Bremen – that confronts an importer will be lower than the target price because of the transportation costs required to ship from Bremen to the final destination. The variable levy, then, needs to be set only at the height of the threshold price to give European farmers a protected market at the target price.

To finance the price support schemes set up for the basic commodities, the EEC established the European Agricultural Guidance and Guarantee Fund. The "guidance" part was intended to help finance technical assistance to European farmers who wished to modernize their operations, thereby increasing their productivity and hence the ability of the customs union to be self-sufficient in agricultural goods. From the beginning, however, the share of the budget allocated to the guarantee part of the fund has dominated, accounting typically for about 95% of the total EAGGF budget. As a result of the expense of maintaining above-world-market prices to European consumers, the EAGGF has also dominated the entire budget of the EEC, as shown in figure 1.1. From

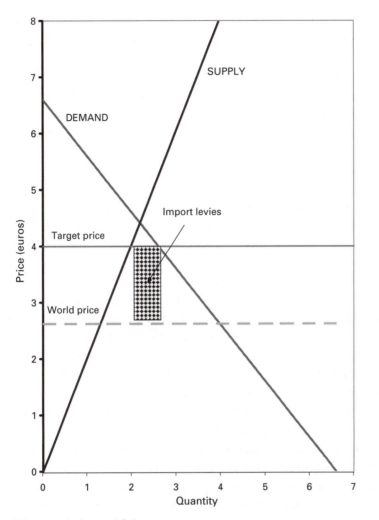

Figure 4.1   Price supports, import deficit

nearly 90% of the EU's budget in the 1968–72 period, it has gradually been trimmed until it is now capped at 45% of the budget.

Despite a very small allocation to guidance over the years by the EU, the technical progress of the agricultural sector has been spectacular. In 1960 15.2 million people were employed in agriculture within the EEC-6; by 1987 that number had dropped to only 5.2 million and the average size of a farm within the EEC-6 had risen from 12 hectares to just under 20. Over the same period the EEC-6 grew in total population but went from providing only 85% of its own agricultural needs to being a net exporter. By 1999 the share of employment in agriculture for the EU-15 had fallen to 4.5%.[10] It is clear that fertilizers and tractors have increased enormously the productivity of both land and labor in western Europe, so much so that labor productivity has increased more rapidly in agriculture than in either services or industry.

Despite the relative increase in labor productivity, however, the ratio of farm incomes to incomes in the rest of the economy has remained quite low, typically 50%, in France, Italy, and Germany. The exceptions are Belgium and the Netherlands, which had relatively advanced agricultural sectors at the beginning of the 1950s. As a result, outmigration from agriculture to the rest of the economy has been rapid, especially in the 1950s and 1960s, when it was regarded by some as the key factor in the economic miracles of West Germany, Italy, and France.[11] The rapid increases in relative labor productivity in agriculture, the result of capital investments stimulated by the generous price support available under the guarantee section of the CAP, did not lead to increases in relative labor income, as they would have in industry or services. The reason is that consumer demand for agricultural output did not rise much at all, even though consumer incomes rose rapidly and the price of agricultural goods fell relative to all other goods. The combination of rapid technical progress in agriculture (enabled by price supports), which created elastic supplies of foodstuffs, and slow increase in demand, caused by inelastic demand in terms of both income and price, has been far more important than the guidance policy of the EEC or of its member governments in achieving the desired goal of self-sufficiency.

The Common Agricultural Policy, however, can take most of the credit for overshooting the goal of self-sufficiency in the 1980s. While maintaining price supports as the primary policy instruments, the agriculture ministers of the EEC responsible for setting the levels of the support prices became increasingly concerned about narrowing the income gap between farmers and the rest of the economy. The result, predictably, was to set prices high enough to provide respectable incomes for small, inefficient farmers. But these same prices provided incentives for even greater production by the more efficient farmers. The response by European farmers led to the situation of export surpluses by 1980, shown in figure 4.2. In this case, domestic supply exceeds domestic demand at the target price and the excess supply has to be bought up and stored, at increasing government expense in the form of mountains of butter and lakes of wine – as were created in the 1980s. It was this situation that pushed the CAP's guarantee expenditures against the limits of revenues available to the European Commission. European farmers responded to the high target prices by steadily pushing the supply curves outward, which in

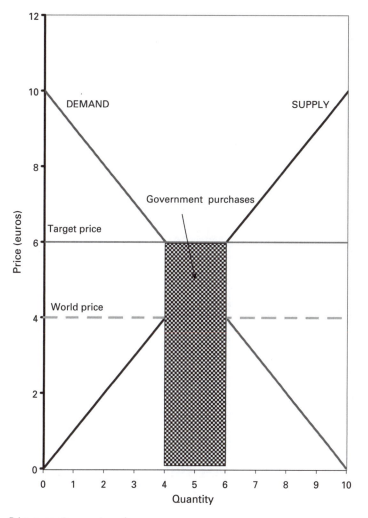

Figure 4.2   Price supports, export surplus

turn increased the excess supply of agricultural products within Europe and increased the expenditures of the EEC on the Common Agricultural Policy.

How did the Council of Agricultural Ministers, responsible for setting the target prices and the crop and animal coverage of the CAP, respond to the increasing pressures on the EEC's limited resources? Not by reducing the target price, as recommended by academic economists, as each country's minister of agriculture was determined to protect the income and investments of his farmers to the best of his ability. Under the parliamentary system of government, the various Cabinet positions are usually filled by politicians recognized

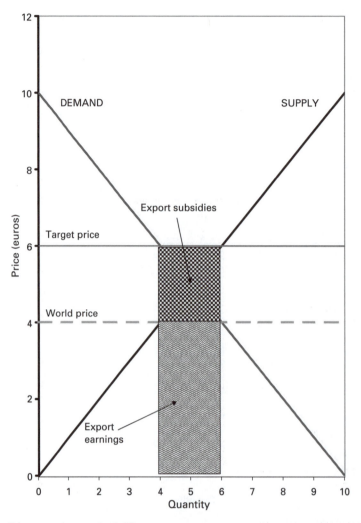

Figure 4.3   Price supports, export subsidies

as defenders of the rights and privileges of the constituencies for each post. In the case of agriculture, it was typical to appoint a politician from the most heavily agricultural region of the country, the one most dependent upon subsidies for continued prosperity. Consequently, the political response to the crisis of overproduction was to cut EEC expenditures by dumping the excess production on world markets at whatever price it would bring, and then simply pay farmers the difference between the target price and the world price for the excess production. The situation of the late 1980s and the 1990s is depicted in figure 4.3. The amount of expenditure required by the EEC to maintain the fixed target price is reduced substantially, but the same incentives for overproduction remain. Further, a new group of interested constituents were brought on board – export houses specializing in finding the best market worldwide for EEC agricultural products.

Direct aid to farmers

British economists recognized the problem that price supports can cause in the agricultural sector when Britain was negotiating its eventual entry into the Common Market. They proposed using a different policy instrument, income supplements called deficiency payments, to achieve closure of the agriculture–industry income gap. Figures 4.4 and 4.5 illustrate how deficiency payments would work in the case of a net importing country and in the case of a net exporting country. The income supplement represents a transfer from consumers to producers via the government, but the net cost to consumers is much less in both cases than it is under a system of price supports designed to keep the same inefficient, high-cost farmers in business. In the case of a net importing country, the cost of the deficiency payments amounts only to the deadweight loss of maintaining inefficient farmers in the economy, a loss that is also sustained under a price support scheme. Consumers, on the other hand, gain consumers' surplus from purchasing a larger quantity of foodstuffs at the much lower world market price. Only part of this is a net gain in efficiency over the alternative of price supports; the rest represents a transfer to consumers from the government, which now gives up the proceeds of the variable levy, and – even more important – a transfer to consumers of producers' surplus from the efficient farmers in the EEC.

In the case of a net exporting country, illustrated in figure 4.5, the system of deficiency payments has even greater advantages over price supports. Again there is a transfer to consumers' surplus from producers' surplus, with some of the consumers' surplus being offset by the deficiency payments, which must come out of general government revenues. There is a net cost to the society: the amount of deficiency payment made to producers for the excess production that is induced by the height of the price support. Previously this was exported; now it is consumed domestically, and consumers still import additional quantities at the lower world price. The efficient producers lose their producers' surplus and the government loses its dumping proceeds, but it lays out a much smaller amount of money to only the most marginal of the agricultural producers. If we draw the implications of this analysis for the

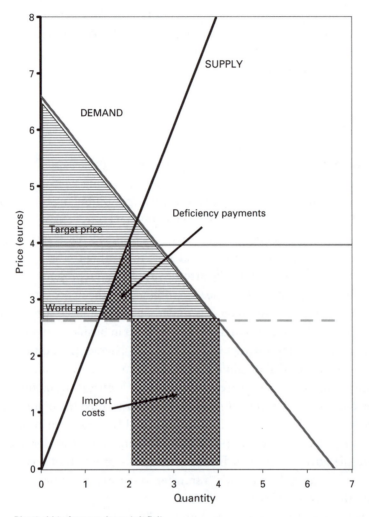

Figure 4.4   Direct aid to farmers, import deficit

political economy of changing from price supports to deficiency payments, we can see that, once a system of price supports has been functioning for some time, there arises a vested interest among prosperous producers and dedicated bureaucrats to maintain price supports as the existing agricultural policy. In 1992 the EEC's Commissioner of Agriculture, Ireland's Ray MacSharry, proposed shifting from price supports to deficiency payments for the smallest farmers in the EEC. To gain the assent of the ministers of agriculture from the member states, he had to propose increasing the actual expenditures on agricultural subsidies during the transition period. Even so, the proposal met

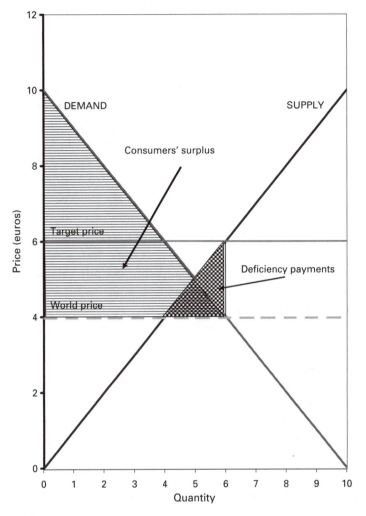

Figure 4.5   Direct payments, export surplus

with violent protest by Continental farmers, leading at one point in the summer of 1992 to a virtual blockade of Paris by farmers parking their tractors and self-propelled combines on the Boulevard Périphèrique.

Nevertheless, the EEC did adopt the bulk of his proposals in May 1992. The total expenditures allowed under the CAP were therefore set at 45% of the total EEC budget, which in turn was limited to no more than 1.27% of EEC gross domestic product, as explained in chapter 1.

The MacSharry reforms were as much a response to international pressure to reform European agricultural subsidies (e.g. GATT negotiations in the

Uruguay Round) as to internal pressures. Support prices were lowered, representing a gain to EU consumers (and the EU's budget) and, of course, a loss to EU farmers. To compensate farmers, the EU decided to grant direct income payments, subject to farmers reducing their use of inputs. For example, cereal producers set aside at least 15% of their arable area; livestock producers limit their herd sizes. In addition, special provisions were made to ease the transition out of agriculture for existing farmers. Export subsidies, however, were maintained, so that the principle of market intervention was still in place. The relative importance of market interventions versus direct aids then depended on the world price of agricultural products covered by price supports under the CAP relative to the target prices set by the agricultural ministers annually. In the late 1990s world prices of agricultural products rose, due in large part to the disruption of agriculture production in the centrally planned economies and their entry into world markets as net importers, coupled with drought conditions in the grain-producing areas of the United States. Consequently, the level of export subsidies required to sustain the EU's support prices for grains fell, which eased the transition to the new system in favor of direct aids over market interventions.

With the collapse of the Soviet Union in 1991, central and eastern Europe, including the Ukraine and European Russia, began importing basic foodstuffs from western Europe, reversing the trade pattern of centuries. On the eve of their accession to the European Union, in 2003, the central and east European candidates for EU membership were still net importers of agricultural products, mainly from western Europe. For a few years these external circumstances reduced significantly the need for export subsidies. But the incentives for reducing production proved to be weaker than the continued price support incentives to increase productivity on the most efficient farms. This was a predictable outcome, given previous US experience with similar "set-aside" programs. When world prices weakened, therefore, export subsidies rose sharply as well.

The welfare effects of these changes were, predictably, difficult to determine, and they have not been made easier by the "decoupling" of EU subsidies to agriculture from actual production. Decoupling means that farmers receiving subsidies under either price support programs or under deficiency payments, both of which were determined in amount by the quantity actually produced by the farmer, would now receive the same amount of subsidy as before, regardless of the amount they produced. This was presumed to reduce the incentive for production. But the price supports remained for precisely those products in surplus, so those incentives remained, as did the productive capacity that

---

Box 4.1 The MacSharry reforms

Arable sector
(i) A reduction of about one-third in the cereal intervention price, which is to fall by 1995/6 to 1,000 green ECU per ton, in three steps. An important degree of protection remains through the threshold price of 155 green ECU per ton.
(ii) Elimination of price support for oilseeds and protein crops.
(iii) Compensation through direct area payments based on historical base areas and regional yields, subject to 15% rotational set-aside for such crops grown by all except small farmers (under 92 tons of cereal equivalent).

Livestock sector
(i) A 15% reduction in intervention prices for beef from July 1993, in three steps.
(ii) Compensation through direct headage payments (premiums) subject to a maximum stocking rate (two livestock units [LU] per fodder hectare) by 1996.
(iii) Increased male bovine and suckler (beef) cow premiums subject to individual limits per holding and to regional reference herd sizes which, if exceeded, reduce the number of eligible animals per producer. There are extra "extensification" headage premiums if a producer reduces the stocking grate below 1.4 LU per fodder hectare.
(iv) A reduction in the ceiling for normal beef intervention buying from 750,000 to 350,000 tons by 1997.

Accompanying measures
(i) Implementation through member state programs with 50% of the cost (75% in less developed regions) borne by the CAP budget.
(ii) An agri-environmental package aimed at more extensive means of production and the use of land for natural resource protection and public leisure.
(iii) Aid for forestry investment and management with up to twenty years' compensation for income loss.
(iv) Various forms of compensation for early retirement, including lump sum or annual payments, for farmers and farm workers over age fifty-five.
Source: European Commission, Directorate-General for Economic and Financial Affairs, "EC agricultural policy for the 21st century," *European Economy, Reports and Studies*, no. 4, Brussels: 1994, pp. 3–40.

---

farmers had built up over the years of relying on stable prices for specific commodities. In terms of our supply–demand diagrams, decoupling has no effect on the demand curves or the support price, and, by increasing the liquidity of farmers, may actually push supply curves outward, worsening the problem of overproduction. It is necessary to reduce, and gradually eliminate, the target levels for price supports, as the European Commission has argued. But political resistance by the farm lobby in all countries, fearful of the effect of falling prices on their ability to service the debt incurred to mechanize and modernize their operations, has repeatedly stalled efforts to reduce, much less eliminate, price supports and the export subsidies that finance them.

The response of the Commission has been to maintain subsidies at constant levels, while gradually redirecting them away from the large, highly productive farms to smaller, less productive farmers deserving of support for reasons other than achieving self-sufficiency or maintaining an export surplus. But this effort has been undermined by "recoupling" subsidies to factors favoring larger farms, such as making subsidies depend on the area that had been under cultivation, or the size of the herd in the case of livestock, or even to subsidize certain inputs that would reduce pollution, or avoid genetically modified organisms or non-organic feed or fertilizer. In an effort to close off these obvious loopholes, the Commission has set limits on the size of herds, areas of cultivation, and amount of inputs that it would subsidize for any given farm. This is the practice known as the "modulation" of subsidies dependent on area or inputs, which, combined with the "degression" of target prices, should eventually solve the problem of overproduction.

Direct, but "modulated," payments in lieu of market interventions also make it feasible to bring the inefficient, heavily agricultural populations of the accession countries into the Common Agricultural Policy. As of 1999 the share of the civilian population engaged in agriculture, forestry, hunting, and fishing was only 4.5% for the EU-15 and went into double digits only in Greece (17%) and Portugal (12.7%). For the countries of central and eastern Europe (CEECs), however, the average was 22%. Nonetheless, only Bulgaria and Romania exceeded this share, and the shares in the other CEEC accession countries fell during the pre-accession period.

To conclude, the agricultural policy of price supports, carried on with enthusiasm, even extravagance, by the EEC since its foundation, when coupled with the technological progress made possible by mechanization and the application of scientific research to the cultivation of crops and the rearing of livestock, has achieved the original goal of self-sufficiency. Indeed, it has gone right on to overshoot the goal and create increasingly unmanageable surpluses and budget problems. The price paid for self-sufficiency has been an increasing sacrifice of economic efficiency.

Welfare and efficiency concerns

To gauge the effects of the various agricultural support programs employed by the European Union, as well as in all the other industrial countries of

Table 4.1 Where agricultural subsidies end up

Policy instrument	Percentage to farm labor	Percentage to farmer-owned land	Percentage to non-farmer- owned land	Percentage to input suppliers	Percentage to cost of resources
Deficiency payment	11.5	14.0	14.0	39.6	20.9
Market price supports	10.4	12.6	13.2	35.7	28.2
Area payment	00.7	46.3	45.0	02.5	05.4
Input subsidy	07.8	09.4	09.4	48.6	24.8

Source: Organisation for Economic Co-operation and Development, *Agricultural Policies in the OECD Countries: A Positive Reform Agenda*, Paris: 2002, p. 10.

the world, the OECD publishes annually its report *Agricultural Policies in the OECD Countries: Monitoring and Evaluation.* At the end of 2002 the OECD followed up its annual report with a declassified working paper by the Joint Working Party on Agriculture and Trade, *Agricultural Policies in the OECD Countries: A Positive Reform Agenda*. This was certainly complementary with, although hardly complimentary to, the EU's attempts to reform its Common Agricultural Policy. The key analysis of the OECD was to highlight the relative inefficiency of each of the EU's means of agricultural support: deficiency payments, market price support, area payments, and input subsidies. For each policy measure, the OECD economists calculated what percentage of a given subsidy would end up as income for various claimants: farm household labor (presumably the main target for politicians), farm landowners (second in priority), non-farm landowners (the rich, rentier class, with few votes but deep pockets), input suppliers, and "resource costs" (the cost to society of making the transfer payment, either by raising taxes or the price of food).

As table 4.1 shows, none of the policies does an efficient job of getting income to the deserving farmer, unless he owns his farm free of debt, and then only if area payments are the policy instrument. Small wonder that economists, regardless of nationality, are opposed to the continuance of these subsidy programs, especially for countries in which self-sufficiency has been obtained or is taken for granted.

Another way of thinking about the efficiency of agricultural policy is to calculate how much extra a society is paying its agricultural producers for their production as a result of a given agricultural policy or mix of policies. This requires calculating a producer subsidy equivalent (PSE) – what would be needed to compensate producers for the removal of all agricultural producer support policies (price supports and deficiency payments) as a percentage of

Table 4.2 Producer subsidy equivalents compared (percentage of value of producers' output)

Country	1986–8	1999–2001
European Union	42	36
United States	25	23
Japan	62	60
Czech Republic	38	19
Hungary	17	18
Poland	4	12
Slovakia	35	20
Norway	66	66
Switzerland	73	70

Source: Organisation for Economic Co-operation and Development, *Agricultural Policies in the OECD Countries: Monitoring and Evaluation*, Paris: 2002, pp. 160–1.

the value of their output at world prices.[12] On this measure, the United States was guilty of raising its average PSE to 28% of agricultural output in 1984–6 from an equivalent of only 16% in 1979–81. Japan also raised its PSE over the early 1980s, but at much higher levels – from 57% to 69%! The EU fell between these extremes, merely raising its average PSE from 37% to 40%.[13] The EFTA countries' agricultural policies give even higher PSEs than in the EU. Over the 1990s progress was made in most countries, but it was still agonizingly slow. Table 4.2 shows that only the Czech Republic made much progress on this measure of policy efficiency. It is interesting that the four accession countries that are also members of the OECD have much lower PSEs than the EU average, while the EFTA countries remaining out of the embrace of the EU and its CAP, Norway and Switzerland, have sustained the highest PSEs of all.

Evaluation

The question arises: why are rich countries willing to pay so much extra for their food supplies? Part of the answer is surely the institutional inertia that keeps policies in operation well after the political forces that created them have lost their power. When price supports were initiated in the 1930s and reinstated in the immediate postwar years, agriculture accounted for a very large share of the jobs in the EEC economies. By 1957 agriculture's share of total civilian employment was still 35.6% in Italy, 16.3% in West Germany, 24.6% in France, and 12.8% in the Netherlands and over 7% in Belgium.[14] This obviously translated into a great deal of political power that could be used to enact government programs very favorable to agriculture. By 1985, however, agriculture's share of civilian employment had fallen to 11.2% in Italy, 5.5% in West Germany, 7.6% in France, 4.9% in the Netherlands, and only 2.9% in Belgium.[15] Clearly, the political clout of the agricultural sector has diminished sharply over the lifespan of the European Economic Community. It is likely that agriculture's continued political success depends on the nature of the institutional arrangement devised for supporting it.

If the agricultural supports come from the EU, into which each member country has paid a share of its value added tax and of its total GDP, then the incentive for each is to get back as much in payments as possible. Because agriculture outlays accounted for 70 to 90% of the EU's budget, setting price supports at levels that subsidize a member country's farmers was clearly the best chance for that country to retrieve its contribution. A similar situation exists in the United States, where each lightly populated state in the Great Plains has two senators to vote in favor of agricultural price supports. In Japan, too, the power of the ruling Liberal Democratic Party resides disproportionately in the rural areas populated by small farmers. When the effective legislature of the EU, the Council of Ministers, is dominated by ministers of agriculture when legislation concerning agricultural subsidies is made, it is not surprising that subsidies, once gained, are not lightly cast aside.

Another part of the explanation for the political success of agricultural interests in modern industrial societies, however, surely must be that the cost of supporting agriculture at an excessive rate has fallen relative to the enormous growth of the rest of the economy. Agriculture's share of the GDP of the EEC-10 had fallen to only 3.3% by 1985. An overpayment of 40%, even if made to the entire agricultural sector, would amount to the equivalent of no more than 1.3% of GDP, which is the self-imposed limit set on total EU spending during the 2000–2006 period.

Finally, for all the overpricing of foodstuffs that the CAP has created for the EU's consumers, their food prices have still risen less than the prices of their non-food goods and services, and food expenditures have fallen even more as a share of household budgets. So the political pressures to undo the CAP have been steadily abating, thanks to the combination of technical progress on the supply side and price and income inelasticity on the demand side. In the last analysis, the costs to any society of inadequate food supplies are far more daunting to consider than the costs of excess food supplies.

Table 4.3 Measures of agricultural policy inefficiency, 1986/7

| Country | (billions of dollars) | | | |
	Producer benefits	Consumer costs	Taxpayer costs	Transfer ratio
United States	26.3	6.0	30.0	1.37
EEC	33.3	32.6	15.6	1.45
Japan	22.6	27.7	5.7	1.48

Source: V. O. Roningen and P. M. Dixit, *How Level Is the Playing Field? An Economic Analysis of Agricultural Policy Reforms in Industrial Market Economies*, Foreign Agricultural Economic Report no. 239, Washington, DC: Economic Research Service, United States Department of Agriculture, 1989.

The second measure of the inefficiency of agricultural support programs – the difference between what society pays and what farmers receive – indicates, however, how much money a society can save by changing the kind of policy it uses to support the agricultural sector. Economists have made an exercise out of calculating the benefits to producers of agricultural supports of different kinds and then comparing them with the costs, whether in the form of higher consumer prices or in government expenditures. For example, comparing the United States, the EEC, and Japan in 1986/7 gives the results shown in table 4.3.

These data show that agricultural support is not just a European problem; the transfer ratios in both the United States and Japan are similar to that of the EEC. Note, however, that the financing of the supports is different. In the United States taxes are paid for the subsidies, while in the EEC and in Japan consumers have paid farmers through higher prices. The EEC has both relatively large tax and consumer costs because domestic prices are kept high and the EEC pays for export restitutions, financed through taxes.

In 1980 British economists estimated the costs to consumers of the excess prices they were paying for foodstuffs in the EEC, the costs to governments of the subsidies made in whatever form, and the amount of extra income actually received by producers. The results are worth reproducing in full (table 4.4), because they show that consumers and governments were consistently paying much more than producers were receiving. On this criterion, the consumers and taxpayers of the EEC paid 1.5 times the amount of extra income received by agricultural producers. Surely, a more efficient redistribution scheme could be devised, if there were the political will to do so.

Moreover, the transfer ratio varied widely among the member states. Tiny Ireland and Denmark benefited greatly because their agricultural sectors, which had concentrated on their comparative advantages for supplying the

Table 4.4 Welfare effects of the CAP by country, 1980

| Country | (millions of dollars) | | | | Transfer ratio |
	Consumers	Taxpayers	Producers	Net	
EEC-9	−34,580	−11,494	30,686	−15,388	1.50
Germany	−12,555	−3,769	9,045	−7,279	1.80
France	−7,482	−2,836	7,237	−3,081	1.42
Italy	−5,379	−1,253	3,539	−3,093	1.87
Netherlands	−1,597	−697	3,081	787	0.74
Belgium-Luxembourg	−1,440	−544	1,624	−360	1.22
United Kingdom	−5,174	−1,995	3,461	−3,708	2.07
Ireland	−320	−99	965	546	0.43
Denmark	−635	−302	1,736	799	0.54

Source: International Monetary Fund, *The Common Agricultural Policy of the European Community: Principles and Consequences*, Occasional Paper no. 62, Washington, DC: 1988, p. 40.

huge British market, now had the protected markets of the EEC-6 to exploit. The United Kingdom, on the other hand, suffered the worst transfer ratio of all the member states. The substantial losses that Britain took from adopting the CAP meant that membership of the EEC continued to be a net economic loss for it well after the difficult years of the 1970s. This factor, more than the clash of personalities between Margaret Thatcher, the British Prime Minister in the 1980s, and Valéry Giscard d'Estaing and François Mitterrand, the French Presidents in the 1980s, accounts for the continued pressures exerted by the British government to reform the CAP, if only marginally, and, failing that, the EEC budget process.

It is interesting to note, in the light of this analysis, how entrenched has become the interest of the prosperous, large farmers in the United Kingdom in maintaining the price support system of the Common Agricultural Policy, now that they have more than twenty years to adapt to it. From accounting for 27% of the OECD's agricultural imports in the late 1960s before entering the EEC and adopting the CAP, the United Kingdom's share had dropped to 11% by 1985. Meanwhile, its share of the OECD's agricultural exports had stayed constant at 6.4%. The implication is that Britain, in common with the original members of the EEC, moved sharply toward self-sufficiency in agricultural products. This is borne out by table 4.5, which compares the self-sufficiency ratios for the United Kingdom and the other EEC member countries in various commodities for 1970–4, 1985, and 1999.

Table 4.5 Self-sufficiency ratios in various foodstuffs for the EEC and its members, 1970–4, 1985, and 1999

	Cereal			Sugar			Butter			Meat		
	1970–4	1985	1999	1970–4	1985	1999	1970–4	1985	1999	1970–4	1985	1999
Belgium–Luxembourg	42	61	57	184	231	162	105	..	131	120	130	182
Denmark	98	134	115	121	239	263	328	198	134	323	322	347
France	159	215	221	154	211	212	113	128	89	95	99	115
Germany	78	100	122	96	132	147	106	112	77	86	91	84
Greece	..	110	67	..	85	..	..	..	30	..	71	58
Ireland	71	102	75	108	141	..	202	..	783	172	199	308
Italy	68	82	80	73	77	109	65	..	75	79	81	76
Netherlands	31	31	21	112	164	..	362	..	152	167	184	236
United Kingdom	65	139	109	35	64	66	18	73	90	70	82	88
Portugal			29			..			125			83
Spain			83			81			92			104
Austria			106			138			99			110
Finland			91			61			128			102
Sweden			131			100			103			98
EEC-15	90	127	115	92	132	..	102	113	99	95	102	107

Source: International Monetary Fund, *The Common Agricultural Policy of the European Community: Principles and Consequences*, Occasional Paper no. 62, Washington, DC: 1988, pp. 28–30; European Commission, Directorate-General for Agriculture and Rural Development, *The Situation in Agriculture, 2001*, Brussels: 2002.

Table 4.5 brings out more interesting aspects of the CAP than merely the incentive it gave to Britain's efficient farmers to expand enormously their output. The self-sufficiency in sugar enjoyed by the EEC-6 in the early 1970s, of course, derived both from their protection of sugar beet farmers, especially in Belgium and France, and from the inclusion in the EEC of Martinique and Guadaloupe as overseas territories of France. Sugar beets were introduced in southern Belgium and northern France at the beginning of the nineteenth century as part of Napoleon I's policy to circumvent the blockade by the British navy of France's access to its sugar islands in the Caribbean, namely Martinique and Guadaloupe. Once Denmark, Ireland, and the United Kingdom adopted the same tariff protection for sugar beets in their agricultural policy, however, their self-sufficiency rose sharply toward the EEC-6's levels.

The same story is repeated for butter and meat. It is interesting that price supports are not used for vegetables and fruit, and that deficiency payments have been the accepted policy for producers of oilseeds. In these categories of foodstuffs, dominated by smaller truck farmers located near cities or owning small orchards, the EEC did not attempt to reach self-sufficiency. The self-sufficiency ratios of the member states changed very little from 1970 to 1985, and that of the United Kingdom actually declined.

Costs of the CAP to the rest of the world

At the Doha, Qatar, summit of trade ministers of member countries in the World Trade Organization, held shortly after the September 11, 2001, terrorist attack on the United States, the EU agreed, with the other industrial nations, that the restrictive trade policies they had all employed since World War II should be removed. The Doha Declaration essentially gave renewed impetus to the Uruguay Round of Agricultural Adjustment (URAA) and prompted the OECD study discussed above. The intent of URAA is to open up international trade to those developing countries with a comparative advantage in trade that would most likely be in agricultural products, especially those best grown or raised in semi- to full tropical climates, but also those coming from temperate zones in the southern hemisphere. The motivation is clear: reducing tariffs on trade in manufactured goods has expanded trade more rapidly than production ever since World War II. Some developing countries have managed to tap into this remarkable engine of growth by finding niches in the production of manufactured goods, at least in the most labor-intensive stages of their production. But other developing countries are frustrated that the markets for their agricultural specialties are either closed off completely or subject to strict quotas by industrial countries.

The EU is an especially egregious offender in this regard, because not only does it impose a variable levy against possible competition to its farmers but it then subsidizes exports of its surplus commodities on world markets, driving down prices for other potential exporters. The commitment of the European Commission to eliminate export subsidies and replace variable levies with fixed tariffs at no more than 25% of the value of the imported product over the next ten years is a welcome initiative. It remains to be seen how far the European Council, composed of the government leaders of the member states, will allow the Commission to deliver on this commitment. In June 2003 the European Commissioner for Agriculture, the Austrian Franz Fischler, could get only grudging acceptance of part of his ambitious plan to do away with price supports entirely. The alternative form of subsidies preferred by the French, Germans, and Spanish is area payments, which are the least effective form of subsidy for farm laborers, but the most efficient in terms of delivering subsidy to the landowners. This is also a form of subsidy that could be subject to reprisals by other trading nations based on subsidy surveillance.

A final problem for the EU's ambition to open up agricultural trade is the trend toward increasing national contributions to agricultural subsidies, as the various new forms of EU subsidies are typically made on a matching basis with subsidies from the member government. In table 4.6 one can see that France, always the largest recipient of EU agricultural subsidies from the beginning of the Common Agricultural Policy, makes by far the largest additional subsidy to its agricultural sector. True, Germany exceeded France in national subsidies in 1993–5, but that was during the initial transition to absorb East Germany's inefficient collective farms into the CAP. And the large expenditures of the United Kingdom in the period 1996–8 were due to the expenses of killing off most of the beef cattle to quell fears of the spread of "mad cow disease" into the human population. Even in 1999–2001, the outbreak of foot and mouth disease in Britain was countered by the slaughtering of 3.5 million farm animals, an expense borne by the British taxpayers. Overall, the individual countries averaged 29% of EU-funded subsidies for their national agriculturists as of 1999. The poorer countries – Greece, Ireland, Portugal, and Spain – rely most heavily on the EU for their subsidies, while the smaller and richer countries supplement the EU subsidies generously. The four largest countries all supplement the EU subsidies to between 20 and 30%.

Table 4.6 National agricultural subsidies within the European Union

Country	(millions of euros)			Percentage of EU subsidies, 1999
	1993–5	1996–8	1999–2001	
Austria	1,359	1,104	896	87.3
Belgium	245	237	341	31.3
Denmark	226	241	247	19.0
Finland	2,248	1,528	1,385	188.6
France	3,481	3,324	3,242	31.8
Germany	3,640	1,882	1,740	26.3
Greece	248	215	223	7.7
Ireland	116	86	240	13.3
Italy	1,080	1,525	1,165	19.4
Luxembourg	30	32	35	101.4
Netherlands	608	983	1,056	77.6
Portugal	186	257	308	37.9
Spain	1,169	685	686	11.0
Sweden	252	299	381	46.8
United Kingdom	837	1,482	1,113	26.8

Source: Organisation for Economic Co-operation and Development, *Agricultural Policies in OECD Countries: Monitoring and Evaluation*, Paris: 2002, p. 88.

Bananas, beef, and bogeymen: the variety of non-tariff barriers

In addition to a trend toward the renationalization of agricultural policies, set in motion by the accession of the three former EFTA countries in 1995 and the adoption of alternative policies that are specific to the felt needs of individual countries, there has been an increased use of non-tariff barriers by the EU since the mid-1990s. All WTO countries have the right to block imports of foodstuffs from another member country on phyto-sanitary grounds – that is, if they have reason to fear injury to either their consumers or to their domestic crops or livestock. The WTO rules provide for impartial scientific experts to determine whether there are valid scientific grounds to block imports of a particular product on health or safety grounds. Before the WTO was created, in 1995, the United States often found that its agricultural exports to the EU were blocked on what it considered spurious grounds, from concentrated orange juice, to processed poultry, to corn gluten in the 1960s, 1970s, and 1980s. Intense negotiations followed and usually resulted in a compromise in which US producers found alternative products to export to the EU, at least until the Common Agricultural Policy could expand its scope to protect those in turn. The process of negotiation, it could be argued, actually encouraged production and product innovations within the agricultural sectors of both trading partners, despite the occasional outbursts of rancor.

The rules of the WTO, however, require that an aggrieved exporting nation (often the United States) invoke the Dispute Resolution Process of the WTO. If a scientific panel finds no grounds for the exclusion of the product in question, the would-be exporter is entitled to receive compensation from the country blocking its exports if that country fails to remedy the situation to allow imports. The last recourse for compensation is for the would-be exporter to impose punitively high tariffs on its imports from the offending country on goods that amount in value to what the WTO's expert panel estimates is the exporting country's loss of earnings from the unfounded trade restriction. Three cases between the United States and the EU have received great attention in the press since the WTO procedures were invoked: (1) bananas subject to restrictive quotas when originating from non-EU affiliated countries; (2) beef products that have had growth hormones injected at some stage; and (3) genetically modified organisms (GMOs), especially corn and soybeans. The three products are obviously quite different, as are the reasons for the EU's exclusion of the products in question, but each case has its own interesting implications for the future of the EU's agricultural policy.

Bananas

The US interest in the banana trade with the EU obviously had nothing to do with domestic producers in the United States, nor did the EU's interest in excluding Central American bananas have anything to do with domestic producers in the EU. Further, the amount of trade involved was really insignificant. In other words, it was an ideal case for both the United States and the EU to try out the new WTO system for resolving trade issues! The problem arose as the EU, an international organization created by international treaty among the member states, found itself bound by three conflicting treaties: the original Treaty of Rome, the 1995 Lomé Treaty with the African, Caribbean, and Pacific countries (see chapter 10), and the WTO treaty, which came into force in 1996. The very last clause in the Treaty of Rome to be agreed upon dealt with the German insistence that they be allowed to continue importing the same quantity of bananas from Central America that German consumers had become accustomed to, especially those in the American occupation zone.

(These same bananas, it's curious to note, were in high demand by East German consumers when reunification occurred.)

France wished to exclude all bananas other than from its former colonies in Africa and the Caribbean, in order to provide those dependencies with an enlarged market for their banana (plantain) exports. The final resolution was to impose import levies on bananas from the dollar area when the German quota had been exceeded. By the 1980s Britain had demanded and received the same preferential access to the Common Market for bananas from its former colonies in Asia and the Caribbean, and so the successive agreements with the African, Caribbean, and Pacific countries, revised every five years, now included non-dollar bananas from a wider area. By the time of the 1995 Lomé Treaty the EU agreed to increase the quota for tariff-free bananas from the ACP countries, but then did this by decreasing the quota for tariff-free bananas from the dollar-area countries, such as Guatemala, Nicaragua, and Ecuador.

Changing a quantitative restriction in this manner, however, violated the WTO rules of trade, which explicitly forbid discrimination by country of origin for any product once it enters a member country. Moreover, it cut into the profits of US firms controlling most of the banana exports from Central America. It took until the expiry of the Lomé Treaty, after five years, and its replacement by the more flexible Cotonou Arrangement in 2000 to allow the EU to work its way out of the conflict among overlapping treaties. In the meantime, the United States tried out reprisals by imposing 100% tariffs on a variety of imports from various EU member countries up to the value of the forgone banana trade. While minor in overall impact, by being targeted to minor items exported from several EU countries, these penalty duties hurt US consumers, angered EU producers, and actually generated increased anti-American hostility within Europe. To make things worse, the EU retaliated by raising penalty tariffs against assorted US products when the WTO ruled against the United States in 2004 regarding tax rebates given to foreign sales corporations. Those duties hurt EU consumers, angered US producers, and increased anti-European hostility within the United States, and did not have the intended effect of forcing the United States to revise its new system of corporate taxation, which it had enacted into law with great difficulty only that year – 2004.

Beef

For many years US beef producers have accelerated the growth of cattle by implanting small amounts of growth hormones, usually testosterone, in the ears of calves. These have the felicitous effect of speeding up the natural growth of the animals so they can be brought to market earlier, typically a full year before normal maturation. On the grounds that these hormones were unnatural and might have some deleterious effects, either on the animals or on consumers eating their meat, the EU has forbidden entry of all US beef, since it is never clear under US Department of Agriculture inspection standards whether a given piece of meat comes from an animal that had growth hormones injected or not.

American scientists have not found any adverse effects from these hormones, either on the animals or on the consumers of their meat. Indeed, they point out that, by slaughtering the cattle before they reach puberty, the amount of testosterone in their meat is actually less than in the European cattle. European scientists have tried very hard to find some adverse effects, without success to date, but in the meantime EU officials find they have support not just from European consumers, fearful of any additives in their food, but also from European producers, wary of cheaper competition from abroad, for the blocking of imports of US beef. To the dismay of US exporters, EU regulators have invoked the "precautionary principle" of regulation: blocking the import of a new product until all possible side effects have been examined and found harmless. As US cattle growers experiment with different hormones and combinations of hormones, in efforts to cut costs or improve quality, the precautionary principle is invoked to require more years of scientific testing. As the amount of beef exported by the United States to Europe has never been very much, it has not been worth the irritation of imposing punitive duties on a few minor items that the United States imports from the EU, so the United States has basically given up on this potential market.

GMOs – a serious issue

The invocation of the precautionary principle for imposing import restrictions on phyto-sanitary and health protection grounds in the case of US beef provided a precedent that led on to a very serious blockage of major imports from the United States – genetically modified corn and soybeans. In 1986 a serious outbreak of "mad cow disease" (bovine spongiform encephalopathy, BSE) was detected in the United Kingdom. The disease, invariably fatal, eventually killed thousands of animals. Once identified as suffering from the disease, cattle were slaughtered and disposed of. Because the disease was similar to scrapie, a brain disease common in sheep, British officials thought it sufficient to eliminate sheep protein from cattle feed, and they saw no danger to humans from mad cow disease as scrapie had never been transmitted to humans in the two hundred or so years it has been observed in Britain.

By 1996, however, the disease was continuing to spread in the British cattle population, and, worse, a number of cases of a similar disease in humans, Creutzfeldt–Jakob disease, began to appear. Finally the British government announced that there was a possibility that "mad cow disease" was transmissible to humans, as were possibly other, similar brain diseases (transmissible spongiform encephalopathies, TSEs). Since then no further use of meat and bonemeal has been allowed in the feed of British cattle, and all cattle that had been fed any form of meat and bonemeal, regardless of the animal source, have been slaughtered and disposed of by incineration. In the meantime, most countries in the world blocked imports of beef from the United Kingdom, including all its trading partners in the EU. Intensive monitoring of cattle stock is now carried out in every OECD country, and occasional cases have been found in other EU countries, but the incidence is low and falling.

"What does this have to do with GMOs?" one might fairly ask. The delay in identifying the source of mad cow disease was due in part to bureaucratic inattention but also to the long gestation period of the disease, at least five years in cattle and probably longer in humans. The implications were twofold: the public was ill-advised to place complete trust in government regulation of food safety; and invoking the precautionary principle by forbidding animal protein as a food supplement to livestock would have saved human lives, as well as millions of cattle. At the same time, GMO food products first began appearing in British supermarkets, the first being a tomato paste that would cling to pasta. This innocuous food product, once it was publicized by consumer advocacy groups to be genetically modified, quickly lost favor with shoppers. Sainsbury's supermarket chain dropped it quickly, but then found that they had to advertise that none of their food products contained GMOs.

Meanwhile, US farmers had planted millions of acres in Bt corn, a genetically modified corn that was resistant to rootworms. Farmers saved money with Bt corn, because they did not have to spray with pesticides and the yield was higher. The EU, however, deployed the precautionary principle and withheld permission to import Bt corn into the Union. Further, given that no effort was made in the United States to tag corn from various fields when stored in silos and then shipped by rail to grain ships, all US corn was banned in the EU market. The closing of a traditional export market, after the planting decisions had been taken, caused considerable loss to US farmers in 1997 and 1998. Then the Roundup Ready soybean was developed by Monsanto Corporation in the United States, a GMO product that resisted the herbicide Roundup, which could then clean a field of all competing weeds, increasing yields. As soy products enter into almost every food process in the United States, American consumers have been ingesting GMOs daily ever since. But, on the precautionary principle, now declared as EU regulatory practice, soybeans were allowed into the EU only for animal feed, not for human consumption.

As of 2003 the EU has passed a directive that, once GMO products have met scientific standards of safety, they may be permitted into the EU. The main legislation that authorizes experimental releases and the marketing of GMOs in the EU, as of October 17, 2002, is Directive 2001/18/EC. This legislation establishes a step-by-step approval process for a case-by-case assessment of the risks to human health and the environment prior to authorizing the placing on the market or release into the environment of any GMO or product containing GMOs. Further, Regulation 258/97/EC on "Novel Foods and Food Ingredients" regulates the authorization and labeling of novel foods, including food products containing, consisting of, or produced from GMOs. All products that may contain some GMO ingredient must be labeled as such, for the information of EU consumers.

In practice, this means that every US product has to be labeled, as there is no possibility under current procedures to distinguish which soybeans or corn have been modified from those that have not. And European consumers have already shown that they are acutely averse to eating anything that has been created, treated, or processed unnaturally. Hence, the United States decided to protest EU practices against GMO foods in the WTO in 2003. From the US perspective, the furor over GMOs in the EU stemmed mostly from the disastrous mishandling of mad cow disease in Britain. Further, the United States sees the EU's precautionary principle on food safety as just another non-tariff barrier designed to keep out competitive products from the rest of the world. Indeed, the WTO finally ruled against the EU in the GMO dispute in February 2006.

NOTES

1. Emile Benoit, *Europe at Sixes and Sevens*, New York: Columbia University Press, 1961, p. 23.
2. European Commission, *A Common Agricultural Policy for the 1990s*, 5th edn., Luxembourg: Office for the Official Publications of the European Communities, 1989, p. 12.
3. "Farms and land in farms, by size of farm: 1880–1954," Series K 61–72, *Historical Statistics of the United States*, Washington, DC: 1960.

4. Benoit, p. 50, note 1.
5. This is an important inclusion and indicates that the EEC was already aware of the problems that exchange rate changes would cause to its pricing policies.
6. International Monetary Fund, *The Common Agricultural Policy of the European Community*, Occasional Paper no. 62, Washington, DC: 1988, p. 31.
7. Organisation for Economic Co-operation and Development, *Agricultural Policies in OECD Countries: Monitoring and Evaluation*, Paris: 2002, p. 71, table 1.7.
8. Ibid., p. 73, table 1.10.
9. European Commission, Directorate-General for Agriculture and Rural Development, *The Situation in Agriculture*, Brussels: various years.
10. European Commission, *A Common Agricultural Policy for the 1990s*, p. 14, note 2.
11. Charles Kindleberger, *Europe's Postwar Growth: The Role of Labor Supply*, Cambridge, MA: Harvard University Press, 1967. See also John Cornwall, *Modern Capitalism: Its Growth and Transformation*, London: Martin Robertson, 1977.
12. Organisation for Economic Co-operation and Development, *Report on Monitoring and Outlook of Agricultural Policies, Markets, and Trade* (mimeographed), Paris: 1988.
13. Ibid., reproduced in IMF, p. 27, note 6.
14. Herman van der Wee, *Prosperity and Upheaval: The World Economy 1945–1980*, translated by Robin Hogg and Max R. Hall, London: Viking, 1986, p. 168; and B. R. Mitchell, *European Historical Statistics 1750–1970*, New York: Columbia University Press, 1978, p. 51.
15. IMF, p. 34, note 6.

5 The euro: the ultimate currency reform?

Overview (1999–2005)

One of the most daunting, but most important, parts of the *acquis communautaire* that the accession countries must agree to take on is the replacement of their national currencies with the common currency of the European Union, the euro. As of 2003, however, only twelve of the fifteen member states had actually adopted the euro as their common currency. The other three – the United Kingdom, Denmark, and Sweden – have opted out for the time being, although each has reserved the possibility of joining eventually. Denmark held a referendum on the issue in 2002, in which the Danish voters cast a negative vote, by a narrow margin, against adopting the euro. Denmark, nevertheless, remains a member of the European Monetary System (EMS), meaning that its monetary authorities are committed to maintaining a virtually fixed exchange rate with the euro. Sweden held a referendum on the issue on September 6, 2003, in which voters narrowly decided against joining the eurozone. The British government had announced earlier, in June 2003, that it still did not feel the economic conditions were right for it to join either the eurozone or the EMS.

The issue confronting each of the ten new accession countries over the next few years, then, is when they should join the common currency and tie their monetary policy to that of the European Central Bank. The alternative is to opt out by following the strategy laid out by either the Danes (pegging their currency to the euro), the Swedes (remain outside even the European Monetary System), or the British (allowing their currency to fluctuate in value relative to the euro and other currencies while setting their own targets for inflation). These issues, which will be dealt with by the governments of "new Europe," are uncannily similar to the issues that were dealt with by the governments of "old Europe" at the end of World War II. Then, as now, individual countries had to balance establishing their legitimacy within restored democratic rule against fostering economic recovery with the aid of foreign capital, all the while maintaining friendly relations with their neighbors. Unlike then, however, when European countries were experimenting with individual ways of coping with the "dollar shortage" (discussed in chapter 2), today's accession countries must deal with the "rules of the game" already in operation within the eurozone. The international money game is now very different from how it was under the Bretton Woods system.

The Bretton Woods era (1958–71)[1]

With the resumption of currency convertibility by the leading nations of Europe in 1958, when the European Payments Union was wrapped up, the multilateral settlement of trade imbalances envisioned in the original Bretton Woods agreement of 1944 could be realized. Indeed, the following ten years saw the full flowering of the possibilities for trade expansion. France and the Netherlands joined in the export-led growth parade initiated by West Germany and Italy, while those two leaders continued to grow rapidly. On the other side of the world, Japan freed the yen, and it too began its export-led ascent to economic supremacy. Underlying this expansion in world trade and world output was a system of fixed exchange rates, with all European currencies pegged to the US dollar. Figure 5.1a shows that this golden decade was initiated by a minor devaluation of the West German mark and the Dutch guilder in 1961 and ended in 1969 with a devaluation of the French franc and a revaluation of the West German mark. The initial decade of the European Economic Community, in short, was one of fixed exchange rates and, effectively, a common currency within the customs union. This monetary regime was accompanied by an enormous expansion of trade among the member countries.

As a result of their common adherence to the rules of the International Monetary Fund, which meant maintaining fixed exchange rates with respect to the US dollar, the member states of the EEC did not have to pay explicit attention to the question of exchange rates with one another, or move toward a common currency as mandated by the Treaty of Rome. By 1968, however, the expansion of trade between France and West Germany had developed into increasing trade deficits for France, which led to the first disruption of the regime of fixed exchange rates within the European Economic Community. The problem arose from the difference in monetary policies followed by France and West Germany: mildly inflationary in France, and strictly stable prices in

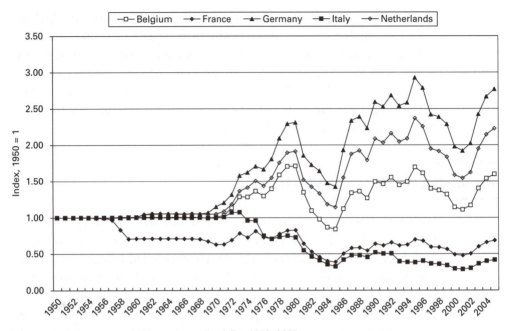

Figure 5.1a   The first six exchange rates on the dollar, 1950–2005

West Germany. With both exchange rates fixed relative to the dollar, a lower rate of inflation in West Germany meant that its real exchange rate was constantly depreciating relative to the dollar, while the higher rate of inflation in France meant that its real exchange rate was constantly appreciating relative to the dollar, and even more so relative to the mark. The continued real depreciation of the mark helped maintain the momentum of West Germany's export-led growth in the 1960s. After further inflation was required in France to quell the labor unrest that erupted in May 1968, a major realignment was agreed upon between the two countries. In 1969 France devalued relative to the dollar by 10%, but only after Germany agreed to revalue against the dollar by an equal 10% (see figure 5.1a).

Before further realignments were necessary within the EEC, however, the Bretton Woods era of fixed but adjustable exchange rates was terminated by the United States. This occurred in August 1971, when President Nixon ordered the Federal Reserve System of the United States to cease paying out gold to central banks of foreign countries when they wanted to cash in part of their holdings of US dollars. Closing the gold window, as this action was termed, enabled the United States to float the dollar against all other currencies, letting it rise or fall depending on the state of the balance of payments. With respect to the currencies of the original six members of the EEC, the dollar fell at differing rates: most against West Germany, then against the Netherlands and

Belgium, and least against Italy (figure 5.1a). This meant that the exchange rates within the EEC changed as well, creating uncertainty among traders and consternation among the bureaucrats charged with administering the price supports of the Common Agricultural Policy.

The snake

In response to the acrimony generated over the realignment of the French and West German currencies, which had been carried out bilaterally in 1969, the EEC launched an ambitious effort to achieve economic and monetary union. The effort culminated in the Werner Report in 1970, and on the basis of that report the EEC proposed to achieve a common currency by 1980 in three stages. Stage I, to begin in 1971 and last for three years, would achieve a "concertation" of national macroeconomic policies with a goal of narrowing exchange rate fluctuations among member currencies within a smaller range than authorized by the IMF (then still +/−1%). Stage II would create a European Monetary Cooperation Fund, controlled by the governors of the individual central banks, which would use its resources to intervene in the foreign exchange markets to minimize exchange rate variations among member currencies. Stage III would see the evolution of this fund into a European central bank managing a common Community currency by 1980.[2] Any resemblance between the Werner Plan of 1970 and the Delors Plan of 1990 is more than coincidental!

The collapse of the Bretton Woods system in August 1971 forced Stage I of the Werner Plan into a series of makeshift arrangements as the individual countries struggled to cope. The final collapse of a managed international monetary system, in March 1972, was followed by the first oil shock, in October 1973, and the second oil shock, in 1979. Concertation was largely put aside in favor of domestic political considerations, and the achievement of consensus over exchange rate policies was not aided by the accession of three new members in 1973 – the United Kingdom, Ireland, and Denmark. What emerged instead was a system of jointly floating currencies anchored to the deutsche mark, which came to be known first as the "snake in the tunnel," while the other European currencies could stay within +/−1.5% of the deutsche mark, and later as the "snake in the lake," when the limits of variation for the other European currencies could not be held fixed.

The first stage in the breakup of the Bretton Woods system was the Smithsonian Agreement in December 1971, whereby a new set of "central rates" among the Group of Ten[3] major industrial countries was agreed on, with temporarily wider bands of 2.25% on either side allowed. The initial reaction of the EEC Council of Finance Ministers to the Smithsonian Agreement was

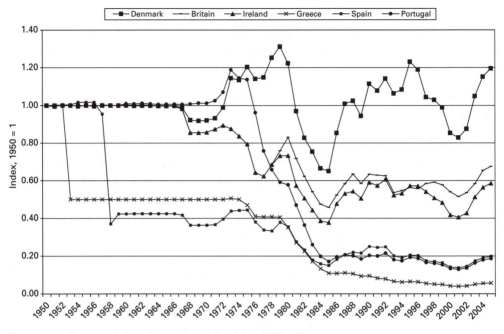

Figure 5.1b   The second six exchange rates on the dollar, 1950–2005

to state that the EEC currencies would maintain this +/−2.25% band with respect to one another, but not with respect to the US or Canadian dollars. A bit later, in March 1972, they determined to maintain margins with respect to each other that were only +/−1.125% from the agreed central rates (the snake), while keeping within the +/−2.25% margins with respect to the other G10 currencies (the "tunnel"). Britain joined only briefly (May to June 1972) as a token gesture of its commitment to membership in the EEC, which was to begin formally in 1973, but then floated from June 1972 on. Italy left the arrangement in February 1973, just before the entire Smithsonian Agreement broke down and generalized floating began in March 1973.

This ended the tunnel, but the snake continued to float, although with a varying membership. By January 1974 France had dropped out of the arrangement, rejoining briefly from July 1975 to March 1976. While Norway and Sweden participated from time to time, the joint float ended up being conducted by West Germany, the Netherlands, Belgium, Luxembourg, and Denmark.[4] Obviously, it was the German Bundesbank that was orchestrating this arrangement and not the European Monetary Cooperation Fund envisioned in the now moribund Werner Report. The disarray of exchange rate policies among the new, peripheral members of the EEC is illustrated nicely in figure 5.1b.

While each major country in the EEC pursued its own national policy to respond to the first oil shock, the West German economy and those linked most closely to it in the snake had the most success. This can be attributed in large part to the effect of West Germany's tight money policy in absorbing a large part of the oil shock through an appreciation of the deutsche mark relative to the dollar. The 1973/4 oil shock consisted of the OPEC countries quadrupling the price of crude oil in dollars. When the deutsche mark and the currencies pegged to it appreciated by 30 to 40% relative to the dollar, they wiped out that much of the price increase for imported oil. Meanwhile, by continuing to depreciate their currencies relative to the dollar, France and Italy magnified the oil shock for their economies. Recognizing their relative failure, the central banks of France and Italy renewed their efforts to imitate the West German policy when they were confronted with the second oil shock, which started in late 1978 and lasted through 1979 into 1980. This led quickly to the formation of the European Monetary System, a greatly modified version of the Stage II envisioned in the Werner Report.

The European Monetary System (1979–92)

The inclusion of France and Italy in the joint float with West Germany against the dollar and yen required some modifications in the arrangements of the EEC. While the formal initiative was launched at the July 1978 meeting of the heads of government of the member countries (the European Council), operation of the European Monetary System did not begin formally until March 13, 1979.[5] The United Kingdom opted out for a variety of reasons, pragmatic and political. Its previous effort at floating with the rest of the EEC had aborted after only one month in 1972; as yet its trade with the rest of the Community had not expanded to the extent hoped for when it had joined; and, most important, its commitment to the development of its offshore oil resources in the North Sea was coming to fruition, foretelling the emergence of Britain as a net oil exporter rather than oil importer, unlike the rest of the EEC. The importance of this was that the price of oil was then (and still is) set in US dollars by the OPEC cartel. West Germany's tight money policies during the first oil shock of 1973/4 had meant that the deutsche mark appreciated relative to the dollar, so the price of oil, while still rising in terms of deutsche marks, did not rise as much as it did in dollars. This was a definite advantage for a net importer such as West Germany and the rest of the EEC, but a definite disadvantage for a net exporter such as Britain.

In the event, the British decision proved right: almost immediately after the launching of the European Monetary System came the second oil shock of 1979/80, set off by the revolution in Iran. This redoubled the price of oil, which had already quadrupled in response to the power of the OPEC cartel in 1973/4. The British decision forced Ireland and Denmark, two small, open economies that had traditionally had the United Kingdom as their major trading partner before they entered the Common Market along with the United Kingdom in 1973, to decide where their future lay. Both opted to stick with West Germany, in essence, and to take their chances on trade with Britain as the pound floated with respect to the deutsche mark. In the short run, this proved especially painful for Ireland, as it found itself priced out of much of its traditional British market and not yet competitive in the rest of the EEC. No doubt the economic costs were judged worth bearing for the political independence from Britain that the decision implied.

More important than the short-run costs for these two small countries, however, was the effect of the second oil shock on the stability of the newly created system. The first oil shock had destroyed permanently the Bretton Woods system of fixed exchange rates, set with adjustable pegs to the US dollar, despite the best efforts to realign rates in the Smithsonian Agreement of December 1971. Would the second oil shock destroy the more modest effort of the Europeans to have a limited area of exchange rate stability within the confines of their customs union? Surprisingly, the EMS survived, expanded in membership, strengthened in effectiveness, and eventually induced even the United Kingdom to join in late 1990.

There were two keys to the survival of the EMS in the face of the second oil shock, reduced growth, greatly increased unemployment, and political turnover in most participating countries. One key was its flexibility, as European analysts argue; the other was the felicity of encountering two favorable shocks in the 1980s. The flexibility was manifest in the frequent realignments, usually to allow France or Italy to depreciate a bit more relative to the West German deutsche mark and the Dutch guilder (table 5.1). The felicity derived from facing first the "Volcker shock" of a sharply appreciating US dollar in the early 1980s, and then the third oil shock in the second half of the 1980s, when the price of oil collapsed. The felicitous shocks were far more important than the flexibility of the EMS members in realigning their rates periodically. All the European currencies, whether they were in the EMS or not, depreciated against the US dollar from 1980 to 1985. This may be called the "Volcker shock," as it came not from any European initiative but from the dramatic change in US monetary policy initiated in 1980 by Paul Volcker, then governor

Table 5.1 Dates and size of EMS realignments (percent change in central rate with the ECU)

	24 Sep. 79	30 Nov. 79	22 Mar. 81	5 Oct. 81	22 Feb. 82	14 Jun. 82	21 Mar. 83
FF	0	0	0	−3	0	−5.75	−2.5
DM	2	0	0	5.5	0	4.25	5.5
IRL	0	0	0	0	0	0	−3.5
ITL	0	0	−6	−3	0	−2.75	−2.5
HFL	0	0	0	5.5	0	4.25	3.5
DKR	−2.9	−4.8	0	0	−3	0	2.5
BFR	0	0	0	0	−8.5	0	1.5

	20 Jul. 85	7 Apr. 86	4 Aug. 86	12 Jan. 87	22 Jan. 90	14 Sep. 92	17 Sep. 92
FF	2	−3	0	0	0	3.5	0
DM	2	3	0	3	0	3.5	0
IRL	2	0	−8	0	0	3.5	0
ITL	−6	0	0	0	−3	−3.5	*
HFL	2	3	0	3	0	3.5	0
DKR	2	1	0	0	0	3.5	0
BFR	2	1	0	2	0	3.5	0
PTA						3.5	−5.0
UKL						3.5	*
ESC						3.5	0

	23 Nov. 92	1 Feb. 93	1 May 93	6 Mar. 95
FF	0	0	0	0
DM	0	0	0	0
IRL	0	−10.0	0	0
ITL	*	*	*	*
HFL	0	0	0	0
DKR	0	0	0	0
BFR	0	0	0	0
PTA	−6.0	0	−8.0	−7.0
UKL	*	*	2.58	2.02
ESC	−6.0	0	−6.5	−3.5

Source: Ecustat, Supplement no. 10, "The Evolution of the EMS," December 1995, p. 50.

of the Federal Reserve System. Volcker targeted limits on the annual growth of the US money supply and let interest rates go as high as the market desired in the face of sharply reduced liquidity in the United States. The dramatic rise in the exchange rate of the dollar worsened the effects of the second oil shock for all Europe, save the United Kingdom and Norway, which were now oil exporters. But it also had the effect of improving the export competitiveness of Europe relative to the United States. Among the oil importers, West Germany was doing no worse than the rest, and there was no chance for any country other than Norway or the Netherlands to imitate Britain by exploiting North Sea oil or natural gas. Even so, realignments were frequent in the first few years of the EMS system under the duress of the Volcker shock. They occurred in September and November 1979, again in March and October 1981, in February and June 1982, in March 1983, and finally in July 1985.

After 1985 the remaining realignments, until the breakaway of the United Kingdom and Italy in September 1992, occurred in the context of new entries coming into the Exchange Rate Mechanism or existing members narrowing their bands from 6% (Italy and Ireland initially, and then Spain, the United Kingdom, and Portugal as they entered the Exchange Rate Mechanism [ERM] of the EMS) to 2.25%. Europeans congratulated themselves on having made the necessary adjustments in central par rates during the shakedown part of the cruise. Having weathered the storm of the second oil shock, they launched the single market initiative.

The revival of investment and growth rates in Europe in the late 1980s is no doubt attributable in part to the opportunities opened up by the Single Europe Act of 1987, though it was already anticipated by the end of 1985. Equally striking, however, from an American perspective was the effect of what might be called the "third oil shock," the collapse of crude oil prices at the end of 1985. This inaugurated a period of relatively cheap energy that was only briefly interrupted during the Gulf War of 1990/1. Moreover, the US dollar fell relative to the other OECD currencies after the Louvre Accord in 1985, making oil prices even cheaper for the European economies. With this fortuitous combination of falling oil prices and a falling dollar, small wonder that the participating currencies in the EMS had no further need for realignment.

From the middle of 1985 until September 1992, indeed, the EMS was hailed as having achieved its goal of stabilizing exchange rates among member states of the EEC, enabling them to move confidently forward to the next step: establishing a common currency. The success in this period owed everything, it appeared, to the economic benefits obtained by member states when they permitted their central banks to accept the monetary leadership of the Bundesbank. The Bundesbank, in turn, was committed by the West German constitution to maintain independence from the central government and to keep inflation under control, meaning less than 3% annually. In effect, the deutsche mark had replaced the US dollar as the key currency for the rest of the European central banks.

The stability of the exchange rates encouraged the member states to press forward with plans for establishing a European financial common market, allowing the free movement of capital among the member states. This required, first and foremost, the elimination of capital controls by individual members, at least as far as the capital exported to other member states. It also required the elimination of restrictions on the ownership by foreigners of financial assets in the EEC, at least if the foreigners were also from the EEC. The initial effects of this limited deregulation of European financial services was very beneficial to those countries that had had the most tightly controlled financial sectors – France, Italy, and Spain. West German and British banks and insurance companies, especially, found previously untapped markets for their efficient operations in mutual funds in Italy, branch banks in Spain, and financial markets in France. Tying their exchange rates firmly to the deutsche mark further encouraged the import of fresh capital to these economies. Consequently, all of the EEC prospered during the late 1980s. It was against this background of increasing prosperity, renewed foreign investment within the EEC generally and especially in the southern tier, financial deregulation, and stable exchange rates that the Delors Plan for achieving, finally, the long-cherished goal of a single currency for the EEC was formulated.

Stage 1, which was already in progress, was to be completed by the end of 1992, when all twelve member states would have committed to maintaining fixed exchange rates with respect to the other eleven currencies. All seemed well until difficulties began to be experienced with the ratification of the Maastricht Treaty by the member states. From early 1987 to June 1992 the EMS and its Exchange Rate Mechanism enjoyed an unprecedented period of stability in the central parities and in the fluctuations around them. Spain and the United Kingdom joined the ERM; Italy and Ireland moved from wide 6% bands for the allowable fluctuations in their currencies to the narrow 2.25% bands. Moreover, when uncertainties over the possible outcomes of the Maastricht summit, held in December 1991, began to put pressure on some currencies, coordinated actions were taken by several central banks to maintain stability in the exchange rates. In November the French and Italians raised their key interest rates and the British were allowed to move closer to the bottom of the 6% band. After the Maastricht summit the Germans raised their discount rate, countering inflationary pressures caused by the mounting costs of reunification, but all the ERM countries except for the United Kingdom followed suit, again to maintain the stability of the grid of fixed exchange rates with one another.[6] By April 1992 even the Portuguese escudo had joined the ERM, and only Greece remained outside the parity grid (figure 5.2).

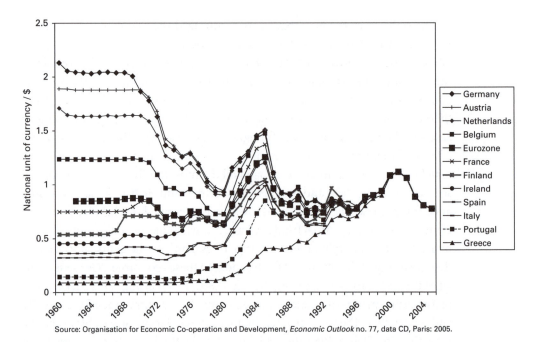

Source: Organisation for Economic Co-operation and Development, *Economic Outlook* no. 77, data CD, Paris: 2005.

Figure 5.2   Leading to the euro, 1960–2005

The first alarm occurred in June 1992, when the referendum presented to the Danish electorate by the government failed to elicit the necessary approval by a majority of Danish voters. Not only did this cast in doubt the viability of the political union foreseen by the Maastricht Treaty, it undermined confidence in the future of the EMS as a stepping stone to monetary union. The political difficulties of both Italy and the United Kingdom made participants in the foreign exchange markets doubt whether those two governments could continue to follow the German Bundesbank in maintaining high interest rates. Moreover, the weakening US dollar was putting balance of trade pressure on all the European economies. Nevertheless, Germany continued to raise its interest rates, and economic difficulties increased for other member states, especially Italy, the United Kingdom, and Spain. Looming in the near future was the upcoming referendum on the Maastricht Treaty in France, scheduled for September 20, 1992. The rejection of the treaty by voters in Denmark was a disturbance, not a disaster. Voters in Ireland had overwhelmingly approved it; perhaps the Danish government had mishandled the presentation of the treaty to its public.[7] If the French referendum failed, however, it would be a disaster. Polls showed that this was quite possible, in fact.

In early September Finland, which had been pegging its currency, the markka, to the deutsche mark in anticipation of applying for full membership and participating in the advantages of the single market, experienced a net outflow of foreign reserves to finance a sudden increase in its import deficit with the former Soviet Union. As a result, Finland was forced to abandon the project and float the markka, which fell sharply. The Swedish krona also came under heavy attack by speculators, leading to incredible interest rates of 75% and then, for a spell, 500%. On Monday, September 14, the Italian lira was permitted to devalue by 7% against the rest of the currencies.[8] Speculative pressures then focused on the British pound. On Wednesday, September 16, the pound sterling was withdrawn (temporarily!) from the ERM, the Italian lira was allowed to float, and the Spanish peseta was devalued by 5% against all the remaining EMS currencies. This effectively ended the ERM for those countries, and the prospect of uniting all the member state currencies into a common currency, as foreseen by the Maastricht Treaty. The foreign exchange markets had decided the fate of EMU – European Monetary Union – before the French voters had their say.

Nevertheless, the French franc remained steadfastly linked to the deutsche mark despite enormous selling pressures against it. The narrow approval of the Maastricht Treaty by French voters on September 20 undoubtedly helped sustain the French government in its determination to maintain the exchange rate of the franc with the deutsche mark. The speculative pressures continued to play against the various currencies that had decided to continue pegging their exchange rate to that of the deutsche mark. At the end of November 1992 both Spain and Portugal devalued their currencies by 6% against the ECU. On February 1, 1993, the Irish pound finally conceded defeat and devalued by 10% against the ECU. By May 1993 both Portugal and Spain had been forced to devalue yet again.

Meanwhile, the French economy continued to suffer slow growth and rising unemployment while British exports began to rebound and the economy revive, apparently in response to the continued lower value of the pound sterling relative to its trading partners in the single market. At the end of July 1993 the crisis culminated when the French government decided it could no longer raise interest rates in defense of the franc and the Bundesbank decided it could no longer extend loans of deutsche marks to the Banque de France. These were starting to increase the supply of German currency circulating in Germany and to undermine the Bundesbank's efforts to control inflationary pressures within the recently unified Germany.

The resolution was to allow the French franc to devalue, but not by realigning relative to the ECU, as had been done by Spain, Portugal, and Ireland, or by withdrawing from the Exchange Rate Mechanism, as had been done by Italy and the United Kingdom. Instead, a novel solution was reached: "temporary" expansion of the allowable limits of fluctuation in the values of the participating currencies to +/−15%. This allowed the French franc to devalue, in fact, by as much as the pound and lira had during the September 1992 crisis. In fact, once the speculators started taking their profits by buying back the now much cheaper French franc, it rose again to within the original +/−2.25% range around its central par rate with respect to the deutsche mark.

The August 1993 solution was viewed as a temporary fix, with the goal of moving toward a common currency still held firm by the French, Dutch, Belgians, and Danes, whose central par rates had remained intact throughout the turmoil. The commitment of the Spanish, Portuguese, and Irish was maintained as well through irregular realignments. At the European Council meeting in December 1993 the composition of the ECU was fixed at its 1989 basket, when the peseta and escudo had been added to it. Hereafter, the ECU is a "hard" unit of account, meaning that in the future any change in a member state's exchange rate can be only a devaluation relative to the ECU, now called the euro.

The successive crises of the European Monetary System from September 1992 to August 1993 forced all the member states of the European Union to resolve the ambiguities of the Exchange Rate Mechanism in one way or another. Economists from the United States and the United Kingdom were virtually unanimous in proclaiming the EMS dissolved. (And good riddance, because of the confusion it caused in foreign exchange markets, the sporadic crises in which caused disruptions to foreign trade.) It would henceforth be better for all the countries concerned to allow their exchange rates to fluctuate freely on the foreign exchange markets. This would use the competitive forces of global product and capital markets to constrain policy-makers in each country to follow sound economic policies that kept their economies competitive with those of their trading partners. If competitive in the product and capital markets, a country's exchange rate would stabilize in the foreign exchange market. Coordination, in short, would occur spontaneously by individual decision-makers responding to the price signals emitted from the common marketplace.

Policy-makers in both Germany and France, however, determined that the solution to the periodic instability of an adjustable peg system would be better solved by affirming that existing exchange rates would be locked at some point on the way to a common currency. With only one currency among them, the problems of coordination would be solved once and for all by centralized authority. The "only" remaining question was how that central authority would make and enforce its decisions. The agreement reached at the Brussels meeting of the European Council on October 29, 1993, between François Mitterrand and Helmut Kohl was to proceed on course with the Delors Plan and begin Stage 2 as planned in January 1994. The Treaty on European Union, better known as the Maastricht Treaty, came into effect in November 1993. The decision to proceed with the next stage of monetary union required by the treaty was taken even as the Exchange Rate Mechanism, which had been characterized by Delors as the "glide path" to a common currency, had crashed.

Instead of a glide path for a common system of currency management that would take off into a common currency centrally managed, the more realistic analogy now was of a convoy of separate ships headed for a common destination but temporarily scattered by stormy seas. Meanwhile, serious construction of the destination site should be undertaken. So the countries remaining in the EMS agreed to maintain their previous central par rates but to allow market rates to diverge up to 15% in either direction from them. No longer would central banks have to stand in one place when attacked by foreign exchange speculators betting on either a revaluation or a devaluation. They could easily slip to the other side and let another set of speculators on the opposite side of the market come to their defense. Meanwhile, the creation of the framework for a single currency could go forward.

Figure 5.2 traces out the annual exchange rate indexes of the euro-12 countries over the period 1960–2005, whether they were in or out of the EU and whether they were in or out of the EMS. The fixed exchange rates of each country's currency relative to the dollar during the Bretton Woods period were dispersed widely. When the Bretton Woods regime of fixed exchange rates collapsed in the period 1971–3, countries with restrictive monetary policies found that their currencies appreciated relative to the dollar (falling downwards to the right on the graph). Countries with expansionary monetary policies found their currencies depreciating relative to the dollar (rising upwards to the right on the graph). The convergence is dramatic through the 1980s and 1990s. Greece never joined the ERM in this period, and once Italy and the United Kingdom dropped out in 1992 neither rejoined until Italy re-entered on November 25, 1996. Spain and Portugal joined the EMS in 1990 but each had to devalue repeatedly, preferring always to be part of the monetary integration of Europe rather than dealing with volatile exchange rates. Their partners in the EMS preferred to let them devalue rather than make interventions in the foreign exchange markets on their behalf, much less to coordinate their own monetary policies with those of the Iberian countries. Their rates within the EMS tracked rather closely those of Sweden and the United Kingdom, both of which have stayed out of the EMS since 1992.

Finland by the end of 1995 was recovering from the shocks to its economy of the early 1990s and formally joined the Exchange Rate Mechanism of the EMS in November 1996, as did Italy. Ireland found itself in the unusual situation of trying to link with the deutsche mark but still being subject to much the same market forces that moved the exchange rate of the British pound sterling up or down. As the pound was weak relative to the ECU in 1993 through 1995, so was the Irish punt. Although it was only devalued once, in February 1993, it was near or at the bottom of the EMS currencies relative to its new central par rate throughout 1994 and 1995. In 1996, however, the pound sterling rose from the middle of the year, and with it also the Irish punt. The French franc managed to stay on course for maintaining its link with the deutsche mark since the mishaps of 1992/3 although by the end of 1996 it was the weakest of the ERM currencies. The Danish situation was dominated by the course of the deutsche mark, but, like Ireland's punt, the Danish krone was pulled down by the importance of its remaining links with the United Kingdom and with the other Scandinavian economies until those currencies began to rise in 1996.

Next on the graph is the Belgium/Luxembourg franc, which seems caught between tracing the course of the French franc or the German mark. In the 1990s the choice was clear: to follow the mark, much to the satisfaction of the Flemish part of Belgium. The thickest line is the calculated average exchange rate of the European Currency Unit, or what would have been the ECU had it been created earlier from the twelve currencies now blended into the euro. The combination of the German mark, the Austrian schilling, and the Dutch guilder shows up as nearly the same thickness as the euro line because the latter two currencies were consistently pegged to the deutsche mark over this period.

Figure 5.2 is a useful diagnostic device because it shows the recent vicissitudes of the EMU adventure very clearly and also because it reveals starkly the "fault lines" that exist in the monetary structure of the EU. There is clearly a deutsche mark bloc in northern Europe, with the French and the Danes trying to maintain their currencies as part of that bloc and Finland trying to rejoin it. There is a second group of "ins" and "outs" that let their currencies depreciate through 1995 either as deliberate policy (the United Kingdom, Italy, and Sweden) or as the unintended consequence of monetary policy dominated by other goals (Ireland, Spain, and Portugal). Greece is entirely another story, as seen in figures 5.1b and 5.2. How can a stable monetary structure be built on such a foundation?

The future

The major advantage of the common currency should be the reduction in transactions costs for individuals and firms doing business across the national boundaries within the EU. But, in order to provide these cost savings to individuals and businesses, banks must make costly investments and find alternative ways of recouping lost revenues from commissions on foreign exchange transactions. A 1996 survey of European banks by *Euromoney* magazine estimated that the costs of converting to euros between 1999 and 2002 would be ECU8 to 10 billion, or an additional 1 to 2% of their operating costs each year for three or four years. For at least three years banks' information technology would have to maintain a dual payment system, denominated in two currencies – its national currency and the euro. Further, the loss of commissions on foreign exchange would constitute a permanent reduction in their revenue base of 5 to 10%.[9] The correspondent banking business across EU borders is now substantially reduced, as any one bank's business can now be consolidated into the largest, most efficient correspondent bank. The article concluded, "In terms of simple return on investment, no sensible banker would actually suggest such a project."[10] All this means is that the large banks in Germany and the state-owned banks in France continue to try to compensate for their lost foreign exchange commissions by devising alternative sources of revenue.[11]

Exchange rate risks are typically hedged effectively for exporters and importers by offsetting contracts with their counterparties, by buying forward contracts in the desired currency, or by selling the current receivables in its currency to a third party. All these require additional market contacts and do have some fixed expenses. The larger the scale of the transactions, typically, the smaller the percentage the fees will be, so for the bulk of foreign trade these commission costs are not a serious impediment. Moreover, the larger and more competitive the market is for forward exchange contracts the lower the fees will be. It is precisely in the tradeoff between going to a market-based solution or going to a financial specialist, such as a Continental-style universal bank, that the British and German businesses differ in their assessment. For the French and Germans the markets are much less competitive than for the British, and so they are more concerned to get special deals from their customary banking houses, which do all their financial business for them, including funding long-term investment projects.

Governments with weak tax bases, such as Greece, Portugal, and Spain, not to mention the EU government-in-waiting and all the governments of the ten accession countries of 2004, necessarily have weak markets for their debt issues as well. How can an investor be confident that a government with uncertain tax receipts and unpredictable demands on its expenditures will pay interest faithfully and redeem the principal when called on? These governments must rely on increases in the money supply they control to cover their expenditures. A counter to the EMU proposal, then, would be to broaden the potential market for the debt issues of governments with weaker tax structures. Indeed, participation in the EMS was a boon for Italian and Irish debt issues, as they continued to pay higher interest rates on their bonds than either the Germans or the French, but had a commitment from the other countries to maintain their exchange rates from depreciating very much.

An alternative for the accession countries, of course, would be to issue debt in the foreign currency of choice for the potential investors. It is not accidental that the first major Euro-bond (debt denominated in dollars by a foreign borrower) issue in the 1960s was to finance the construction of the Italian *autostrada*. But this alternative denies the government in question the possible benefits of seigniorage. Excessive issue of its currency would increase the burden of servicing the debt denominated in foreign currency. Moreover, the government then has to compete with other issuers of bonds to keep its creditworthiness competitive. No European government has enjoyed doing this in the past and it is unlikely that the governments of the central and east European accession countries will enjoy it in the future.

The existence of different levels and kinds of government debt already issued by the member states, however, raises further problems. Each government will still be required to service its own debt from its own tax base, even though every government's debt is denominated in the same currency – the euro. There is no intrinsic problem with this: every state in the United States issues its own debt denominated in the common currency of the US dollar. But every state has a balanced budget requirement, so each new issue of debt has to be backed by a specified source of revenue dedicated to servicing it. This is necessary because no state now has the right to redeem its debt with money that it has created.

A similar problem to that now facing the European governments, however, arose when the currency union of the United States was formed with the adoption of the constitution in 1789. Alexander Hamilton, the first US Secretary of the Treasury, decided to assume the debts that the separate states had issued during the preceding years, including the expensive war years of the American War of Independence. Combining all their bond issues into one large issue that was backed by the customs revenues and land sales of the new federal government enabled Hamilton to create a broader market for US debt than would have been possible otherwise. Nothing is foreseen at present for a similar refunding operation in Europe, but the same pressures of differential debt burdens and abilities to service them that prompted Hamilton to do his assumption of state debts were present in the European Union of fifteen member states, and will only increase within the European Union of twenty-five member states.

The Commission's counter-argument to this scenario is that the sheer volume of euros will create a demand for them in other countries to hold as a reserve currency. Indeed, if demand for a country's currency by others depends on the size of its trade with the rest of the world, it would appear at first sight that the euro will be in greater demand than the US dollar, given the greater importance of the European countries as a group in world trade. If true, then the euro will become the world's favorite currency to hold for reserves by central banks and international businesses.

However, it is not true to say that demand for a reserve currency is determined in this way. First, the EU trades mostly with itself, which is why it dominates world trade when intra-EU trade is counted as foreign trade. If we take just the trade of the EU with the non-EU world, it turns out that in the 1990s the United States alone had more trade with the rest of the world than did the EU. Another way to see the point is to realize that the deutsche mark reserves once held by central banks and businesses in the rest of the EU are no longer necessary for them, because their own currency, the euro, is the same as the German currency needed for payments there. Euros are not foreign reserves for any European bank or firm that is within the EMU, by definition. Only the rest of the world will still need a European currency for financing trade, and it will need dollars more than euros.

This point has been readily recognized. What is less obvious is that the value of the dollar as a reserve currency for central banks, and especially for banks and firms around the world engaged at all in foreign transactions, rests not so much on the volume of trade flows denominated in dollars as in the volume of capital flows denominated in dollars. It is the liquidity of the US capital market, seen first in the size and ease of transfer among secondary holders of its national debt, and then made truly unmatchable by its broad and deep markets for private equity and bonds, that makes the dollar – or, rather, dollar-denominated financial instruments – so attractive to the rest of the world, including Europe. A study by the Bank for International Settlements concluded

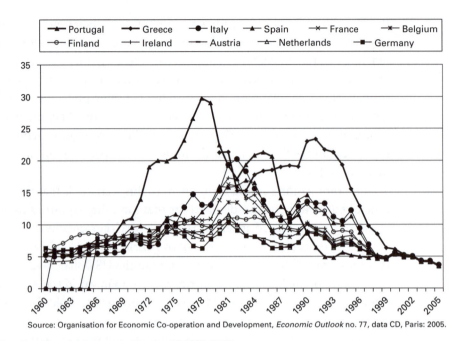

Source: Organisation for Economic Co-operation and Development, *Economic Outlook* no. 77, data CD, Paris: 2005.

Figure 5.3   Long-term interest rates, "Euroland," 1960–2005

that the superior liquidity of US dollar financial instruments explains "why virtually all mean-variance analyses of optimal reserve portfolios find the actual proportion of US dollar holdings to be well above that suggested by efficiency considerations alone."[12]

The same study concluded that increased volatility in exchange rates experienced by currency peggers, such as members of the ERM, tended to boost the dollar share of reserves. If a central bank holds reserves to offset volatile changes in a country's, or firm's, balance of payments, then it surely will see the advantage of holding those reserves in the most liquid financial asset available. Again, we come to the conclusion that it is not the common currency that is vital for the success of the single market but the additional market for credit.

With such an uncertain future for the euro and a present economic situation characterized by continued high unemployment and slow growth, the question for an economist is: what economic motivation could be driving European governments toward adoption of the common currency? A good part of the answer can be seen in figure 5.3, which shows the dramatic fall in the rates of interest paid by European governments on the stock of their outstanding debt and their convergence to historic lows. With the average debt to GDP ratio now in "Euroland" of 80%, and average interest rates falling to 3.5%, the reduction in interest payments alone has enabled governments to reduce their deficits by nearly one percentage point of GDP on average.[13] The deficit reduction from the effect of falling interest rates is obviously highest for those countries with the highest ratios of debt to GDP and with the highest interest rates at the beginning (Italy, Portugal, and Spain), but it has been significant for all. The reduced interest payments have enabled governments in Euroland to sustain the payment of continued unemployment benefits, thereby reducing the political pressure to reform wage policies or remove structural rigidities in their labor markets.

This is unfortunate, because the long-run pressures on all European governments are mounting in terms of future pension liabilities. High unemployment, as now concentrated among older and younger workers, is continuing to exacerbate the problem of the future funding of retirement benefits for an aging population. High unemployment among older workers encourages early retirement, intensifying pressures on pension funds. High unemployment among younger workers reduces their future employability and productivity, reducing the growth of the tax base. In short, the continued high unemployment in Euroland that has characterized the adoption of the common currency under the tutelage of the Bundesbank is generating greater fiscal pressures for their governments in the future, even as the transition has reduced fiscal pressures in the present.

Ultimately, each country will have to turn to a greater use of capital markets, both to encourage the funding of new enterprises that can create new employment and to provide investment opportunities for pension funds. Hopeful signs of this necessary transformation can already be seen in Germany. The financial sector there is trying to surmount the daunting costs of reunification by developing venture capital mechanisms and equity markets for small and medium-sized enterprises. The "relationship banking" that has been the hallmark of German universal banks since the nineteenth century has proven incapable of mobilizing adequate finance for the reconstruction of the east German economy. If there is no "relationship" between west German banks and east German entrepreneurs, there can be no lending! At the same time, German banks are beginning to reform their practices to approach more the arm's-length lending and investment practices of their American and British counterparts. Perhaps the German financial sector, if it is reformed rapidly enough, can provide more useful leadership for the rest of the eurozone in the coming years than the Bundesbank is providing at present. In short, the future of the euro depends upon the growth of capital markets in the eurozone.

NOTES

1. This section is drawn from chapter 7 of Larry Neal and Daniel Barbezat, *The Economics of the European Union and the Economies of Europe*, New York: Oxford University Press, 1998.
2. Charles Kindleberger, *A Financial History of Western Europe*, 2nd edn., New York: Oxford University Press, 1993, pp. 443–4.
3. The Group of Ten was formed in the early 1960s as a caucus of the leading members of the IMF to discuss and initiate changes in IMF legislation. It consisted of the G7 – the United States, West Germany, Japan, the United Kingdom, France, Italy, Canada – plus the Netherlands, Belgium, and Sweden. Although Switzerland is not a member of the IMF, a representative of that country is often included in the meetings.
4. The history of the snake is given in *European Economy* 12 (July), 1982.
5. Horst Ungerer, *The European Monetary System: The Experience, 1979–82*, Washington, DC: International Monetary Fund, 1983, p. 1.
6. "The ERM in 1992," Study no. 5 in *European Economy* 54 (December), 1993, p. 145.
7. In contrast to the Irish government's technique of distributing brief pamphlets that high-lighted the advantages Ireland would enjoy in a single market, the Danish government, at great expense, made widely available complete copies of the full treaty. Even Jacques Delors admitted later that the wording required in EEC documents to gain the approval of the entire European Council made many parts of them unintelligible.
8. This was done by devaluing the lira by 3.5% against the ECU and revaluing all the other currencies by 3.5% against the ECU.
9. *Euromoney*, September 1996, pp. 94–5.
10. Ibid., p. 99.
11. One such source would be preferred access to TARGET, the interbank payments clearing system among banks on the European continent. The French and German banks proposed this as early as 1996, with the implicit support of both governments. Needless to say, the British banks objected mightily, and in response hastened the implementation of their more advanced computer technology so as to facilitate payment clearings with allied banks elsewhere in Europe.
12. Scott Roger, *The Management of Foreign Exchange Reserves*, Economic Paper no. 38, Basle: Bank for International Settlements, 1993, p. 68.
13. International Monetary Fund, *World Economic Survey*, Washington, DC: 2000, pp. 126 and 132.

6 The European Central Bank in action

When the euro was introduced as a unit of account for the initial eleven member countries deemed eligible to join the common currency on January 1, 1999, the European Central Bank officially assumed responsibility for the monetary policy of those countries. The mandate of the ECB was laid out in article 105(1) of the Treaty on European Union, namely "to maintain price stability." The political independence of the ECB was guaranteed twofold: first, by requiring that the national central banks in each member country be formally independent from their national governments; and, second, by making the decision-making authority of the Governing Council of the ECB formally independent from the European Union. The only indication of the close connection between the institutions of the EU and the ECB is the treaty requirement that, "[w]ithout prejudice to the objective of price stability, the [Eurosystem] shall support the general economic policies in the Community," such as "sustainable and non-inflationary growth" and a "high level of employment." First and foremost, the objective of ECB monetary policy is price stability; only if it is confident that the growth of the money supply or a reduction in interest rates will not threaten price stability is it even expected to use its power to influence growth or employment.

In practice, the ECB has interpreted this mandate to mean that it should not pay attention to the exchange rate of the euro with respect to any other currency, whether that of another country in the European Union or in Europe, much less with respect to the dollar or yen. Formally, decisions about euro exchange rates are reserved to the respective finance ministers of the member states, but obviously the ECB would have to implement whatever exchange rate decisions were made at the EU level. Because both Japanese and American monetary policy-makers pay close attention to other economic factors as well as to the goal of price stability, the exchange rate of the euro with respect to the dollar has varied widely since its introduction. Figure 6.1 shows the course of the monthly exchange rate of the euro with respect to the dollar since its introduction in 1999. For historical perspective, figure 6.1 also shows the

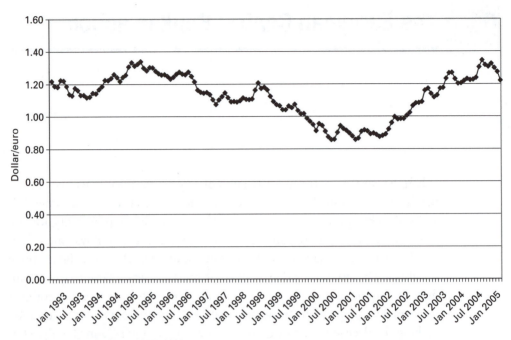

Figure 6.1   US dollar/euro, 1993–2005

exchange rate of the ECU, the EMS basket currency that was the forerunner to the euro, for the six previous years. Obviously, neither the US Federal Reserve System nor the EU European Central Bank has bothered to stabilize the single most important exchange rate in the world economy! To date, the only period of concern arose when the dollar/euro rate fell from 1999 to 2001 at the same time that inflation rates in the eurozone countries remained above the target rate of 2% annually. By the end of 2002 the dollar/euro rate began to rise, however, recovering the previous averages of around $1.20 to the euro by 2004.

Beginning its existence on January 1, 1999, the euro at first could exchange for $1.1674, then rose in a few days to a height of $1.1808. Over the next two years, however, the value of the euro with respect to the dollar continued to fall, reaching a low of $0.8285 in late October 2000. The prolonged fall of the euro occurred as the US economy and especially its stockmarket boomed, but the decline of the euro continued even after the US stockmarket crashed in March 2000. None of the textbook determinants of exchange rates seemed to explain this sustained fall in the euro over this period. While US interest rates were higher than EU interest rates and the growth of the US economy was higher than that of the euro-area economy, there was no change in the

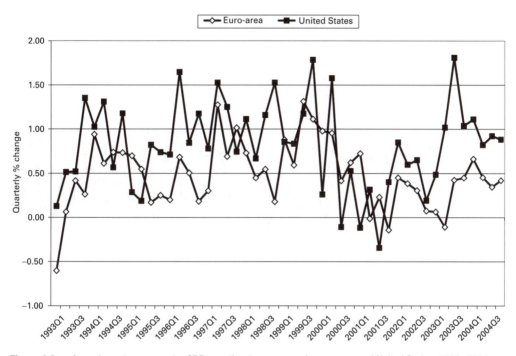

Figure 6.2 Annual quarter-on-quarter GDP growth rates compared, euro-area and United States, 1993–2004

relative interest rates or growth rates, or even, for that matter, in the relative inflation rates that would account for the continued decline in the euro over that period. Figures 6.2–6.4 show the OECD quarterly estimates of the euro-area and US determinants of exchange rates over the period preceding the formal introduction of the euro – 1993Q1 to 1998Q4 – the "break-in" period of the euro – 1999Q1 through 2001Q4 – and the full operation of the euro within the euro-area – 2002Q1 through 2004Q3. The changes in relative interest rates, especially the short-term interest rates, which are the most responsive to policy actions by the central banks, do seem to explain some of the changes in the dollar/euro rate both before and after the "break-in" period. One explanation could be that adjustment to the new institution dominated exchange rate movements over the three years from the introduction of the virtual euro (when financial institutions and governments used it as their unit of account but the legacy currencies continued to circulate as notes and coins) to the completion of the new currency, when euro coins and notes replaced the legacy currencies.

In retrospect, it appears that international financial institutions, especially the major international banks and their corporate clients, were making

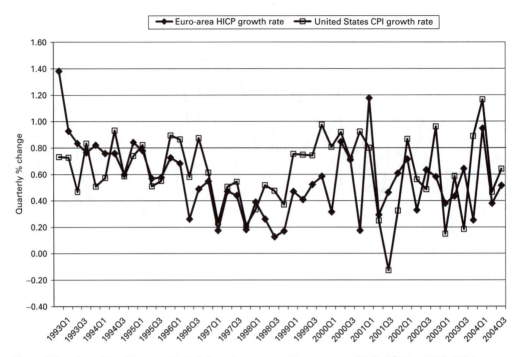

Figure 6.3 Annual quarter-on-quarter inflation rates compared, euro-area and United States, 1993–2004

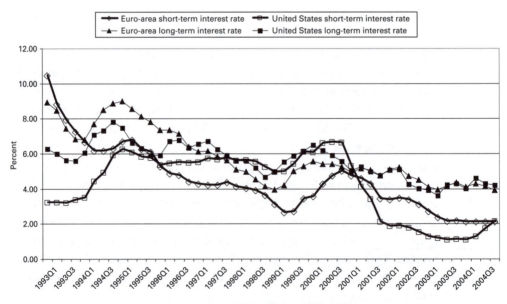

Figure 6.4 Interest rates compared, euro-area and United States, 1993–2004

adjustments in their portfolios in response to the new "rules of the game" put into place by the ECB. Following the commitment of the US government, beginning in 2002, to fund the expenses of the military operations in Afghanistan and then Iraq the euro rose steadily, reaching a peak of $1.3622 at the end of 2004. Over this period interest rates were higher in the euro-area than in the United States, as the Federal Reserve System committed itself to historically low interest rates to help the US economy revive after the shock of the terrorist attacks of September 11, 2001. Henceforth, perhaps, the textbook explanations, which presume stable institutional arrangements, will reassert their validity for understanding the long-run movements of the euro/dollar rate. (No textbook tries to explain the short-run volatility of all exchange rates in today's global economy!)

The European Central Bank

Structure

The structure of the European Central Bank is unique, as befits its unique origin, and this may help to explain the otherwise odd behavior of the exchange rate of the dollar/euro during its initial three years of operation. The uniqueness stems from its complete independence from government authority. Not only is the ECB independent of the European Union, it is doubly independent of the governments of the member states belonging to the common currency. While the euro-area governments do appoint the President and the Vice-President of the ECB, their terms are then fixed in duration. The four members of the Executive Board are also appointed by the European Council, but, again, their appointments are for fixed, staggered terms, so that the turnover of personnel responsible for decision-making is minimized. While these six individuals make up the Executive Board of the ECB, which carries out and oversees its daily operations, they are responsible to the Governing Council of the ECB. The Governing Council includes the six members of the Executive Board plus the individual governors of the national central banks that belong to the common currency as of 2004. That means that, since Greece's joining in 2002, it has had eighteen members. Those governors, while representing their respective countries, are also appointed for fixed terms by their governments, with the notable exception of Italy; that country's governor is appointed for life. The individual governments are bound not to interfere with the central bankers as they manage the monetary policy set by the ECB. To cap it off, the treaty establishing the European Community states explicitly in article 108:

While exercising the powers and carrying out the tasks and duties conferred upon them by the Treaty and the Statute of the ESCB [European System of Central Banks], neither the ECB, nor a national central bank, nor any member of their decision-making bodies shall seek or take instructions from Community institutions or bodies, from any government of a Member State or from any other body. The Community institutions and bodies and the governments of the Member States undertake to respect this principle and not to seek to influence the members of the decision-making bodies of the ECB or of the national central banks in the performance of their tasks.

In addition to the Executive Board and the Governing Council, there are regular meetings as well of the General Council, which adds the heads of the national central banks in the European Union that are not yet part of the common currency. With the accessions of May 2004 the General Council now includes twenty-five heads of central banks plus the six members of the Executive Board. The General Council, of course, has no voice in determining ECB policy or operations, but the intent is that eventually all member states will adopt the euro, at which time it will be dissolved. In the meantime, its role is to monitor the progress of the non-members of the ECB, taking on the functions that were performed by the European Monetary Institute (EMI) in the preparation period for the euro.[1] It is also the formal mechanism by which the non-members of the euro are kept abreast of the actions and thinking of the ECB in carrying out the monetary policy of the euro-area.

Since the accessions of 2004 the statutes of the ECB have been amended to keep the number of governors of national central banks that have voting rights in the Governing Council at fifteen. It seems doubtful as of 2006 that the three incumbent members of the EU who have not yet joined the euro will join in the foreseeable future. But all ten of the new member states do intend eventually to join the euro. Once there are more than fifteen governors of national central banks, voting rights will be allocated to different groups of countries. Up to twenty-one governors, there will be two groups: the first will consist of the five largest and richest countries in the euro-area, and the second will be the remaining eleven to sixteen countries. The first group of five will have at least four of their number retaining voting rights while the second group will rotate in ten of their number to exercise their votes. When there might be twenty-two or more member states in the euro-area, the allocation of voting rights will split into three groups, now with four of the top five countries rotating in to vote, eight of the next twelve rotating in, and three from the bottom group of six to eight rotating in to vote their interests. To date, the maximum number of member states anticipated to join the euro is twenty-seven, implying that provisions are made for all the twenty-five current members to join the euro eventually and then assuming that Bulgaria and Romania will join as well at some stage, depending on when they enter the EU and then meet the criteria for admission to the euro.

Strategy

How does this complex organization, designed to placate the varied interests of the current and future member states of the European Union, accomplish its mission of assuring price stability within the euro-area? The first pillar of the ECB's strategy has to be its economic and monetary analysis of the euro-area economy as well as individual indicators of developments in particular sectors or regions of the economy. These analyses allow it to determine whether measures need to be taken to offset shocks to the economy regardless of their effect on the growth rate of the money supply. The economic analyses, however, also allow the Bank to ignore events if it deems them to be transitory in nature, or self-correcting providing that price stability is maintained. Indeed, after the initial break-in period with the "virtual euro," the Bank has maintained very stable monetary conditions, certainly by comparison with the US Federal Reserve System, or, for that matter, by comparison with the Bank of England or the Bank of Japan.

The goal of price stability first had to be given operational content. A target rate of 2% annual inflation was set for the eurozone as a whole. Recall that the Maastricht criteria included setting the limit on a member country's debt/GDP ratio at 60% and a limit on a member country's deficit/GDP ratio at 3%. Both these ratios can be maintained in equilibrium if a country's nominal GDP grows at 5% annually.[2] If one expects the trend growth of real GDP to be 3%, then to get a trend growth of nominal GDP of 5% the rate of inflation should be 2% annually. The 2% annual rate of inflation, as one might infer from the graphic in figure 6.5, can be achieved given the historical experience of the leading countries within the European Monetary System. To achieve it, the ECB relies on the relationship between real economic growth, financial deepening, and inflation. The theory is that in the long run the trend growth rate of nominal GDP (equal to the trend growth rate of real GDP plus the average rate of inflation) will equal the trend growth rate of the money supply plus the average rate of change in the velocity of money (the rate at which

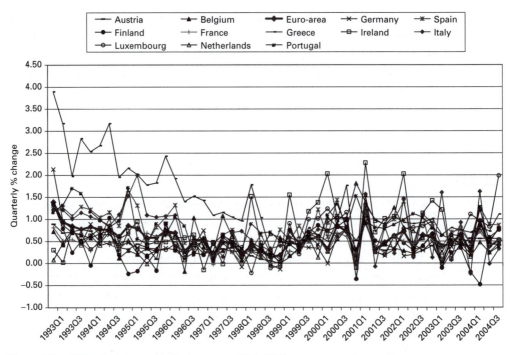

Figure 6.5   HICP rates compared in the euro-area, 1993–2004

the money supply turns in a year relative to the size of the nominal GDP). In equation form:

$$\Delta y + \Delta p = \Delta m + \Delta v$$

In the past, the trend growth of real GDP (Δy) has been between 2% and 2.5% and the rate of change of velocity (Δv) has been from −0.5% to −1.0% annually. Both these variables are driven by forces in the economy other than monetary policy. Real output is determined by the growth of factors of production, capital and labor, and technology while velocity is determined by financial innovations. A central bank empowered with a monopoly on the supply of money in an economy should then be able to control its growth rate (Δm). To reach a target rate of inflation (Δp), then, of 2.0% annually, all a central bank has to do is keep the growth rate of money at a steady 4.5%, assuming that the growth rates of real GDP and the rate of decline of money velocity are independently driven. This reference rate, announced by the Governing Council in December 1998 and confirmed in subsequent reviews, constitutes the first pillar of the two-pillar strategy of the ECB.

The control of the rate of growth of the money supply then comprises the second of the two pillars of the strategy of the European Central Bank. But only the circulating currency (M_1) of the euro money supply is controlled directly by the ECB. Bank deposits and time deposits in savings institutions make up the rest of the money supply (M_3). The relationship between these other components of the money supply, only indirectly controlled by the ECB's policy instruments, and the rate of inflation in consumer prices is subject to change over time, especially as private agents use the new currency in novel ways in a constantly evolving economy.

The second step was to design a measure of price stability, which was not as straightforward as a non-economist might think. Toward this end, the European Monetary Institute began to construct a "harmonized index of consumer prices" (HICP) for each member state. The intent was to have a similar basket of goods going into the construction of each country's consumer price index, albeit with weights specific to the average consumption pattern of the goods in that country. Then, weighting each country by the size of its GDP, the aggregate HICP for the euro-area could be determined. Figure 6.5 shows the progress of this measure for all twelve euro-area countries since 1993, when the Treaty on European Union was ratified.

After the ratification of the Maastricht Treaty the inflation rates of the eventual members did converge perceptibly, edging toward the eventual target set by the ECB of a 2% increase annually (0.5% on a quarterly basis, which is what is shown in figure 6.5). Even Greece, which did not meet the Maastricht criteria initially and had to delay entry until 2002, just in time to convert the drachma to the actual euro coins and notes, was successful in bringing down its inflation rates to join the cluster around the target rate. After the introduction of the "virtual" euro in 1999, however, the inflation rates all rose above the target rate. Surely this was the result of the continued depreciation of the euro relative to the dollar, meaning that the euro-area as a whole was importing inflation by being forced to pay higher prices for goods and services imported from outside the area. Since the introduction of the actual coins and notes, however, inflation rates have settled around the target rate, with the dispersion of inflation rates continuing among the diverse member countries.

For some time now, the inflation rates in the least advanced countries have been noticeably higher than those in the most advanced and largest countries. The efforts of the ECB to constrain overall inflation rates have led some critics to suggest that too much attention is paid to the high inflation rates in Ireland, Spain, Greece, and Portugal and not enough to the low inflation rates in Germany, France, Belgium, and the Netherlands. But, given the low levels of per capita income initially in the first four countries, compared to the high levels in the latter four, the mere process of price convergence meant that inflation rates would have to be higher in Spain and the other low-income countries while they were catching up with the richer countries. The case of Ireland, which did catch up with the average level of per capita income in the euro-area over this period, and in which inflation rates moved from above-average to average rates, bears out this conjecture.

This phenomenon reminded economists of the so-called "Balassa–Samuelson effect," which had been noticed in the early years of the Bretton Woods system, when countries with low levels of per capita income joined the fixed exchange rate regime of the International Monetary Fund and then began to experience higher rates of inflation. It also raises concerns about what the accession countries will experience in their inflation rates during the transition period as they try to meet the Maastricht criteria and adopt the euro in turn. As of 2006 several accession countries have already delayed their target dates for joining the European Monetary System, which is the first step toward adopting the euro and committing to fixed exchange rates with the eurozone countries.

Policy

While the Bank has both discount rate and open market operations at its disposal in principle, it necessarily must rely most heavily on its discount rate instrument to affect monetary conditions. Open market operations depend on a central bank having at its disposal large amounts of government debt that it holds and that it can sell or buy on the open market from the private sector. Given the limited capital of the European Central Bank and the dispersion of euro-area government debt among the twelve member states, the Bank has limited ability to affect the government debt market directly. It has managed to get the Governing Council to agree to impose a very modest, 2.5%, reserve requirement on the national central banks, but mainly to give the Bank some working capital, not as a tool for monetary policy by varying the reserve rate.

Figure 6.6 shows the policy actions of the ECB from its initial assumption of its duties through April 2005. The discount, or rediscount, rate instrument is, essentially, the lending rate of the ECB to its member banks. Banks needing liquidity for short periods of time, sometimes just overnight, can borrow the funds they need from the ECB at the lending rate. Banks finding that they have more cash on hand than is needed to meet payments can deposit these funds

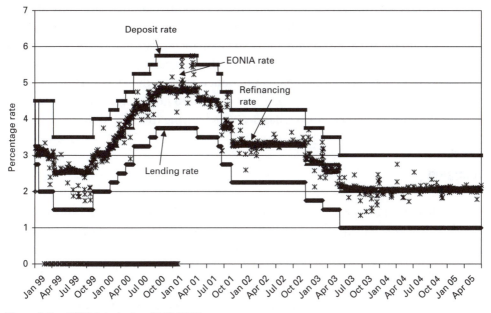

Figure 6.6   ECB interest rates, 1999–2005

with the ECB and earn the lower deposit rate. The spread between the two rates has been kept at a constant two percentage points, basically to encourage banks to lend and borrow with each other within that spread. The European Overnight Interest Average (EONIA) is the daily rate for interbank lending within the euro-area, and, although volatile at times, it has kept within the spread set by the ECB. The other rate of interest is the refinancing rate, the rate at which the ECB offers fresh infusions of euros to the member banks. The process by which the ECB carries out this form of open market operations, which it considers its most important instrument of monetary policy, deserves fuller explanation.

Open market operations in the ECB model are carried out by the ECB offering to the member banks a fixed amount of euros at a set interest rate. Banks then bid for the amount of euros they want to have at that interest rate, and, since June 2000, for the amount of euros they want at slightly higher rates. The total amount bid by all the member banks is then divided up among them pro rata. The ECB then holds the eligible assets that have been offered by the member banks, usually in the form of government debt, and earns the average rate of interest bid on the bonds it now holds. By varying the interest rate on which it will provide fresh infusions of euros to the banking sector, the ECB determines the interest rates that banks use in dealing with each other.

This is why the average rate of EONIA in figure 6.6 fluctuates daily around the refinancing rate, which is set weekly by the ECB. The lending rate is then set at one percentage point above the refinancing rate and the deposit rate at one percentage point below, to create the two percentage point spread. It is evident that most of the changes in policy came in the ECB's first three years of operation. Since June 2003 it has decided to hold a steady course. Indeed, the volatility of the EONIA has decreased during this period as well.

Conclusion

To date, the operations of the European Central Bank in conducting the monetary policy of the euro-area have to be considered a success from its viewpoint. The new currency has been introduced throughout the euro-area and is accepted by the citizens as the one legal tender for all financial transactions. No financial crises or disruptions to the flow of payments have occurred. Moreover, after some difficulties in holding the overall inflation rate at the announced target rate of 2%, inflation has stabilized and seems to be converging among the member countries.

The question raised by an increasing number of analysts and European politicians, however, is whether the viewpoint of the European Central Bank is the appropriate perspective to take for managing the common currency of the European Union. The perspective of the ECB is that if it accomplishes this one goal – price stability – then all the other goals that preoccupy the leaders of the European Union – continued growth of the economy and full employment of the labor force – will be that much easier to accomplish. Confidence in price stability enables decision-makers within the economy, at every level from the central government down to individual households, to proceed with more confidence and to achieve their full potential. The political leaders of Germany, France, and Italy, by contrast, find themselves confronted with sluggish economic growth, continued high unemployment levels, and rising discontent among their voters. They must envy the members of the ECB's Governing Council with their fixed terms of office and their indifference to political discontent.

Economists studying the ECB have also raised doubts about its performance. It is not clear, for instance, that 2% inflation rates are appropriate for achieving the other economic goals that preoccupy political leaders. Given that average deficit and debt ratios to GDP have risen above the 3% and 60% levels picked in 1992 when the Maastricht criteria were formulated, and that average growth rates of real GDP have slipped well below the anticipated trend of 3% and have had difficulty reaching even 2% over the past decade, a reasonable argument can be made for higher rates of inflation, and higher rates of money growth. Certainly, the economic structures of France, Belgium, and Italy have been built on a foundation of higher rates of inflation in the past, while the economic structure of united Germany could benefit from higher rates of inflation than drove the prosperous years of West Germany. The counter-argument of the ECB economists is that structural changes in the respective labor and capital markets of the member states are needed to bring down unemployment rates and to speed up capital formation and economic growth. But these structural changes are very resistant to political pressures within each European country.

It may be that the political independence of the European Central Bank is its ultimate weakness, making it tone-deaf to the sounds of discontent arising among the electorate in Germany, France, and Italy. Created by international treaty under special circumstances, the ECB may eventually succumb to these pressures, precisely because it has no independent source of political strength. An example of the political forces at play came with the modification of the Stability and Growth Pact in 2005 by the decision of the European Council, over the publicly voiced objections of the ECB. It may be that a central bank can perform its tasks better when it is politically independent, but it cannot afford to be politically indifferent when deciding what tasks to undertake and how to undertake them.

NOTES

1. The EMI was created in January 1994 to prepare for the introduction of the euro by coordinating the statistics and policy assessments of the EU's national central banks. Headed by Alexandre Lamfalussy, who had recently retired as managing director of the Bank for International Settlements, and who had begun his career in the BIS when it coordinated the European Payments Union (discussed in chapter 2), the EMI constituted Stage 2 in the introduction of the euro. Stage 3 was the adoption of the euro as a formal unit of account on January 1, 1999, when the European Central Bank replaced the EMI and absorbed its staff and functions.

2. This follows from the formula $d = bg$, where $d = D/Y$ (the ratio of the government deficit to GDP, both in nominal terms), g = the growth rate of nominal GDP, and b = the ratio of government debt (B) to GDP, both in nominal terms. Because the stock of debt increases each period by the amount of the deficit, $D = B'$, by definition $B' = b'Y + bY'$, so $D = b'Y + bY'$. Dividing both sides by Y, $d = b' + b(Y'/Y)$. If $b' = 0$, meaning no change in the ratio of government debt to GDP over time, we have $d = bg$.

7 The single market: from eliminating non-tariff barriers to enforcing competition

The adoption of the single currency in 1999 was considered the natural follow-up to the single market initiative, which had been declared operational from the end of 1992 with the ratification of the Treaty of Economic Union. But the success of the common currency has highlighted the incomplete implementation of the single market to date. While the EU Commission continues to urge further reforms to make the single market truly operational across national boundaries within the EU, an increasing number of special interest groups have raised objections to any EU measures that might increase competition for jobs. It is no coincidence, then, that delays in implementing single market directives and regulations are most noticeable for those countries within the eurozone that have experienced sluggish growth since the introduction of the euro – Germany, France, and Italy. In contrast, the United Kingdom, Denmark, and Sweden – all remaining resolutely out of the common currency – are exemplary in transposing EU single market regulations and directions into national law. Even Norway and Iceland, remaining outside both the eurozone and the European Union to date, implement single market initiatives from Brussels more rapidly and more completely than France or Germany. The tradeoff between protectionism via national regulation versus protectionism via flexible exchange rates proves important in practice for European policy-makers.

Non-tariff barriers

The essential purpose of the Single European Act (SEA) was to remove the remaining barriers to trade among the partner countries within the customs union established in 1958. These barriers, while not transparent like uniform tariffs, had become increasingly visible within the EEC as trade expanded rapidly among the member states during the 1960s and early 1970s. In addition to the quantitative restrictions and tariffs on trade discussed in chapter 3, all sorts of non-tariff barriers (NTBs) can distort trade patterns. But, while tariffs are so-called "transparent" barriers to trade, because exporters can see through them to the domestic market, non-tariff barriers are far more difficult to detect and to eliminate. Examples are discriminatory regulations and taxation on foreign firms that make them less able to compete against domestic firms, customs and other border controls that increase cross-border transport costs, and closed or restrictive bidding for public contracts. For thirty years only the most blatant NTBs were attacked by the various negotiations of the successive rounds of the General Agreement on Tariffs and Trade. Although small steps were made in the Tokyo Round of the 1970s, the international community seriously addressed these sorts of trade barriers only with the Uruguay Round, which began in the 1980s but was not concluded until 1995. From the US perspective, the single market initiative of the Europeans was merely a subset of the general thrust of the Uruguay Round negotiations, which focused on NTBs as the main remaining obstacle to the continued expansion of international trade. From the EU perspective, the SEA was a positive reaction to the problem of "euro-sclerosis" among the economies of Europe. It was also a renewal of the momentum toward "ever closer union" that required effective institutions at the EU level.

The effects of these indirect, non-tariff barriers are very similar to the effects of transparent barriers, except that governments do not receive revenue directly from them. Basically, they create the same economic distortions as tariff barriers: they reduce consumers' surplus and decrease allocative efficiency. As with explicit tariffs, domestic producers benefit from NTBs, but only at the cost of the economy as a whole. In a 1987 survey conducted in the then twelve member states, 20,000 firms ranked the seriousness of the barriers. On average, they were ranked in three tiers, in order of most to least important:

(1) technical standards and regulations, administrative barriers, and frontier formalities;
(2) freight transport regulations and value added tax differences; and
(3) capital market controls, public procurement, and the implementation of Community law.

These were the areas targeted by the Single European Act, legislated by the EU in 1986.[1]

The Single European Act – Europe 1992

The much-publicized "Europe 1992" program was initiated with the European Commission's 1985 White Paper, supervised by Lord Cockfield (then the

Commission Vice-President). The White Paper was designed to identify market barriers and to propose changes to eliminate them. It was to be used as a guideline and not "to harmonize or standardize at any price." Even approximations of the proposals would be a significant movement toward unity.[2] The structure of the plan was a brilliantly constructed piece of international relations. It set a tight, specific timetable that ensured that individual members would be less likely to stall on efforts; otherwise they would be left behind. In addition, its acceptance was to be made under qualified majority voting in the Council of Ministers so that the program would not get bogged down before even starting. Finally, the program was to be implemented by attaining hundreds of small, specific workable steps so that the momentum from the document would be carried through. The success of the Single European Act that implemented the "Europe 1992" program within the context of member states pursuing their own national interests has been ascribed to its qualified majority voting rule and the overall reduction in special interest group conflicts.[3] To this can be added the tight schedule and the breakdown of goals into bite-sized pieces.

The countries formally adopted the White Paper with the signing of the SEA in February 1986, which entered into effect on July 1, 1987, after each member state had ratified it. The document identified three areas of constraints that needed attention by EC competition policy:

(1) *physical barriers*, such as customs and border controls;
(2) *technical barriers*, such as product safety rules, public procurement policies, and limits on types of labor and capital flows; and
(3) *fiscal barriers*, such as different tax rates and laws.

Physical barriers

Before 1985 horribly bureaucratic paperwork was required to move goods across national boundaries, and cargoes were subject to many inspections that were required for health and safety reasons. As a simple example, if a truck (lorry) made a 750-mile trip within the United Kingdom it would take about thirty-six hours. If, however, the same truck were to go from London to Milan it would take about 60% longer, fifty-eight hours, even netting out the channel crossing. The cost of the London–Milan trip would obviously be higher, even without considering the delay in delivery deadlines, and the costs of inventory management and storage. This difference was mainly due to all the documents (each in the languages of the countries being crossed) required by border controls, which were needed to ensure that all the various trucking regulations were being observed.

Far more costly, though, were the administrative costs of the barriers. In a study done by the accounting firm Ernst and Whinney, the direct costs of border controls were estimated at ECU8.4 to 9.3 billion, and of that amount ECU7.5 billion were accounted for by the administrative costs of cross-border trade.[4] To combat this, the members first of all simply initiated a common form, called the Single Administrative Document (SAD), and then, by the beginning of 1993, eliminated the need for even this document except for goods deemed for military use. By January 1993 all hauling quotas in and out of a country were abolished, and non-domestic trucks were granted cabotage freedom – that is, they were allowed to carry goods from point to point within the domestic market as long as this was shown not to cause severe harm to domestic truckers. By 1993 goods were largely able to flow freely across the EEC – something that had only been envisioned earlier. However, problems still arose from illegal restrictions on cross-border goods' flows. The number of complaints about unwarranted border restrictions received by the Commission increased from 202 in 1994 to 259 in 1995.[5]

Technical barriers

The technical barriers were, of course, difficult to resolve. Through the 1980s countries largely had their own regulations, affecting goods and, even more importantly, services. In the original EEC treaty technical barriers were forbidden, but countries could impose special regulations for health and safety reasons (article 36). However, member states were highly regulated, and all sorts of standards and regulations controlled their markets. It was estimated that before the SEA there were over 100,000 different technical regulations and standards in the member states. Regulations can seriously impede trade without being clearly directed toward trade. For example, in the French market prior to the passage of the SEA, tile manufacturers pushed stringent standards for tile construction with the national standards authority, AFNOR. Although the French were not able to make the standards legally binding, they were required for all public construction, which constituted 40% of the market at the time, and were often required for insurance for builders. These conditions in practice precluded far cheaper Spanish and Italian tile from the French market.[6]

The abuse of this safety clause changed with the landmark *Cassis de Dijon* case in 1979. Germany forbade cassis, a liqueur made from blackcurrants, to be imported as a liqueur because it failed to meet its alcohol content standards. The German importer (Rowe-Zentral AG) took this to the Court of Justice and the Court ruled that, because cassis met French standards and did not jeopardize German health or safety in its status as a liqueur, it could not be kept out of the German market. This effectively established the "mutual recognition principle" for such cases: the lawful products of one member can have access to all members, given no security or safety problems. Because of this decision, many more cases came before the Court.

With the push for the single market, the Commission published its "New Approach to Technical Harmonization and Standards" in 1985.[7] This established the means for countries to conduct cooperative efforts in setting and policing common standards for goods, indicated by the near-ubiquitous CE mark (for *Communauté européenne*) placed on goods that meet the requirements. These are the standards that are often lampooned by the media – reports, for example, of the standard minimum length for condoms of 6.7 inches! It has been very hard for the EC to establish rules that are consistent across the member states for all sectors. It would be vastly harder still to attempt rules for all products across all sectors. Not surprisingly, the process has been slow and difficult in protected areas such as motor vehicles and pharmaceuticals. However, progress has been made, and the convergence of rules and standards has made trade easier and cheaper to conduct. Annual updates of the progress made, or yet to be made, in achieving the goals of the single market are posted on the European Union website: http://europa.eu.int/comm/internal_market/en/update/score.

Another broad area taken under the heading of a "technical barrier" is public procurement – the purchases of the members' governments, and state subsidies. As one would expect, governments, in office at the discretion of the domestic population, buy and subsidize domestic products. In 1992 the Commission estimated that only 2% of the ECU600 billion public market was bought from firms outside the home country.[8] This was an area closely watched by the United States because the growing telecommunications market was controlled by member governments, and the highly competitive US firms were worried that they would not be able to compete in those markets. Although the SEA was very clear on establishing open, transparent bidding across all enterprises, article 29 allowed members to discard bids with less than half EEC content and to allow a 3% price preference to EEC bids.[9] Government subsidies to firms are also precluded, although member states are often loath to discontinue their financial support to preferred sectors or their indirect incentives for business investment. One example was the continued subsidies by the German government to Volkswagen in Saxony, which were made in direct disregard for the Commission's block on the payments.[10]

Regulations covering professional services and the service sector generally were also addressed. The banking and insurance industry, for example, has been the target of several formal initiatives from the Commission, designed to allow capital to flow more freely and to facilitate the convergence of the European economies. Economists have argued that harmonizing limited regulations within the framework of the SEA for Europe will reduce the possibility of regulatory capture and collusion that characterized the banking and insurance industry before 1992.[11] The apparent success of the Commission's regulations to create a single market in banking and insurance despite the loss of foreign exchange commissions as a result of the introduction of the euro, discussed in the previous chapter, has prompted the Commission to expand its initiatives into the service sector more generally. Barriers to trade within services include the reluctance of EU countries to accept each other's standards and norms or sometimes to recognise the equivalence of professional qualifications. Remedial action by the Commission was initiated in 2005, as its action plan to develop an integrated financial market by 2005 was completed. This allowed savers a wider range of investment products from the *European* supplier of their choice as well as reducing bank charges for cross-border payments. (Popular resistance to the Commission's initiative, however, was reputed to be a major factor in the French rejection of the proposed EU constitution in June 2005.)

Intellectual property, the bane of GATT law, has also been very difficult for the Commission. The establishment of common rules for a mutually recognized trademark has been nothing short of a battle among the states. The EU has also had difficulty in applying standards for high-tech patents. The rejection in March 1995 by the European Parliament of the draft directive on the protection of biotechnological patents was an early example of how a lack of common patent rules puts European industry at a competitive disadvantage.[12] Ten years later the European Court of Justice actually affirmed the right of individual countries within the EU to set their own regulations with respect to biotechnology.

Fiscal barriers

Differences in taxation are at the heart of fiscal barriers. By treaty, each member state of the European Union is required to adopt a system of value added taxation. In the EU tax system, the bulk of the taxes collected by governments are taxes paid by firms and levied on the basis of the value added by a firm in its production of goods or services. The value added is calculated as the gross

Table 7.1 How to tax McDonald's French fries (dollars)

Stage of production	Sales	Non-firm costs	Value added	Sales tax, 10% final sales	Turnover tax, 10% sales each stage	Value added tax, 10% value added each stage
Agricultural suppliers	$100	$0	$100	$0	$10	$10
Farmer	$300	$100	$200	$0	$30	$20
Wholesaler	$600	$300	$300	$0	$60	$30
Processor	$900	$600	$300	$0	$90	$30
Retailer	$1,000	$900	$100	$100	$100	$10
Total	$2,900	$1,900	$1,000	$100	$290	$100

sales revenues of the firm minus the costs of inputs it purchases from other firms. By the time a given product or service has moved up through the various stages of production, the total value added tax collected should equal the total sales tax that would have been collected if a government had simply levied the tax on the final point of sale. Table 7.1 illustrates how the value added tax (VAT) works in practice, using as an example the production of McDonald's French fries. The table traces $1,000 of French fries sold by a McDonald's outlet somewhere in the world back through various intermediate stages, such as:
- a processing firm that slices and packs the potatoes it has bought in bulk from;
- a wholesaler who has collected and graded the potatoes it bought from;
- a farmer who grew the potatoes using inputs he or she purchased from suppliers of machinery and fertilizer. Under a simple sales tax of 10%, the final sales of $1,000 of French fries yields $100 of tax revenue to the government, collected from the McDonald's outlet that sold them. Under a VAT of 10%, the final sales also yield $100 of tax revenue to the government, but now the revenue is collected in portions from each firm that contributed to the final supply of French fries. The McDonald's outlet is liable for only the last $10 of the total tax, proportional to the part of the total value added that the outlet provided by preparing the French fries for the consumer at the moment of final sale.

The table also compares an alternative form of tax, little used these days, called a turnover tax. Under this form of taxation, a government collects a fixed percentage of the total sales of a product, regardless of the stage of production. If it were to use the same high percentage as the value added tax or sales tax on potatoes of 10% in the table, it would collect $290, or nearly three times the amount of VAT or sales tax. Obviously, this would create incentives for firms to integrate vertically, above and beyond the incentives that McDonald's may have to grow its own potatoes. In the context of the early days of the European Coal and Steel Community, for example, German coal and steel firms had been vertically integrated to a much greater degree than were either Belgian or French firms. It was clear that using the VAT instead of the turnover tax would remove at least that incentive for the German coal and steel firms to recreate the cartels that existed before World War II.

Two other advantages of VAT should be noted as well. Perhaps most important is that it minimizes the issue of class conflict over the share of government that should be paid by taxes on labor or capital or rentiers. This is because the total value added by a firm is in fact equal to the total income that is earned by each factor of production employed in the firm. The total income of the firm may then be divided up among the owners, managers, and laborers of the firm in whatever way suits the firm. Instead of imposing differential income tax rates on the different sources of income, the government imposes the same tax rate on all incomes created by a firm.

The second advantage of VAT is that it provides incentives for honest reporting with respect to the tax base. Obviously, firms at each stage of production have an incentive to overstate their costs from other firms, and an incentive to understate their revenues from sales to other firms. But the two incentives offset each other in a VAT system. The two theoretical advantages may, however, be offset by the disadvantage of the extra bookkeeping costs required by all firms as well as the extra monitoring costs desired by the government.

In practice, the member countries of the European Union have always applied a wide variety of rules for taxation, and of rates for excise taxes and value added taxes. Of course, these differences distorted trade, as businesses and consumers avoided taxation in high-taxed areas. As standards were harmonized, rules for kinds of goods to be taxed also became more similar. However, trying to get the actual tax rates to converge has proved difficult for the EU. Not only are the rates different but they differ in how they are actually applied. For example, some countries do not place any tax on purchases of food and clothing; others give reduced rates for such goods.

Before 1992 average VAT rates varied by over ten percentage points across countries. Countries with high rates and extensive programs, such as Denmark, were nervous about accepting Community control of rates and thus were ambivalent about deepening integration. In 1991, however, member states agreed that rates should be harmonized and they further agreed to standardize rates at 15% or more, to abolish luxury rates, and, for countries with zero rates on special items such as food, to allow lower rates for a transition period. As late as mid-1997, however, the new Labour government in the United Kingdom was allowed to reduce its VAT rate on household gas and electricity bills from 8 to 5%, instead of eliminating it entirely or raising it to 15% as required by the agreement.

The collection of taxes from cross-border sales still posed a problem. The Commission had originally proposed simply collecting the value added tax in the country of origin for each sale, but member states opted for payments in the country of destination. The "destination principle" forces buyers and sellers in each country to report their activities to their respective tax authorities. Sellers to another country get a rebate on their value added tax; buyers from another country then pay their country's VAT on imports from other member states. Before January 1, 1993, if someone bought some good worth more than ECU600 in one member state and transported it to another, he or she had to declare the item and could receive a rebate of the VAT already paid, but he or she would then have to pay the VAT of the country into which he or she was importing the good.

This lengthy, complicated process is no longer applicable as long as the good is for the person's own use and is not for resale. Now such goods can be bought in one country and freely transported to another. Because exports carry with them the exporting country's taxes, the tax authority of the importing country will later bill the exporting country to get its taxes. In short, the settling of tax balances between the two states is done by the tax authorities, not the traders. Sales by exporters are monitored inside each country instead of at the borders, as before. To coordinate information relating to sales among traders and states, all member states are linked via a computerized system (VAT Information Exchange System, VIES) that keeps the VAT registration numbers of all the traders along with their cross-border transactions. The system is still complicated, but actual trading is no longer subject to long delays with shipments being held up at borders. Since the 1992 agreement there has been some progress toward the general harmonization of VAT rates, but delays in installing the new system and double-checking by tax authorities on tax payments and rebates with businesses has kept transactions costs higher than was intended by the SEA.

In addition to general consumption taxes, certain goods have special excise taxes placed on them – for example, petroleum products, alcoholic beverages, and tobacco. These differences are relatively minor, though, and have small effects relative to the differences in the VAT rates and bases. Areas in which the Commission has paid special attention are mineral oils and alcohol. It is clear

Table 7.2 Excise duty and VAT per liter of beer (euros)

Country	Excise duty	VAT	Total
Germany	0.10	0.02	0.12
Spain	0.10	0.02	0.12
Luxembourg	0.10	0.02	0.12
France	0.13	0.03	0.16
Greece	0.14	0.03	0.17
Portugal	0.15	0.03	0.18
Italy	0.18	0.04	0.22
Netherlands	0.21	0.04	0.25
Belgium	0.21	0.04	0.25
Austria	0.26	0.05	0.31
Denmark	0.46	0.12	0.58
Sweden	0.86	0.22	1.08
United Kingdom	0.99	0.17	1.16
Ireland	0.99	0.21	1.20
Finland	1.43	0.31	1.74

Source: European Commission, *Update on the Internal Market: Scoreboard no. 10*, Luxembourg: 2002.

that VAT and excise rates do not have to be identical across all the members for the SEA to become operative; neighboring states in the United States have different rates with no border controls. The range of rates can be up to five percentage points apart before cross-border trading starts to become significant in the US experience. The United Kingdom has long argued to allow market forces to drive tax rates, not the Commission. In any case, member states have agreed that excises will not be lower than a set Community minimum rate for goods covered – for example, for unleaded gasoline (petrol) ECU287 per 1,000 liters.[13] Picking beer as an example of a universally consumed, and taxed, item, the Commission reported the differences in VAT and excise rates across the EU-15 countries shown in table 7.2.

In addition to consumption taxes, countries vary as to their corporate taxation. Until 1990 very little was accomplished in this area. However, with the attempt to decontrol capital movements in the EU, tax distortions were also examined. In 1990, after decades of consideration, directives on the taxation of cross-border mergers were issued. Following that, the Ruding Report of 1992 estimated that the variations in tax base assessment and tax rates caused major distortions and predicted that the market would be slow to correct these failings. In response, the Commission recommended a corporate tax range of 30 to 40%, the harmonization of tax base assessment, and the elimination of the distinction between domestic and foreign companies in cross-border activities.

In fact, corporations have had great difficulty with EU law. The long-standing proposal for a European Company Statute (ECS) has been held up by problems with member states agreeing to the conditions of worker partici-pation. The ECS would provide the format for a company that would operate EU-wide and would be governed by a single Community law applicable in all member states. Companies established in more than one member state would benefit greatly, since they would not need to organize each subsidiary differ-ently according to the various different national statutes. The Ciampi Report, from the Competitiveness Advisory Group, estimates that such organization costs European businesses about ECU30 billion a year.[14]

Progress report

Of course, there has been much slippage among these three areas. At the out-set 287 proposals were made, but some were either too sensitive or difficult to undertake, so they were broken down further and the original proposals evolved to 302. By the beginning of 1996 93.4% of the national measures had been enacted in order to implement the Community's single market legisla-tion. However, member states' acceptance of single market legislation varied considerably: Denmark, the Netherlands, Spain, and Sweden were substan-tially above the Community average of 93.4%; Greece, Germany, and Austria were substantially below. As we saw above, most of the failures to implement measures of the SEA were in the areas of public procurement, intellectual property, and insurance.

By 2001 it appeared that all countries were making progress toward full implementation in national law of the directives required for the single market. A goal was agreed upon to have all but 1.5% of the directives in place by 2002. But slippage then occurred; the goal of 98.5% compliance was not reached in 2002, although it seemed attainable as 98.2% of the directives were in place in national law among the fifteen member states. It became clear by April 2003 that some backsliding had occurred, however, as the Commission regretfully noted then that only 97.6% of the directives were in place. Part of this was due to the continued flow of new directives generated by the Council, but delays of two years or more in implementing the older directives indicated political or administrative resistance to the EU directives.

It is interesting that France, Germany, and Italy, presumably the political leaders of European unity, were the worst offenders, while the United Kingdom, Sweden, Denmark, Finland, and Spain were the best performers. The economic aspects of the single market appear to be more attractive to the late arrivals than they are to the founding fathers! But it may also be true that those countries that remain outside the common currency of the euro, and therefore can still have fluctuations in their exchange rates with the rest of the single market to absorb shocks to their economies, encounter less political resistance in implementing the single market directives. Norway, for example, as a member of the European Economic Area, but not the European Union or the euro, has the highest implementation rate of all.

It appears likely, then, that the accession countries will also make rapid progress in implementing the internal market directives, given that their motivations for membership are overwhelmingly economic. It is precisely the lower prices in the accession countries, which average less than 50% of the price level in the EU-15, however, that account for the increasing resistance of the established members toward implementation of the internal market. The reason for the lower prices in the accession countries is that their wage levels and rents are, so far, much lower than in the incumbent countries. How rapidly their wages and their rents will rise toward the higher levels in western Europe depends on how rapidly labor markets and capital markets are integrated. These are even more sensitive issues than VAT or excise tax rates on consumables, however, and require separate chapters.

Price convergence took place very quickly between the new members and the incumbent members in the two previous enlargements, one with countries having much lower prices than the existing members (Greece, Spain, and Portugal relative to the nine incumbent members in 1980) and one with countries having significantly higher prices than the existing members (Austria, Finland, and Sweden relative to the twelve incumbent members in 1990). The price convergence was driven in two ways: one, with prices continuing to converge among the incumbent countries; and, two, with prices in the accession countries converging even more rapidly to those of the incumbent countries.[15] Part of the process of price convergence, therefore, is driven by the encouragement of competition within the single market by the efforts of the Commission, as well as by the unceasing stream of directives intended to eliminate the artificial barriers to competition among the member states.

Competition policy

The Competition Directorate has emerged as one of the most powerful instruments of the European Union's economic policies. All mergers above a certain size have to meet the approval of the Commission, which is charged with the responsibility of determining if the proposed merger is likely to improve or harm competition within the market, or markets, affected if the proposal is implemented. All mergers, regardless of size, are required as well to meet the standards of competitive behavior expected within the single market, and member states are charged with the responsibility of enforcing competition within their borders according to single market directives. This is, in reality, a complete reversal of the Common Market's competition policy. In the early 1960s the primary concern of industrial policy in each European country was to allow firms in key industries to reach a size sufficient to realize the economies of scale that were thought to be the key to the success of American firms in the aftermath of World War II. National champions in each industry were encouraged to emerge and mergers that tended to create such champions were encouraged as a consequence.

Worse, from the perspective of the Competition Directorate, however, was the tendency for some national governments to provide substantial state subsidies toward the creation of national champions in particular industries where economies of scale were important. As the forces of competition are unleashed within the single market, however, the reliance of many state-owned or state-subsidized enterprises on subsidies has increased. Subsidy surveillance by the Competition Directorate has, therefore, been required to make sure that competition is occurring on the same terms throughout the European Union. From the viewpoint of final consumers, of course, subsidies provided by taxpayers in one country may simply benefit consumers in the other countries. So the justification for subsidy surveillance by the Commission seems more a concern by smaller countries to keep larger countries from subsidizing their own companies to a greater extent than is possible for the smaller countries.

The response of the member states to the exercise of the enforcement powers conferred upon the Commission, which are intrusive to say the least, as they include the power to seize the records of firms accused of violating the rules of the single market, has been to create justifications for continuing the subsidies other than maintaining a "national champion." One justification would be to maintain a plant or firm in a depressed region of a country, or to aid the industry to meet EU environmental standards, or to fulfill another objective of the

EU such as restricted fishing in the Mediterranean or North Sea. It is clear that heavy reliance upon state subsidies for firms in the accession countries that were previously wholly owned by the state will not be permitted; nor will they be eligible for EU aid in the future.

Conclusion

The benefits of a common market, realized after the elimination of internal tariffs on manufacturing products within the customs union by 1968, were increasingly offset afterwards by an increasing reliance by the member states upon non-tariff barriers. These were successful in creating niche markets for national firms in a wide range of products as economic growth and structural change occurred throughout Europe. Individual governments became committed to continued subsidies, whether granted directly to state-owned enterprises or national champions, or granted indirectly through idiosyncratic technical standards or government purchasing preferences that protected national firms from competition by other European firms.

The variety and pervasiveness of national preferences for national products that had arisen over literally centuries of past experience creates a massive agenda for the European Union. From the initial 287 non-tariff barriers that were identified when the single market initiative was launched in 1985, by 2005 no fewer than 1,530 directives and 377 regulations had been required to continue the creation of a truly single market for manufactured goods within the European Union.

Services, which have become much more important than manufacturing in all European economies, are still not subject to the detailed monitoring and control required for a single market. National preferences and regulations still prevail in banking, insurance, law, real estate, and stockbroking, despite the intent of the Single European Act to create a single market in services as well as in goods. Enrique Barroso, the Portuguese President of the European Commission, encountered serious opposition by politicians in the largest EU states when he proposed a general services directive for the single market. Most probably it was fears of the "Polish plumber" displacing unionized plumbers throughout the older member states that mobilized some of the negative votes against the new constitution in France and the Netherlands. The one area where a single market in services does seem to be firmly established throughout the European Union is in higher education, perhaps because it is a service industry that is not regarded as critical for the employment of fellow citizens.

NOTES

1. G. Nerb, *The Completion of the Internal Market: A Survey of European Industry's Perception of the Likely Effects*, European Commission, Directorate-General for Economic and Financial Affairs, Brussels: 1988, as quoted in M. Emerson, M. Aujean, M. Catinat, P. Goubet, and A. Jacquemin, "The economics of 1992," *European Economy* 35 (March), 1988, p. 44.
2. See the *Bulletin of the EC* no. 6, 1985, p. 18.
3. See Ludger Schuknecht. "The political economy of current European integration," in Hans-Jürgen Vosgerau, ed., *European Integration in the World Economy*, New York: Springer-Verlag, 1992, pp. 677–702.
4. Costs per consignment were estimated at an average of ECU67 for imports (with a low of ECU26 for Belgium and a high of ECU130 for Italy) and ECU86 for exports (with a low of ECU34 for Belgium and a high of ECU205 for Italy). See Emerson et al., p. 48, note 1.
5. European Commission, *Report on the Status of the Single Market*, Luxembourg: 1996, section 1.
6. Emerson et al., p. 53, note 1.
7. For an analysis of this "new approach" see Jacques Pelkmans, "The new approach to technical harmonization and standardization," *Journal of Common Market Studies* 25 (3), 1987, pp. 249–69.
8. Desmond Dinan, *Ever Closer Union? An Introduction to the European Community*, Boulder, CO: Lynne Rienner Publishers, 1994, p. 345.
9. Ibid., p. 346.
10. The Commission attempted to block subsidies of DM241 million ($163 million) to Volkswagen plants in Saxony. While Germany was trying to reverse the decision, Saxony had already disbursed DM92 million. "Bonn and EU resort to court," *Financial Times*, September 12, 1996, p. 2.
11. Xavier Vives, "Banking competition and European integration," in Alberto Giovannini and Colin Mayer, eds., *European Financial Integration*, New York: Cambridge University Press, 1992, p. 18.
12. European Commission, *The Single Market in 1995*, Luxembourg: 1996, section 1.
13. For the list of minimum rates for all the covered items, see the DG10 website: http://europa.eu.int/en/comm/dg10/incom/xc5/ewfqa/ewfq0902.htm#09.02.00.
14. European Commission, *The Single Market in 1995*, note 12.
15. European Commission, *Update on the Internal Market: Scoreboard no. 12*, Luxembourg: 2004, p. 25.

8   The single market in labor: from refugees to Schengen

In chapters 3 and 7, we saw how the elimination of trade barriers, whether they were transparent tariff barriers or opaque non-tariff barriers, affects the flow of goods and services among countries. The underlying assumption in the economic theory we used is that goods and services are traded but the factors of production responsible for producing them – capital, labor, and land – remain fixed in each country and do not move across their respective national borders. For labor and capital to be allocated efficiently across regions within each country that is part of an economic union, however, they must be allowed to move freely from one location to another. If each factor moves to where it can receive the highest return within an economic union, then total output for the union as a whole will be maximized. Only with the free movement of the factors of production across the borders of the member states can total output for the economic union reach its full potential.

Figure 8.1 illustrates this reasoning by contrasting the situation for labor as a factor of production in West Germany and Italy during the economic miracle period of the 1950s (the period is described in more detail in chapters 12 and 15). The demand for labor in each country is determined by the marginal product of labor (MPL in the figure). West Germany's demand for labor decreases from left to right, showing that marginal product falls as the quantity of labor used with a fixed amount of capital and land increases. Italy's demand for labor also decreases with increasing quantity, but from right to left. The two countries are juxtaposed so that the supply of labor for each country, taken as fixed in both cases, meets in the center of the diagram (read West Germany from left to right, Italy from right to left). The marginal product of labor in West Germany was consistently higher than in Italy, mostly because the quality and quantity of capital available per worker was greater in West Germany than in Italy. The supply of labor, however, was roughly the same.

Figure 8.1a shows the situation that arises if no migration of labor or capital is allowed between the two countries. The real wage in each country is determined by the intersection of the demand and supply for labor in that country.

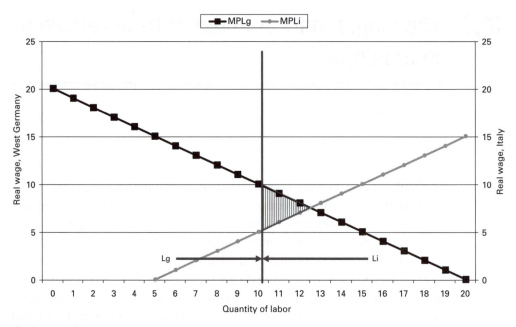

Figure 8.1a Separate labor markets

The result is that real wages are higher in West Germany than in Italy. They can remain higher as long as no movement of labor (or capital) is allowed between the two. The implication, however, is that the total output of the two countries combined remains less than it could be if labor were allowed to move freely. If some of the Italian workers with low marginal products could move to West Germany and produce higher marginal products, for example, the loss of output in Italy would be less than the increase in output in West Germany and the total product available would increase. The loss of potential output is given by the area of the triangle in the center of the figure.

In the course of the 1950s arrangements were made to allow Italian workers to migrate temporarily to West Germany. These culminated with the provision for the free movement of labor within the European Economic Community made by the Treaty of Rome. Figure 8.1b illustrates the result that could have happened with migration. Equilibrium would be reached by equalizing the marginal products of labor in each country and paying labor the same real wage in both West Germany and Italy. This could be done simply by moving the required number of workers from Italy to West Germany (Li to Lg in figure 8.1b). Total output for the two countries combined would then rise by the amount of the triangle in figure 8.1a.

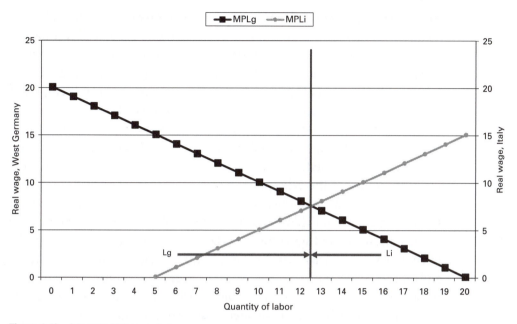

Figure 8.1b Integrated labor markets

Of course, the additional product may not be shared equally between the two partner countries, although the figure is drawn deliberately to show that as a possibility. Even with equal gains to each country, however, political conflicts will arise within each country over the way the gains will be distributed initially. The entire gain to West Germany, for example, has gone to the owners of capital, not labor (this is the area of the triangle above the new real wage). Moreover, the laborers in West Germany would have seen their real wage fall so the amount of income they lost would now be redistributed to capital. Obviously, business owners in West Germany would find this attractive and be enthusiastic supporters of labor migrants and, later, guest worker programs. Equally obviously, labor unions would oppose immigration, at least of workers competitive with their members. (They might, however, accede to increased numbers of workers in occupations or sectors that were complementary to those of their members. In this case, they could share in the gains that would accrue to owners of capital.)

On the Italian side of the diagram, by contrast, all the gains of increased output go to the workers (the area of the triangle below the new wage). In addition, the remaining workers in Italy also gain at the expense of Italian capitalists as their real wages rise due to the decreased supply of workers remaining in Italy. In Italy, therefore, the redistribution of income is from capital to labor.

No wonder Italian labor unions favor the emigration of competitive laborers, while Italian capitalists are displeased by the resulting increase in real wages.

Of course, nothing as extreme as depicted in figure 8.1b was allowed to happen in practice, even though the Treaty of Rome is explicit about attaining the freedom of movement of labor for both employed workers and self-employed workers.[1] Workers in the "public sector" have special status, however, and the prohibition of national discrimination does not extend to workers who can be shown to be directly or indirectly involved with the "exercise of public authority," or with "state matters." Given the size of the civil service in most European countries, these exceptions have kept a large portion of the European labor force out of a "common market." In general, though, the EEC achieved free movement for individuals relatively rapidly after its creation and by 1970 for manufacturing and agricultural workers. However, countries had very different welfare and social security systems, different health insurance systems, and different educational systems. All these made moving very risky and costly for workers and for families. The result by 1980 was that the number of EEC national citizens who were permanent residents in a different EEC country was minimal compared to the number of foreigners from outside the EEC present in each country. For example, most West German citizens resident in France were the wives of French men and most French citizens resident in West Germany were, likewise, the wives of German men. North Africans were the dominant group of foreigners in France while Turks were the largest single group of foreigners in West Germany.

Meanwhile, the increased labor demands generated by the expansion of manufacturing activity within the customs union were met by increased guest worker programs. These had first been devised in the immediate aftermath of World War II as a way of finding an appropriate means of barter, especially between France and Italy. But it was not until the Berlin Wall was constructed in 1961, which cut off the continuing influx of German-speaking migrants from East Germany and beyond into West Germany (see chapter 12), that guest worker programs began in earnest. By 1974, when the first oil shock had put all industrialized nations into recession and a situation of rising unemployment, each industrialized member state had substantial populations of guest workers, from Luxembourg to West Germany. They came from Spain, Portugal, Yugoslavia, Greece, Algeria, Morocco, Tunisia, and – especially – Turkey. Meanwhile, the movement of labor among the member states seemed to repatriate people back to their country of origin within the EEC. The movement was especially marked in Italy. Later, when first Greece and then Spain and Portugal became members of the EEC, these countries, which had been a major source of emigrants to the industrial heartland of Europe, saw a similar reflux of their citizens. It appeared that, as trade in goods increased among the member states of the customs union, the movement of people within the customs union stagnated, and even reversed. As employment opportunities increased in their home countries, migrants returned to their friends and families.

What explains this behavior, in obvious defiance of the goals expressed in the Treaty of Rome to allow workers to move anywhere they pleased, when they pleased, within the economic union? At the time of the repatriation, part of the explanation was the aging of the original emigrants, who found retirement much more attractive back in their home village or neighborhood. Among the younger emigrants, however, it was now much easier for, say, a Spanish national to return to his or her place of employment in the EEC if opportunities for employment in Spain did not work out. In fact, as we will see in the next chapter, entry into the EEC for these three countries (Greece, Spain, and Portugal) elicited large inflows of investment capital, which made new employment opportunities more attractive than in the older member countries. But the most interesting economic aspect of the repatriation phenomenon is that it illustrates a tradeoff between expanding trade among the members of the customs union and expanding labor mobility. Trade and migration within the European Union have proven, time and again, to be substitutes rather than complements.

Guest worker programs, 1961–74

The effect of the customs union in diverting the pattern of trade toward partners within the customs union and away from previous trade partners that remained outside the customs union was pronounced, as we saw in chapter 3. Trade diversion continues to characterize the functioning of the customs union with each successive expansion of membership. The obvious reaction by firms located in countries excluded from the customs union is to locate their production facilities inside the new tariff wall. By investing in new plants within the customs union, of course, American and British firms helped continue the rapid industrialization and the "golden age" of economic growth for the original six members of the Common Market. In such a situation, economic theory (the Rybczynski Theorem)[2] predicts that the labor force within a country experiencing inflows of capital must shift into the expanding sectors where investment is taking place. In the initial postwar adjustment period of the 1950s most European countries found it easy to take labor from the rural areas with uncompetitive agriculture and put it to use in urban areas expanding on the basis of modern industry. By the 1960s, however, agriculture was no longer a source of cheap labor. The Berlin Wall, built in 1961, actually cut off the supply of German migrants from the backward agricultural regions of East Germany and eastern Europe to West German industry. But the supply of labor from agriculture to industry was drying up within the Common Market in general, and continued to wither as the Common Agricultural Policy took effect.

Consequently, the continued expansion of the Common Market's industrial labor force was based increasingly during the 1960s on a variety of so-called "guest worker" programs. Bilateral agreements were made between a host country, say Germany, and an origin country, say Turkey, that so many qualified workers from Turkey each year could be hired by German firms for fixed-term contracts, usually one year, but renewable at the discretion of the German firm and the Turkish worker. It was understood that German wages would be paid to the guest worker for the duration of his or her employment, and that the guest worker would send back to his or her home country the bulk of his or her earnings, benefiting the Turkish economy as well. It was ironic, but understandable in the light of the Rybczynski Theorem, that the most visible mark of foreign direct investment in West Germany, the Ford Motor plant outside Frankfurt, was also the largest single employer of Turkish guest workers.

For the Common Market countries, and, indeed, for much of western Europe as well, the 1960s were clearly a case of "demand-pull" migration. Moreover, the guest workers, being less skilled – or, certainly, less trained initially – than the native workers, were complements to the more skilled or more highly trained native workers, as well as complements to the new capital invested in the receiving country. Consistent with the economic motivation of the EEC as an intergovernmental organization, however, each member country of the EEC made its own bilateral agreement with each sending country. So West Germany focused on first Austria, then Yugoslavia, and finally Turkey, while France dealt with first Italy, then Portugal, Greece, and finally Spain, with agreements eventually with Algeria, Morocco, and Tunisia – the so-called Maghreb countries of North Africa.

Restrained migration, 1974–85

The various oil shocks during the period from 1974 through 1985, however, brought an abrupt end to the golden age of economic growth, and to the investment booms within the original six member states of the Common Market. They also terminated, permanently, the guest worker programs. In their place came a series of misguided and ultimately futile efforts to repatriate the mass of foreign workers who had become part of the industrial and service sector labor force within the Common Market. Each country developed its own set of programs intended to send back their unwanted foreign workers to their home countries. Lump sum buyouts of varying generosity were the initial tactic employed in each case. In each case, the results were disappointing from the viewpoint of the host country, revealing two important economic principles. First, given that the foreign workers were segregated into the least skilled parts of the production process in any given industry or service, they really were complements to, and not substitutes for, the rest of the native workers, who were more skilled or more highly trained. Removing all the Turkish workers from the West German auto industry, for example, would have meant making most of the remaining West German workers idle as well. Second, no matter how large the one-time payments made to a foreign worker leaving West Germany or France, he or she had to compare those payments to the loss of future wages he or she could make by staying in West Germany or France. For, once the foreign worker was out of the country, there was little chance that he or she could be let back in the country once the economy recovered.

Further missteps were made by the West German authorities when they saw former guest workers, determined to maintain their eligibility for employment in West Germany, bring their spouses and children to the country. When the West German government then cut off children's allowances until the children had been in West Germany for over one year, young Turkish families responded by bringing in their older relatives to take care of the children. Consequently, a Turkish population consisting mainly of young male workers in 1973 became a larger Turkish population consisting more of multigenerational families by 1985. All this occurred while West German unemployment rates, in common with the rest of continental Europe, rose to permanently higher levels. Given that all the members of the European Community had ceased their individual guest worker programs, it is odd that they did not move toward a common external policy with respect to labor migration. Instead, they refocused their attention on the internal mobility of labor within the customs union.

Schengen Agreement, 1985–2006

In article 8A of the Single European Act, member states agreed to create common policies for political asylum, immigration, visas, and police measures (terrorism, drug smuggling, etc.). Although each of these was addressed in various conventions, only those relating to border formalities were enacted under the Schengen Agreement. In 1985 France, West Germany, and the

Benelux countries agreed to allow the free movement of persons along their borders, and they actually achieved this goal in March 1995. In 1993 Italy, Spain, Portugal, and Greece also agreed to allow this. Eventually, all members of the European Union save the United Kingdom and Ireland implemented the common Schengen Information System for controlling access to the European Union. In addition, Norway and Iceland have joined the system as part of their commitment to participate in the single market. Even Switzerland, where the voters keep rejecting aspects of the European Union other than the customs union in various referendums, ratified its acceptance of the Schengen Convention in 2005. The ten accession countries that joined in 2004 also had to agree to implement the Schengen Information System by 2007. Signatories to the Schengen *acquis* agree on a common set of rules for checking the papers of individuals entering their external frontiers, so that once an individual had entered one of the countries from outside the group he or she could travel freely within all the other countries without further formalities.

All sorts of strategic and security issues plague the Schengen Convention, and it has not been fully incorporated into the *acquis* of the European Union. On the one hand, this means that non-members of the European Union can feel free to sign up to it without encumbering themselves with the other rules and directives of the EU. Liechtenstein, for example, has begun negotiations for entering the Schengen Convention, while the other microstates in Europe – Andorra, Monaco, San Marino, and Vatican City – as well as the territories of Greenland and the Faeroe Islands have arranged for free travel with the adjacent signatories. On the other hand, even the original signatories feel obliged to suspend the rules whenever they feel the need. After the July 2005 bombing attacks of London public transport by terrorists, for example, France imposed border controls. Even after Austria signed up to the Schengen Convention immediately after its official entry in the EU in 1995, Germany continued to exercise controls at the German-Austrian border for two years. Moreover, the right to travel within the Schengen countries does not carry with it the right to work, which is still subject to regulation by each individual country. While some progress has been made among the signatories to have a common policy with respect to refugees, there is still no common migration policy.

Common labor force problems, 1985–2006

A compelling reason why there has not yet been a common approach taken to what has emerged as a common problem among the European Union members

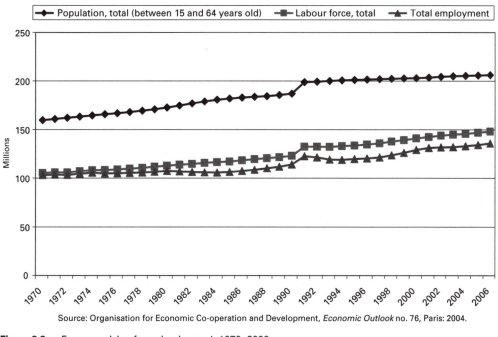

Source: Organisation for Economic Co-operation and Development, *Economic Outlook* no. 76, Paris: 2004.

Figure 8.2   Euro-area: labor force development, 1970–2006

is that each country has tried to maintain its own version of the social compact binding labor, capital, and government to act cooperatively in their mutual interest, as discussed in chapter 1. In practice, each successive shock to the European economies, beginning with the onset of general inflation in 1971, continuing with the successive oil shocks of the 1970s and 1980s, and resuming with the collapse of the Soviet Union after 1990, has been met by reassuring labor that its interests are protected. This means that public employees are maintained in their jobs with continuing regular increases in real wages, and that private employees covered by union contracts are promised the same protection of employment and wage. The result, predictably, has been increases in the unemployment rates of workers not protected by virtue of belonging to a union or to a civil service. Figures 8.2 and 8.3 show the development of the employment situation in the twelve countries participating in the eurozone as of 2006, compared with 1970, when the golden age of economic growth began to come to an end.

Figure 8.2 shows the gradual growth of the population eligible to participate in the labor force by virtue of being old enough to leave mandatory schooling (fifteen years and above) and young enough not to be forced into retirement (under age sixty-five). The sudden jump in 1991 reflects the addition of the

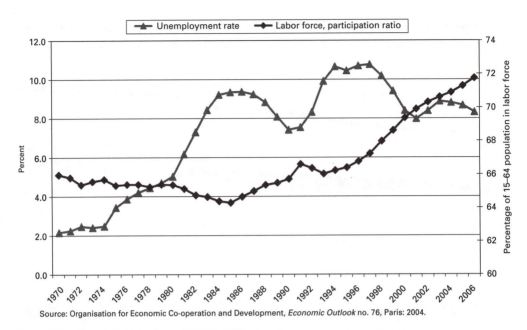

Source: Organisation for Economic Co-operation and Development, *Economic Outlook* no. 76, Paris: 2004.

Figure 8.3   Euro-area: unemployment, 1970–2006

former East Germany's population with the formal reunification of West and East Germany in that year, as discussed in chapter 12. More remarkable is the large difference in the number of people old enough to be in the labor force and the number who actually declare themselves in the formal labor force. The participation rate of the eurozone population stayed around two-thirds of the eligible population, rising only slightly in the 1990s to just over 70%. For comparison, the US labor force participation rate has remained slightly above three-quarters during this period, which is perhaps the main reason that per capita incomes have remained higher in the United States – a higher proportion of the population actually produces income in the United States than in the EU. Given that the gap between the labor force and actual employment has widened over the last thirty years and remains high, it is useful to examine the relation between the participation rates of the EU labor force and the unemployment rates, shown in figure 8.3.

Figure 8.3 shows clearly the inverse relationship that exists between participation rates and unemployment rates. As employment opportunities rise, the additional workers drawn into employment come not only from the currently unemployed but also from the currently non-participating population. Moreover, the apparent "natural rate of unemployment" in the eurozone has been gradually reduced at the same time that the average participation rate of the working age population has increased. Closer examination of the composition of these changes show that the positive results have arisen from policy changes initiated by several countries within the eurozone, but not yet adopted across all members. While the East German population increased the size of the potential labor pool for the eurozone, it also increased the participation rate. East Germany, in common with the rest of the Soviet bloc countries, required the full participation of women in the labor force. While that participation rate for women has fallen after reunification and the adoption of West German employment policies, which have kept German unemployment high in both the western and eastern parts of the country, other countries have adopted policies that have increased the participation rate of women and, consequently, reduced the unemployment rate. The most success to date has been enjoyed by the Netherlands, which will be analyzed further in chapter 16, but the key factors are clear – just difficult for other countries to imitate.

The Dutch took as their example the policy changes initiated in the United Kingdom as part of the labor market reforms introduced by the Conservative government of Margaret Thatcher in the 1980s. The key initiative by the Dutch was to allow employers to hire temporary workers. The advantage of temporary employees for employers is that they are not bound by union contract rules to show cause for terminating employment – it is understood that the job is "temporary." Of course, if the worker proves his or her value to the employer by exemplary on-the-job performance, the employer is free to hire the individual permanently. The temporary job, in other words, can become a probationary period of indefinite duration.

The success of temporary employment, first shown in the United States and then in the United Kingdom, in increasing participation rates and lowering unemployment rates illustrates an important economic principle. Employers are less likely to hire workers in the first place the more difficult it is for them to dismiss unsatisfactory employees, because of laws and union contracts, once they are on the payroll. The advantage for employees is that their actual take-home pay is usually higher than they would get from a permanent position, mainly because unemployment taxes are not levied on such workers' incomes, at least initially, when they are clearly temporary workers. And, permanent employment may be possible if the worker proves his or her worth to the firm during the period of temporary work. These positive effects of temporary employment are further increased for the employee if the job is part-time or flextime, as the extra downtime allows a non-participating person to continue his or her previous commitments to some extent. A mother, for example, may adjust her work times around the school schedules of her children. Anyone may adjust for classes to improve his or her skills, or, in a more extreme case, for rehabilitation sessions for chronic drug users. While flextime and part-time employees increase the difficulties faced by managers in organizing the work flow in the firm, difficult workers' contracts can be terminated more readily if they are temporary, rather than permanent, employees.

The Dutch reforms have not been imitated in other countries, for a variety of reasons. Perhaps the major objection to them is the reduction in eligibility for both long-term unemployment insurance, for the chronically unemployed, and for disability payments. In each case, the former recipient of generous welfare payments must either make an effort to search for alternative employment, taking training classes for acquiring new skills if there is no demand for the individual's previous skills, or show evidence of continued disability despite continued medical treatment or therapy. The reduction of benefits long taken for granted within a society is very difficult to implement politically, and more difficult the more diverse and divided politically the society. Even in the case of the Thatcher reforms, discussed in chapter 14, it may have been a fluke of the British political system that enabled them to take effect. Even the positive effects of the Dutch reforms, however, look dubious to other countries. Dutch women historically had by far the lowest participation rate in the labor force of any European country, and the Dutch rate still remains below that of other European countries. Moreover, a very high percentage of the new jobs taken by Dutch women remain part-time, which raises the question of how much gain in household income and citizen satisfaction can be expected in other countries undertaking similar reforms in their labor markets.

Future labor force problems

A common problem for all European countries, not just those that have adopted the euro as a common currency, is the continued slow, even negative, rate of growth of the native population. The rapid aging of the European populations, combined with generous pension commitments to the current labor force, poses serious problems for the future. In part, they can be ameliorated by increasing the participation rate of the working-age population in the labor force. If participation rates remain at their 2001 level (68.3%), the natural rate of increase of the population suggests that the eurozone labor force will grow over the period 2002–2010, but only at a snail-like pace of 0.04% annually. If, on the other hand, a widespread adoption of British/Dutch labor market reforms has the desired effect of raising participation rates to the US level (76.8% in 2001), the labor force will grow at a more respectable pace

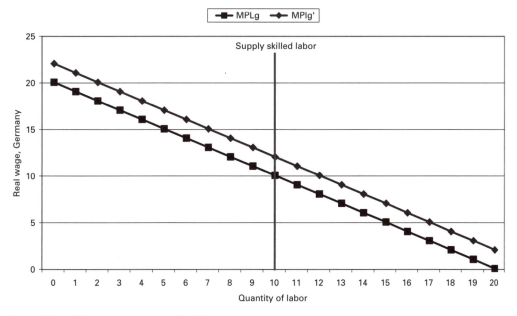

Figure 8.4a   Effects of migrants on skilled labor

of 1.4% annually.[3] Even that rate, however, will prove deficient in covering the burgeoning demands of the retired population. Demographic projections indicate that the population of people over sixty-five in the European Union will rise from 14.1% in 1990 to 18.6% in 2020, while the working-age population will decline from 67.1% in 1990 to 65.1% in 2020.

It is increasingly evident that an alternative strategy to temporary employment opportunities for native workers may well be temporary, but longer-term, employment opportunities for migrants. The guest worker programs of the 1960s will not be resurrected, given the political difficulties they created for governments in the 1970s, but the experiences from those earlier programs provide a rationale for a common EU migration policy. The key to the generally positive economic effects of earlier migration surges to the EU countries lies in the apparent complementarity of the foreign workers to the native workers. As argued above, if foreign workers are generally less skilled, or less specifically trained for jobs in the host country, an increase in their supply increases the marginal productivity of the more skilled and more highly trained native workers and therefore the demand for their services. Figures 8.4a and 8.4b illustrate the economic logic of this empirical finding from the past.

In figure 8.4a, the demand curve for German skilled labor shifts upward, thanks to the complementary inputs of unskilled labor now provided by the

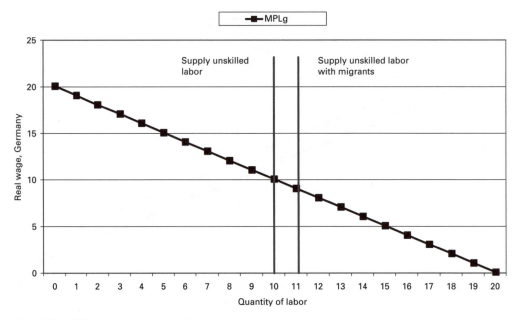

Figure 8.4b   Effects of migrants on unskilled labor

new migrants. Skilled laborers are better off, and their employers are happy to pay the higher real wages, given the increased productivity of the skilled labor force. In figure 8.4b, by contrast, the supply curve for German unskilled labor shifts outward, again thanks to the inputs of the new migrants, who are near substitutes for the unskilled German laborers. Wages for unskilled German labor are driven down as a result. German employers and consumers, of course, are better off, as are the skilled German workers. The overall effect of new migrants on the host country then depends on the relative weight of skilled versus unskilled labor in the native labor force and upon the relative weight of skilled versus unskilled labor within the migrant labor force.

Past experience with the large immigrations of mainly unskilled labor into EU countries in the 1960s was quite positive for the host-country economies. Social tensions proved to be costly for cities with high concentrations of immigrant populations, however; 10% seemed to be the critical point. By the 1980s, moreover, the wage rates of native workers had become increasingly fixed by minimum wage regulations and union contracts, so that the effects of further immigration were revealed in different ways. Unskilled labor, rather than seeing its real wage decline, saw instead its unemployment rate increase. Skilled labor, rather than enjoying increased real wages, saw employers reaping higher profits. In terms of figures 8.4a and 8.4b, the responses occurred along the quantity axes rather than the wage axes. Political tensions in response to increased migration became exacerbated as a result.

Further increases in the labor force, say by renewed immigration pushes from distressed economies in the former Soviet Union or former Yugoslavia, then create increased unemployment among less trained or less skilled workers in the European Union. Rising unemployment may then occur even if the increased supply of less skilled workers helps increase the wages of more skilled, and union-protected, workers. If the immigrant flows are composed of more skilled workers, especially from heavy industry, then the wages or employment of native skilled workers may be at risk as well. In heavily unionized France, for example, fear of Polish plumbers competing freely with French plumbers was used as a campaign tactic in the successful vote against ratification of the EU constitution in 2005.

In the coming years, however, the demographic pressures will become more pressing from more distant sources of growing populations, especially in north Africa, the Middle East, and central Asia. Population growth in the ten accession countries that joined in 2004 is not projected to be much higher than the 3.3% projected for the original fifteen member countries over the period 1994–2025. Turkey, with its population of over 70 million in 2003, however, was projected to grow nearly 60% over the same thirty-year period.[4] The populations of all north African countries are projected to grow even more rapidly than Turkey's. Formulating a common immigration policy for the EU as a whole, therefore, will be much more of a challenge to policy-makers than continuing the gradual creation of a common labor market within the customs union.

NOTES

1. See article 7 of the treaty for the general commitment to forbidding discrimination and article 48 for details on how it is applied to various types of workers.
2. The relevant economic theory is called the Rybczynski Theorem after the Polish economist who first formulated it in mathematical terms. He noted that even the capital-intensive sectors of an economy need labor, so that imports of capital to an economy require that the economy shift some of its labor force from labor-intensive sectors to the capital-intensive sectors, with the effect of changing its terms of trade even more sharply in favor of the capital-intensive sector.
3. Véronique Genre and Ramón Gómez-Salvador, *Labour Force Developments in the Euro Area since the 1980s*, Occasional Paper no. 4, European Central Bank, Frankfurt: 2002, p. 7.
4. United Nations Population Fund, *The State of World Population 1994*, New York: 1995.

9 The single market in capital: from Bretton Woods to Maastricht

The Single European Act of 1986 declared a commitment by each member state to four freedoms: free movement of goods, services, labor, and capital. As far as the movement of goods was concerned, the Act simply addressed the non-tariff barriers that impeded the full operation of the customs union with its tariff-free trade area, as discussed in chapter 7. Services, other than in the distribution of goods including the finance of distribution, are largely non-tradable in any event. Labor, as discussed in chapter 8, has not moved nearly as much as is possible in theory, due to the advantages of working in one's home country and producing tradable goods and services. The free movement of capital, by contrast, was a major change in national economic policy, and twenty years later it is by no means fully established within the European Union, especially with respect to the ten accession countries that joined in 2004. While the rigidity of national labor markets in response to the challenges of the single market and the common currency can be understood in terms of domestic political pressures, the resistance of national capital markets to the challenges of the single market and the common currency is less easily understood. The barriers to free movement of capital within the European Union have become more visible and appear more susceptible to action by the Commission and the European Central Bank. In the process of adopting the common currency and then of enlarging the membership of the European Union, however, some unexpected developments occurred that highlight the complexity of modern capital markets and the challenges remaining for Europe.

Under the Bretton Woods system, which governed international financial relationships between Europe and the United States until 1971, each European country maintained a system of capital controls. Capital imports denominated in a foreign currency were segregated into distinct banking accounts within each European country and subjected to specific regulations designed to prevent sudden withdrawals or attacks upon the foreign reserves held by each central bank. In this way, the trilemma that confronts open economies – the impossibility of a country maintaining simultaneously the desirable policies of (1) fixed exchange rates, (2) an independent monetary policy, and (3) the free import of capital – was resolved in favor of fixed exchange rates and an independent monetary policy for each European country. With the adoption of the euro as a common currency, however, the trilemma was resolved in favor of fixed exchange rates and the free movement of capital within the European Union, and each country that adopted the euro as its currency gave up its independence in setting monetary policy, as discussed in chapter 6.

Optimists believed that a common financial market would emerge easily once the hassle of calculating differences in exchange rates among the European currencies was removed by the replacement of all the legacy currencies with the new common currency. More important was the removal of uncertainty over the course of future exchange rates, when investors might want to repatriate their earnings or investments. In practice, it appears that large investors within the European Union had already devised adequate techniques for protecting themselves from exchange rate fluctuations, unlike small investors, consumers, or workers. What remained as obstacles to a common financial market were national rules and regulations, covering everything from how to set up a company to governing it, to listing its bonds or equity shares on a national stock market, and to protecting its intellectual property, whether in the form of patented technology or trade secrets. Moreover, the national practices in every case had worked well for each country over the previous forty years, creating sustainable market niches for national champions and for their counterparts in the financial sector. Removing these impediments to the operation of a truly single market in capital throughout the European Union remains a major task.

Theory

It is obvious to economists why the European Union would benefit from the creation of a truly single market in capital. Just as we described the advantages for Italy and West Germany of a single labor market in the previous chapter with a simple general equilibrium diagram, we can demonstrate the advantages of a single capital market for Italy and Germany. Again, however, the distribution of the resulting gains in overall product may create issues that have to be dealt with in the political arena.

Figure 9.1a, similar to figure 8.1a, shows the problem with capital controls and separate equilibrium prices for capital in the two countries. This time, however, we posit that the returns to capital, r, are higher in Italy than in

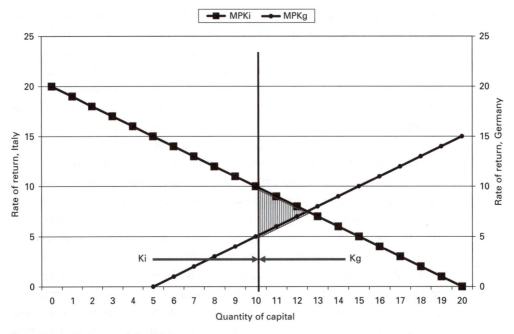

Figure 9.1a   Separate capital markets

Germany (recall that we posited earlier that wages, w, were higher in Germany than Italy). As long as capital controls, buttressed by differences in the regulation of companies within Germany and Italy, remain in effect, owners of capital in Italy gain higher returns than owners of capital in Germany. Figure 9.1b, similar to figure 8.1b, shows that returns to capital fall in Italy and rise in Germany once the barriers to cross-border investments are removed. While the overall product of the two economies increases by eliminating the deadweight loss triangle in figure 9.1a, savers in Germany have gained while savers in Italy have lost. The political influence of employers and owners of capital in Italy can be very effective in blocking such capital movements, even if they may not be as numerous and well organized as the laborers in Germany. (Yet another scandal broke out in Italy in summer 2005 when the revered governor of the Banca d'Italia was accused of blocking the takeover of an Italian bank by a German bank in favor of merging the Italian bank with another Italian bank.)

History

To understand why barriers to capital mobility persist within the EU, despite twenty years of efforts at eliminating them in concert with the adoption of the

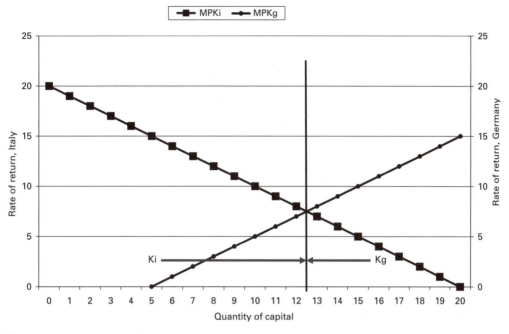

Figure 9.1b   Integrated capital markets

common currency, we have to acknowledge the previous success of the individual efforts of the member states to encourage capital formation. Immediately after the end of World War II national incomes were depressed, and all efforts were devoted to rebuilding the war-torn economies. Historically high rates of investment relative to GDP arose as a result. With the planning efforts encouraged by Marshall Plan administrators within each country, albeit in different ways depending on the specific needs of the country, high rates of investment were maintained during the period of Marshall Plan aid. The political pact among government, labor, and capital that emerged during the success of the European Payments Union, described in chapter 2, managed to sustain high rates of investment throughout the 1950s and into the 1960s. During this period the higher the ratio of investment to GDP the higher the rate of growth of GDP overall, which created conditions for full employment and rising incomes. Figure 9.2 plots the average ratio of gross domestic capital formation (I) to gross domestic product (Y) over the period 1960–73 for each of the fifteen countries that constituted the EU by 1995 against their average rate of growth of gross domestic product (measured in 2000 PPP dollars) for the same period.

Figure 9.2 shows just how effective the focus on high investment rates was during the golden age of economic growth. Countries such as the United

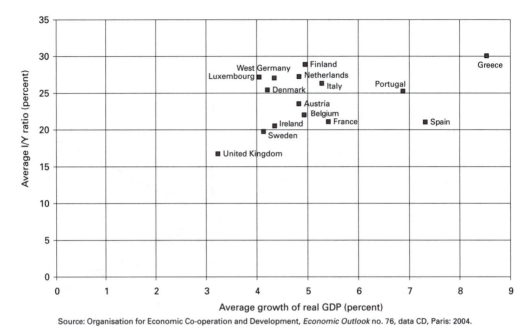

Source: Organisation for Economic Co-operation and Development, *Economic Outlook* no. 76, data CD, Paris: 2004.

Figure 9.2   Investment and growth during the golden age, 1960–73

Kingdom and Ireland, which failed to encourage capital formation to the extent practiced in West Germany and France, found their citizens falling farther behind the prosperous Continentals. Clearly, the efforts of most countries to keep their rates of investment up at the historic highs paid off in terms of continued high rates of economic growth. Countries such as the United Kingdom and Ireland, which did not maintain such high rates of investment, also lagged well behind the rest of western Europe in terms of overall economic growth. The consequences of such laggardly behavior eventually became felt by the British and Irish voters, leading to the first expansion of the European Union to include the United Kingdom, Ireland, and Denmark in 1973.

To see the economic consequences more clearly, figure 9.3 plots the initial level of per capita income in 1960 on the Y axis in each of the fifteen countries that had joined the EU by 1995 against the average annual rate of growth of per capita income over the golden age of economic growth, which lasted until the end of 1973. Only six of the countries were actually members of the European Economic Community over this period, but all six continued to enjoy historically high rates of economic growth while maintaining high rates of investment.

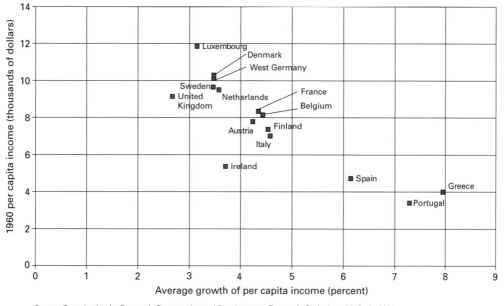

Source: Organisation for Economic Co-operation and Development, *Economic Outlook* no. 76, Paris: 2004.

Figure 9.3   Convergence in the golden age, 1960–73

The downward slope to the right of the scatter plot in figure 9.3 shows a clear pattern of convergence among the European economies in this period. If a country began the period with a relatively low level of per capita income, reflecting low levels of labor productivity, it could expect higher than average rates of growth of per capita income over the ensuing period, provided that it maintained high rates of investment. The points for the United Kingdom and Ireland lie below and to the left of the general pattern, showing that their growth rates of per capita income were lower than should have been the case had they followed the rest of western Europe in terms of economic policy. The country chapters in Part II will argue that a key part of the British and Irish differences in economic performance during the golden age of economic growth arose from their stringent controls on the import and export of capital.

Policy

Individual countries joining the EEC adopted the value added tax on transactions of goods and services, but, given the annual basis for calculating the tax, goods that were not purchased by a final consumer within a given tax year were not subject to the tax. Effectively, this meant that consumption goods were taxed but capital goods, most of which last much longer than one year after being put to use, were not. Consequently, VAT is often referred to as a consumption tax, which helps to explain the higher rates of saving in the EU countries than in the United States. Moreover, the rates of saving in the United Kingdom and Ireland rose after they adopted VAT upon entry to the EEC in 1973.

Indicative planning, carried on in most European countries even after the initial impetus from the Marshall Plan had lapsed, also helped keep investment ratios high. By reducing uncertainty over which sectors were expected to expand most rapidly over the ensuing plan period, indicative plans also encouraged private investment in those sectors. If the leading sector did not respond sufficiently, moreover, in most countries the government could be counted on to help along the investment decisions, either through activity by the nationalized industries or through helpful finance, subsidies, or tax breaks, each government acting individually.

The role of the EEC in all this activity was confined in the Treaty of Rome to watching out for unfair competition, while observing indulgently the creation of national champions in each country. The guiding economic principle was that large-scale enterprises needed to exist in order to realize economies of scale. Until 1989 EEC control of industrial concentration was put into effect by applying articles 85 and 86 of the Treaty of Rome. These encouraged the formation of large firms if they increased economic efficiency, and left the determination of whether that was the case to the individual member states. The new regulation in 1989, however, gave the Commission the exclusive responsibility to oversee mergers of a Community-wide dimension; smaller mergers would still be the work of the member states. "Community-wide dimension" was taken to mean an aggregate worldwide turnover of more than ECU5 billion, or when Community-wide turnover of each of at least two of the parties is more than ECU250 million, or the parties concerned do not have more than two-thirds of their Community turnover within one and the same member state.[1]

Since 1989 the work of the Competition Directorate has expanded enormously. By 1996 there were 1,280 cases pending; during that year 447 new antitrust cases appeared while only 388 were closed. Over the ensuing decade, however, the expansion of staff numbers and the Directorate's enforcement capability, as well as a better understanding throughout the member states of the criteria established by the EU for evaluating the implications of proposed mergers or cartel activity for the single market, have gradually brought down the number of cases pending, as well as the number of new cases.[2] In the meantime, however, a new concern has arisen that takes up more time and has far-reaching implications for the regulatory activities of the Commission, especially with the enlargement of 2004: state aid.

State aid

The number of cases appearing before the Commission that concern distortions in the competitive environment within the single market created by state aid by national, regional, or municipal governments within the EU has not declined over the past decade. Moreover, the Commission is determined that the same rules it has been applying to state aid within the fifteen member states will also be applied with the same rigor to the ten accession states. Consistently, the Commission has felt that the level of state aid given to particular industries and firms by national governments is too high. The defense that "everybody else does it" is no longer accepted. Consequently, more and more long-established practices within the member states have been challenged by the proactive efforts of the Competition Directorate of the Commission.

The terms of reference of the Competition Directorate have been expanded to services, although the cases of state aid in the sectors of agriculture, fisheries, transport, and coal have been reserved for other directorates. With the wrapping up of the European Coal and Steel Community in 2002, however, the coal situation has come under the watchful eye of the Competition Directorate, as has the ongoing merger activity and restructuring of the European steel industry. This aspect of the EU's regulatory activities makes it quite distinct from the United States, or the national governments within the EU. State and municipal aid to enterprises seeking the best location within the United States is accepted as part of the competition among governments, for example. Not so any more within the EU.

The role of financial markets

Despite the success of the common currency in lowering the costs of servicing government debt for the member states, similar results have not occurred for corporate debt issued in the private sector. Indeed, one of the reasons given for the two-year decline of the euro relative to the dollar was that the common financial market created for government debt had lowered the costs of borrowing for the private sector, but investment in the booming US stockmarket was much more attractive than investment within the European Union. To remedy this situation, the European Council called on a Committee of Wise Men to examine the regulation of European securities markets and to make recommendations for improving the competitiveness of EU capital markets compared to those in the United States and in the United Kingdom.

The six-member committee was chaired by Alexandre Lamfalussy, the former managing director of the Bank for International Settlements and a former director of the European Monetary Institute, which was the precursor to the European Central Bank. The Lamfalussy Report, submitted in February 2001, recommended far-reaching reforms (see box 9.1) to be undertaken by the European Union and urged that special procedures be deployed so that the reforms could be made as quickly as possible.[3]

Box 9.1 Summary of the Committee of Wise Men's recommendations

Economic benefits of integrated markets
Carry out research work and publish quantitative estimates as soon as possible and continuously benchmark progress toward an integrated European financial market.

Supply of equity and risk capital for small and medium-sized enterprises (SMEs)
Ensure appropriate environment is developed in the EU.

Differences in legal systems and taxation; political, external trade, and cultural barriers
Must not be ignored if full benefits of integrated European financial methods are to be assured. Furthermore, establish comprehensive list of external trade barriers to be removed in the next trade round.

Priorities of the Financial Services Action Plan
Adopt by end-2003.
Single prospectus for issuers.
Modernize admission to listing.
Home-country control for all wholesale members and definition of professional investor.
Modernize investment rules for UCITS (undertakings for the collective investment of transferable securities) and pension funds.
Adopt International Accounting Standards.
Single passport for recognized stockmarkets.

European regulatory and supervisory structures
Encourage convergence to ensure European Securities Regulators Committee works efficiently.

Clearing and settlement
Further restructuring necessary; pursue work in the Investment Services Directive (ISD) review, especially for wholesale capital markets, and the Giovannini Group (a group of market

participants that advises the Commission regularly on economic and financial matters); consider whether regulatory framework needed; examine general systemic issues, in the context of monetary policy and smooth functioning of payment systems; on competition issues – careful examination is required by the European Commission.

Managing prudential implications of integrated markets
Strengthen cooperation between financial market regulators, institutions in charge of micro- and macro-supervision, and cross-sectoral regulators.

Resources
Improve the allocation of resources devoted to the task of building an integrated European securities/financial market.

Training
Improve the deployment of best regulation and common understanding throughout the European Union.

The main action plan lay wholly within the competence of the European Union institutions, and the Lamfalussy Report urged that it be completed by the end of 2003. In the event, most aspects of it were in place by the end of 2005, when the market for financial services within the European Union could truly be said to be Community-wide, rather than divided up among the individual member countries. Other recommendations that required the cooperation of member governments and of their various institutions, such as stock exchanges and accounting standards, proved more difficult to implement.

Nevertheless, substantial progress has been made on each front, despite the deep differences between US and EU financial sectors. Credit has to be given to the United Kingdom and its market-oriented financial sector, which has provided both the model and the expertise needed for implementing reforms in the capital markets of continental Europe. The opportunities for the private sector to export capital into the accession countries of central and east Europe has also highlighted the desirability of making it easier to mobilize capital across national boundaries generally.

Some stumbling blocks remain, due to the difficulties of integrating the separate stock exchanges within Europe that over the years have been deeply entrenched, self-regulating organizations, each with its own standards for membership, listing rules, settlement procedures, and even times of operation.[4] With the adoption of the euro, much progress has been made in the market for government debt, as explained in chapter 5, but more obstacles appear progressively in integrating the European markets for corporate debt and, especially, for public equities. The Commission must also confront the uncertain nature of technological change, which is rapidly transforming the structure of European stockmarkets, before it can determine the appropriate regulations needed to help create a common financial market. The self-interests of users, owners, and managers of the national securities markets vary among the member countries of the European Union – and, indeed, within the eurozone as well. Experiments with combining clearing and settlement operations with the trading operations of an exchange are under way in the United Kingdom, Germany, and France, but all with different technologies. The Scandinavian securities markets are experimenting with combining trading operations with derivatives markets. EuroNext is combining the trading operations of the Amsterdam, Brussels, Lisbon, and Paris stock exchanges. The recently demutualized London Stock Exchange, long the leading securities market in Europe, has been the object of takeover bids by Deutsche Börse, EuroNext, OMHEX, and even an Australian entity. Each bidder represents a different business model that may dominate in Europe if it can include the customer base of London. Meanwhile, the US markets are reorganizing as well in order to maintain their dominance in the global financial market.

Especially troubling has been the provision of capital to small and medium-sized enterprises in continental Europe, most of which have relied upon banks for their external finance, or chosen to avoid banks by retaining large portions of their earnings in order to self-finance investment projects. The difficulties with bank-oriented finance for SMEs arise for firms trying to market new technologies or products based on new technologies. In the United States, venture capital firms have emerged with the object of identifying the entrepreneurs most likely to succeed in bringing to market the "next new thing," and the success of the Silicon Valley firms over the course of the 1990s was an object lesson for the policy-makers of Europe.

The difficulty in imitating the US model was highlighted by the short life of the Neumarkt, the German stock exchange formed precisely to market small and medium-sized firms. It was modeled explicitly on the NASDAQ stockmarket (founded in 1971) in the United States, which had succeeded as the preferred venue for venture capitalists to launch initial public offerings for new technology firms such as Microsoft and Apple. Neither private German investors nor German financial institutions showed any enthusiasm for making such high-risk investments, however, and the exchange was soon closed down. NASDAQ is the initialism for National Association of Securities Dealers Automated Quotations, which implies large numbers of dealers (i.e. traders willing to buy or sell securities on their own account, not just charging commissions to customers) actively searching for underpriced securities. Such large numbers of dealers do not exist in continental Europe, where most stock

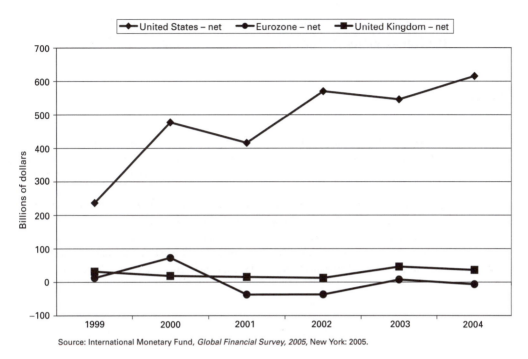

Source: International Monetary Fund, *Global Financial Survey, 2005*, New York: 2005.

Figure 9.4   Net capital flows compared: United States, United Kingdom, and eurozone

exchanges are dominated by a few large firms that will match orders within their own customer base before taking orders to the stock exchanges. Much more experience with public companies is needed in Europe before capital markets of the depth and breadth of American and British stock exchanges can be created.

Figure 9.4 sums up the dilemma facing the euro-area countries, by comparing the net capital inflows (or outflows) of the twelve euro-area countries since the establishment of the euro in 1999 with the capital flows for the United States and the United Kingdom. Despite the intent of the EU leaders to make the euro the alternative international currency to the US dollar in the global financial market, the net flows of international capital have been largely neutral, even slightly negative, with respect to the euro countries as a group. By contrast, the capital markets of the United States, despite the collapse of the dot.com boom in 2000, have attracted the bulk of the world's investment capital. Even the UK economy, much smaller than the combined GDP of the euro-area, has consistently attracted capital from the rest of the world to invest in its economy. To date, then, the successful introduction of a common currency in most of the EU countries has served mainly to highlight the problems with structural rigidities in the national markets for capital as well as for labor.

NOTES

1. "Competition and integration: Community merger control policy," *European Economy* 57, 1994, p. 11. In late 2005 the commissioner in charge of antitrust policy for the EU, Neelie Kroes, called for the right to scrutinize deals even if the companies involved conduct the bulk of their business in one EU member state.
2. European Commission, *European Union Competition Policy, 21st Report*, Brussels: 2001, p. 54.
3. The Committee of Wise Men, *Final Report of the Committee of Wise Men on the Regulation of European Securities Markets*, Brussels: European Commission, 2001.
4. Heiko Schmeidel and Andreas Schönenberger, *Integration of Financial Market Infrastructures in the Euro Area*, Occasional Paper no. 33, Frankfurt: European Central Bank, 2005.

The EU inside and out: regional policy and development aid

Students viewing an official map of the enlarged European Union may be struck by the emphasis on the regional boundaries inside the borders of each member state, including even the smaller countries. They are usually puzzled as well by the insets showing the overseas territories of France, Spain, and Portugal, which are nowhere near continental Europe. Both features reflect historical legacies of ethnic conflicts within the nation states of Europe and of imperial adventures overseas. Both features also reflect the economic policies of the EU, designed to resolve such ethnic conflicts permanently within Europe and to eliminate imperial rivalries among European powers overseas.

Inside the European Union, regional policy programs have been an increasing part of the budget expenditures over time and will continue to grow in importance with the addition of the central and east European countries and their ethnic rivalries. Outside the European Union, development strategies for former overseas colonies have confronted increasing challenges from the globalization of international trade and finance, which has undercut the value to the former colonies of "imperial preference" or "Community preference." Both policies, one directed to reduce economic inequalities within the European Union, and the other directed to reduce economic backwardness in former colonies, received their basic impetus from the accession of the United Kingdom in 1973. Each subsequent enlargement of the membership of the EU has brought with it a reorientation of both regional and development policy, driven mostly by the political needs of the new members but shaped as well by an evaluation of the economic effects of previous policies.

Regional policy

The EU's regional policy aims to further social cohesion in the process of European integration by reducing the economic disparities among and within EU member states. Since the early days of the EU, regional policy has grown

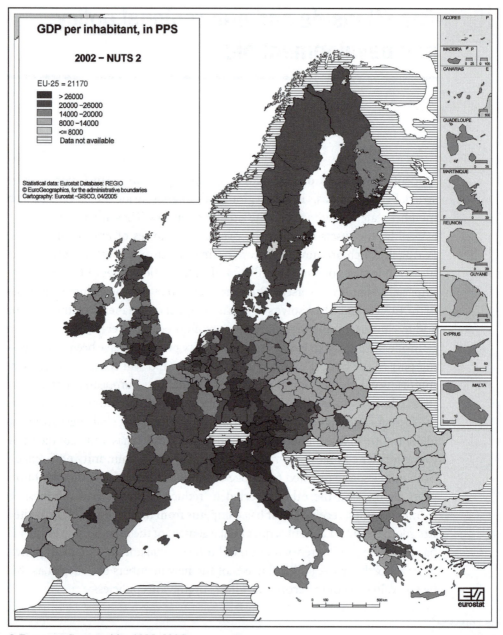

© European Communities 1995–2006

Figure 10.1   The regional diversity of the European Union, 2002

               NB: PPS = purchasing power standards, to adjust for differences in price levels among the EU countries.

in importance, so that today it holds second place as a share of EU total expenditures, after the Common Agricultural Policy. While only 3.8% of the EU budget was devoted to regional policy in 1980, it rose to 18% in 1989 and 30% in 1993, and by 2006 had risen to nearly 36%. The EU's regional policy will become even more important with the challenges of the central and east European countries now in the Union. To understand the economic issues of the EU's regional policies, it is useful to review how they evolved. Each enlargement of membership or major change in trade, agricultural, or monetary policies has caused the EU to revise the terms of its regional policy. Revisions have usually occurred in response to new political forces, combined with a recognition that previous policies have largely failed to reduce the initial economic disparities.[1] We can distinguish six phases to date.[2]

Phase 1 (1975–8)

The active regional policy of the EU started only in 1975. When the United Kingdom became a full member of the EEC, in 1973, British critics of the Community argued that the United Kingdom gained little from the CAP, as the British agricultural sector was small in comparison with the other EEC member states. The criticism came to a peak in 1974, when a Labour government replaced the Conservative government that had been responsible for the accession terms of 1973. The new government pressed for new accession conditions pertaining to finances, and backed its case by putting EEC membership to a popular referendum in 1975.

In response to these pressures, the Community that year established the European Regional Development Fund (ERDF), which provided a financial source from which the United Kingdom could also benefit from EEC membership. Although there was no explicit legal base in the Treaty of Rome for funding regional policy, the referendum in the United Kingdom did receive a majority for remaining as a member, and regional policy has remained part of the EU ever since. The ERDF disbursed its modest allotment of funds to the member states according to pre-set quotas. There was no focus or emphasis on really disadvantaged regions. It was left up to the individual countries to apply the funds to supplement their national regional policies and to set their goals according to strictly national political considerations.

Phase 2 (1979–84): the Commission becomes more than a treasurer

As the Commission's role was no more than to keep track of the disbursements made under the original design of the EEC's regional policy, it subsequently tried to obtain some discretion in administering the regional policy funds. The Commission scored a small success in 1979, when the ERDF was split into two parts: one with 95% of the ERDF resources, distributed by fixed quotas as before, and another with 5% of the ERDF resources. The Commission determined by its own authority which regions would be supported by this 5% of the ERDF. These Specific Community Programs were selected according to EEC communal criteria, and the EEC could implement regional policy programs regardless of whether the regions involved were supported by their national states. Although this reform was quantitatively insignificant, amounting to just 5% of the ERDF's modest budget, it was qualitatively remarkable, as the EEC was now able to run a regional policy for the first time independently from national regional policies.

Phase 3 (1985–7): the Iberians knock on the door

Portugal and Spain became members of the EEC in 1986. Their entry caused the main areas of conflict to switch from the relation between the Commission and the Council to the relation between the "rich" and the "poor" member states. The addition of Spain and Portugal to Greece (which had joined the EEC in 1981), Ireland, and the Mezzogiorno part of Italy increased the demand for regional funds from the EEC. The main contributing countries were willing to accept this increase only if the main recipient countries submitted to conditions about how to spend these resources. In addition, the continuing economic failure of regional policy to narrow income inequalities revealed the problems with the previous system. These problems included a lack of concentration of resources, a rigid quota distribution among the member states, and the fragmentation of the regions receiving aid.

The southern enlargement of the EEC therefore had a strong impact on regional policy. The ERDF was restructured into two types of programs: "Common Programs," financed by the EEC; and "National Programs of Communal Interest," co-financed by the EEC and the relevant member state. In addition, the fixed national quota system was replaced by a system of fixed EEC shares for the co-financing of national programs. These shares were determined in advance for three years. As a result, the position of the Commission as a policy-maker was reinforced. Even though the "National Programs of Communal Interest" formally guaranteed national autonomy in regional policy, in practice the member states adopted the preferences of the Commission for regional policy in order to get subsidies from the ERDF. Hence, at this step of EEC enlargement, the changes in the decision-making process for regional policy and its impact on the members' behavior were at least as relevant as the increase of the regional policy budget.

Phase 4 (1988–93): the single market compensation payments

As the EEC intended to finish the project of a single market in 1992, the intra-EEC controversies on the regional effects of increased economic integration again became a major topic. The poor member states – Ireland, Greece, Portugal, and Spain – made the argument, based on past experience within the original member states of the Common Market, that the single market would strengthen regional disparities. Anticipating that they would suffer losses from deeper market integration, the four poorest states claimed that they should be compensated by the winners from deeper market integration through an increase in regional policy expenditures. Indeed, the budget on regional policy was doubled from 1987 to 1992 as a concession by the eight rich states to the four poor states in order to obtain their agreement to the single market project. Moreover, the Single European Act legally confirmed the regional and cohesion policy of the European Economic Community for the first time. Ever since, the reduction of regional disparities has been an official policy aim of the EEC.

The EEC tried to concentrate its activity in 1988 by devoting regional policy expenditure to five "objectives of convergence":
(1) promoting the development and structural adjustment of lagging regions;
(2) converting regions seriously affected by industrial decline;
(3) combating long-term unemployment;
(4) facilitating job training for workers; and
(5) promoting rural development through structural aid.

The EEC also combined the different funds that had arisen: the ERDF, which is still the most important fund; the European Social Fund; and the "guidance portion" of the European Agricultural Guidance and Guarantee Fund, which was originally a part of the agricultural policy. The result of the political bargaining process among the member states on this issue reflected their different political interests, however, more than an attempt to concentrate regional policy expenditures more effectively. It was political rather than economic considerations that ended with criteria that managed to give each member state some share of the regional funds.

Phase 5 (1994–9): single currency compensation payments and northern enlargement

As the reform of the regional funds in 1988 was triggered by the single market project, the reforms that determined the regional policy from 1994 up to 1999 were provoked by the single currency project and by the northern enlargement of the EU. Of lesser importance might be the fact that the five objectives of convergence of 1988 had been modified a little and that a sixth objective had been added when Sweden and Finland joined the EU, so as to account for the needs of the less populated northern regions. Even the rich northern countries were now eligible to receive funds under Objective 6. While this reform of the objective system was, again, due to the political compromise to give each member state a share of the regional funds, the introduction of a new fund – the Cohesion Fund – merely duplicated the EU strategy that had already been applied in 1988.

To facilitate the completion of the single currency project of the European Monetary Union (the second stage started in 1994, another step in deepening the EU), the poor countries had to be compensated. This was especially true as the European Monetary System criteria of convergence implied far-reaching reductions in public expenditure in these countries, which would have caused a dramatic cut in the necessary investment on public infrastructure. The Cohesion Fund, devoted especially for infrastructure in traffic and environment, directly subsidized the countries that had a per capita GDP below 90% of the Community average. In other words, it was specially designed for getting the agreement of Spain, Portugal, Greece, and Ireland to the Monetary Union. The funds paid up to 85% of projects in these countries. The Cohesion Fund was initially projected to finish at the end of 1999, the end of the financial forecast at the time, but it is now a permanent fixture in the EU budget.

Phase 6 (2000–2006): no reforms for the eastern enlargement

In summer 1999 the EU had to make projections for regional policy over the next seven years for the financial perspective of 2000–2006.[3] At the time, the EU projected that at least the Czech Republic, Estonia, Hungary, Poland, Slovenia, and Cyprus would be members of the EU by some point during the planning period. Indeed, by 2004 not only those countries became members but also Latvia, Lithuania, Slovakia, and Malta – ten in all. Only Cyprus and Malta could be considered ineligible for regional aid under the previous provisions. Most of the remaining eight countries were eligible for Objective 1 aid under the existing criteria. In its "Agenda 2000"[4] the EU decided to handle this enlargement without any deep reform of its finance system. This decision meant that the EU could not follow its traditional strategy of raising the budget for side payments to certain member states in order to get their agreement to further integration or further enlargement. As all the joining countries were relatively poor, much poorer on average than had ever been the case in previous enlargements, and were therefore candidates for regional policy subsidies, handling the eastern enlargement with the same budget mechanism that already existed for the EU-15 made it necessary to reform the existing regional policy dramatically and to reduce the subsidized regions to those really in need.

The decision was made in two steps. The first was to restrict the access of the new member states to the structural funds during their transition period, typically five years, after formal entry in 2004. Spain insisted that the allocation of structural funds among the EU-15 recipients remain the same through 2006. This was Spain's condition for agreeing to the Nice Treaty anticipating enlargement in 2004.

The second step was to restrict access to the structural funds for the 2007–2013 budget term to regions in which the average per capita income over the past three years was less than 75% of the three-year average per capita income of the EU-25. This is a radical reduction from the former rule of restricting access to regions with less than 90% of the per capita income of the EU-15. It is in line with the general move toward limiting the scale and scope of the EU budget in the future, as discussed in chapter 1. Figure 10.2 shows that this new rule as of 2005 would restrict expenditures by the EU's structural funds to only 84 of the 268 regions then recognized by the Commission.

As expected, most of these regions are in the new accession countries. Nevertheless, some remain in the former EU-15 member states, showing that some regions have eluded the best efforts of the EU to date to reduce income inequalities among regions. The most resistant cases appear to be in southern Spain, southern Italy, western England, and northern Scotland. Indeed, of the nine most extreme cases of regional inequality within the EU-25, five cases are in the EU-15, and only four are among the ten new members. The next most extreme case is in Romania, scheduled to enter the EU in 2007.

Finally, the Commission has been given more authority over the allocation of funds by reducing the number of objectives to three, and making each broader in scope. Implicitly, the increased vagueness of the objectives gives the Commission more latitude to decide which national applications are the truly deserving cases. Objective 1 regions, which take 70% of the funds, are those where "development is lagging behind," as defined above. Objective 2 regions include those areas facing structural difficulties, while Objective 3 regions are a catchall for modernizing policies and systems of education, training, and employment.

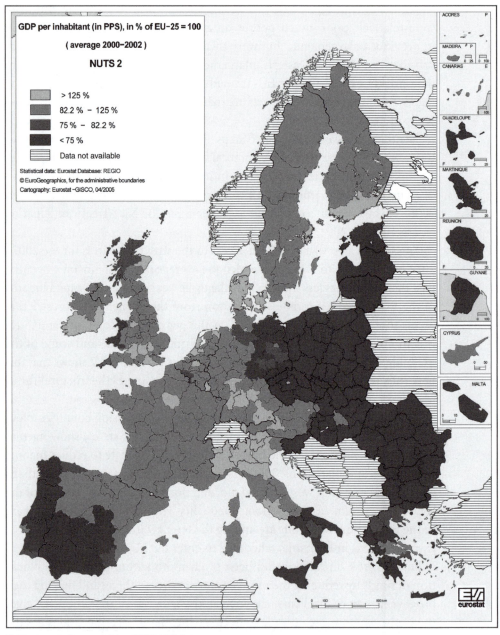

GDP per inhabitant (in PPS), in % of EU-25 = 100

(average 2000–2002)

NUTS 2

- > 125 %
- 82.2 % – 125 %
- 75 % – 82.2 %
- < 75 %
- Data not available

Statistical data: Eurostat Database: REGIO
© EuroGeographics, for the administrative boundaries
Cartography: Eurostat –GISCO, 04/2005

Figure 10.2   The eligibility of EU regions for structural funds, 2002

NB: PPS = purchasing power standards, to adjust for differences in price levels among the EU countries.

As the Commission has pointed out,[5] however, all the cases of moderate inequality among regions occur among the EU-15 incumbent countries, which is some vindication, perhaps, of the past efforts by the EU and national authorities to mitigate inequality. Nevertheless, statistical analysis by Michele Boldrin and Fabio Canova suggests that most of the convergence of regional incomes within the EU-15 came as a result of general economic growth, not as a result of any redistribution of largesse within individual countries. Consequently, the criteria for funding regional initiatives have become increasingly based not so much on need, which just determines eligibility, but more on implementing proven policies from previous success stories in other regions. Constructing factories or infrastructure in a given region, such as the Mezzogiorno in Italy, has too often simply increased job opportunities in the advanced regions with capital goods industries that take advantage of the orders placed for factory machinery or construction equipment. Indeed, there already seems to be a "growth pole" effect occurring with the new member countries, with the growth pole typically the region around the capital city. Immediate order flow to the private sector, in other words, is the key to stimulating economic growth in a region. The record of government transfers, even on a huge and continuing scale, has not been encouraging, as the chapters on Germany and Italy demonstrate.

Development policy

Formal development of the EU's development policy, unlike its regional policy, actually began in 1957, as the Treaty of Rome recognized in articles 131 and 136 the obligations of member states to help their colonies economically. To help meet these obligations of the colonial powers (mainly France and Belgium at the time), the European Development Fund (EDF) was set up in 1958. While the disbursements of the EDF are under the supervision of the Council, the funding has always consisted of contributions from the concerned member states. As decolonization proceeded rapidly in Africa after the independence of Algeria was recognized by France, a formal treaty, Yaoundé I, was signed between the former African colonies and the EEC in 1963, to cover aid disbursements by the European Development Fund over the next five years, 1964–9. Since then, succeeding agreements – Yaoundé II (1969–74), Lomé I (1975–9), Lomé II (1980–4), Lomé III (1985–9), Lomé IV (1990–4), Lomé IV revised (1995–9) – have been worked out between the existing membership of

---

Box 10.1 The evolution of the Cotonou Agreement

Yaoundé I (1963)
Benin, Burkina Faso, Burundi, Cameroon, Central African Republic, Chad, Congo (Braz-
    zaville), Congo (Kinshasa), Côte d'Ivoire, Gabon, Madagascar, Mali, Mauritania, Niger,
    Rwanda, Senegal, Somalia, Togo (eighteen total)

Yaoundé II (1969)
Kenya, Tanzania, Uganda (twenty-one total)

Lomé I (1975)
The Bahamas, Barbados, Botswana, Ethiopia, Fiji, The Gambia, Ghana, Grenada, Guinea,
    Guinea-Bissau, Guyana, Jamaica, Lesotho, Liberia, Malawi, Mauritius, Nigeria, Samoa,
    Sierra Leone, Sudan, Swaziland, Tonga, Trinidad and Tobago, Zambia (forty-five total)

Lomé II (1979)
Cape Verde, Comoros, Djibouti, Dominica, Kiribati, Papua New Guinea, Saint Lucia, São
    Tomé and Príncipe, Seychelles, Solomon Islands, Suriname, Tuvalu (fifty-seven total)

Lomé III (1984)
Angola, Antigua and Barbuda, Belize, Dominican Republic, Mozambique, Saint Kitts and
    Nevis, Saint Vincent and the Grenadines, Vanuatu, Zimbabwe (sixty-six total)

Lomé IV (1990)
Equatorial Guinea, Haiti (sixty-eight total)

Lomé IV revised (1995)
Eritrea, Namibia, South Africa (seventy-one total)

Cotonou (2000)
Cook Islands, Marshall Islands, Federated States of Micronesia, Nauru, Niue, Palau (seventy-
    seven total)

---

the European Union and the expanding number of countries deemed eligible for preferential treatment in trade and aid.

From the eighteen African countries covered in Yaoundé I, every five years there has been a renegotiation and redefinition of the economic relationships between the ever-expanding membership of the EU and, as a consequence, the number of ex-colonies, trusteeships, or overseas territories for which European countries feel some responsibility. By 1999, at the end of Lomé IV revised, there were no fewer than seventy-one countries gathered under the rubric of African, Caribbean, and Pacific countries that were guaranteed preferential access to EU trade and aid (see box 10.1).

In 2000, however, a new agreement was signed in Cotonou that made sub-stantial changes in the administration of EU development aid. Not only was the banana regime, discussed in chapter 4, revised to conform to the WTO rules for trade agreements, but the long-standing policies of the EU for providing aid to the ACP countries, STABEX and SYSMIN (see below), were eliminated as well. For the future, the disbursements of the European Development Fund will be geared, as in the case of structural funds, toward policies that provide long-term growth prospects to the recipients. The ninth EDF was allocated fresh funds of €13.5 billion over the following five years. Added to the €9.9 billion left over from previous allotments, the EDF has more funds at its disposal than ever. The failures of STABEX and SYSMIN to meet the test of effective economic policies help illustrate some hard economic lessons for both donor and recipient countries – lessons that will guide EU allocations of aid toward the ACP countries in the future.

STABEX and SYSMIN

STABEX was the part of the European Development Fund devoted to stabilizing the export earnings of the ACP countries. Initially limited to just a few commodities and a few countries, it was later supplemented by a separate funding scheme for minerals, called SYSMIN. STABEX focused thereafter on agricultural exports such as coffee, cocoa, bananas, and peanuts, while SYSMIN dealt with specific minerals such as copper, cobalt, and uranium. Thanks to the effectiveness of international cartels in petroleum and diamonds, these minerals were excluded from the program. Rather than try to stabilize international prices for primary commodities or to stabilize the national output of a primary commodity for the individual countries, then, these programs simply stabilized the total export income earned by the specific products. Worse, they may have had the unintended consequence of maintaining the reliance of recipient countries on monocultures that promised little for future economic growth.

From the viewpoint of development policy, STABEX recognized that export earnings were a major source of economic growth for countries just beginning to participate in the international trading system. Not only could the earnings be used to finance the import of capital goods needed for industrialization or the improvement of social infrastructure, the market orientation of the export sector toward more advanced economies provided a role model and learning laboratory for the rest of the economy. Given that the initial exports of less developed countries would continue to be primary commodities, either agricultural or mineral, earnings would be subject to supply shocks specific to the country. Even if global demand for a given commodity or mineral might be price-inelastic, each individual country would be a price-taker as it provided only a small part of the world's total supply. If a country, say Gabon, suffered a shortfall in its annual banana crop due to the ravages of a tropical storm, STABEX provided funds to help make up the loss of earnings for that year. If the funds were used to replant the plantations and improve the access roads, and even improve packing facilities to improve the quality of the delivered product, earnings would recover the next year. A bumper crop that led to above-average earnings, on the upside, would yield larger than average earnings, a portion of which could be put aside in the STABEX fund.

From the viewpoint of the EU, the funding of STABEX could never lead to excessive demands requiring additional resources from the European Development Fund, or, worse, from a specific EU member country. As a stabilization fund, STABEX was presumed to be self-financing: excess earnings in good years would be used to make up losses in bad years. The contrast with the policy adopted for domestic agricultural producers, the Common Agricultural Policy, should be obvious. The CAP provided specific price supports for European farmers, while STABEX provided the ACP farmers only with general income support.

The idea in each case was the same – that the stabilization of earnings from the production of a specific commodity would encourage producers to make long-term investments that would increase productivity over time. In the case of price supports for European farmers, however, the funding required by the government increased proportionately with the increase in output, while in the case of income support for ACP farmers the funding remained stable over time. As productivity increased in the case of price supports, output increased as well, leading to self-sufficiency – a desirable goal for the EU. It also led to increased EU government expenditures. If productivity increased in the case of income supports for ACP farmers, by contrast, they had little incentive to increase total output as their total earnings could not increase. Instead, the less efficient farmers would leave agriculture, providing cheap resources for the manufacturing or service sectors. Best of all, there would be no increase in EU government expenditures.

The adverse consequences of this kind of income support policy for long-term economic growth should be evident, once it is explained in terms of the incentives provided to the private sector. In the best case, where the STABEX and SYSMIN schemes worked, the recipient country was locked into its primary source of export earnings instead of diversifying into other crops or minerals. Given the limited market for most primary goods, concentration

---

Box 10.2 The Millennium Development Goals (and targets for 2015)

Goal 1   Eradicate extreme poverty and hunger (reduce population with <$1 a day by one-half by 2015).

Goal 2   Achieve universal primary education (for both boys and girls by 2015).

Goal 3   Promote gender equality and empower women (equal education for boys and girls through all levels of education by 2015).

Goal 4   Reduce child mortality (reduce under-five mortality by two-thirds by 2015).

Goal 5   Improve maternal health (reduce maternal mortality ratio by two-thirds by 2015).

Goal 6   Combat HIV/AIDS, malaria, tuberculosis, and other diseases (halt and begin reversing spread by 2015).

Goal 7   Ensure environmental sustainability (integrate principle of sustainability into country programs and reverse loss of environmental resources).

Goal 8   Develop a global partnership for development (develop further rule-based, open, non-discriminatory system of trade and finance).

Source: United Nations, *The Millennium Development Goals Report, 2005*, New York: 2005.

---

on one product proved inimical to long-run growth. As the STABEX and SYSMIN systems evolved in subsequent agreements, the range of commodities was increased as well as the number of countries participating. Moreover, the Commission increased its restrictions on how funds could be spent by recipient countries. Emphasis was put on improving the marketability of the product or on diversifying the country's exports. Recipient countries, however, could easily justify the funds in terms of their ongoing development projects, and saw the EU's funds as mere supplements to their overall grant aid.

In actual operation, the EU delayed disbursement of funds to an increasing extent, trying to force recipients into compliance with the evolving EU strategy for economic development. It took basically half a century of experimentation with STABEX and related domestic schemes, however, such as marketing boards throughout sub-Saharan Africa, to convince policy-makers in both the ACP and the EU countries that the policy was doomed to failure and that both sets of countries would be better off with a redesigned aid policy.

Toward this end, the EU has put its full support behind the Millennium Development Goals (see box 10.2), worked out under the leadership of the United Nations. The goals focus on people and their welfare rather than on infrastructure projects, as in the past. Moreover, they require cooperation by the recipient states in forming feasible action plans. The EU in particular has pledged to increase aid expenditures to 0.7% of national income by 2015, with an intermediate goal of 0.56% in 2010, taking account of the reduced incomes of the ten accession countries. In return, the EU will expect recipient countries to respect human rights, follow the rule of law, and abide by the international rules governing trade and finance. In this respect, the EU is applying the success of its accession strategies for the ten new member states, discussed in chapter 19, to its client states. As with the change in regional policy, the change in development policy has a twofold advantage: (1) it reduces the future budget pressure on the EU and therefore on the individual member states; and (2) it increases the incentives for recipients of EU funds to make permanent economic improvements for the benefit of their citizens.

Conclusion

Both the regional policy and the development policy of the European Union originated in political motives to reduce antagonisms created by the extreme inequality of economic outcomes, whether within the member states of the EU or among their former colonies and dependencies. In each case, policy initially was essentially a redistributive exercise: money collected from the rich governments was handed to the poor governments. The economic outcomes for the individuals involved, however, did not live up to initial expectations. Individuals taxed by the rich governments became increasingly resentful of the tax burden that did not create any obvious benefit for them, much less obtain gratitude from the individuals in the poor regions or ex-colonies. Individuals in the recipient regions or countries became increasingly aware of the continued gap between their economic status and that of the taxpayers in the rich regions and countries, especially as the movement of people, whether interregionally or internationally, became easier and more prevalent over time.

The causes of the increasing malaise among all concerned can be understood in hindsight as being the result of adverse incentives that operated in both the private and public spheres in the application of the redistributive regional and development policies. Obviously, some government agencies – and, indeed, many individuals – were winners from the redistributions that occurred. Ultimately, however, they were temporary players in a permanent zero-sum game. Time will tell if the new strategies, certainly more cost-effective, will prove to be positive-sum games in which all players, present and future, rich and poor alike, can be gainers.

NOTES

1. An especially discouraging appraisal of the EU's regional policies to date can be found in Michele Boldrin and Fabio Canova, "Europe's regions: income disparities and regional policies," *Economic Policy* 32, 2001, pp. 207–53.
2. A more detailed analysis can be found in Larry Neal and Gregor van der Beek, "The dilemma of enlargement for the European Union's regional policy," *The World Economy* 27 (4), 2004, pp. 587–607.
3. European Commission, *Unity, Solidarity, Diversity for Europe, Its People, and Its Territory: Second Report on Economic and Social Cohesion*, Brussels: 2001, pp. 147–56; European Commission, *First Progress Report on Economic and Social Cohesion*, Brussels: 2002.
4. European Commission, *Agenda 2000*, Luxembourg: 1997.
5. European Commission, *Regions: Statistical Yearbook 2005*, Brussels: 2005, p. 41.

11   The EU: the other economic superpower?

The confrontations of the United States and the European Union over various trade issues seem to have increased over the years as the EU has expanded in size and improved its institutional capacity for protecting the economic interests of its member states. The issues confounding the resolution of the Doha Round of trade negotiations, begun in 2001, highlight the differences in approaches of the two economic superpowers. Both, however, are committed to the rule of law in governing international trade through the operation of the World Trade Organization, created in 1995 at the conclusion of the Uruguay Round of the General Agreement on Tariffs and Trade. The EU and the United States both consistently account for about 20% of international trade even as the total volume of trade increases annually more rapidly than world production. Once they agree on the rules and regulations to govern the administration of trade under the oversight of the WTO, the rest of the world finds it efficient to adopt the same procedures.

Nevertheless, the two economies dominate not only international trade and the world economy but also the number of disputes brought before the WTO. Of the 1,349 measures in force in mid-2004 by WTO members under the rubric of "anti-dumping" actions, the United States deployed by far the largest number, 293. India, belatedly opening up its economy to the forces of globalization, was in second place, with 216. The EU was not far behind, with 165, followed by China and South Africa, with eighty-five and eighty-four measures in force, respectively. This means that these five economies accounted for over a half of the anti-dumping actions taken by the 148 members of the WTO. China's exporters were subject to the highest number of initiations of anti-dumping investigations undertaken in the previous year, fifty-nine, but the United States and the EU were subject in turn to twenty-three and nineteen investigations, respectively.

The irony is that, each time the United States initiates a dispute against the EU over some restriction on the access of US products to the single market, the EU finds cause to initiate a dispute against the United States. Indeed, the US Congress requires the US Trade Representative to present an annual report on restrictive trade practices in the rest of the world, the bulk of which identifies obstacles that US exporters have found in the European market (Office of the United States Trade Representative, *2005 National Trade Estimate Report on Foreign Trade Barriers*, Washington, DC: 2005). To counter this, the European Commission issues its own trade report annually documenting the obstacles that European exporters have encountered in the United States and other non-EU markets, as well as giving information on tariff schedules and formalities that EU exporters will encounter, country by country, product by product (http://mkaccdb.eu.int, the EU Market Access Database). In addition, the WTO issues regular *Trade Policy Reviews* for each member country and especially for the United States and the European Union (these are available for downloading from http://www.wto.org).

Even though the trade rounds have demonstrated that the European Union can form a powerful, unified negotiating bloc, the diversity of interests across the member states has made trade arrangements very complicated, with individual members demanding special features that suit their own needs. This makes it very difficult for the EU to respond to alternatives offered by its negotiating partners, since any change in position has to meet the approval of all the member states. While there has been a common trade policy, its development has been greatly affected by member state interests. It is useful, in light of the increased importance of international trade for the rest of the world and the rules established by the WTO, to review the historical process by which the European Union established its role as the sole representative of the combined interests of the member states in matters of foreign trade.

The General Agreement on Tariffs and Trade (GATT)

The international, institutional framework of multilateral trade from 1948 until 1996 was the GATT, the predecessor of the WTO. Under the agreements reached in successive rounds of negotiations among the members (there were eight rounds over the nearly fifty years of GATT's existence), the European countries conducted their external trade policy individually until the establishment of the European Economic Community in 1958. From comprising in 1950 mostly the United States, Canada, and the OEEC countries, GATT membership rose over the years with each round of trade negotiations.

From ninety-two members in 1986, when the Uruguay Round began, GATT membership had risen to 114 when negotiations ended in 1993. By the time of the first ministerial meeting of the World Trade Organization, in Singapore in December 1996, membership had risen to 126, with another thirty waiting to join, and by the end of 2005 the total stood at 149. Moreover, while GATT dealt only with trade in manufactured goods at the beginning, the WTO currently covers non-tariff barriers, trade in services, agriculture, trade-related investments, and trade-related intellectual property rights among its member countries. Little wonder that the successive rounds of negotiations have lasted longer and longer before reaching agreement.

The GATT rested on two main principles that continue with the WTO: trade liberalization and non-discrimination. The non-discrimination rule is implemented by the most favored nation (MFN) clause in all trade agreements among members. This stipulates that trade concessions granted to one member must be granted to all members. It would appear, therefore, that the EU conducts discriminatory policy, since it has eliminated barriers only among members. However, the GATT allowed regional trade arrangements so long as the common tariffs were not higher than the average of its members' tariffs prior to the arrangement (article 26). Because the Treaty of Rome satisfied these conditions, it was allowed under the GATT. The GATT also provided a Generalized System of Preferences (GSP) for developing countries, whereby developed countries are ensured non-discriminatory trade and the developing nations get concessions on manufactured products. In 1995 the GSP was revised to help support more strongly the industrialization of developing countries, their export diversification, and their realization of higher export earnings.

With the Doha Declaration of 2001 the WTO committed its members to promoting sustainable development in the developing and transition economies. The developing countries believe this requires market access in the developed world for their exports of agricultural goods and labor-intensive manufactured goods, especially textiles. The developed countries believe that sustainable development requires market access for their capital goods and advanced services in the developing countries. The mutual reduction of tariffs on manufactured goods was relatively straightforward under the GATT negotiations. Mutual market access for quite different types of goods and services, however, presents much more complicated issues to resolve.

Dillon Round (1960–1) Under the Dillon Round, the six-member EEC agreed to reduce its planned common external tariff by 20 %. While the United States promoted the integration of western Europe at the time and supported

European nations acting as a unified economic and political force in principle, each country signed the agreement individually.

Kennedy Round (1963–7) By 1963 the six countries presented a united front in the negotiations, which resulted in a reduction of tariffs by an average of 35%, and for some industrial goods 50%. These reductions were to be carried out by 1972. The United States demanded that some agricultural products be included in the reduced tariffs and the EEC did reduce variable levies on some goods.

Tokyo Round (1974–9) In the Tokyo Round, tariff reductions were on average 33% for manufactures, mainly machinery, chemicals, and transport equipment. The conference attacked the widespread use of non-tariff barriers and signed seven agreements dealing with the various forms of NTBs (as discussed in chapter 7). In addition, the EEC demanded that there be some attempt at tariff harmonization on a worldwide basis. The "Swiss formula" was used, which allowed high tariffs to fall more rapidly than lower tariffs so that gradual convergence occurred over time.[1]

Uruguay Round (1986–94) The Uruguay Round was the first international trade round of the post-Cold-War era. This round, the results of which were formally agreed to in 1994, marked a new era for international trade. Agricultural trade was explicitly considered, along with services. A new body, the World Trade Organization, was created to oversee global trade, as a successor to the GATT. Tariff levels were further reduced. Given the changes due to the SEA, the EEC was deeply divided over whether further liberalization would proceed with agriculture. In fact, the EEC refused to cut agricultural subsidies by the scheduled deadline of December 1990. However, in May 1992, as we saw in chapter 4, the EEC finally agreed to reform the CAP, with further reforms in 2002.

Doha Round (2001–2006) The EU has encountered difficulties in making acceptable proposals to the developing countries for access to its agricultural markets, as has the United States. Cotton is the problem for the US negotiating position, while sugar beet is the problem crop for the EU's negotiating position. Further, the EU is constrained by an agreement reached, with difficulty, in 2002 to maintain the level of its continued agricultural subsidies (even the "decoupled" ones) until 2013. The United States put pressure on the EU by offering to eliminate all its export subsidies if the EU would do so sooner than 2013. These issues, creating headlines in 2005 at the Hong Kong Ministerial Conference of the WTO, simply highlight the different political constraints that bind the United States and the EU when negotiating the future rules and regulations for the continued expansion of international trade.

Economic comparisons of the EU and the United States

Every EU document since the creation of the Common Market in 1958 has compared the area, population, and gross domestic product of its combined member states with that of the United States and Japan. Until recently, this exercise served mainly as a calibration device, serving on the one hand to reassure the United States that its pre-eminence was not being challenged even economically, and on the other hand to reinvigorate the EU supporters that much remained to be accomplished if they were to reach the goal of economic parity. With economic parity, the EU elite anticipated that political parity would follow as a matter of course.

In 2004 the population of the EU-25, formed that year, far exceeded that of the United States: 459 million to 294 million. The EU-25 GDP, calculated in PPP euros by Eurostat, actually slightly exceeded the US GDP: €10.3 trillion to €10.2 trillion. Only in terms of land area did the United States still exceed the EU-25: 9.6 million square kilometers to just under 4 million square kilometers. In terms of per capita income, obviously, the United States could still claim leadership: €34,700 to €22,400. Even there, legitimate doubts could be raised about the relative economic performances. A higher proportion of adult Americans actually participated in economic activity than in the EU: over 75% in the United States, compared to just below 70% in the EU. Further, those American workers labored on average far more hours per year than the European workers, with their long paid vacations and generous leaves for sickness, maternity, and paternity. The contrasting participation rates in the respective labor forces in the EU and the United States raise microeconomic issues, as discussed in chapter 8. Either the extra taxes imposed on labor throughout the EU compared to the United States reduce the incentives of Europeans to participate in the formal labor force, or, perhaps, the workers in the EU experiencing the benefits of employment and income stability have come to value leisure opportunities more highly than US workers, who prefer income opportunities. The contrasting performances in terms of the standard macroeconomic policy goals – economic growth, low inflation, and high employment – are clear, however.

Figure 11.1 compares the level of real GDP in terms of purchasing power parity dollars in 2000 for the entire period 1960–2005. It illustrates nicely the distinguishing feature that contrasts the two super-economies: stable growth in the EU versus more volatile and more rapid growth in the United States. The EU-15 countries in aggregate have opted for stability in overall growth, whether

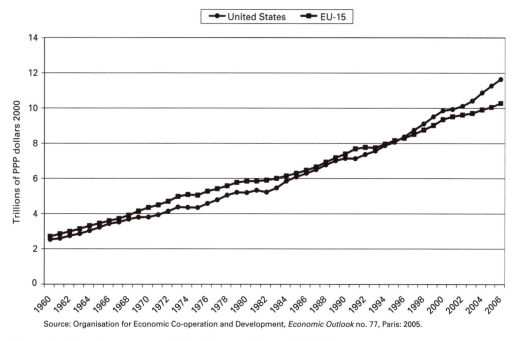

Source: Organisation for Economic Co-operation and Development, *Economic Outlook* no. 77, Paris: 2005.

Figure 11.1   Gross domestic product, United States and EU-15, 1960–2005

they were formally part of the European Union or not (recall that, while our figures include the fifteen EU countries as of January 2004, the EU had only six members in 1960, and did not reach fifteen until 1995). The United States, by contrast, fell behind the EU-15 rates prior to the oil shocks of the 1970s, but by 1982 it had begun a period of catching up again that lasted until 1992. The sudden rise in EU GDP then came from the addition of East Germany to the EU-15 total. The US economy also suffered a brief setback due to the Gulf War, which began at the end of 1990. Since the reunification of Germany, however, the US economy has continued to outperform the combined efforts of the EU-15 economies, despite a sharp setback in 2001 with the collapse of the dot.com bubble.

Figure 11.2 demonstrates that the volatile, more rapid growth of the US economy in aggregate is largely driven by more volatile, more rapid growth in per capita output compared to the EU-15 aggregate. The scale in both figures is arithmetic, so the worrisome slowdown in the productivity growth of both economies since the oil shocks of the 1970s is not immediately apparent. Has the relative success of the US institutions in promoting economic growth since the 1980s come at the expense of the other macroeconomic policy goals of low inflation and high employment? The answer is "no," as inflation rates on

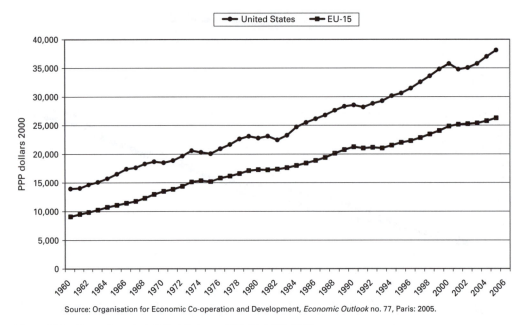

Source: Organisation for Economic Co-operation and Development, *Economic Outlook* no. 77, Paris: 2005.

Figure 11.2   Per capita output, United States and EU-15, 1960–2005

average for the EU-15 have been close to the US average while unemployment rates in the United States have remained well below those of the EU-15 since the 1980s.

Figures 11.3 and 11.4 show that after the oil shocks of the 1970s and the collapse of the Bretton Woods monetary arrangements, discussed in chapter 5, the economic policy performance of the United States improved dramatically relative to that of its European counterparts. The average inflation rate for the United States, given by the annual rate of change in the GDP deflator, rose sharply with the oil shocks of the mid-1970s, as did the average inflation rate for the twelve countries now in the eurozone. Nevertheless, from the 1980s on the inflation rate in both superpowers has fallen and remained low. The most dramatic contrast is in the pattern of unemployment rates after the 1970s. In response to each successive macroeconomic shock, the unemployment rates in both economies rose. Nevertheless, unemployment typically remained at permanently higher levels for the EU-15, while in the United States it fell back to previous levels quickly. Both the inflation rates and the unemployment rates for the EU-12 or EU-15 are weighted averages of the diverse experiences of the individual countries, the policies of which have varied over time and from one another.

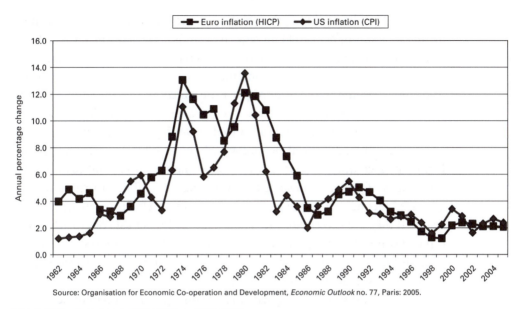

Source: Organisation for Economic Co-operation and Development, *Economic Outlook* no. 77, Paris: 2005.

Figure 11.3 Euro-area and US inflation, 1962–2005

Source: Organisation for Economic Co-operation and Development, *Economic Outlook* no. 77, Paris: 2005.

Figure 11.4 Unemployment rates, United States and EU-15, 1960–2005

Figures 11.5 through 11.7, therefore, compare the US experience in achieving higher levels of per capita income than all the EU-15 countries. The technique, popularized by Robert Barro and Xavier Sala-i-Martin,[2] relates the average rate of growth of per capita income over a fixed period for a group of countries to the initial level of per capita income of each country at the beginning of the period. The idea is that the country with the highest level of per capita income has the most advanced technology and institutions for the effective use of the advanced technology, while the other countries lag behind. If the other countries, however, have the same incentives and institutional capabilities of the most advanced country, they should be incorporating the advanced technology of the leading country in an effort to catch up to the leader. If they are successful, they should have a higher rate of growth of per capita income over any given period. Economists then expect to see an inverse relationship showing up between the initial level of per capita income and the subsequent average rate of growth of per capita income.

Economic historians distinguish three distinct periods of economic growth over the period 1960–2005, for which the OECD has compiled national income statistics for its member countries. From 1960 to 1973 most OECD countries experienced the last years of the "golden age of economic growth" that spanned the period 1950–73. The next thirteen years, thanks to a succession of oil shocks and policy shocks, destroyed any illusions that governments had mastered the techniques of managing their economies to maintain high growth, low unemployment, and stable prices. From 1986 to 2005 the globalization of the international economy spread rapidly, as more countries imitated the successful economic strategies that had emerged during the preceding period of intensive experimentation with new economic policies.

Figures 11.5 through 11.7 take these three periods – "miracles," "shocks," and "globalization" – and compare the United States with the fifteen countries that eventually comprised the European Union by 1995. In each figure, a line is drawn to indicate what the theory of neoclassical growth might predict as the "unconditional convergence" of the sixteen countries. If each country had the same set of economic institutions and incentives to achieve higher levels of per capita income, they should lie along the "unconditional convergence" line. For countries that lie above the line, economists expect to find special conditions that account for higher than expected rates of growth of per capita income. Likewise, special conditions should explain countries that lie below the line in each period.

In the "miracle" period, most countries in continental Europe, especially the original six members of the European Economic Community, clustered along

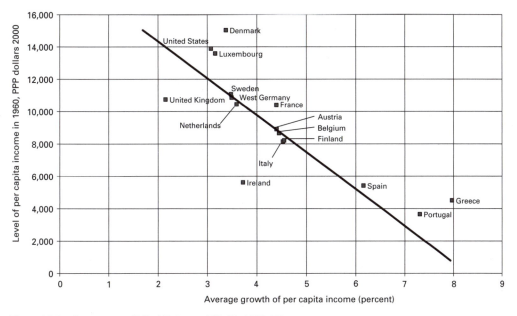

Figure 11.5   Convergence, United States and EU-15, 1960–73

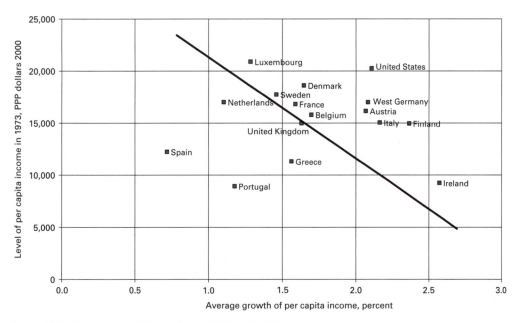

Figure 11.6   Convergence, United States and EU-15, 1974–85

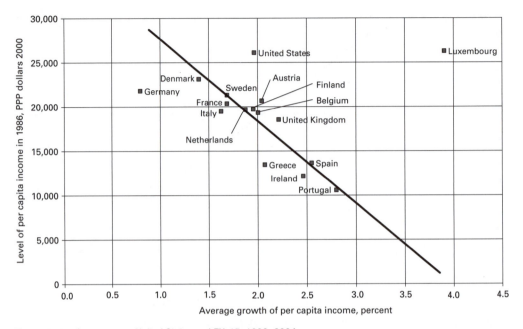

Figure 11.7   Convergence, United States and EU-15, 1986–2004

the unconditional convergence line inserted in the graph. France, under the new economic regime instituted with the establishment of the Fifth Republic in 1958, did better than expected, making up for less rapid growth in the last years of the Fourth Republic. Spain, Portugal, and Greece also did better than predicted, due to new arrangements that helped them individually tap into the rapidly growing economies of continental Europe. Denmark and Luxembourg, for special reasons, also had higher growth of per capita incomes, even with the already very high levels in 1960. Strikingly, the United States, which by 1960 was consumed with angst that it was losing its economic leadership to the emerging powerhouses of West Germany and Japan, still did better than one would predict. This result suggests that the policy initiatives of the United States in this latter period of the golden age of growth sufficed to keep it growing more rapidly than it would have with the institutional arrangements of the European Union countries. The United Kingdom and Ireland both suffered inferior rates of growth, especially given that their per capita incomes were low by comparison with the successful economies in the EEC.

In the following period, 1974–85, the successive shocks of the collapse of the fixed exchange rate regime of the Bretton Woods system, the two oil shocks of 1974 and 1979, and the Volcker shock of 1980[3] scattered the sixteen countries away from any consistent unconditional convergence of levels of per capita income. The line inserted for illustrative purposes would never emerge from regression analysis, as each country needs at least one special condition to explain its performance in this period. Part II of this book explains the experiments undertaken by the individual countries in Europe and the results that occurred. The important point is that the experiments of the United States – beginning with the Volcker shock to reduce inflation there, continuing with the deregulation of the financial and transportation sectors, and concluding with the tax cuts of the first Reagan administration – ended by maintaining the economic leadership of the United States relative to the European countries. To date, only the United Kingdom has attempted to imitate these policy regimes, for reasons that are explored in the country studies of part II.

Finally, the "globalization" era, which began in 1986 with the start of the Single European Act and the collapse of crude oil prices when the OPEC cartel disintegrated, appears to have created an even stronger convergence pattern among the European Union countries. The outliers are Luxembourg (positive) and Germany (negative), but the special conditions needed to explain each case are obvious – EU administration is concentrated in Luxembourg, and the reunification problems for Germany. The interesting case is that once again the US economy, even though beginning with the highest per capita income in 1986, still had a higher rate of growth of per capita income than predicted by the catchup process of the EU-15 countries.

Conclusion

The variety of national experiences among the now twenty-five member states of the European Union helps to explain both the differences in overall performance of the EU and US economies and the differences in approaches of the EU and the United States to the WTO negotiations. To grasp fully the range of economic issues that confront the European economies and the functioning of the European Union, it is necessary to take a closer look at the individual economies. Part II takes up the major countries in order of the size of their economies, and then the rest of the countries in order of the basic economic problems that face their political leaders. Resolution of these issues will occupy the best efforts of policy-makers in Europe at both the national and EU level. The outcomes to date are of great interest to economists, as the European economies have experimented with a variety of approaches to similar problems:

(1) how to maintain high levels of per capita income with continued growth when confronted with external shocks or internal dissatisfaction;

(2) how to maintain price stability and high employment; and, above all,

(3) how to adjust to the rapid changes in technology and trade relations that have occurred and will continue to occur in the twenty-first century.

We begin by looking at the largest economy in Europe and the fifth largest in the world, ranking behind the United States, China, India, and Japan in terms of PPP US dollars: Germany.[4]

NOTES

1. See www.wto.org/english/tratop_e/agric_e for a full explanation of the various formulas used to make tariff reductions. The Swiss formula is $Z = X - [(AX)/(A + X)]$, where Z is the reduction in the tariff rate each year, X is the initial tariff rate, and A is the adjustment coefficient, which is also the limit for the final, lower tariff rate if reductions continue indefinitely. (They never do!)

2. Robert Barro and Xavier Sala-i-Martin, *Economic Growth*, 2nd edn., Cambridge, MA: MIT Press, 2004

3. Paul Volcker, chairman of the Board of Governors of the US Federal Reserve System from 1979 to 1987, instituted a new policy regime of controlling the rate of growth of the money supply instead of moderating the level of nominal interest rates. The result was a sudden, sharp peak in interest rates and a rapid strengthening of the US dollar exchange rate. See also chapter 5.

4. See http://www.imf.org/external/pubs/ft/weo/2006/01/data/dbgimin.cfm for regular updates.

Part II

The economies of Europe

12 Germany: problems with reunification

Introduction

Sixteen years after the reunification of West Germany with East Germany, in 1990, Germany's economic problems and policies continue to weigh on the future of the European Union and the other economies of Europe. Its size and relative weight within the EU increased sharply and permanently after reunification, but it has not yet been able to come to grips with the twin challenges of incorporating the East German economy while restructuring an economic system that remains the envy of the rest of Europe. Germany's twin problems are more difficult to solve because of the way reunification was carried out. After the narrow election of Angela Merkel as Chancellor in the elections of 2005, and the compromises she needed to form a new government, it is still not clear that the problems can be solved.

The former Chancellor, Gerhard Schröder, lost the election he called in order to gain legitimacy for the labor market reforms he had initiated at the beginning of 2005 – the Hartz IV program. Developed by a 2002 commission headed by Peter Hartz, Volkswagen's personnel director, the various reforms proposed in successive stages of Hartz I, II, III, and IV merely tried to reduce gradually some of the most obvious rigidities of the German labor market while adopting new rules that had worked well in other countries. Both major parties in Germany, the Christian Democratic Union/Christian Social Union (CDU/CSU) and the Social Democratic Party (SPD), recognized the need for labor market reforms, but differed in how to pay for them. The Hartz IV reforms required workers receiving any kind of social insurance to apply for employment if they were capable of working. This requirement added nearly 400,000 to the unemployed rolls by forcing people long out of the labor force to re-enter it. Even so, over 100,000 more became unemployed as a result of the sluggish economy and the ongoing restructuring of both the West and the

Table 12.1 Germany: basic facts

Area	357,021 km²	9.0% of EU-25
Population (July 2005 estimate)	82,431,390	18.0% of EU-25
GDP (2004 estimate, PPP)	$2,362 billion	20.3% of EU-25
Per capita income (PPP)	$28,700	106.7% of EU-25 average
Openness ([X+M]/GDP)	76.5%	65% with EU-25
Birth rate (per 1,000)	8.33	Death rate (per 1,000) 10.55

Sources: Central Intelligence Agency, *World Factbook, 2005*, available at http://www.cia.gov/cia/publications/factbook; Statistical Office of the European Communities, *Europe in Figures: Eurostat Yearbook 2005*, Brussels: 2005.
NB: Openness measures the total value of exports and imports as a percentage of GDP.

East German economies. Unemployment had never been higher in Germany than when Schröder first took office in 1998 (over 4 million) and he promised to reduce it sharply while in office. By the time he left office, at the end of 2005, unemployment had risen to over 5 million, demonstrating that he had done no better than his predecessor in tackling the problems of reunified Germany.

As early as 1995/6, then Chancellor Helmut Kohl made valiant efforts to liberalize the West German economy along the lines initiated by the Americans and British, and to reduce West German tax rates while liberalizing its labor markets and privatizing some state enterprises. The persistent malaise of the German economy since the reunification of 1990 can be traced back, however, to Kohl and to the German Economic and Monetary Union of July 1990 that he created. The essential feature of the monetary union that has plagued German policy-makers ever since was the overvaluation of the East German currency, and therefore the money wages of East German workers. The exchange rate of the deutsche mark, the West German currency, with the ostmark, the East German currency, was set close to one to one, so that on average only 1.2 ostmarks were required to purchase 1 deutsche mark. Any realistic exchange rate would have required at least six ostmarks, and perhaps as many as twelve, to purchase one deutsche mark. The political consequences of this decision were dramatic: the East German voters, recognizing how advantageous these economic terms were, voted in a referendum held in April 1990 to abolish the East German state and to join West Germany on the terms provided in the Basic Law of the Federal Republic of Germany. The Basic Law has always specifically allowed new states, or *Länder*, to be added. The five new states that comprised the former East Germany were formally added to the Federal

Republic in October 1990. With this reunification of Germany, a formal peace treaty was then signed with the Federal Republic of Germany by the Allied powers – France, the United Kingdom, the Soviet Union, and the United States. Germany became once again a fully sovereign nation state.

The economic price for this long-sought political prize has proven to be much higher than anticipated. Part of the reason is the hubris of West German policy-makers in 1989/90, who, knowing that the East German economy was at most 10 percent the size of the West German economy, felt that absorbing the most advanced and competitive economy of the eastern bloc would be well within the capability of the most advanced and competitive economy of western Europe. But the major part of the increased price has been the realization of just how backward and uncompetitive the infrastructure, technology, and machinery of East Germany were compared with Western standards. This meant that East German wages and prices, now set in West German deutsche marks, were too high to be competitive in the West German market. Unemployment rose sharply in East Germany, where the workers were now entitled to unemployment benefits at the generous West German levels. These payments added to West Germany's financing burden. East German backwardness also meant, however, that the costs of reunification now included the costs of rebuilding the entire infrastructure of East Germany. Everything – roads, electric power generation and transmission facilities, railroads, airports, telephone systems, water and sewage treatment and distribution plants – had to be rebuilt to bring it up to West German standards.

These costs are being met almost entirely by West Germans. A special "reunification tax" has been levied on West Germans and higher VAT rates imposed on all consumption goods. The European Union, as explained in previous chapters, is not capable of contributing adequate resources to meet this kind of shock. Moreover, initially it objected to making the East German states eligible for structural funds designated for backward regions, or even for counting East German farm production under the provisions of the Common Agricultural Policy, given its limited budget. The possibility of foreign investment in the privatized enterprises of East Germany was sought by the Treuhandanstalt, a temporary agency set up by West Germany to dispose of the state enterprises of former East Germany. But the problems of high wages, obsolete plant and equipment, and deficient infrastructure were especially discouraging to foreign investors, who lacked the cultural and family ties with East Germany that many West German firms possessed.

The problems of mobilizing sufficient resources to bring East Germany up to the economic level of West Germany have been made worse by the restrictive monetary policy of the Bundesbank. The central bank of unified Germany momentarily lost control in 1990 of the German money supply when East German ostmarks were converted into deutsche marks at fixed conversion rates. But, between the fall of the Berlin Wall in November 1989 and the establishment of German Economic and Monetary Union in July 1990, the East German government produced many more ostmarks. The result when they were converted into deutsche marks was an unusually sharp rise (by West German standards) in the price level. The Bundesbank responded by curtailing the growth of the future money supply. This strengthened the deutsche mark on the foreign exchanges, which was good for paying for the imports required to rebuild East Germany, but bad for the traditional export-based industry of West Germany.

Further, the strengthening of the deutsche mark as a result of the Bundesbank's response to the currency union with East Germany meant that EU members of the European Monetary System also saw their currencies strengthen and their exports other than to Germany and each other fall off. The result, starting in 1990, was a marked slowing in real output, a rise in already high unemployment rates, and an actual decline in real output per capita throughout the European Union. In this sense, Germany's EMS partners paid a price as well for Germany's reunification; but, in addition, as their lower incomes reduced their demand for German exports, their economic slowdown made it even more difficult for West Germany to bear the costs of reunification. West Germany's unfortunate experience with the costs of reconstructing East Germany, the most advanced of the eastern bloc nations, also cast a pall over the European Union's enthusiasm for extending aid to the transition economies of central and east Europe. An unintended consequence is that German firms are investing in new plants and service centers in the accession economies more enthusiastically than they have been investing in the former East Germany.

How did Germany, the powerhouse economy of continental Europe for a century and a half, get into this quandary? It would appear that the decades of successful economic performance had embedded rigid institutions in the mentality of the German population, making it difficult for political leaders to change course even when it became clear that a change of course was necessary.

Macroeconomic policy indicators: 1960–2005

Figure 12.1 traces out the growth rates, inflation rates, and unemployment rates of West Germany from 1960 through 1990, and of unified Germany

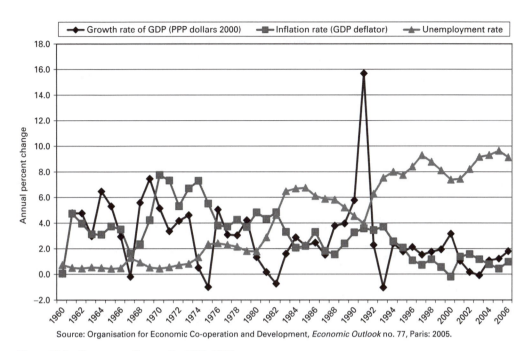

Source: Organisation for Economic Co-operation and Development, *Economic Outlook* no. 77, Paris: 2005.

Figure 12.1   Germany: policy results, 1960–2005

from 1991 on. The growth rate of real GDP[1] shows clearly that the economic miracle of the 1950s was slowing down in the 1960s. The underlying causes were mainly a slowdown in the rate of population growth, mostly due to falling birth rates but partly due to the Berlin Wall cutting off the refugee flow from East Germany in 1961. To the extent that the reduction in the growth of the supply of German workers was offset by importing larger numbers of guest workers, technical progress in West German industry was discouraged. Despite the signs of longer-term problems, the unemployment rate remained very low and inflation was kept low until the sharp rise in oil prices in October 1973, with the result that the West German economy was still the marvel of Europe. The first oil shock took full effect in 1974, raised unemployment rates (permanently, as it turned out), and reduced the growth rate to an absolute decline in 1975. Both the growth rate and the unemployment rate recovered dramatically, however, in comparison with those of the rest of Europe, until the second oil shock in 1979.

Perhaps the reason for both phenomena was the striking control over inflation that was maintained by the Bundesbank, in a period when inflation rates in the rest of the industrialized countries typically exceeded 10%. In the post-Bretton-Woods period of floating exchange rates, the relatively low rate of

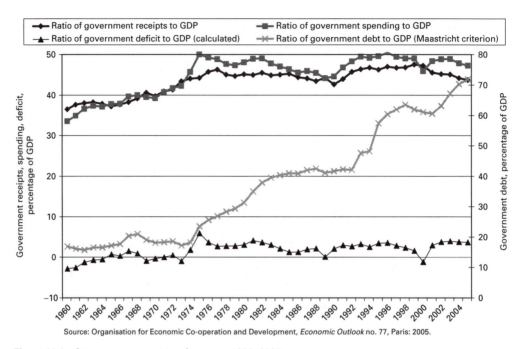

Source: Organisation for Economic Co-operation and Development, *Economic Outlook* no. 77, Paris: 2005.

Figure 12.2   Germany: government performance, 1960–2005

inflation in West Germany compared with its major trading partners translated into a substantial strengthening of the deutsche mark in the foreign
exchanges. Because oil was priced in dollars, each strengthened deutsche mark
could purchase more dollars, and therefore more oil. While West Germany's
exports could have been hurt by the stronger deutsche mark, which raised their
price to foreign customers, most of West Germany's exports were to its trading
partners in the European Union, which had even higher rates of inflation. As
the costs of producing West Germany's export goods were reduced, in that the
costs of imported raw materials and fuel were reduced by the stronger deutsche
mark, West Germany's exporters actually gained competitiveness relative to
the rest of the European Union.

West Germany's success in weathering the first oil shock with this strong
currency strategy encouraged its closest economic partners in the EEC to imitate the strategy. The central banks of Italy and France, unlike the Bundesbank,
were completely under the control of their respective central governments. So
first they had to get the agreement of their governments to restrict money
supply growth. This they accomplished by establishing the European Monetary System in 1978, as described in chapter 5, which required them and the

Benelux countries, Denmark, and Ireland to maintain exchange rate stability with the deutsche mark and each other's currencies. To maintain stability, the other central banks in the EMS had to restrict the growth of their respective money supplies to the rate established by the Bundesbank for the West German money supply. The second oil shock in 1979/80, however, disrupted the exchange rates agreed on, and cast some doubt on the wisdom of West Germany's restrictive monetary policy as well. While inflation remained under control, West Germany's unemployment rate was notched up permanently another few percentage points and GDP growth fell to the lowest rates since World War II.

A change of government from the SPD, led by Helmut Schmidt, to the CDU/CSU alliance, led by Helmut Kohl, occurred in the summer of 1982. Chancellor Kohl then led West Germany for the longest period in German history, until his election defeat in 1998. Initially, Kohl chose to challenge the strength of the West German unions, the continued wage demands of which despite low inflation, one could argue, had prevented West Germany from increasing its exports at a time when the deutsche mark was relatively weak compared with the dollar. But the strong dollar did not increase imports from Europe; rather, it led to increased imports from Asia and Latin America. Moreover, the British economy was then showing renewed vitality (chapter 14) stemming from the vigorous liberalization policies of the Prime Minister, Margaret Thatcher. But West German economic performance did not improve under Kohl until the single market initiative began to take effect and Spain and Portugal entered the EEC; their combined effect showed up after 1987. In common with the rest of oil-importing Europe, West Germany also benefited from the collapse of oil prices in 1986, the third oil shock.

German exports boomed to the rest of the now expanded EEC in anticipation of the growth potential of the single market, to be achieved by the end of 1992. Growth rates rose to near the rates of the wonderful 1960s; unemployment, while still high, began to decline noticeably. Only inflation seemed troublesome, as it began to rise to rates high enough by 1990 to make the Bundesbank nervous. We shall never know how long this renewed growth would have lasted under the scenario envisioned by the EEC, which was to incorporate the rest of western Europe into the customs union after the completion of the single market. As the member states of the European Free Trade Area were all trading partners principally with West Germany, the free trade area for West German exporters would have expanded and West German economic policy would have been focused on exploiting these trade opportunities. So the growth spurt could have continued for at least a few more years.

History, with the helping hand of Helmut Kohl, changed course in 1990 with the reunification of Germany. East Germany, larger in population than any of the EFTA member states, the applications for membership of which were being delayed until after the completion of the single market, was immediately absorbed into West Germany – and into the EEC as well. The consequence is that an entirely new set of challenges and possibilities for the German economy have been created, quite independently of the internal dynamic of European unification embodied in the institutional framework of the European Union. As figure 12.1 shows, however, the West German policy-makers have largely responded to date by maintaining the courses of action that have sustained them since the end of World War II. The initial inflationary impulse of reunification, caused by the conversion of many more ostmarks than anticipated into deutsche marks, was rapidly brought under control by the Bundesbank. The cost, however, was to increase unemployment to yet higher levels, concentrated in the east, but still higher in the west than before reunification. And growth, initially projected to regain its pre-1990 rates, has stagnated at the rates of the early 1980s. But a few years of adversity in the face of an enormous challenge were not going to undo all at once the policy framework that had proven so successful for forty years.

Unfortunately, the stagnation of the German economy after reunification has lasted much longer than anticipated. After the initial enthusiasm for reunification, shared by West and East Germans alike, had tapered off and the work of reconstruction had begun in earnest, some hard lessons about the inherent limitations of the West German postwar social economy model began to sink in. The initial institutions set up by the West German government when it took charge of economic policy from the Western occupying powers relied on the import of labor and the construction of housing and factories to accommodate them. Labor, for its part, accepted stable wages in exchange for full employment and cheaper consumption goods, as explained in chapter 2. The monetary reform of 1948, as explained below, reinforced the social contract between the government, business, and labor. By contrast, the institutional arrangements of West Germany imposed on East Germany were intended to bring the stability and comfort of the West German social system to the East German population. Instead of labor coming from the east to make capital in the west more profitable, as in the 1950s and 1960s, the monetary union of 1990 maintained labor in the east, but also discouraged private capital from putting the labor force in the east to work. To understand the contrast in policies and the differing economic results of the two periods, it is useful to review the economic history of West Germany.

Wirtschaftswunderzeit: 1945–57

It was up to the four Allied powers – the United States, the Soviet Union, the United Kingdom, and France – to decide what to do with Germany after its complete defeat and unconditional surrender on May 8, 1945. Agreement had already been reached at the Yalta Conference in February 1945, which included only Roosevelt, Stalin, and Churchill, that postwar Germany would be divided up among them and administered jointly from Berlin. Basically, the Soviet Union took the eastern third, including Berlin, the United Kingdom took the northern third, including the great ports of Hamburg and Bremen and the industrial heartland of the Ruhr, and the United States assumed responsibility for the southern third. France was included later for an occupation zone of its own, but the Rheinland-Pfalz and Saarland *Länder* and the southern halves of the Baden and Württemberg *Länder* had to be carved out of the American zone to constitute it. These arrangements were confirmed and clarified at the Potsdam Conference in July 1945, attended this time by Truman (Roosevelt had died in office in April), Stalin, and Churchill/Attlee (Attlee replaced Churchill during the conference due to the result of the British general election). France objected to the terms immediately, as it had not been represented at either Yalta or Potsdam. Both France and the Soviet Union wanted reparations in kind and as soon as possible. The British resisted the idea of reparations in principle, while the Americans maintained ambivalence, most charitably explained by a desire to hold the wartime alliance together as long as possible. Due to differences in objectives among the Allies and to changed leadership in the United States and the United Kingdom, conflicts arose immediately among the Allies over the implementation of the Potsdam agreements.

The French occupation zone included the coal resources of the Saarland, which provided the most economical way of smelting and refining the iron ore of Lorraine. French hopes were that continued occupation would lead eventually to the incorporation of the Saarland into France, much as Alsace-Lorraine had been incorporated into Germany from 1871 to 1914 and again from 1940 to 1944. But even these coal resources were deemed inadequate for French reconstruction purposes, so French policy became focused on gaining access to the coal and iron facilities of the Ruhr basin, which had been assigned to the British. Like the French, the Russians wanted to dismantle Germany's factories, to eliminate the threat of renewed armament or, perhaps, to replace their own factories that had been destroyed during the war. While they had access to the industrial plants of Silesia (now part of Poland), Upper Saxony, and Branden-burg, the bulk of the factories lay in the Ruhr, which was in the British zone. They repeatedly proposed placing the Ruhr under international supervision so that a large part of its output could be directed to rebuilding efforts outside Germany. The Americans were left with responsibility for maintaining order among a growing population of refugees with a large occupation army, both of which could be supplied only through the British zone.

As these conflicting objectives for access to the British zone were played out, the British found the expenses of maintaining a large standing army and caring for a large refugee population in their area of Germany, the one most flattened by Allied bombing, to be simply overwhelming. Their policy, born out of immediate expense and remembrance of the reparations failures after World War I, quickly came to be one of reconstructing German industry and rebuilding housing in their zone. American official policy was presumed to be given by the infamous Morgenthau Plan, in which the American Secre-tary of the Treasury proposed to dismember Germany politically, dismantle its factories, and maintain per capita income in Germany at the lowest level in Europe. This would ensure an end to the German problem, which had caused three major wars in Europe in less than a century. American mili-tary forces occupying the American zone, however, found that they had the expense of housing and clothing millions of refugees from the east, and this had to be done so as to maintain any kind of order. So they never imple-mented the Morgenthau Plan in practice, save for continuing the dismem-berment of Germany politically for awhile. By September 1946 American policy was, in practice, converging with British policy. It became mutually convenient for both to combine the operation of their zones from January 1947 on as Bizonia. This became the basis for the formation of the Federal Republic of Germany, established as a separate, independent (but not yet sovereign) state in May 1949, now including the French zone as well. This was the final result of four years of experimentation and conflict among the victorious Allies as to how to deal with defeated Germany. The new state of West Germany was clearly committed to cooperation with the Allies in the rebuilding of western Europe. The following chapters will discuss how committed other Europeans were to the restoration of German economic might, but, clearly, both the Americans and British were. Their consensus pro-vided the political framework within which West Germany's economic miracle occurred.

Economic historians in recent years have revised considerably our view of how miraculous the economic recovery of Germany from World War II was. Certainly, to observers at the time, the devastation wrought by the Allied round-the-clock bombing for two years and the complete overrunning of German territory by the remorseless advances of the Russian, American, and British armies seemed total, and as unconditional as the surrender extracted from Admiral Dönitz in May 1945. The re-emergence of West Germany as the strongest economy in Europe by the mid-1950s seemed an almost incredible tribute to the combination of the German work ethic and American generosity. Scholars sifting through the archival materials that have become increasingly available in the past twenty years, however, have identified more mundane factors that help explain both the miracle of recovery and the role that West Germany played in the economic integration of western Europe.[2]

The first revision to come was a reassessment of the loss of capital stock to the German economy caused both by the brutal combination of Allied bombing, artillery barrages in the ground advance, and the "scorched earth" defensive strategy of the retreating German forces. Allied bombing, it turned out, had flattened buildings and disrupted transportation links, especially at harbors and rail yards, but left machines largely intact. German factory managers were explicitly ordered by Albert Speer, the minister in charge of armaments production, not to destroy the machinery but, rather, to disable the abandoned plants so they could be restarted quickly in recovery from defeat. In fact, the capital stock of just the West German economy was larger at the end of the war than at the beginning, thanks to the large investments made during the war. Moreover, it was readily convertible to the production of civilian goods, unlike much of the British and American manufacturing plant, which used specialized machinery for the mass production of military items. So the German economic miracle began with excess capacity in its relatively modern and up-to-date manufacturing capital stock.

The second revision came in reassessing the refugee and displaced person problem. Approximately 11 million individuals poured into the western occupation zones of Germany in the ten years after the war. Nearly the same number left Germany – inmates of concentration and extermination camps, prisoners of war, and foreign workers – but the total population of postwar Germany, including the Soviet zone and Berlin, had actually grown by more than 10% between May 1939 and October 1946. Importantly, it had shifted location considerably, out of the great cities such as Berlin and Hamburg and into more rural areas of Schleswig-Holstein, Lower Saxony, and Bavaria. Internal as well as international migration was the dominating characteristic of the German population.[3] Moreover, the new population was German-speaking, and after 1950, when 3.6 million refugees fled the Soviet zone to come to West Germany, it was well educated and at prime working ages. Perhaps most important, all 11 million immigrants, as well as the larger number of internal migrants, were highly motivated to work hard and save stringently in order to restore their material situation as quickly as possible. Hence, the excess capacity of West German manufacturing plant could be staffed immediately by new workers eager for employment and easily trained. Ironically, the Russian policy of pushing Germans out of eastern Europe and encouraging them to leave even East Germany provided more assistance to the recovery of the West German economy than all the American aid.

Marshall Plan aid did not materialize until early 1948, by which time the forces described above had already served to begin economic recovery at a rapid rate. Moreover, the total aid given to West Germany was substantially less than that given to the United Kingdom and France, and even less than that provided to Italy. American aid of $1.62 billion given under the GARIOA (Government and Relief in Occupied Areas) program until mid-1950 slightly exceeded the $1.56 billion given under the Marshall Plan.[4] As a share of total capital formation, West German Marshall Plan aid was small, save in the first year. Nevertheless, Alan Kramer argues that even the aid given to the United Kingdom and France was important for West Germany's recovery, for two reasons. First, US aid to its western Allies removed their claims on West Germany's industrial plant for reparations, in turn removing much of the uncertainty over the final ownership of West Germany's excess capacity and allowing West German entrepreneurs to resume the restoration and conversion of their capital stock to civilian production. Second, the Marshall Plan aid was directed into sectors, such as cement, coal, and electricity, where price controls were maintained, discouraging private investment in those vital sectors.

The currency reform of June 1948 marked a sudden resurgence of the West German recovery, which seemed to have stalled in the preceding months. Part of the reason for the temporary slump was the severe winter, following the very severe winter of 1946/7, but most of it probably stemmed from the withholding of goods from the market until the new currency, the deutsche mark, was actually introduced into circulation. A large, informal, quasi-barter economy had arisen because of the inflation created by the occupation currency introduced by the Allies. The occupation Reichsmarks quickly depreciated, because there was no central control of the amount issued. While the Americans and British cooperated in the control of their share of the occupation currency, the Russians were determined to pay occupation expenses and to extract reparations in kind by issuing more and more of the currency – a case of competitive seigniorage. Germans in the western zones avoided the price and wage uncertainty created by the depreciation of the occupation currency by substituting other universally recognized standards of value, namely American cigarettes and chewing gum.

The new currency, the deutsche mark, introduced in 1948 by Ludwig Erhard, was issued just for the combined American and British zones (Bizonia), and the issue was strictly controlled by the incipient central bank, the Bank Deutscher Länder. The Russians responded by creating their own currency for their occupation zone and imposing the blockade on Berlin. The French responded by combining their occupation zone, which had been carved out of the American zone in the first place, with Bizonia, thereby creating, briefly, Trizonia. The terms of the currency reform are interesting in light of the similar transition problems faced in the early 1990s by the former communist countries, and especially by the soaking up of the East German currency that occurred in July 1990. The deutsche mark was exchanged one to one for the first forty old Reichsmarks in June 1948. In two months another twenty deutsche marks could be obtained, again at the one-to-one rate. But all other financial assets, checking and savings accounts to mortgages and insurance policies, were cashed in at the rate of 1 deutsche mark per 10 Reichsmarks. In other words, the money supply in one fell swoop was reduced by nearly 90%. Holders of physical assets such as inventories of merchandise, factories, land, or houses benefited greatly. Savers in financial assets were again, as after World War I, wiped out. The incentives to the West German population were clear: to obtain more than 60 deutsche marks of the new money they had to be willing to put either their real assets or their labor skills on the market.

Contrary to the advice of the Allied economists, Ludwig Erhard, a free-market economist appointed by the Allies to be Finance Minister of the new West German government, removed most price controls. This temporarily boosted the prices of consumer goods, encouraging dishoarding by merchants and also generating increased tax revenues for the government via their turnover taxes, excise duties, and customs revenues. Erhard's gamble may have been driven mostly by his laissez-faire ideology, but his confidence must have been boosted by observing the Italian success in the previous year with lifting price controls rapidly. Moreover, he maintained rent controls and rationing for some basic foods, as well as price controls on utilities and basic coal and steel supplies for industry. This meant that both supply and demand could expand for manufactured consumer goods without quickly running into constraints of rising prices for inputs on the supply side or of consumer essentials on the demand side. It also meant that workers could accept continued low wages, knowing they would be adequate to provide at least housing and basic food. Further work effort was stimulated by exempting overtime wages from income tax. Whatever the innate propensity of Germans to work hard, they were certainly given the appropriate incentives by Erhard!

While the economic demands of the uprooted and impoverished Germans were strongest for scarce consumer goods, the productive capacity of the West German manufacturing sector was best suited for producer goods. These were precisely what was needed in the rest of war-torn Europe, however, so the resurgent West German economy was export-oriented from the beginning of the recovery process. Further expansion of West Germany's productive capacity in these sectors was encouraged by accelerated depreciation allowances on investment for the tax liabilities of business firms. The tight money policy followed by the Bank Deutscher Länder tended even then to raise the value of the deutsche mark relative to the currencies of its trading partners, which would have hurt exports had there been any major competition. In September 1949, however, in common with the other European countries, the deutsche mark was devalued by one-third. Even so, future European demand for West German machine tools, equipment, and vehicles might very well have been limited had it not been for the creation of the European Payments Union in 1950 and the fillip to export demand for the Europeans that was created by American financing of the Korean War. But, with that, the West German economy was firmly on its course of export-led growth, which continued until, ironically, the creation of the Common Market in 1958.

To reprise, the key elements in the West German economic miracle of the period 1948–58 were excess capacity for the production of producer goods, an elastic supply of well-educated, highly motivated workers, and an incentive structure that permitted rising standards of living for moderately paid West German workers thanks to an appreciating deutsche mark. These were exceptional conditions, which help in large part to explain why the West German growth experience in this period was also exceptional. They also highlight the contrast with the period 1990–2005 for unified Germany.

Slowing down: 1958–73

While 1958 was marked by a brief slowdown in the rate of expansion of the West German economy, in common with the rest of western Europe, the turning point in its miracle period has to be 1961. It was in this year that the Berlin Wall was erected to complete the closure of the border between East and West Germany in order to stop the flow of refugees, which it did. The free movement of labor within the Common Market, mandated by the Treaty of Rome, might have been expected to induce an influx of Italian workers into Germany to make up the shortfall of labor required to staff the still rapidly expanding capital stock of West Germany. In fact, the Common Market increased the export opportunities for Italian manufacturers and their demand for labor rose, reducing the supply of Italian laborers to the rest of Europe. Accustomed to docile labor recruited from the underemployed population of the West German countryside or from the exploited population of East Germany, West German industry responded by initiating the Gastarbeiter (guest worker) program.

The Gastarbeiter program succeeded wildly. Meanwhile, West German capital stock continued to grow, as it had become the favorite destination for direct investment by British and American firms. Firms that had been exporting to West Germany because of its growing demand for consumer goods and low tariff barriers were now concerned to some extent that their West German market might be lost thanks to a high common external tariff, but mostly they were eager to have a European base from which to export to the rest of the Common Market, where high tariffs and quantity restrictions had kept them out previously. It was natural for British firms to locate in the British occupation zone and for American firms to locate in the American zone, comprising the southern *Länder* of Hessia, Baden-Württemberg, and Bavaria. These became the growth poles of West German expansion in the 1960s, and the destination of choice for the guest workers. These were recruited from various countries, originally Spain, then Yugoslavia, and finally Turkey. Turkey, with its large, growing population and rapid structural change as a result of being an American military client state, proved capable of supplying all the workers German industry could desire. German workers did not mind as much as one might think (from later developments) because their superior education and prior training kept them in superior jobs, whereas the temporary foreign workers took the lowest-paid, least skilled positions available. By 1971 West Germany's export-led economic expansion had raised its share of world trade to 10%, nearly the same share enjoyed by the German Empire in 1913 (12.1%).[5]

West German firms could continue to be competitive in their export markets by lowering their average unit costs thanks to the low-paid guest workers taking the least skilled positions. The tight money policy of the Bundesbank, combined with the fixed exchange rates of the deutsche mark with the other currencies of its trading partners in the Western world, also meant that the real exchange rate of the deutsche mark kept falling, making German goods more competitive. Nevertheless, the West German rate of investment slowed down in this period, because West Germany's export markets had also slowed their growth and West German firms were barely able to keep the market shares that they had built up over the past decade. Investment that did occur was designed to make maximum use of the elastic supply of low-paid, unskilled foreigners. This meant it was not as technologically advanced as capital invested by competitors not so favorably supplied with cheap labor, such as the United States.

The use of guest workers for low-skill jobs also meant that these entry-level jobs were not available for on-the-job training for young West Germans or for West German women. West German youth remained committed to the apprenticeship program, funded jointly by the government and by business. This was, and still is, a model program for providing access to human capital for the native population of a country. But it is inflexible in the numbers trained for each skill and occupation. So slow-growing sectors will have a backlog of potential entrants, who are forced into unemployment while waiting for a job appropriate to their training to open, while rapidly expanding sectors will have unfilled positions. The option of guest workers enabled export-oriented firms to meet their labor requirements without urging changes in the composition of apprentices in their favor. Moreover, it discouraged West German women from entering the labor force in greater numbers, so that their participation rate in the labor force failed to rise any further during the 1960s. It is true, nonetheless, that women's education levels rose substantially, as West Germany expanded greatly its institutions of higher learning and filled them up largely by admitting women.

To sum up, the reliance on foreign workers for the continued growth of labor inputs until 1973 enabled Germany's golden age to continue, albeit at gradually reduced rates of growth and of investment. But it was storing up future problems, in that the capital equipment installed was not at the cutting edge of modern technology, exports remained concentrated on product lines for which markets were not expanding as rapidly as before, and the stock of human capital in the manufacturing sector was no longer growing as rapidly as in the 1950s.

The three oil shocks: 1974–85

If the shock of the Berlin Wall was insufficient to change the growth strategy of West Germany, one could be forgiven for wondering whether the oil shocks beginning in October 1973 might not do the trick. In fact, the German strategy for confronting the oil shocks had already been established in the way it dealt with the earlier shock of the collapse of the Bretton Woods system in August 1971. The Bundesbank, the successor to the Bank Deutscher Länder, established in 1957, was committed to maintaining price stability within West Germany. In a world of rising prices, led by a rapidly growing supply of US dollars in the international economy, this meant a steady appreciation of the deutsche mark. In the era of fixed nominal exchange rates, lasting from 1949 to 1971, the deutsche mark actually depreciated as West Germany kept a lower rate of domestic inflation than existed in its trading partners. The Bundesbank was committed to this strategy by law, in order to prevent any risk that the financial assets of small savers might be dissipated by inflation, as had happened in the aftermath of both World War I and World War II. Part of the reason West German industry could keep nominal wage increases low was that West German workers were assured that their pensions would maintain their real purchasing power after retirement, thanks to the anti-inflation commitment of the Bundesbank.

When exchange rates became flexible in 1971 the nominal exchange rate of the deutsche mark rose sharply relative to most of its trading partners, including the United States. This raised the price of West German export goods to its customers, unless West German producers either lowered their prices in terms of deutsche marks or raised the quality of the product to the foreign importers. In fact, they did both, but each strategy decreased profit rates and led to lower rates of investment in West Germany. On the benefit side, the cost of imports was reduced. This kept down wage demands insofar as West German consumers could benefit from the lower prices of imported consumer goods, and it reduced the costs to West German industry of a wide range of raw materials and intermediate goods, including imported petroleum.

One of the ways that West German exporters had raised the quality of their products to foreign buyers was to move beyond producing a variety of specialized machinery to setting up entire "turnkey" factories, especially in developing countries trying to build up a modern manufacturing sector from scratch. The idea was that, at final delivery, the buyer would simply turn the key on and the factory would be ready to produce at full capacity immediately. Payment for such factories was arranged through long-term contracts in which the customer would deliver intermediate products to the West German exporter for a number of years at fixed, below-market, prices. A wide range of such deals were quickly completed with Iran, for example, at the outset of the first oil shock in October 1973. These arrangements, actually initiated with the Shah of Iran's father by Hjalmar Schacht in the 1930s, continued to provide strong trading relationships between West Germany and Iran through the overthrow of the Shah in 1978 and into the 1990s. The combination of such fixed-price contracts for the long-term delivery of oil and the continued appreciation of the deutsche mark relative to the dollar helped West Germany weather the effects of the first oil shock much better than, say, Italy or France.

Nevertheless, the oil shock caused sharp reductions in demand throughout Europe, West Germany's primary export market, and West German output fell as well, with a noticeable rise in unemployment rates. Attention turned to the presence of the guest workers, who, it was felt, should be returned promptly to their home countries, preserving their jobs for West Germans. Unfortunately for this strategy, which had great appeal politically, West German employers had concentrated their employment of guest workers in only one or two stages of the production process. Eliminating all of them in any one firm, therefore, meant closing down the entire production process until new workers could be found to replace them. And the new workers would have to be willing to accept the low wages and status that went with that part of the production line. It turned out not to be feasible to solve the unemployment problem simply by eliminating the foreign workers.

Moreover, a surprisingly large number of such workers had proven so valuable for their employers that they had been in the country for as long as ten years. That meant that they could apply for West German citizenship, and in any case they were eligible for unemployment relief, as long as they stayed in the Federal Republic. To discourage this, the government tried at first to bribe them to return to their home country, usually Turkey. But the amounts required to get any response turned out to be higher than the government felt it could afford. The next alternative attempted was to eliminate children's allowances for any West German employee whose children were not physically present in West Germany. This led to an influx of fresh foreign immigrants, comprising primarily children and their mothers, grandparents, and aunts to take care of them. The problem of the Turkish population for West German social stress was alleviated only when employment opportunities increased in Turkey itself for a period of time in the mid- to late 1980s.

The social stresses within the Federal Republic were heightened by the second oil shock of 1978/9. Unemployment rose again and the economic miracle definitely seemed to be at an end. It didn't help that after the OPEC oil ministers doubled the price of oil again, in dollar terms, in 1979 the dollar began to strengthen relative to the European currencies, including the deutsche mark, in 1980. This exacerbated the effects of the second oil shock for all of Europe, including West Germany. The underlying institutional arrangements that had propelled West Germany back to being the pre-eminent economy of Europe came under renewed scrutiny. Wendy Carlin identifies three key institutions that differentiated Germany from much of southern Europe, and certainly from the United States and the United Kingdom. These are: (1) the co-determination principle of corporate governance, which required each West German corporation to have on its board of directors representatives of its labor force and of the general public; (2) an elaborate system of apprentice training jointly administered by federal, state, and local governments as well as private businesses; and (3) the practice of universal banking in the financial sector, so that banks lending to business could also own part of the borrowing firms.[6]

Co-determination had the initial benefit of satisfying West German workers that, if the profits of the firms employing them went up as a result of their moderate wage demands, these profits would in turn be used to expand capacity and create more jobs. The presence of union leaders on the board of directors meant that business managers, in turn, could be confident that wage demands would be kept down long enough to allow new investments to become profitable. This device for coordinating the decision-making process of management (to invest or not to invest) and labor (to strike or not to strike) may have been instrumental in moderating West German labor union demands for wages, maintaining high rates of investment by West German business, and keeping unemployment rates low until the oil shocks of the 1970s. Of course, an elastic supply of labor, first from eastern Europe under Soviet domination, then from East Germany, and finally from Yugoslavia and Turkey, helped do the same things.

When the effects of the second oil shock kept persisting into the early 1980s, however, the negative aspects of co-determination received more attention. If labor shedding, downsizing, or purging the workforce became necessary to maintain competitiveness in an industry, then labor and consumer interests represented on the boards of directors were sure to resist. In short, the institutional device was useful for its initial purpose – to establish the legitimacy of the new capitalist economic system in a country imbued with a corporatist tradition – but dysfunctional when it came to making rapid adjustments to changed economic conditions.

The second institution, an active apprentice program in industry available to all West German school leavers on a competitive basis, kept up the level of human capital in the West German economy. By its design, it combined the generally useful skills of literacy and numeracy through the formal education system with specifically targeted skills in particular trades through the apprenticeship service. Apprentices completing their term of service found employment readily with the company they had served. West German industry could underpay entry-level workers while they were apprentices and part-time students, and after pre-screening and training them hire them in as fully productive members of the production team. This avoided the free-rider problem caused when firms might lose young workers to competitors after having invested time and money in training them to be productive in their own system. The benefits of this system were clear with a stable structure of occupations in the economy, which was the case through the 1950s and the 1960s. But, faced with the structural changes required to meet the challenges of the successive oil shocks in the 1970s, the system was inflexible. Occupations with stagnating employment opportunities continued to be supplied with trained apprentices, who waited longer and longer for appropriate jobs to open up that would reward them for the skills acquired. Meanwhile, sectors where demand was rising rapidly found it difficult to recruit new workers, the most promising of whom were already committed to prior apprentice programs.

The third institution, the close relationship between German banks and business firms, has been much admired in the rest of Europe, and, indeed, in many developing countries. The theoretical advantages of banks taking equity in the companies borrowing from them have been spelled out clearly. Being privy to management decisions made by a business customer helps remove what economists call asymmetric information. This means that borrowers are much better informed about what they intend to do with the proceeds of a loan and how well their project is paying off than their creditors are. This is especially the case with stock- or bondholders in the American or British financial systems, who typically only observe how the capital markets evaluate their financial assets and know little about the operations of the companies issuing their stocks and bonds. The downside of such close relationships has become clearer to the Germans, especially in the 1990s, but has long been appreciated in economic theory (as well as in Anglo-American banking practice). This is that the bank itself can become hostage to bad business decisions in which it may have participated or approved initially. Moreover, knowing the intentions and probity of an individual business person is no guarantee that his or her product will sell profitably in a rapidly changing and competitive marketplace.

To sum up, the vaunted institutions of West Germany, all of which certainly helped maintain its exceptional growth record in the golden age of 1950–73, proved increasingly incapable of meeting the challenges of the 1980s and 1990s. Expanding exports continued to be the key to general economic success in the Germany that had emerged after World War II, and increasingly the best way to expand exports was to expand the market it had come to dominate, the European Economic Community. This was the fourth, and perhaps most important, institution maintaining West Germany's economic success. This explains the eagerness of West Germany to expand the membership of the EEC, bringing in the United Kingdom, Ireland, and Denmark in the first expansion of 1973, then the premature accession of Greece in 1980, and finally the inclusion of Spain and Portugal in 1986.

From single market to United Germany: 1986–90

A number of positive events occurred in 1986 to reinvigorate the West German economy and rouse it from the prolonged stagnation that had followed the recession of 1980/1. The expansion of the European Economic Community to include Spain and Portugal stimulated a surge of foreign investment in those two low-wage countries. Whether the new production and distribution facilities were financed by American, Japanese, or European firms they required construction equipment and machines, both of which were West Germany's most competitive exports. The imminent passage of the Single European Act stimulated renewed business investment throughout the EEC, including West Germany. The third oil shock rapidly lowered the price of imported oil. Moreover, the American commitment to weakening the dollar in order to stimulate US exports further reduced the cost of imported oil for West Germany. Finally, the third oil shock removed the pressures on the currencies of the participants in the Exchange Rate Mechanism of the EMS, so they were all allowed to appreciate in lock step with the deutsche mark. The strengthening of the EMS as a result led to increased momentum for completing the single market in 1992, as well as for formulating the outlines of the Maastricht Treaty, as discussed in chapter 7. But it also helped maintain West Germany's access to its primary export market: the rest of the European Economic Community.

The expansion did have one blemish: it failed to make much of a dent in the historically high rate of unemployment that had arisen during the second oil shock. This led to the formulation of the hysteresis hypothesis for European unemployment, a hypothesis that obtains a great deal of credibility for the rest of the European Union countries as well. Briefly, the idea is that employers are selective in the workers they lay off during a recession. They focus on the workers whose productivity is lowest relative to their wage, which means those who are older, less skilled, less educated, less healthy – in short, less capable of increasing their productivity relative to their wages. And they are less likely to hire these disadvantaged workers back during an expansion. Such workers could, in theory, offer their services for lower wages, but union rules of wage determination by acquired skill and seniority restrict employers from accepting such offers. Further, generous unemployment benefits, 63 to 68% of the last net wage for up to two years and 56 to 58% thereafter, limit the extent to which long-term unemployed workers would be willing to work for lower wages in the first place. The result is a growing proportion of long-term unemployed in the ranks of the unemployed. These outsiders become less and less attractive to potential employers the longer they remain unemployed, and their skills stagnate or become obsolete.

The other blemish became increasingly evident as negotiations proceeded both on how to lower non-tariff barriers within the EEC as the Single European Act was implemented and on how to lower non-tariff barriers with the rest of the world as GATT negotiations continued in the Uruguay Round. This was the extent to which parts of the West German economy had become dependent for their success on non-tariff barriers, which had risen as rapidly as – or more rapidly, in some cases, than – tariff barriers had fallen. Under GATT rules, import quotas could be imposed against certain countries on specific products if it was found they were selling at less than the cost of production. These could be held off if the offending country, usually Japan, agreed to a voluntary export restraint (VER). West Germany, in common with the other countries in Europe, resorted to these with increasing frequency in the late 1970s and early 1980s. They continued to employ them even with the expansion of the late 1980s. These specific quotas and VERs were administered at the national level, not at the Community level.

True, West Germany was not the worst offender in the Community in the use of these forms of non-tariff barriers (France and Italy are discussed in following chapters). But it also compounded the effect of these by providing subsidies to certain declining, or "sundown," sectors. Perhaps the most egregious example was coal, which was produced at $100 a ton to maintain employment for coal miners, and electric power plants and steel mills were subsidized for using it rather than being able to buy American coal for $10 a ton. Agriculture was another example, of course. Given the declining numbers employed in these sectors and their diminished political influence within West Germany, more and more opposition arose to the continuation of non-tariff barriers, which took the form of nationally tailored subsidies.

The reunification shock, 1990–2006

Both the bloom of the expansion and the concern about the blemishes were put aside in the throes of the political shock of reunification with East Germany. The first manifestation of the shock was the huge influx of young, prime-working-age East Germans into West Berlin and into West Germany via Hungary and Austria. Some economists saw in this collapse of the Berlin Wall and the physical reconnection with East Germany the possibility of a reprise of the postwar economic miracle. This had been prolonged by the continued infusion of eager, skilled refugees from East Germany until the Berlin Wall was built in 1961. Now that it had been torn down, perhaps the expansion under way in the late 1980s could also be prolonged. This scenario, however, had been upstaged for fifteen years by another drama – what to do with unwanted guest workers. Now that the Turkish problem was on its way to solution (see chapter 20), the West Germans did not care to see that drama repeated. The key to solving the Turkish dilemma had been to invest in Turkey itself, providing employment opportunities there in the production of goods for the West German market. This seemed the obvious thing to do with East Germany.

As explained previously, the German Economic and Monetary Union of July 1990 implemented this strategy. The essential element was to convert the East German currency into the deutsche mark at a rate of one to one for the equivalent of two months' wages and at 2 ostmarks for 1 deutsche mark above that amount. Meanwhile, basic foods, utilities, and rental prices would be maintained under control. In short, East Germans were being paid very well not only to vote for reunification on West German terms but also to stay put in their subsidized housing and buy Western-made consumer goods with their deutsche marks. So West German firms were denied the possibility of an influx of cheap, easily trained, and highly motivated workers. The vaunted institutions of co-determination and specially tailored apprenticeship programs for training workers served as serious institutional obstacles to exploiting the positive possibilities of reunification.

All the same, East Germany constituted a large new market for West German firms, so initially they could make higher profits from the increase in domestic demand for their goods. As the unrealistically high exchange rate for the East

German currency also put the contractual wages of East German workers well above their productivity level, however, unemployment rose. Not only did this increase the subsidies in the form of unemployment benefits that now had to be paid by West Germany to East Germany, it also decreased the attractiveness of East German enterprises to foreign investors. Only West German firms and entrepreneurs could be induced to invest in the state enterprises being privatized in East Germany. The highly prized German social safety net for its citizens meant both that the price of reunifying with East Germany was raised and that it would have to be paid mainly by West Germany.

The West German financial system was also imposed on East Germany, while the financial system of East Germany was rendered immediately bankrupt by the terms of the currency conversion. For all East German financial interme-diaries, it took at least 2 ostmarks of their assets to get 1 deutsche mark, while most of their liabilities were charged against them at the rate of 1 ostmark per 1 deutsche mark. Given the importance of bank finance for business investment in the West German system and the importance of close relations between bank lenders and business borrowers in that system, this meant that, while only East German firms and entrepreneurs knew the local profit opportunities, it was only West German firms and entrepreneurs that could get financing to exploit them. So the last of the unique West German institutions associated with the postwar economic miracle, the system of universal banking, turned out to be an obstacle rather than an asset in meeting the challenge of refurbishing the East German economy.

The measure of these failures was the turnaround of the German trade account from healthy surpluses in the late 1980s to deficits in the early 1990s. Unemployment actually began to rise in West Germany as well as in East Germany. Some signs of improvement seemed to appear by 1994, and espe-cially in 1995, as an export surplus began to emerge once again. By mid-1996, however, this was petering out, and on reflection it seems that what was hap-pening was that a significant percentage of exports, as usual concentrated in machinery and equipment, were going to equip German factories being relo-cated outside Germany – and, indeed, outside western Europe (see chapter 19 on the transition economies of central and eastern Europe). The export surplus in goods and services in this case corresponded to a reduction in employment opportunities in Germany rather than an increase.

The expense of reunification shows up in the continued deficits of the Ger-man government, which repeatedly violated the 3% of GDP limit set by the Stability and Growth Pact. Figure 12.2 shows how the aftershocks of reunifi-cation created an unprecedented period of fiscal stress for Germany. Earlier,

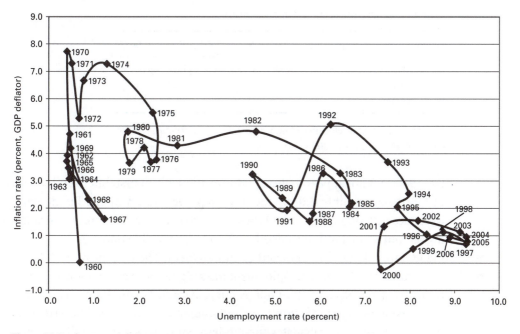

Figure 12.3   Germany: inflation versus unemployment, 1960–2006

the government had encountered regular deficits while confronting the successive oil shocks of the 1970s. As the opportunities for expanded exports arose in the late 1980s with the adoption of the single market initiatives within the European Union and the enlargement to include Portugal and Spain, the government's deficits declined and the ratio of debt to GDP leveled off at a very respectable 40%. This record of fiscal prudence is rapidly fading into the past as a result of the costs of reunification. The new Schröder administration attempted to regain budgetary balance from the late 1990s, but this came at the expense of unemployment, as shown in figure 12.1.

Figure 12.3 demonstrates the dramatic change in the economic environment facing the German labor force after the oil shocks of the 1970s, then the reunification shock of 1990 and the aftershocks created by the effects of monetary union. During the 1960s a steep, but discernible, inverse relationship appeared between inflation and unemployment rates, giving some credence to the idea that policy-makers in advanced economies faced a trade-off between controlling inflation or controlling unemployment. This was the so-called Phillips curve, named after the physicist who detected a similar inverse relation between unemployment and inflation rates for the British economy during the twentieth century. The first inflationary shocks of the

Table 12.2 German unemployment, national definition

Unemployment rate (percent)	2002	2003	2004	2005	2006 Q1
United Germany	9.8	10.5	10.6	11.7	11.3
West Germany	7.7	8.4	8.5	9.9	9.6
East Germany	17.7	18.2	18.4	18.7	18.2

Source: Economist Intelligence Unit, *Country Report, Germany*, London: October 2005, p. 29; July 2006, p. 31.

late 1960s did not appear to disrupt this relationship at first, but the oil shocks of the 1970s certainly did. By the time steps were taken by the Bundesbank to reduce inflation rates in the 1980s, unemployment rates were significantly higher, but some kind of tradeoff seemed to be possible once again, albeit at higher rates of both inflation and unemployment. The reunification shock of 1990, however, shoved unemployment rates higher once again. Only the most recalcitrant devotees of the Phillips curve paradigm could see a consistent relationship between inflation rates and unemployment rates. (Nevertheless, the OECD regularly calculates the modern equivalent of the Phillips curve, NAIRU – the "non-accelerating inflation rate of unemployment.") For Germany and most EU countries, however, NAIRU keeps shifting outward, if erratically. This implies that the "natural rate of employment" has become unstable as well, driven back and forth by erratic economic policies.

A closer examination of German unemployment rates, moreover, reveals that the rates in the former East Germany are more than twice those in the former West Germany. Table 12.2 shows that the attempt at labor market reforms by the Schröder government came in response to unemployment rates rising in *both* West and East Germany. The lack of private investment in East Germany, despite the roughly $70 billion a year in government expenditures on public infrastructure in East Germany, keeps unemployment high there. The continued extra "reunification tax" levied on West German individuals keeps unemployment high there as well.

One hopeful sign that the German efforts to bring the East German public infrastructure up to the levels of West Germany may finally be beginning to pay off is the resumption of growth in German exports. Figure 12.4 shows that the export-led growth of the West German economy began to tail off even in the late 1960s, but was certainly hurt badly by the reunification shock of the early 1990s. Since 2000, however, export growth has resumed, so much so that in 2004 German exports actually totaled more in dollar terms than those of the United States. Closer examination of the direction of German exports and the

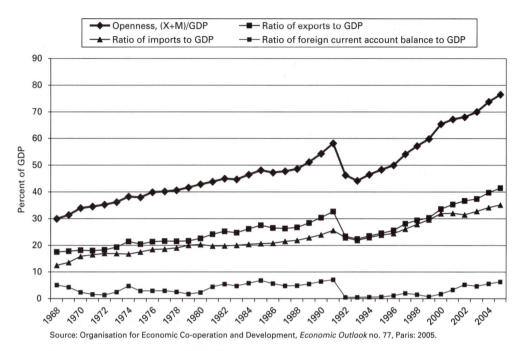

Source: Organisation for Economic Co-operation and Development, *Economic Outlook* no. 77, Paris: 2005.

Figure 12.4   Germany: foreign sector, 1968–2005

composition of goods, however, shows that capital goods produced by West German factories are exported to the central and east European economies to provide jobs for their workers, rather than for East German workers. Hungary, the Czech Republic, and Slovakia have all reduced their corporate tax rates much below those in Germany in order to encourage investment in their transition economies. Meanwhile, workers in east and central Europe are not paid nearly as much as East German workers, who are now paid in euros at close to West German wage rates.

Conclusion

West Germany must respond to the challenge of reunification with East Germany in its own way, which needs to be different from the approach it developed toward the partition of Germany at the end of World War II. The postwar arrangements were induced by the various initiatives of the Allies, to which the CDU government of Chancellor Konrad Adenauer responded eagerly, albeit on the basis of institutions that were tried and true from the pre-Nazi era – universal banks, an independent central bank, strong municipal governments, highly organized trade associations, and a commitment to honor social obligations such as health insurance, education, and pensions. The success of the West German institutions within the structure provided by Allied postwar arrangements encouraged the rest of Europe to try to imitate them, to the extent that their own cultures and political constraints permitted. Moreover, the various administrations of the Federal Republic have, by and large, worked faithfully to expand and strengthen the international arrangements that provided a felicitous environment for their own institutions. This has meant a strong commitment to the military alliance of NATO, the economic market of the European Union, and all the specialized groups for European cooperation that have arisen since World War II.

This commitment manifested itself quickly after German reunification as Chancellor Kohl pushed for the EEC to move quickly beyond the single market to the Treaty on European Union, which led to the prompt signing of the Maastricht Treaty and its eventual ratification in 1993. But, even though support for backward agriculture and depressed regions has become the focus of the EU's budget over the past twenty years, very little aid has been forthcoming from the EU to help West Germany resuscitate the economy of East Germany. Consequently, the expenses of reunification have been borne almost exclusively by West Germany. Given the enormity of this project, it is perhaps not surprising to learn that, despite German leadership in promoting and passing the Single European Act and the subsequent Treaty on European Union, Germany in 1995 was one of the three most laggardly member states in implementing the directives of the single market into national legislation. Moreover, public opinion polls consistently showed that the majority of German citizens were opposed to the common currency for the EU that replaced the deutsche mark in 1999–2002.

Imposing West German institutions upon East Germans after a separation of forty-five years (two generations) has not met with the economic success initially expected and hoped for. After sixteen years of all-out effort by the taxpayers of West Germany to remold East Germany into the image of West Germany, it is clear that even the economic institutions of West Germany need alteration. While some of the changes required are obvious to most – lower tax rates in general for both business and labor, more diversity among industries and regions in setting wage agreements, and, above all, more flexibility in the labor market – questions remain as to how to make the changes and how rapidly they can take effect. How long can separate rules for unemployment, retirement, and medical benefits persist between West and East German workers? How should the changes be financed, especially given the commitment of successive West German governments to balanced budgets and a strong currency? For example, the eventual agreement of the EU Council at the end of 2004 that the expenses of reunification against the German government deficit would not be counted for the purposes of enforcing the Stability and Growth Pact was helpful for Germany. But easing Germany's continued problem of reunification in this manner was not helpful for the process of developing a common set of institutions for the governments of the European Union. Modifying the economic and political institutions of unified Germany, it turns out, also requires modifying the economic and political institutions of the European Union. In that process, however, the interests of other countries, with their own problems to deal with, need to be considered as well. We turn next to the country that has the most to gain if Germany and the European Union succeed in modifying their economic institutions, and the one that has benefited the most from the existing institutions: France.

NOTES

1. Due to the volatility of foreign exchange rates, all international economic comparisons are now made in purchasing power parity exchange rates, which adjust for the different price levels within each country. In the early 1980s the US dollar was overvalued in the markets compared with its domestic purchasing power, while in the early 1990s it was undervalued. Using the market exchange rates to compare the United States with Europe, it appears that the US economy has slowed down markedly compared with that of the EU. Adjusting for the large swings in the exchange rates, which are not passed on to domestic price levels, however, shows that the US economy has grown more rapidly than the EU economies over the past decade. The PPP exchange rates used in this book are the 2000 US dollar equivalents as calculated by the Organisation for Economic Co-operation and Development in Paris.

2. The best single source for reviewing these revisions is Werner Abelshauser, *Wirtschaftsgeschichte der Bundesrepublik Deutschland 1945–1980*, Frankfurt: Suhrkamp, 1983. Both Carlin (note 6) and Kramer (note 3) summarize his findings, while still finding an important role for both Marshall Plan aid and the currency reform of 1948.

3. Alan Kramer, *The West German Economy, 1945–1955*, German Studies Series, New York: Berg, 1991, p. 12.

4. Ibid., p. 149.

5. Karl Hardach, *The Political Economy of Germany in the Twentieth Century*, Berkeley: University of California Press, 1980, p. 228.

6. Wendy Carlin, "West German growth and institutions, 1945–90," in Nicholas Crafts and Gianni Toniolo, eds., *Economic Growth in Europe since 1945*, Cambridge: Cambridge University Press, 1996.

13   France: problems with assimilation

Introduction

Until the French voters rejected the proposed constitution for the European Union in the referendum of 2005, France had been the political leader of the Franco-German alliance to keep moving Europe toward ever-closer unity. France had led the "deepening" process for the European Union, from the Schuman Plan of 1950 to the Nice Treaty of 2002, primarily to ensure that a resurgent Germany would be enmeshed entirely in a democratic rule of law for Europe. The rejection of the constitution, the change in parliamentary leadership, and the outbreak of widespread riots by alienated, and unemployed, north African youth throughout France in the fall of 2005 have forced the French political leadership to shift emphasis. Preserving French identity and economic interests within the enlarged European Union now take priority over initiatives to strengthen EU institutions. Rather, initiatives are now directed toward strengthening the executive leadership within France, for example by placing the Commissariat du Plan directly under the Prime Minister in October 2005. From now on, this agency, set up originally to oversee the operation of the Monnet Plan after World War II, will be comparable to the Council of Economic Advisors to the President of the United States. These policy shifts are a response to the continued high unemployment rates and sluggish growth of the French economy, which began at the same time as the slowdown in the German economy. Both countries' economic problems were the result of the "reunification shock" in Germany and the way each country responded to the challenges of reunifying Germany. The previous chapter reviewed the consequences of the German Monetary and Economic Union of 1990, which was implemented for political reasons. This chapter looks at the consequences of the *franc fort* policy in France, also initiated in 1990, which consisted of keeping the French franc as strong as the deutsche mark, whatever the cost.

Table 13.1 France: basic facts

Area	547,030 km^2	13.8% of EU-25
Population (July 2005 estimate)	60,656,178	13.3% of EU-25
GDP (2004 estimate, PPP)	$1,737 billion	14.9% of EU-25
Per capita income (PPP)	$28,700	106.7% of EU-25 average
Openness ([X+M]/GDP)	59.1%	67% with EU-25
Birth rate (per 1,000)	12.15	Death rate (per 1,000) 9.08

Sources: Central Intelligence Agency, *World Factbook, 2005*, available at http://www.cia.gov/cia/publications/factbook; Statistical Office of the European Communities, *Europe in Figures: Eurostat Yearbook 2005*, Brussels: 2005.

(As the European Central Bank was going to be located in Frankfurt, Germany, there was an ironic pun intended as well!)

With the strengthening of the deutsche mark after 1990, maintaining an equally strong French franc required restrictive monetary policy, which led to higher unemployment and slower growth. Ever since the formal adoption of the euro as the common currency in 1999, France has been subjected to the same restrictive monetary policy as the rest of the eurozone. As discussed in chapter 6, the attitude of the European Central Bank in response to the unemployment problems of various economies within the eurozone is that individual countries must liberalize their labor markets as a long-run solution. In the meantime, there will be no monetary easing to provide short-term palliatives. For the French government, and for French economic institutions in general, this change in monetary policy means that unemployment has remained high, while unions, farmers, pensioners, and government functionaries are all aware of the threats to their traditional emoluments. Each group takes action when it perceives a threat to its existing benefits, and its actions receive support from the other groups as well. Overall, the French public considers its existing privileges from membership in the European Union to be permanent fixtures, while resisting intensely the possible costs from new programs or new members of the EU. Since the formal adoption of the euro and acceptance of the restrictive monetary policy of the European Central Bank, the French government has found it increasingly difficult to meet the Stability and Growth Pact, which it had agreed to as part of the *franc fort* policy. Indeed, French defiance of the 3% of GDP restriction on deficits preceded the German violation, and will persist as long as unemployment remains high.

France, geographically fated always to be the heart of western Europe, has dealt throughout its history with challenges to its integrity from each of the six sides of its roughly hexagonal shape. The Romans from Italy, the Moors from Spain, the English from the Atlantic and the Channel, the Habsburgs from all directions, and in modern industrial times the Germans, from either the east or the northeast, have all threatened its integrity. Under Charlemagne and Napoleon I, France in turn attempted to unify Christian Europe under its enlightened rule. Either defeated or badly bloodied by German forces repeatedly from the Battle of Waterloo in June 1815 until D-Day in June 1944, French strategy has been militarily defensive and politically offensive, attempting to coordinate through diplomatic relations a system of alliances that could thwart German expansionism while maintaining a credibly strong military defense. From the end of World War II until the present day the relationship between France and Germany has determined the political architecture of western Europe, which in turn determines the economic policy of the EU. With the sea change in French domestic economic policy after 1990, however, one may expect a comparable change in the political architecture of Europe.

The reunification of Germany in 1990 was accepted by France in return for the German commitment to deepen the political structure of the European Union, which led to the signing of the Treaty on European Union in 1992 (the Maastricht Treaty) and its ratification by all twelve member states of the European Union by the end of 1993. A key provision was to revise the treaty to clarify both the internal political structure of the EU and the external political role of the EU. Further, this had to occur before European monetary union took effect, in 1997 or 1999. The need to clarify the political environment for the planned monetary union was the basis for the Inter-Governmental Conference of 1996, which concluded with the Treaty of Amsterdam, ratified in 1999. The key issue then, as now, was how to make the European Union function effectively with a steadily increasing number (potentially twenty-seven) of member states with much greater diversity in size, structure, and objectives than ever before. Ten years later, it is obvious that these issues still plague the European Union.

Enlargement in the first round after completion of the single market enclosed Germany on the south (Austria) and the north (Sweden and Finland) but gave potentially much greater voting power to German interests. The inclusion of Malta and Cyprus as representatives of France's Mediterranean interests only partially offset Germany's increased political weight. It was the resulting imbalance between France and Germany, it could be argued, that led to the eventual enlargement taking in ten new members at one go instead of just a few in each successive round of enlargement, as originally envisioned. The outcome of that unprecedented enlargement, however, has refocused French political concerns toward domestic economic issues.

Macroeconomic policy indicators: 1960–2005

Figure 13.1 traces out France's economic success after joining the European Economic Community in 1958. Almost immediately, French economic growth rates began to catch up with, and then surpass, those of West Germany, averaging over 5% annually until the first oil shock in 1973/4. Part of the reason for France's participation in the economic growth miracles of western Europe in the 1960s was indeed the beneficial effect of the Common Market, as explained in chapter 3. But a larger part was probably played by the decolonization carried out by General Charles de Gaulle. De Gaulle was elected President of France in 1958 under a new constitution that set up the Fifth Republic. Withdrawing from Algeria eliminated much of the fiscal drain on successive French governments caused by the futile attempts to regain control of their prewar colonies in Algeria and Indochina. The former colonists returned to France with their labor, skills, and capital in large numbers thereafter, which helped stimulate growth in the domestic economy. De Gaulle's economists also carried out a monetary reform, creating a nouveau franc equal to 100 anciens francs while devaluing the nouveau franc relative to the dollar and the rest of the European currencies at the same time.

De Gaulle's reforms and the export opportunities provided by the Common Market brought the rate of French economic growth up to and then beyond the levels of West Germany and Italy. But the massive structural changes created by rapid growth led to rising social tensions. These exploded in the events of May 1968. Then university students incited what became a nationwide strike to protest against President de Gaulle's economic policies, as well as his educational policies. Calm was restored only by the Grenelle Agreements of 1968, which, basically, granted the demands of the workers and students. This exacerbated French inflation relative to the continued low inflation rate of West Germany, putting more pressure on the fixed exchange rate regime between France and West Germany that had existed since 1958. At the end of 1969, after acrimonious discussions, the Franco-German exchange rate was adjusted, first by a devaluation of the French franc and then by an equal revaluation of the German deutsche mark, to create a 20% devaluation of the franc relative to the deutsche mark.

In the subsequent shocks to the European financial system, however, France continued its loose monetary policy and let inflation rates rise ever higher. The first shock was the collapse of the Bretton Woods system in August 1971, which meant that the dollar floated against all other currencies for the first time since

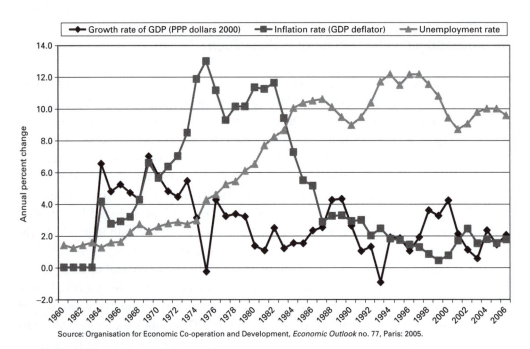

Source: Organisation for Economic Co-operation and Development, *Economic Outlook* no. 77, Paris: 2005.

Figure 13.1   France: policy results, 1960–2005

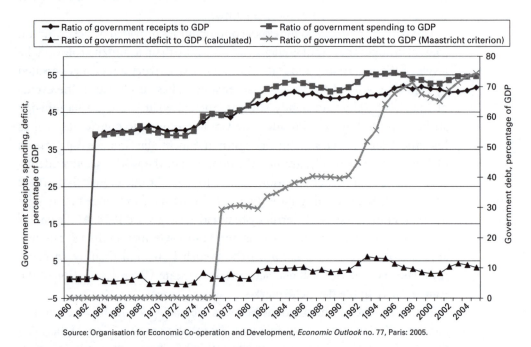

Source: Organisation for Economic Co-operation and Development, *Economic Outlook* no. 77, Paris: 2005.

Figure 13.2   France: government performance, 1960–2005

World War II. The dollar float caused all intra-European exchange rates to come unstuck as well, as each set its own course against the dollar. Initially the French franc appreciated against the dollar, as French authorities tried to keep the franc rate with the deutsche mark steady. However, the first oil shock, starting in October 1973, caused the French government to respond with an expansionary monetary and fiscal policy. This led to a rapid depreciation of the franc against the dollar and especially against the deutsche mark, which continued to appreciate against the dollar. But depreciation of the franc did nothing to abate the continued rise in unemployment, and the GDP growth rates continued to fall, albeit not as badly as in other OECD countries hit by the first oil shock.

The hardline socialist policies that François Mitterrand imposed as President in the early 1980s proved disastrously unsuited to coping with the second oil shock of 1979. Mitterrand held out the promise of renewed technological advance, financed by the central government, which enlarged its capacity enormously by nationalizing banks and basic industries. While this strategy might have promoted growth in the long run, in the short run it provoked massive capital flight. Moreover, the fixed exchange rates with Germany agreed to under the European Monetary System facilitated the flight of capital from France, even though France tried to tighten its controls on capital movements and devalued the franc repeatedly within the framework of the EMS.

In contrast to the growing success of Margaret Thatcher in the United Kingdom, who was pursuing a counterstrategy of privatization, Mitterrand was obliged to reverse his economic strategy by 1983 and begin to denationalize many of the firms he had hastily nationalized. Since 1985 the French franc has been stable against the deutsche mark, putting to one side the attacks on the franc in 1992 and 1993. The results were to decrease inflation sharply and, with a lag, to improve growth rates gradually, which almost reached 5% again in 1988. By the late 1980s unemployment rates had started to decline slightly as well. The single market initiative was proving its worth for the French economy as well as for the West German economy. But, having tied its economic policy so closely to that of West Germany when the West German economy was setting the standards of performance for all Europe, France now had to cope with the same economic consequences as Germany confronted the reunification shock of 1990.

Like Germany, France weathered the reunification shock with little change in inflation, a sharp contrast with its performance during the oil shocks. Also like Germany, France suffered a drop in growth rates, especially in 1993, when the franc was attacked on the foreign exchanges by speculators who believed it would have to devalue in view of the continued loss of reserves. Even without having to deal with forcibly unemployed East Germans, France managed to increase its unemployment rate to well above 10%! By linking its economic policy – tight money, balanced budgets, and gradual liberalization and privatization – to that of Germany, France ended up sharing in the economic costs of Germany's reunification, even though it contributed very little toward the actual financing of reunification. If misery loves company, however, the shared economic travail of the two largest economies in Europe initially strengthened their political commitment to expand and deepen the institutional framework of the European Union.

The problems for the French policy-makers of assimilating the euro and the restrictive monetary policy of the European Central Bank, along with the increased influxes of labor from east and central Europe, show up clearly in figure 13.2. The French government's habit of running deficits to confront each external shock was evident even before the oil shocks of the 1970s. But the habit has run amok since the German reunification shock of 1990. Not only have deficits remained consistently above the 3% of GDP limit set in the Stability and Growth Pact, the level of government debt to GDP has soared. In 2005 it was well above the initial limit of 60% set in the Maastricht Treaty, and it continues to rise. How did this governmental habit get started, and why is it so hard to break?

The travails of the Fourth Republic: 1945–57

Occupied by Nazi Germany from May 1940 until late 1944, and omitted from the postwar planning conferences carried on mainly between the Americans and British but including on key occasions the Russians, France emerged from World War II politically isolated, internally divided, and economically devastated. Unlike Germany, France had stagnated throughout the 1930s, shifting from one misguided policy to another, with the result that national income in 1939 was no higher than it had been in 1929. Quickly defeated by the German invasion of 1940, France was ruthlessly taxed by the Nazi occupation forces for the remainder of the war. French industry was directed toward supplying consumer goods for the German market, where industry was diverted entirely toward producing military goods. The French capital stock, far from being expanded and updated, as in Germany, was simply allowed to wear out, while skilled French workers were deported to work in the factories seized by the Nazi forces in central and eastern Europe. Caught in the fierce fighting accompanying the advance of the Russian forces toward the end of the war, most of these French workers never returned.

Under the political leadership of General de Gaulle, who had been installed in London during the war as leader of the Free French, the Fourth Republic was established in 1945 as a parliamentary democracy, revenge against Nazi collaborators was quickly carried out, and Jean Monnet, known today as the Father of Europe, proposed his Plan de Modernisation et d'Équipement. The Monnet Plan was officially adopted as a four-year plan in 1946 and was extended later for two years to coincide with the funding of the Marshall Plan. Monnet's vision was to focus on building up the basic sectors in France that had been the key to German economic and military superiority. These were coal, steel, cement, electricity, transport, and agricultural machinery. As many of the large firms in precisely these sectors had been nationalized immediately following the war, all that seemed necessary to implement the plan was to indicate to the respective managers what was needed as inputs in each sector to achieve its goals for increased output by the end of the plan. The key French agency, the Commissariat du Plan, had no direct power to allocate resources, but concerned itself instead with acquiring information on the input-output structure of the economy and disseminating this information to the leaders of each sector. Hence the phrase "indicative planning" is used to describe the French method. (Recall that the Commissariat du Plan was put under the Prime Minister's office at the end of 2005.)

If financial constraints seemed to be inhibiting certain sectors from expanding as rapidly as desired, recourse could be had to loans from any of the four largest banks, all of which had been nationalized, or to government subsidies directly upon approval by the Treasury, which had unlimited recourse to loans from the Banque de France. All three sources of finance – nationalized commercial banks, the Treasury, and the Banque de France – were under the supervision of the Minister of Finance. Unfortunately for the success of Monnet's plan, however, the banks were concerned more with regaining their financial health than with fulfilling his vision by making large loans to nationalized enterprises that had no track record of repaying their debts. Moreover, the government was limited in its ability to subsidize investment due to chronic budget deficits. No firm tax base had yet been established, but wage demands by the workers in the nationalized industries and in the government had to be met in order to establish the postwar legitimacy of the new government. Consequently, inflation became a chronic problem, which further inhibited banks from providing the requisite financing for long-term projects. By the end of 1947 little progress had been made, while the French franc encountered the first of many balance of payments crises that were to afflict it over the coming years.

While France was one of the initial members of the International Monetary Fund, the 44% devaluation of the franc at the beginning of 1948 was well above the 10% limit beyond which members had to agree they would not devalue without prior approval from the Fund. France's unwillingness to cede its tenuous sovereignty to a new, untried international agency at this moment seriously undercut its ability to attract foreign loans from private sources. The Fund had been unwilling to accept the French devaluation because France had proposed at the same time to introduce a two-tier exchange rate. For capital account transactions, in which it was to French advantage to have an over-valued franc, the new rate was fixed artificially and applied to all transactions approved under the French system of tight capital controls. For obtaining scarce dollars, however, exports and imports of goods and services would be at a floating rate, most likely well below the fixed rate for capital transactions. Faced with the refusal of the Fund to approve what could have become the first of multiple exchange rates for the franc, the French went ahead and devalued anyway. The reluctance of its major trading partners, Italy and Belgium, to trade with it on terms that could be rendered so disadvantageous suddenly and without consultation forced France into making bilateral barter agreements with each. Constrained in its ability to earn foreign exchange from exporting, France limited imports of consumption goods to 3% of French consump-tion of the particular item. Such bilateral agreements and quota restrictions confined the possible expansion of French trade and damaged the long-run possibility of attracting foreign investment.

Smaller devaluations were carried out later in 1948 and in 1949, though now in consultation with the Fund. But the saving grace for the financing of the Monnet Plan clearly came from the funds provided to France under the Marshall Plan. More than any other recipient, France directed its American aid monies toward purchases of the construction materials and machinery required to expand the output of its targeted six sectors. Even so, it found its output targets continually frustrated in coal and steel, where inputs from the coal fields of Belgium, the Saarland, and the Ruhr basin were essential. The costs of transport and the much larger amounts of coal than iron ore needed in the smelting and refining of steel meant that it was only rational to send French iron ore to German coal and bring back the finished steel products for use in France. Toward this end, the initial French policy was to try to incorporate its occupation zone of the Saarland into the adjacent French province of Lorraine, with its rich iron ore mines. France also pressed for international control of the

Ruhr basin, where it could have a decisive voice in determining the allocation of coal between German domestic use and export to Belgium and France. The French finally accomplished a diluted version of their goals when the International Control Authority for the Ruhr was established in March 1948, with the United States, the United Kingdom, France, West Germany, and the Benelux countries all having a voice. To placate the West Germans and to ensure the success of the Monnet Plan, the French Prime Minister, Robert Schuman, proposed his plan for a European Coal and Steel Community (see chapter 2 for a discussion of the ECSC).

The Schuman Plan and the consequent expansion of the European coal and steel capacity managed to save the Monnet Plan, which perhaps was unfortunate for France. The attempt at unbalanced growth within an economy that was trying to be as self-sufficient as possible while restoring authority over distant colonies that had been lost during World War II proved ineffective for increasing the growth rate of the whole economy. True, the output of the six key sectors increased, but shortages of consumer goods led to increased wage demands by workers and chronic balance of payments problems. While GDP growth was certainly higher than during the 1920s and 1930s, in retrospect this was due to a prolonged "catching up" effect. This was especially powerful for France given how backward it was in 1945 relative to Germany and, in particular, the United States. But unlike Italy and West Germany, where the catching up effect was reinforced by rapid productivity advances in the export sectors, France had no leading sector to provide the kind of productivity advances that could have raised French real wages without causing inflation and balance of payments difficulties. Moreover, the expenses of trying to regain control of Indochina and to maintain control of Algeria and to take its place in defeated Germany as a full-fledged occupying power with the British, Americans, and Russians proved a constant drain on government finances and French savings.

The loss of Indochina in 1954 and the humiliation of defeat in the Suez Crisis of 1956 led to increased vigor in the Algerian fight for independence and decreased political will in France, where parliamentary divisions led to frequent changes of ineffectual governments. After Suez both the United Kingdom and France suffered speculative outflows of their already reduced holdings of gold and dollars. For France, there were increased drains as well on the government's budget to finance the intensified war in Algeria. These financial pressures led to closer cooperation with the IMF and World Bank, something the French had resisted until then, seeing these twin pillars of the Bretton Woods system more as instruments of American hegemony than as precursors of a truly international monetary system. They also saw a need to intensify their cooperation with West Germany and the Benelux countries, which were enjoying continued economic growth and rising prosperity. This stimulated their accession to the Treaty of Rome in 1957 to set up the European Economic Community as an overdue complement to the European Coal and Steel Community. The change in France's economic policy, forced upon it by the costly losses in Indochina, Suez, and now in Algeria, was made permanent by a signal domestic political event as well.

The triumph of the Fifth Republic: 1958–69

In 1958 General de Gaulle, leader of the Free French during World War II from London, who had stepped down from power in January 1946 in disgust at the political gridlock of the Fourth Republic, was called back to be Premier of France. He proposed a referendum on a new constitution to form the Fifth Republic, saw it pass approval for a stronger presidential form of government, and was elected the first such President, taking office in January 1959. De Gaulle's decade of rule, however, had really started in 1958, when he became Premier with nearly dictatorial, if temporary, powers, and ended in 1968, when his party forced him to make political concessions after the general strike of May 1968. Formally, he was President from January 1, 1959, until April 1969, when he resigned after a second referendum on constitutional reform failed to pass. De Gaulle's initial political reforms that created the Fifth Republic were quickly complemented by economic reforms, starting with currency reform. This replaced the ancien franc, as it became called, with the nouveau franc. The new currency was exchanged for the old at a rate of 1 nouveau franc to 100 anciens francs, so immediately two zeroes were lopped off all prices and wages. This made it seem much stronger, but, at the same time, the currency was devalued against the dollar.[1]

The currency reform was part of the Rueff Plan, devised by Jacques Rueff, de Gaulle's first Finance Minister. He also attempted to bring inflation under control in order to maintain the competitive advantage of the devalued franc as long as possible. To do this, Rueff abolished cross-indexation between agriculture and industry, which had kept up the level of subsidies to French farmers as industrial prices rose in response to liberalization. He also cut public subsidies for food and nationalized industries, which led to a rise in their prices. Cuts in social transfers, family allowances, repayments of medical charges, and ex-servicemen's pensions were also implemented in order to reduce government spending. Revenues were raised by increasing corporate taxation. All in

Table 13.2 Destination of French exports, 1952–84 (percent of total)

	Former French colonies	Non-EEC OECD	Original EEC
1952	42.2	27.3	15.9
1958	37.5	24.4	22.2
1962	20.8	27.9	36.8
1968	13.5	27.0	43.0
1973	9.2	27.5	48.6
1984	9.3	30.7	37.3

Source: William J. Adams, *Restructuring the French Economy*, Washington, DC: Brookings Institution, 1989, p. 178, table 22.

all, the Rueff Plan prepared France well for competition with West Germany. This had been inaugurated by the Treaty of Rome, which came at the same time that the European currencies became mutually convertible for transactions on the current account. The two events in combination meant that 90% of French trade was now open to price competition, primarily from West Germany. The effects of competition were temporarily forestalled, however, by maintaining very high tariffs. In 1958 tariffs averaged 17%, compared with 6.4% in West Germany.[2] Only after 1966, when the Common External Tariff had been progressively reduced by the Dillon and Kennedy Rounds of negotiations under the General Agreement on Tariffs and Trade, did French industry truly feel the effects of international competition. By that time, high levels of investment had made some firms, at least, competitive in European markets.

The pattern of French trade continued to change over the next ten years. The EEC countries kept replacing the franc zone countries (existing and former colonies of France) in both exports and imports, but at a more rapid pace than before the customs union was formed (see table 13.2). Oddly, the commodity structure of France's foreign trade did not change much in terms of the relative importance of agriculture and manufacturing within both exports and imports. Agriculture remained between 13 and 16% of exports, while manufacturing stayed between 50 and 55% of exports. However, within manufacturing there was a reversal in the relative importance of semi-manufactures, which fell from one-third of exports to one-fifth, and machinery and transport equipment, which rose correspondingly.[3]

Despite the improved growth performance resulting from the combined effect of de Gaulle's reforms and the steadying management of aggregate demand by his economists, unemployment rates rose gradually until 1968. Moreover, the Rueff reforms had shifted the distribution of income in favor of capital, away from labor, and real wages had fallen as prices rose more rapidly than nominal wages. The gradual culmination of these processes helped to provoke the events of May 1968, when university students incited what became a nationwide strike in protest at President de Gaulle's economic and educational policies. Unemployment rates were still very low, especially by comparison with the years since, and inflation rates seemed tolerable, especially by comparison with the immediate postwar years. Nevertheless, France's inflation rates were significantly higher than those in West Germany throughout the 1960s. By the end of 1968 it was clear that the exchange rate that had been fixed by de Gaulle's financial experts when he came to power in 1958 was no longer sustainable. Finally, in August 1969, the franc was devalued, this time by 10% against the dollar. Then, at de Gaulle's insistence, the deutsche mark was floated in September and revalued in October by the same percentage as the franc had devalued. By this time, however, de Gaulle had resigned in dismay at the concessions extracted by the unions from parliament despite his powers as President. His successor, Georges Pompidou, proved more facile in dealing with political pressures, but the Gaullist political movement would be divided from then on.

The de Gaulle era was marked at both its start and its end by dramatic political events, which brought about major changes in the French political system. Economic historians, however, have been surprised at how smoothly the French economy seemed to grow relative to the rest of Europe, despite France's having more serious political disruptions than its neighbors. It seemed that high, smooth rates of growth were necessary to maintain the tentative social consensus in a society that was being torn apart by the stresses of adjusting to the modern economy. In just the period 1948–62, for example, nearly 2 million people moved out of agriculture, reducing the absolute size of the rural population by one-third. The southern, mountainous region called the Midi was in danger of depopulation, while all the outlying regions lost population to the magnetic attractions of the Paris basin. Manufacturing absorbed only 170,000 of the rural migrants, construction another 550,000, and the rest, over 1 million strong, went into the service sector. Moreover, despite the obvious attractions of the high-growth sectors in manufacturing for new labor, the wage gap between manufacturing and agriculture remained relatively constant. Even the skill differentials within manufacturing did not change over time. In other words, the tremendous quantity adjustments that were made at great personal cost to literally millions of French citizens did not have the desired or expected impact on relative incomes by sector, gender, or qualification.

The smoothness of aggregate French growth may be held accountable in part for this odd pattern of structural adjustment, made, apparently, not so much in response to price signals emitted by the market as to "indications" provided by the planners. In fact, it has been accepted that French demand management was able to sustain the confidence of capitalists, so that they continued to maintain high rates of investment, financed mainly out of retained earnings by the firms. This was the *auto-financement* of French business, or self-financing without recourse to outside debt or equity in the capital markets, or even very much to credit from the banking sector. Closer examination of each successive five-year plan and the specific goals announced by each at the beginning, however, shows that the latent tensions in the French economic fabric were very much at work. While most plans came very close to their announced goals by the end of each five-year period, the usual pattern was to note serious shortfalls emerging after two to three years into the plan, the diversion of substantial government resources to make up the shortfall in the last two or three years, and then the announcement of success once again at the conclusion of the plan period. Meanwhile, the next plan would be devised to cover over the weaknesses or unplug the bottlenecks that had emerged during the course of the previous plan. As long as this held, the private sector could avoid fulfilling its presumed obligations in each plan and focus on exploiting the opportunities that would emerge from expanded activity by the public enterprises. Few countries had the central government capacity to mobilize resources so quickly for specific objectives without further political debate or decision-making. Attempts in other countries to imitate the French success with indicative planning usually faltered, as they stimulated effective resistance to a plan's objectives by interest groups that felt they would be losers in the process.

As French economic success became apparent in the early 1960s and the course of the Common Market appeared increasingly attractive to other countries in Europe, the United Kingdom changed its mind and decided to apply for membership in 1963. De Gaulle objected and single-handedly vetoed British membership, arguing that the Common Market was not ready for new members. The United Kingdom applied again in 1967, just as the elimination of internal tariff barriers was about to be achieved and the EEC was clearly a solid success as a customs union. This time de Gaulle objected on the grounds that the United Kingdom was not ready for membership! It is clear in retrospect (and was obvious at the time to many) that de Gaulle's resentment of his treatment by the British and Americans while leader of the Free French in exile in London during World War II had turned him into an Anglophobe, if he hadn't been one before. This helps account as well for his removal of France from

NATO and the ouster of American forces from France. But it also seems clear that his views were shared by many French, and his sense of history was surely acute in recognizing that, while France geographically is at the heart of western Europe, it could not play the central role necessary for its long-run survival without achieving greater economic success (and military power). Toward this end, he committed France to the Common Market and ever-closer economic and political relations with West Germany, but with France in control of the speed and pace of European integration.

The successive shocks of devaluation, oil, Mitterrand: 1969–85

France confronted the end of the Bretton Woods system in August 1971 and the first oil shock of October 1973 while still adjusting to the end of the de Gaulle era. French policy was still in the Gaullist mode, so the collapse of the US dollar as the key currency of the Bretton Woods system was welcomed. It seemed to give France a fresh opportunity to play a major role in shaping the international economy. The favorite French prescriptions for reform were either to devalue the dollar against gold or to substitute some other commodity standard, such as oil, for gold. The first proposal, which was the official French position for a long time, would have had the effect of greatly enlarging the value of the foreign reserves of the Banque de France relative to those of the Bundesbank. The Banque de France consciously tried to maintain a higher proportion of gold and dollars in its reserves, while the Bundesbank built up large reserves of dollars. Neither the Americans nor the West Germans could see much advantage in giving such a windfall simultaneously to the French, the Russians, and the South Africans, so the French proposal was never seriously considered. Moreover, French domestic monetary policy made it an increasingly weak negotiating partner in the deliberations that followed the breakup of Bretton Woods.

It was at this time that the policy changes that had been made in 1968 and 1969 to placate the discontented French workers came to bear on French inflation rates. The minimum wage had been increased by 35% in June 1968, with other wages raised 10 to 15%, and the length of the working week had been cut. But most dangerously, in light of the inflationary oil shock of 1973/4, wages had been indexed formally to prices, which produced a wage-price spiral that could not end once one or the other had started to rise. The social peace that had been gained by the Grenelle Agreements in 1968 was not to be forsaken easily. French real incomes would not be allowed to fall despite the rise in oil prices, the adverse balance of payments, and the claims of the OPEC oil producers upon French national income. The result of this determination to maintain French real incomes was an increase in inflation and a sustained rise in unemployment – the combination that came to be termed "stagflation." France was not alone in this experience, and, in fact, its economic performance in terms of both inflation and unemployment appears to be roughly the European average, while its growth of output held up well compared with that of the rest of Europe, dropping only by half from the average rate enjoyed in the "golden age" of growth.

Unfortunately for the Gaullist vision of France's role in Europe, the West German response to the end of Bretton Woods and the first oil shock was quite different. As described in chapter 12, West Germany chose to maintain low inflation rates throughout. The predictable result was a further depreciation of the French franc relative to the deutsche mark. France had joined the European "snake" in April 1972 to demonstrate European solidarity in face of the depreciating dollar and to maintain the feasibility of financing the Common Agricultural Policy, as explained in chapter 5. But the difference in inflation rates between France and West Germany, which came to dominate the snake, forced France out with the first oil shock. It tried to re-enter again in July 1975, only to be forced out once more in March 1976. This was when the anti-inflationary measures devised by Raymond Barre seemed the best political alternative.

In the meantime, the government of Georges Pompidou, de Gaulle's successor as President in 1969, welcomed the third attempt by the United Kingdom to join the Common Market. Edward Heath's Conservative government made the final push, with negotiations carried out in 1971/2 in common with Ireland, Denmark, and Norway. Part of the French motivation at this time was probably to bring in a counterweight to the increasing stature of West Germany within the affairs of the EEC, and part was probably to gain access to the markets of the sterling area. But most of the initiative came from the British side, which successively adopted a value added tax (VAT), changed its agricultural policy to the price support system of the Common Agricultural Policy, accepted the Common External Tariff against the sterling area countries, decimalized its currency, and floated the pound from the middle of 1972, while the EEC countries tried to maintain for a while longer their new par rates with the dollar. Faced with this overwhelming turnabout in the United Kingdom's attitudes and practices, France had to accede to its entry.

With the United Kingdom entering, Ireland and Denmark had little choice but to join as well, and both looked forward to taking advantage of the

Common Agricultural Policy. Norway, meanwhile, put the matter to a popular referendum, in which it was defeated, as it was again in 1994. When the Greek colonels' regime of some seven years was replaced by a democratic government led by a conservative politician, Constantine Karamanlis, in 1974 France also pushed for Greece's rapid entry, in order to solidify the legitimacy of the new democracy. It was less forthcoming, however, on the possibility of entry of Portugal and Spain. Both these countries had emerged from authoritarian rule only a year later than Greece, but the authoritarian regime in each had a much longer history to overcome. France was at the center of a nine-member European Economic Community from 1973 onward and a ten-member EEC from 1980. During the oil shocks the deepening process of the Community was put on hold, while the first major steps at widening the EEC were made. French national interests were very much in evidence in this shift of direction in the process of European integration.

At the same time, France under the presidency of Valéry Giscard d'Estaing (1974–81) opened up other initiatives for international cooperation outside the Community. His director of the Treasury, Jacques de Larosière (later to become managing director of the IMF), was instructed to work out a mode of cooperation with the United States within the framework of the International Monetary Fund. These meetings culminated in the world's first economic summit, held in 1975 at the Château de Rambouillet in France. The heads of government of the seven leading industrial economies – the United States, Japan, West Germany, France, Italy, the United Kingdom, and Canada – met in an informal "house party" at the eighteenth-century château with their Foreign and Finance Ministers in attendance. This was the forerunner of the annual G7 (now G8 with the addition of Russia) meetings, where current economic problems are discussed and common policy positions are announced. It was also the stimulus for the now semi-annual meetings of the European Council, the meeting of the heads of government of all the member states of the European Union. This meeting, at first an informal method of policy coordination, has now been formalized as part of the European Union's set of institutions. The Rambouillet summit led directly to the second amendment of the articles of the IMF, which acknowledged the changed role of exchange rates in the world. No longer would the IMF uphold fixed exchange rates, but instead it would "assure orderly exchange arrangements and promote a stable system of exchange rates."[4] Cooperative interventions in the foreign exchange markets could occur by mutual agreement, but the object was to keep the system stable, not the exchange rates as such.

By 1976, when the Barre Plan was introduced in France, extreme anti-inflationary measures seemed called for. Rather than continue to devalue the franc, the Barre Plan tried to control the government budget by cutting subsidies and raising taxes. The intent was to eliminate the need for the Banque de France to increase the money supply by covering the increasing government deficit and thereby fueling further inflation. However, the Banque de France continued to increase the money supply by making exceptions for exports, for investment in energy-saving equipment, and for housing construction. The government also had to help finance investment in the six new strategic industries it was targeting for expansion. Reflecting the technological changes that had occurred in the thirty years since the Monnet Plan, the strategic industries in the Barre Plan were offshore technology, office information systems, electronics, robots, bio-industries, and energy-saving equipment. Again, any investment in these was facilitated by government finance, so France's inflationary spiral, begun by the wage increases of 1968 and continued by the practice of wage indexation, was exacerbated by the first oil shock.

To rein in these pressures on the Banque de France, Barre promoted the entry of France into the European Monetary System. By committing the French government to maintaining a stable central par rate with the other members of the EMS, which meant primarily with West Germany and the Benelux countries, with their perennially strong currencies, Barre hoped to force it into allowing the Banque de France to pursue an equally tight money policy instead of acceding to the demands of France's numerous pressure groups. The Barre Plan was effective in reducing the rate of inflation – just in time for the second oil shock. This sent unemployment soaring again, and, with no short-term solution available to French policy-makers to cope with labor unrest, the conservative government fell in the presidential elections of 1981. François Mitterrand became the new President and immediately began to carry out a set of socialist economic reforms.

He began by nationalizing more industries, especially the largest remaining private banks, imposing price controls, raising wages, and installing worker councils in the major firms. It was definitely a counterstrategy to the tight money policy of West Germany and Benelux and to the privatization and deregulation initiatives under way at the same time in the United States and the United Kingdom. There was certainly no thought initially of devising a common European strategy to cope with what, after all, had been a series of common shocks to all the member states. These had been the collapse of the Bretton Woods system of fixed exchange rates, with dollar deficits fueling the rise of international reserves and prices; the two oil shocks in 1973 and

1979; and the "Volcker shock" of 1980/1. The latter shock was the result of the US Federal Reserve System changing its policy from stabilizing the interest rate on US government debt to stabilizing at a much reduced rate the growth rate of the US money supply. But all these shocks had affected every European country in much the same way. It is a mark of the failure of the European ideal, articulated by Jean Monnet, that this decade-long string of common threats to the economic security of Europe should have seen such a variety of individual national initiatives seeking to meet them separately, with no thought of the consequences of their actions for the rest of Europe.

As it turned out, Mitterrand's "socialism in one country" strategy proved disastrous. With the French franc holding its strength relative to the other European currencies in the EMS and the property rights of business firms threatened throughout France, capital flight began in earnest. The dollar became stronger all the time as the Volcker strategy took hold, so much of the flight capital even went to the United States, in addition to the traditional safety perch of Switzerland. An example of the strength of the incentives for capital flight created by Mitterrand's initial policy was that the French Rothschild's actually set up a US branch, the first time this storied international banking firm had dealt directly in the United States. Within the EMS, France had to devalue repeatedly against the other currencies. And this time the devaluations had no effect in maintaining French exports. Instead, they simply raised the price of oil further and accelerated the pace of capital flight.

By 1983 Mitterrand (and the French electorate) realized the error of his economic policy and began to reverse it. The key actor in effecting this turnaround was his Finance Minister, Jacques Delors, later to become famous as the architect of the European Monetary Union. The first steps were to halt nationalization and firm up France's commitment to the European Monetary System in order to avoid further devaluations. In fact, this proved successful in stabilizing the franc and halting further capital flight. It did nothing, of course, to reduce the rate of unemployment, which remained uncomfortably high. And it did nothing to restore the high rates of growth that had kept domestic peace during much of the 1950s and 1960s. At the center of an enlarged European Economic Community, France by the mid-1980s was also at the heart of the economic stagnation afflicting most of western Europe. The situation was aptly dubbed "Eurosclerosis." But the initiative out of this predicament came again from France. Jacques Delors, passed over at the direction of François Mitterrand for the office of Prime Minister in the Socialist government in 1984, resigned as Finance Minister to become President of the European Commission. Over the next ten years his initiatives in promoting the establishment of the single market and then of European Monetary Union led to at least a modest resumption of growth and a resurgence of hope.

From ECU to *franc fort* 1986–2006

The single market initiative emanated directly from the European Commission under the leadership of Jacques Delors. Yet it fell on fertile soil. Big businesses throughout western Europe were upset at the continued restrictions of trade across national boundaries and envious of the rapid economic recovery under way in the United States, where deregulation seemed to be stimulating a flurry of investment activity. Even the United Kingdom, with the privatization initiatives of Margaret Thatcher, the Prime Minister, was growing more rapidly than the traditional leaders of western Europe's growth league. A conservative majority in the French parliament in 1986 forced Mitterrand into a policy of "cohabitation" with the conservative Prime Minister, Jacques Chirac. Blocked by political circumstances from domestic innovations in economic policy, Mitterrand supported the efforts of Delors to increase the vitality of European integration. When it seemed that the dispute over the harmonization of VAT rates would prove insoluble, for example, it was France that broke the logjam by changing the structure of its own rates first. The resurgence of investment and the rise in the rate of economic growth that anticipated passage of the Single European Act in 1987 helped Mitterrand win re-election as President in 1988.

This success solidified his commitment to the European Monetary System. Since 1985 there have been no further changes in the central par rate between the French franc and the deutsche mark. Later, to facilitate accomplishment of European Monetary Union, France passed legislation to make the Banque de France legally independent from the credit demands of the government, the first time that this had been considered since its founding in 1801. The commitment of France to a stable currency and a fixed exchange rate with the deutsche mark and the deutsche mark bloc encouraged other countries to join in the EMS as well. By April 1991 every member state had joined except for Greece, and the future of the system seemed assured.

This was when the pressures of German reunification began to be felt. Thanks to the artificially maintained system of fixed exchange rates within the EEC at the time, these pressures were transmitted to the rest of the member states. As the deutsche mark rose in value relative to other currencies in the world, especially the dollar, exports were hurt and imports encouraged.

This was fine for directing resources toward the reconstruction of the German economy, but it was not in the economic interests of the other member states to cut short the economic expansion that had barely begun in response to the single market initiative. Now, for strictly political reasons that had much more to do with the future architecture of Europe and Mitterrand's place in world history than with domestic elections, much less the domestic economy, France remained committed to the EMS. The Maastricht Treaty that embodied this commitment was barely passed in a referendum in France in 1992. The narrowness of this vote surely played a major role in provoking the crisis for the Italian lira and the British pound sterling that followed shortly afterward.

The power of the conservative Gaullist party was clear in the French parliament, which saw the continued high rates of unemployment as an opportunity to restrain the role of the unions and to liberalize the operation of the labor market. An ailing Mitterrand did nothing to aid the Socialist party in the presidential election of 1995, although the continued high unemployment rates did lead to the defeat of the presidential ambitions of the Prime Minister, Edouard Balladur. But, instead of a Socialist president, it was the other conservative candidate, Jacques Chirac, who won the presidency by promising to attack the problem of unemployment first of all. In office, however, Chirac retained the commitment of France to partnership with Germany and to join with Germany in a common currency. Chirac even conceded to the renaming of the common currency, from "ECU," which had distinct francophone overtones, to "euro," which sounds completely different when spoken by a German.

Rather than pressure Germany explicitly to change the way it was handling the shock of reunification with East Germany, France chose instead to undergo a sympathetic travail of sluggish growth and rising unemployment, but stable prices. The unanticipated result has been to help make its German partner larger and stronger relative to France. By the mid-1990s it appeared that, rather than directing the course of European integration toward its own national self-interest, which had been the logic of French policy through the resignation of President de Gaulle in 1969, France found itself letting the course of European integration be determined by German initiatives. The valiant efforts of President Chirac, first elected in 1995 and re-elected in 2002 to redirect EU policies in favor of French economic interests, have failed repeatedly. French defiance of the Stability and Growth Pact, moreover, has undermined its moral authority to lead the EU politically. National economic policy will have to pre-occupy French political leaders until the problems of assimilating the large and

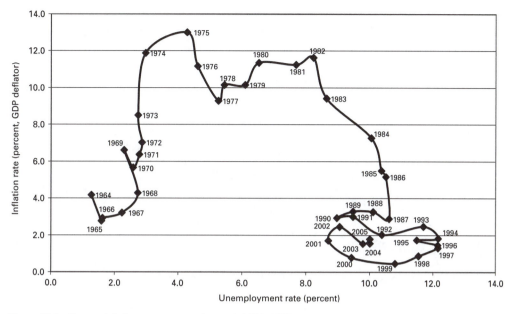

Figure 13.3 France: inflation versus unemployment, 1964–2005

growing immigrant population in the French labor force and of recovering competitiveness in international markets are overcome.

Figure 13.3 shows that the unemployment problem in France has stabilized at even higher levels than in Germany, with each reduction in overall inflation creating a new, higher plateau for the "natural" rate of unemployment. Figure 13.4 shows that low rates of inflation for France have not improved its competitiveness. Unlike Germany, moreover, French industry has not found investment in central and eastern Europe to be attractive. Imposing the *franc fort* policy on its former colonies in Africa, moreover, has simply increased the cost of imports. The solutions to French difficulties, however, can be found in the policies initiated in the 1980s by Margaret Thatcher in the United Kingdom. These are taken up in the next chapter.

Conclusion

As France confronts the domestic problems of increasing numbers of strikes and ever-rising rates of unemployment under the administration of President Chirac in his successive terms of office, it has come to regret some of the terms of the Maastricht Treaty. Those terms, set by Jacques Delors, a former Finance

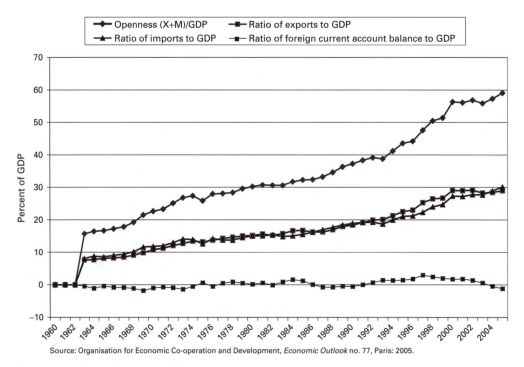

Source: Organisation for Economic Co-operation and Development, *Economic Outlook* no. 77, Paris: 2005.

Figure 13.4   France: foreign sector, 1964–2005

Minister of France, seemed very much in the long-term national interests of France. But the initial efforts of Chirac and Alain Juppé, his first Prime Minister, to initiate the labor market reforms necessary to comply fully with both the monetary policy of the common currency and the restrictions on fiscal policy ran into immediate resistance. Chirac's response, calling elections to give Juppé a parliamentary majority that would approve the reforms, backfired, as a Socialist majority was elected instead. The Socialists' attempt to solve the unemployment problem was to restrict further the hours of work for French labor to thirty-five hours a week.

This legislation, universally ridiculed by economists as resurrecting the "lump of labor" fallacy and resisted intensely by French business, was redolent of the forty-hour week legislation passed by the Popular Front government of France in 1936. That legislation persisted into the post-World-War-II period, and worked well during the "golden age" of economic growth that lasted until 1973 in Europe. But the collective memories of French voters failed to recall that Léon Blum's efforts to raise wages, reduce hours of work, and maintain fixed exchange rates had failed to revive the French economy before World War II overtook it.

Despite this analysis, the initial implementation of the thirty-five-hour legislation in January 2000 worked surprisingly well. In retrospect, part of the apparent success was the result of the initial weakening of the euro's exchange rate, which helped French exports, as shown in figure 13.4. More important, probably, was that the law at first applied only to firms with more than twenty employees, and those firms were allowed to apply the thirty-five-hour week on an average basis for the entire work year. This meant that employees could work more then thirty-five hours some weeks and fewer hours in subsequent periods. French employers welcomed the increased flexibility in the use of labor and put it to good use. After January 2002, however, the law was extended to firms with fewer than twenty employees. Smaller firms had less opportunity to shift regular employees around. The bad results for employment overall that economists had predicted from the outset then began to appear.

Economic historians can see the dilemma facing France as clearly, no doubt, as French politicians and voters see it. On the one hand, the European Union and its predecessors in economic integration have helped maintain peace in Europe between France and Germany for over fifty years – which marks a record for the duration of peace in Europe since the beginning of the military revolution in the sixteenth century. It seems vital to the national security of France to strengthen as much as is feasible the institutional arrangements that have provided this opportunity for continued economic growth and prosperity. On the other hand, these same fifty years have seen periodic social turmoil within France, episodes that have led to major changes of economic policy and political governance. It may be time for such an episode to occur again.

NOTES

1. The French franc was originally set at a par value of 119.107 francs to the US dollar on December 18, 1946, when France finally decided to join the International Monetary Fund. It insisted on not having a par value with the IMF from January 26, 1948, to December 28, 1958. In the meantime, however, its market value was kept at 350 francs per dollar from the devaluations of September 1949 until November 1957. Then, under the pressure of domestic inflation and speculative attacks on both the French franc and the British pound after the fiasco of their joint effort in 1956 to regain control of the Suez Canal in Egypt, the franc fell to 420 francs per dollar, a 20% decline. De Gaulle's economists carried out further devaluation such that the currency stood at 490 francs per dollar in December 1958. They also set the par value of the French franc with the IMF at 493.706 to the dollar at the end of 1958. Then, on January 1, 1960, they introduced the nouveau franc, with a par value of NF4.93706 to 1 dollar. Ultimately, this represented a 40% devaluation from the beginning of the war in

Indochina to the conclusion of peace terms with independent Algeria. From the end of World War II, this was a 315% rise in the value of the dollar relative to the French currency!

2. Stephen A. Resnick and Edwin M. Truman, "An empirical examination of bilateral trade flows in western Europe," in Bela Balassa, ed., *European Economic Integration*, Amsterdam: North-Holland, 1975, p. 63.

3. Christian Sautter, "France," in Andrea Boltho, ed., *The European Economy: Growth and Crisis*, Oxford: Oxford University Press, 1982, p. 454.

4. Harold James, *International Monetary Cooperation since Bretton Woods*, New York: Oxford University Press in conjunction with the International Monetary Fund, 1996, p. 271.

14 The United Kingdom: after Thatcher, what next?

Introduction

After a rocky start to its membership in the European Union, the United Kingdom has gradually moved up from being the fourth largest economy in the European Union to being the second largest by 2004. Throughout its erratic relationships with the European continent since the end of World War II, the United Kingdom has had a different perspective on economic policies from the majority consensus within the European Union. While taking the lead in organizing a European response to the Marshall Plan initiative in 1948, it was a reluctant participant in the European Payments Union in 1950 and abstained entirely from the European Coal and Steel Community. When the European Economic Community was formed in 1958 it was the United Kingdom that took the initiative to form an alternative group, the European Free Trade Association. This comprised seven countries around the borders of the six founding countries, and was seen as a viable alternative to the future of European trade relations during the 1960s. (Now it has only Iceland, Liechtenstein, Norway, and Switzerland as members.) When the United Kingdom finally abandoned the EFTA group and joined the EEC in 1973 the Bretton Woods system of fixed exchange rates had finally collapsed, and then the oil shocks of the coming decade started in October 1973.

During the successive oil shocks of the 1970s the United Kingdom gambled on developing its own petroleum resources in the hazardous North Sea area, while the Continental countries attempted to strike long-term contracts with various exporting countries within the OPEC cartel. After a brief period within the European Monetary System, from October 1990 to September 1992, the United Kingdom has maintained a flexible exchange rate policy toward the rest of the world, including its trading partners in the European Union. Since that time the British economy has consistently outperformed both the

Table 14.1 United Kingdom: basic facts

Area	244,820 km^2	6.2% of EU-25
Population (July 2005 estimate)	60,441,457	13.2% of EU-25
GDP (2004 estimate, PPP)	$1,782 billion	15.3% of EU-25
Per capita income (PPP)	$29,600	110.0% of EU-25 average
Openness ([X+M]/GDP)	58.4%	57% with EU-25
Birth rate (per 1,000)	10.78	Death rate (per 1,000) 10.18

Sources: Central Intelligence Agency, *World Factbook, 2005*, available at http://www.cia.gov/cia/publications/factbook; Statistical Office of the European Communities, *Europe in Figures: Eurostat Yearbook 2005*, Brussels: 2005.

German and the French economies in terms of economic growth, inflation, and unemployment. Since 1997, after Italy rejoined the European Monetary System so that it could join the first group of euro countries in 1999, the United Kingdom has outperformed the Italian economy as well. What accounts for this turnaround in economic fortunes? More puzzling, what accounts for the reluctance of the European economies to imitate at least part of the British example in economic policies?

To be in or not to be in? This question about their relations with Europe has plagued British policy-makers since the end of World War II. As the one major country in Europe that avoided domination by the Nazi war machine during World War II, the United Kingdom served both as the supply depot for American material support and as the launching pad for American military force against Nazi-occupied Europe. In this critical position, British leaders managed to play an equal role with their American counterparts in formulating Allied policies, from high politics (Churchill and Roosevelt) to military strategy (Montgomery and Eisenhower) to international finance (Keynes and Morgenthau). Following the war, however, the United Kingdom was in no position to play on equal terms with its superpower partner across the Atlantic. Two economic factors, one external and one internal, were to plague the United Kingdom for the next three decades.

Externally, British war finance created enormous debts, denominated in pounds sterling, that the United Kingdom owed to its sterling area trading partners in order to maintain British forces around the world and to supply vital materials to the war effort in Europe. Offsets to the debts were arranged with Canada, Australia, and South Africa; US aid came under the provisions of the Lend-Lease Agreement; but India and Egypt held large sums on account. Against total liabilities of over £3 billion (£1.7 billion to India, Burma, and the

Middle East) at the end of 1945, Britain had available less than £0.5 billion in gold and dollar reserves.[1] These reserves would have been lost immediately to the United Kingdom's creditors if the sterling balances could have been converted into gold or dollars at the exchange rate agreed on at Bretton Woods with the Americans (and the independent countries in the sterling area). Indeed, an American loan of $3.75 billion granted in 1946 on condition that the pound resume convertibility just on current account transactions was exhausted by mid-1947, within weeks of convertibility being allowed. The United Kingdom now needed more imports from the dollar area than from the sterling area, while the sterling area needed more imports from the United States than from the United Kingdom. So the result was that exporters throughout the sterling area turned in their sterling proceeds for dollars to pay for imports from the United States. Scarred by this episode, the British authorities became obsessed with exchange rate policy and available foreign reserves. They continued to block the sterling balances from being converted into dollars or gold, which meant keeping trade within the sterling area from becoming fully integrated within the multilateral trading system desired by the United States. Indeed, the blocked sterling balances were not fully eliminated until 1979, as part of the conditions for an IMF loan to Britain.

The internal problem stemmed from the promise of the wartime government that British labor would be paid for its wartime sacrifices by payments deferred until the war was over. This created a monetary overhang domestically as well. Eliminating it in the French fashion, by allowing rapid inflation, would have caused a rapid devaluation of the pound on the current account. This would have increased immediately the burden of the sterling balances, which had been pegged to the dollar and gold. Eliminating it in the Italian fashion, by financial repression on the financial sector, would have reduced its foreign exchange earnings, which were important for covering the United Kingdom's traditional deficit on trade. As a result, the wartime measures of price controls and rationing had to be continued until the early 1950s, with some lasting until 1954. These were the domestic counterpart of the blocked sterling balances to overseas creditors.

To ensure the ending of a war economy, British voters elected a Labour party government in the first postwar election. Labour immediately implemented its program of introducing the modern welfare state, characterized as "cradle to grave" insurance, and nationalized basic industries to ensure that workers continued to be employed and were not laid off in massive numbers, as had been the case after World War I. Only after Margaret Thatcher was elected

Prime Minister in 1979 was any concerted attempt made to undo national-ization or to limit the power of labor unions. Nationalization reduced the government's tax base while its commitment to extensive entitlements increased its peacetime expenditures. Labour's social policy therefore made British governments very aware of fiscal policy and its uses, while the use of price controls and rationing effectively ruled out paying much attention to monetary policy.

At first, the United Kingdom took the lead in organizing the European response to the US initiative of the Marshall Plan, and benefited correspond-ingly as the largest single recipient of Marshall Plan aid. But, under the Euro-pean Payments Union, the bulk of British trade proved to be with its former trading partners in the sterling area and with the United States, rather than with the other European members. This may help explain why it had no part in the Schuman Plan, much less the European Coal and Steel Community, which were entirely Continental enterprises. When the idea of forming the European Economic Community and Euratom arose, Britain continued to opt out, preferring to rely on its special relationship with the United States. These decisions must be seen in retrospect as stemming from British preoc-cupation with the perils of decolonization, which in the case of India and Egypt were complicated by settlement of the wartime sterling accounts, as well as reflecting the non-European orientation of British trade. While West Germany and Italy were recovering rapidly in the 1950s, France and Belgium were lagging, so it was not yet clear that British economic strategy was inferior to the European.

This did become clear during the 1960s, however, as the original six mem-bers of the EEC enjoyed continued high and smooth rates of economic growth, while Britain's growth rate continued to lag. Perhaps it was the low savings rate of the United Kingdom that kept its rate of investment down, and there-fore slowed the modernization of its industry. Perhaps it was the exceptional openness of the UK economy, which meant that any expansion of exports from devaluation was quickly offset by an increase in the price of imports and the cost of living; this led to increased wages and a loss of the devaluation effect in the price of exports. Perhaps it was the aggressive, undisciplined behavior of British labor unions, which called strikes at the least provocation to any craft in any plant, with no attempt to pay attention to broader interests in the way that national and industrial unions maintained labor peace on the Continent.

Whatever the diagnosis, it appeared that it would be better for the United Kingdom to have improved access to the European trade area. Even though the Common External Tariff against British exports was reduced as a result of the Dillon and Kennedy Rounds in the GATT negotiations, there would always be a price wedge between European and British goods and border controls that would disadvantage British manufacturers. So the United Kingdom made a belated application to join the EEC in 1963, only to be rejected because of President de Gaulle's hostility to the British (and American) vision of Europe's future. Even when a Labour government reapplied in 1967, France rejected its application. It was not until de Gaulle was replaced by President Pompidou in 1969 that British membership could be accepted. And then it took a Conservative government led by Edward Heath to renew the British application. By the early 1970s American preoccupation with the Vietnam War, and then its unilateral abrogation of the Bretton Woods system in 1971, ended the special financial relationship with the United Kingdom that the Bretton Woods Treaty had codified. This had the effect of making the Europeans much more receptive than previously to accepting UK membership. In 1973 it finally joined the EEC, along with two of its closest European trading partners, Ireland and Denmark.

Ironically, within a year of its joining the European Economic Community the first oil shock had occurred (the OPEC oil embargo of October 1973), and the fundamental differences in economic strategy between the United Kingdom and its European trading partners reappeared. While each European country formulated its own, specifically national, response to the quadrupled price of imported oil, only the United Kingdom and Norway had access to the one potential major source of crude petroleum in western Europe – North Sea oil. For Norway, having opted out of the British initiative to join the EEC in 1973 (although coming very close, as again in 1995), the strategy was clear. This was to invest heavily in offshore drilling platforms to tap the North Sea oil fields and to do everything to keep the price of oil high in the meantime, so as to ensure that the costs of developing the production facilities over several years could eventually be repaid. It did not take long for this to become the announced British strategy as well. Both countries benefited more than they lost, therefore, from the second oil shock in 1979, when OPEC doubled the price of oil.

But, until the second oil shock, the United Kingdom's investment in North Sea oil created more problems, because it had to finance the outlays while paying extraordinarily high prices for the necessary imports of fuel. The pound weakened against the dollar in 1976, raising the cost of imported oil further. A loan from the IMF was conditional on the United Kingdom finally unblocking the last of the sterling balances left from World War II. Inflation rose even more than in the Italian case and unemployment also soared. Despite an improvement in the British external accounts in 1977 and 1978, a series of labor disputes in the winter of 1978/9 brought general discontent to the country as a whole. In May 1979 a Conservative government headed by Margaret Thatcher was elected, and the Thatcher revolution was launched just as the second oil shock hit the industrialized world.

Thatcher was determined to limit the power of the unions, to privatize the basic industries that had been nationalized, to reassert British military power, and, in general, to undo the democratic socialist experiment that had begun in the United Kingdom after World War II. In her view, it had been given a fair test and had failed miserably. One element of this grand strategy was to win back concessions from the European Economic Community, which had become an increasing, if still relatively minor, drain on British finances. The United Kingdom had always recognized that adoption of the EEC's Common Agricultural Policy, which relied on price supports instead of income payments, would impose a net drain on the UK economy. The United Kingdom imported most of its food supply from abroad, although like the rest of postwar Europe it was less reliant on imports than before the war. Nevertheless, it would now have to impose the high variable levies of the EEC instead of finding the cheapest source of supply, say from Canada or New Zealand. To compensate for this, British negotiators insisted on expanding EEC expenditures on regional development projects for backward regions, including those affected by a declining industrial base (northwest England and south Wales, for example). The two oil shocks that followed UK entry into the EEC, however, also raised agricultural prices worldwide in addition to creating an industrial slump. This made the agricultural shortfall worse and exacerbated the problems of the United Kingdom's declining regions, so at first the compensation scheme did not work as hoped.

It proved impossible to change the CAP to British tastes, especially as both Ireland and Denmark benefited enormously from it. Thatcher insisted therefore on obtaining an explicit rebate on the United Kingdom's excessive net contribution to the EEC's budget. This caused much antagonism toward the United Kingdom, and prevented the UK government from taking an effective role in setting the rest of Community policy. Finally, in 1984, a permanent rule was agreed on for determining the size of the British rebate. This may have helped increase British influence in the EEC initiatives that followed: first came the agreement to enlarge the EEC to include Spain and Portugal (against the reluctance of France, Italy, and Greece); second, and more important, was the single market initiative in 1985. The United Kingdom's support for the Single European Act created a momentum that surprised both the Eurocrats and the British, leading as it did to the Treaty on European Union in 1992. UK cooperation with the EEC strategy culminated with the entry of the United Kingdom into the European Monetary System in October 1990, although this was motivated less by a burst of Euro-idealism than by an attempt to get the recurring problem of inflation under control by constraining the flexibility of the exchange rate. Ironically, entry into the EMS occurred just one month before Thatcher was eased out of office by her own party and replaced by her Chancellor of the Exchequer, John Major.

Under Major's leadership, the United Kingdom pressed for the rapid completion of the single market and expansion to include the states of central and east Europe as quickly as possible, in order to solidify their newly elected, democratic governments. In this it made common cause with Germany. However, it drew back on the Maastricht Treaty, withdrew from the European Monetary System in September 1992, and since then has fought a series of battles over EU initiatives. These have ranged from the terms of qualified majority voting with expansion of the Council of Ministers to include Austria, Finland, and Sweden to objections to the terms imposed by the EU for assisting the United Kingdom in dealing with mad cow disease. In each instance the United Kingdom has ultimately lost its case, thereby diminishing its influence in setting the course of EU policy for the future. Remaining out of the common currency has created further tensions, as fluctuations in the sterling/euro exchange rate have major effects on the competitiveness of British manufacturers, hurting them when the pound appreciates relative to the euro, or on the welfare of British consumers, hurting them when the pound depreciates relative to the euro.

The United Kingdom, with its extensive connections with its former colonies around the world and long-term concern about terrorist attacks, from the IRA since the 1970s and from Al Qaeda since 2001, is not a party to the Schengen Accord for ease of movement among EU countries. Moreover, the United Kingdom was the sole member of the European Union to not sign the Social Chapter when it was adopted in December 1989. After the election of Tony Blair as Prime Minister at the head of a Labour government in 1997 the United Kingdom did sign the Chapter. By then, however, the Social Chapter was understood to suggest minimum standards for the protection of workers' interests across the EU, while leaving implementation to national legislation. Harmonization, in other words, was not sought in the case of social and employment legislation, unlike other fields of EU law. In the case of capital, mention has already been made of the United Kingdom's continued resistance to the German and French desires to harmonize levels of taxation across the

EU. Only gradually has agreement been worked out on how to calculate the basis of corporate taxation; rates of corporate taxation are still at the discretion of the individual member states.

In its presidency of the EU during the second half of 2005 the United Kingdom did manage to open negotiations for the eventual accession of Turkey, and to hammer out eventually a budget perspective for the EU for the following seven years, 2006–2013. In particular with respect to the allocation of revenues and expenditures among the twenty-seven members expected to comprise the EU over the period of the financial perspective, the United Kingdom's role as the perennial outsider to the EU's initiatives proved useful. Blair offered a reduction in the UK rebate from contributions to the revenues of the EU if France agreed to a reduction from the expenditures of the EU on the Common Agricultural Policy, from which France is the largest recipient. France's refusal to bend on the terms of the CAP until 2013, however, allowed the United Kingdom to keep most of its rebate intact as well. Regional aid was capped per country according to specific limits depending on the size of a country's total GDP as well as the level of its per capita GDP relative to the EU average. Overall, the growth of the EU budget over time was projected to fall gradually as a percentage of the EU's total GDP, from 1.27% to 1.10%. The projected fall in the EU budget met the desires of the original EU-15 to limit the future role of the EU as an agent of redistribution from rich to poor countries; keeping the eventual level slightly above the 1% preferred by Germany helped assuage the disappointment of the ten accession states that they could not expect to be treated as generously by the EU as previous poor accession states had been.

Macroeconomic policy indicators: 1960–2005

Figure 14.1 shows the course of growth rates, inflation, and unemployment for the United Kingdom from 1960 to 2005. The growth rates of the 1960s were smooth and high by historical standards for the United Kingdom, but well behind those generally experienced on the European continent. Unemployment rates, likewise, were low by historical standards but still above those in the economic miracle leaders in the EEC. Moreover, inflation was definitely more of a struggle for British policy-makers than for West Germany or France, approaching double digits even before the first oil shock in 1974. This clearly hit the United Kingdom harder than it did any of the other large countries in Europe. Unemployment rates doubled, growth rates of GDP turned negative

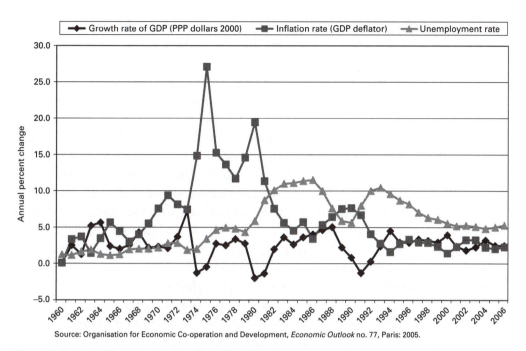

Source: Organisation for Economic Co-operation and Development, *Economic Outlook* no. 77, Paris: 2005.

Figure 14.1   United Kingdom: policy results, 1960–2005

for two years running, and the inflation rate peaked at a record 27% in 1975. Small wonder that the United Kingdom was a supplicant to the International Monetary Fund and had to meet the stringent terms imposed at the insistence of both the United States and West Germany.

It is interesting to note that the economic indicators were all improving in 1977 and 1978, despite the worsening political situation for the ruling Labour party. If the beginning of the Thatcher revolution was, in fact, the prime mover for these macroeconomic indicators in the years 1979–81, one would have to infer that it was a disaster. Inflation shot up again close to 20%, unemployment rates jumped, never returning to their pre-Thatcher levels, and growth rates turned negative once again. Of course, the full panoply of Thatcher economic reforms was not yet in place, or even begun as far as privatization and monetary policy were concerned. The second oil shock in 1979 and then the "Volcker shock" of 1980/1[2] were the dominant forces acting on the British economy, as they were on the rest of the European economies. The second oil shock, which doubled the price of oil, did not affect the United Kingdom directly, since it exported as much oil by then as it imported. However, it certainly reduced worldwide demand in general and demand for British exports in particular. Worse, the British suffered even more than the EMS countries because in 1980, when the EMS currencies and most of the rest of the world's currencies began to fall against the dollar, the pound kept on rising. This further reduced the United Kingdom's export competitiveness.

The recovery of the British economy from the double shocks inflicted by OPEC and the United States was more rapid and more effective than that of its European trading partners. Even so, it took time, and it seems doubtful, given the extra pain that the British had endured in Thatcher's first years in office, that the reforms she initiated would have been allowed to continue if she had not won re-election in 1983. Her re-election, in turn, was partly due to her ability, under the British system, to call for an election when popular opinion was still favorable due to the British victory in the war over the Falklands/Malvinas Islands off Argentina. Under Thatcher's continued leadership inflation rates fell sharply and leveled off close to their 1960s levels, while growth rates rose well above the 1960s rates by the late 1980s.

Eventually, even the double-digit unemployment rates began to decline, in contrast to the Continental experience, where they remained high. Confidence in the validity of the new policy regime rose even further as the United Kingdom seemed to be gaining more than the other large economies from the implementation of the single market program. The one, continuing, problem was the tendency for inflation to pick up with recovery in the economy. This has been the perennial problem facing UK economic policy-makers since the end of World War II, but it was especially frustrating that a determined policy to limit the growth of the money supply could not solve it. Thatcher finally relented under pressure from successive Chancellors of the Exchequer to try controlling inflation the way the French and Italians had – by joining the European Monetary System. The United Kingdom finally joined in October 1990.

This decision, coming at the same time that Germany completed its reunification, enabled the British economy to share fully the economic shocks of German reunification. Growth rates fell and unemployment rose, though inflation rates did fall as hoped. Only by withdrawing from the European Monetary System in September 1992 was the United Kingdom able to restore some measure of the healthy growth it had experienced at the height of the Thatcher era. And unemployment rates again began to edge down, as did inflation rates despite the absence of the EMS constraints on exchange rates. Small wonder that doubts and fears about the economic wisdom of joining in the European march to a common currency by 1999 were felt most strongly and voiced most loudly in the United Kingdom, and within the ruling Conservative party at that.

After the election of Tony Blair and the return to power of the Labour Party in the general election of 1997 the British economy remained on course, resulting in his re-election in 2001, and again for a third term in 2005. The main issue for Blair with respect to Britain's relation to the European Union was whether to join the euro, which would require re-entry into the European Monetary System. It appeared that Blair was committed to bringing the United Kingdom in, but only if the public approved the idea in a popular referendum. His Chancellor of the Exchequer, Gordon Brown, made the first step toward British entry into the common currency by immediately announcing that the Bank of England would have operational independence from the Treasury under the Labour government. Independence of the central bank is a prerequisite for any country desiring to join the eurozone, and the Bank of England had been under the direct control of the Chancellor of the Exchequer ever since it had been nationalized by the Labour government in 1945. Moreover, Brown then said that the only governmental expectation of the Bank of England was that it would keep inflation under control, which is precisely the mandate of the European Central Bank. Brown also made it clear, however, that he would not recommend the United Kingdom to join the euro until five criteria were met in addition to the United Kingdom meeting the five Maastricht criteria (discussed in chapter 6) that would allow the United Kingdom to join if it applied for membership.

Brown's five criteria were as follows.

1. Would joining EMU create better conditions for firms making long-term decisions to invest in the United Kingdom?
2. Would adopting the single currency make British financial services more competitive?
3. Are business cycles and economic structures compatible so that UK citizens and others in Europe could live comfortably with euro interest rates on a permanent basis?
4. If problems do emerge, is there sufficient flexibility to deal with them?
5. Will joining EMU help to promote higher growth, stability and a lasting increase in jobs in the United Kingdom?

Discussion in the United Kingdom ever since has focused on deciding whether any or all of these criteria were being met or, if not, would be met if the country did join the eurozone. A quick look at figure 14.2 makes it evident that the United Kingdom has always been able to meet the five Maastricht criteria under the Labour government, with debt/GDP ratios comfortably under the 60% limit and the deficit/GDP ratio also remaining under the 3% limit of the Stability and Growth Pact, unlike Germany, France, or Italy, at least until

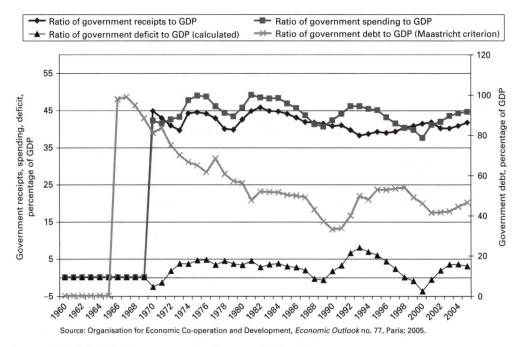

Source: Organisation for Economic Co-operation and Development, *Economic Outlook* no. 77, Paris: 2005.

Figure 14.2 United Kingdom: government performance, 1960–2005

the budget of 2005/6. Consequently, attention must focus on Brown's five criteria. Figure 14.1 shows that inflation remains under control in the United Kingdom at close to the rates achieved in Germany and France by the European Central Bank's monetary policy there. But the British pattern of unemployment and growth rates of GDP, the best indicators of business cycle movements, are clearly different from those in Germany, France, or Italy. Those three countries, however, have had similar patterns since joining the common currency, so one argument is that the United Kingdom's economy would fall into line as well once it joined the eurozone.

That raises the fundamental issues of inducements to invest, effects on the financial services industry, resilience to shocks, and, ultimately, whether the United Kingdom could meet the macroeconomic policy goals of high growth, low inflation, and low unemployment better under the administration of monetary policy by the European Central Bank than by the Bank of England on its own. By the end of 2005 it was clear that the United Kingdom continued to attract more foreign investment into its economy than either France or Germany, presumably because the tax rates on companies and regulations over company formation and employment were more favorable in the United Kingdom than on the Continent. While maintaining a fixed exchange rate with its dominant trading partners within the EU would probably add to these inducements for investment, there might be more pressure on the United Kingdom to raise corporate taxes and impose restrictions on its labor market if it joined the eurozone.

The United Kingdom's financial services industry has continued to thrive even while remaining outside the euro. Indeed, the banking sectors in both Germany and France are in the throes of more serious pressures to change their long-held business plans while British joint-stock banks continue to expand. Finally, while the United Kingdom has more flexibility in its labor markets and fiscal regime to respond to external shocks than is the case in Germany and France, there seems little cause to put those British institutions to the test within a monetary system that, to date (end-2006), shows little advantage to be gained for the United Kingdom.

From great power to withdrawal from east of Suez: 1945–57

While free from actual invasion during World War II and firmly allied with the United States in the final victory, the United Kingdom found the price of winning to be very high indeed. If it were to maintain its wartime equality with the United States in determining global strategy, it had to sustain a large military force in peacetime. Of course, the United Kingdom had to maintain equal standing with the United States in the occupation and control of defeated Germany. In addition, however, vital British interests ranged from Hong Kong in the Far East to Newfoundland in the North Atlantic, with especial focus on India and the sea routes between Britain and India. Of special concern to a naval power with no domestic petroleum sources was continued access to the oil reserves of the Middle East. Attempts to regain control, however, were resisted everywhere by nationalist independence movements that had gained momentum throughout the interwar period and now seemed to be erupting everywhere. Consequently, military expenditures remained extremely high despite the election in 1945 of a Labour government committed to the improvement of domestic living standards.

Part of the British response was to persuade the United States to take a bigger role in the protection of the Mediterranean sea lanes by coming to the support of anti-communist movements in Greece. In addition, the United States recognized the importance of maintaining the rights of exploitation to the Iranian oil fields, rights that seemed to be jeopardized by Russian troop advances to the north of Iran. But the major response had to be coming to terms with the independence movement in India, the crown jewel of the British Empire since the middle of the eighteenth century and the source of the majority of the United Kingdom's land forces. Trade with India was considered, rightly, as the primary economic asset to the United Kingdom of the sterling area. Not only did imperial preference grant British exports of manufactured goods preferred access to the huge Indian market, but the earnings from providing the necessary shipping, insurance, brokerage, and financing services to sustain the trade were a valuable source of foreign exchange earnings. The United Kingdom's overall surplus on the current account with India was hoped to offset its deficit with the United States and continental Europe, much as it had before World War I and again during the 1930s.

Providing political independence to Indian nationalists while maintaining the economic ties that had grown over two centuries meant reducing the drain on military resources that reasserting colonial control over a vast country would require while increasing the chances of restoring the United Kingdom's surplus on overseas transactions. Key to the success of this strategy was maintaining the inconvertibility of the sterling balances that the colonial administration of India had built up during the war. A gradual reduction of these debts would then be possible by means of resuming an export surplus with not only India but the entire sterling area, which included Australia and New Zealand as well as South Africa, Malaysia, Egypt, and the remaining British colonies scattered around the globe. But to make this strategy work required limiting the access of these traditional British customers to the now much-preferred American market. The most effective way of doing this was to make the sterling balances inconvertible save against specified transactions with the United Kingdom.

In fact, this strategy worked well for its immediate purpose. The United Kingdom quickly removed its import deficit, which had continued for a couple of years after the war due to the need to restock its industrial and distribution system for civilian goods, but it did so mainly by increasing exports to the sterling area in the late 1940s. The export surplus with the sterling area, however, only partially reduced the overhang of sterling balances accumulated during the war and immediately afterwards. It did nothing toward increasing the United Kingdom's reserves of gold or dollars. Without such reserves, it was in no position to play equal partner with the United States in the IMF or in financing the reconstruction of the rest of western Europe. The United Kingdom did earn some dollars and gold from limited exports to the dollar area and received huge sums first in the form of relief from the United Nations Relief and Rehabilitation Agency, the Anglo-American Loan of 1946, and the Marshall Plan. The United Kingdom, in fact, was the largest recipient of Marshall Plan aid. But it offset all this, and more, by capital exports. Some of the capital went toward the reduction of the sterling balances through trade with third parties, some toward building up British military establishments overseas, and some toward restoring British direct investments abroad. Rather than applying American aid directly toward rebuilding export capacity, as was the case with West Germany and the Netherlands, or toward restoring basic industries such as energy and steel, as was the case with France and Italy, the United Kingdom chose to use it to make the process of transition toward peacetime more gradual and less disruptive to the British people.

The sterling strategy – maintaining preferential trade arrangements between the United Kingdom and the former colonies while keeping sterling inconvertible with gold and the dollar – helped the British government maintain a sense of control over the twin processes of decolonization abroad and peacetime conversion at home during the critical five to seven years after the war. Both decolonization and conversion proceeded more gradually and with less political trauma for the United Kingdom than it might easily have had to endure otherwise. The pound sterling was maintained unchanged as the unit of account not only for the British economy but for the entire sterling area as long as the sterling area lasted (until 1958). Currency reform along either the French or West German models was avoided, as was Italian-style inflation. Colonies were lost, true, but without the United Kingdom's suffering casualties on the order that had become all too familiar during World War II. On these terms, which, after all, were paramount to British politicians, the strategy has to be judged a brilliant success.

It did have unfortunate long-term consequences, however, in separating the United Kingdom economically and politically from both the United States and Europe. British leaders constantly found themselves holding fast to untenable positions against either American or European initiatives and then yielding with bad grace and limited reward for the concessions made. When, in September 1949, it finally took the obvious step of devaluing the pound against the dollar, for example, it had to devalue the pound by fully 30%, from $4.03 to $2.80. But, with over one-third of its imports and nearly one-half of its exports with the sterling area and with most of western Europe devaluing by as much or more against the dollar, this translated into a mere 9% overall devaluation against the currencies of its trading partners. In coming into the European Payments Union, at the insistence of the Americans, the United Kingdom had to give up its network of bilateral agreements with each European country in which trade deficits beyond certain agreed limits were paid off in sterling.

Only when the United Kingdom, in effect, was allowed to act as the banker for the entire sterling area in its dealings with any of the European countries was it satisfied with the EPU arrangement. The British obsession with maintaining the preferred trading relationships within the sterling area meant continued resistance to US plans to liberalize trade patterns and reintroduce multilateral settlements of financial imbalances.

It also meant resistance to European initiatives for dealing with the dollar shortage. For example, the French and Germans devised the Schuman Plan without any thought of British participation. The immediate casualty of British intransigence was the American proposal for an international trade organization to oversee the removal of non-tariff barriers to trade and the reduction of tariff barriers. In its place, the makeshift arrangement called the General Agreement on Tariffs and Trade, begun in October 1947, continued to be the framework for international trade negotiations until the World Trade Organization finally superseded it in 1995. The United Kingdom was to pay a high price in later years for this early estrangement from the United States and Europe.

Domestically, the sterling strategy allowed the Labour government, elected in July 1945, to continue in power until 1951. By that time it had successfully completed a large part of its initial agenda, which was to implant the fundamental elements of democratic socialism into British society. Labour sought to do this first by enacting the basic elements of the welfare state as spelled out in the prewar Beveridge Report, which had recommended "cradle to grave" support of British citizens by the state. This meant, first, a national health system with access based on need rather than ability to pay, and then free universal education and benefits for unemployment, retirement, and death. The national health system was the only part actually installed that placed any demand on government spending during Labour's term in office. And that spending was exceeded by the agriculture and food subsidies the government continued from wartime in order to complement the "sterling strategy."

Agricultural subsidies were needed to decrease food imports and relieve strain on the balance of payments. Food subsidies were needed to placate labor demands for higher wages. In fact, real wages actually fell on average during the Labour government. The explanation for this paradox is that organized labor, represented by the Trades Union Congress (TUC), was willing to soft-pedal demands for higher wages in return for a commitment to the welfare state and acknowledgment of its power to organize at the plant level by individual trades. This created a fragmented and mutually competitive structure of labor unions, any one of which could strike and extract improved working conditions or emoluments for its members, who could be limited to, say, the machinists in a particular plant. The structure of British labor unions fragmented by craft and plant contrasted with the national and industrial unions that dominated in continental Europe. However, in these early years, British labor unions, faced with the daunting task of reabsorbing some 7 million members of the armed forces, were quite content to increase their membership base without insisting on higher real wages. Unfortunately for the future progress of British labor productivity, both the unions and the firms were also happy to expand output on the basis of traditional work practices and plant organization. Later, these practices became entitlements, and were used to resist the technical advances taking place rapidly in continental Europe.

Beyond establishing the welfare state, Labour's leaders were also determined to seize control of the "commanding heights" of the economy. Drawing on the lessons learned regarding government control of resources during the wartime mobilization, they sought to accomplish this by nationalizing the basic industries of the nation. They started with the Bank of England in 1946 and moved steadily on to coal, gas, and electricity by 1948, with rail and canal transport, telecommunications, civil aviation, and steel thrown in for good measure by the beginning of 1951. Once in formal control of these basic sectors, however, the Labour government seemed to have no particular objective, other than to provide ample employment opportunities and to keep prices of output controlled as part of the overall strategy to avoid inflation. There were no plans drawn up as in the French example to change the structure of the economy.

Overall, what the Labour government did accomplish was to expand output and employment rapidly, while keeping down the level of consumption. This allowed both investment and exports to expand, driving unemployment down to record lows and removing the fear of a balance of payments problem. Meanwhile, the government's budget tended toward regular surpluses, as tax revenues rose and the costs of the welfare state commitments proved to be ones for future generations rather than the present. This meant that successive Chancellors of the Exchequer increasingly saw the budget as a means of controlling the inflationary pressures on the economy by varying the size of the surplus. Deliberate manipulation of the budget surplus or deficit to control the state of the economy was initiated by Hugh Gaitskell, Labour's Chancellor of the Exchequer from 1949 to 1951. His policy was then continued by R. A. Butler, who succeeded him as the Conservatives' Chancellor in 1951. This fiscal tinkering to the exclusion of any grand strategy for the economic direction of the country received the derisive label of "Butskellism" from the *Economist* magazine.

The "sterling strategy" effectively terminated with the denouement of the Suez Crisis of 1956. This stemmed from the failed attempt to regain joint Franco-British control of the Suez Canal from Egypt following its nationalization earlier in the year by President Nasser. The military operation combined elements of the British, French, and Israeli armed forces in a joint exercise conceived by the British and French. It failed, and, worse, brought down on the French and British the opprobrium of both the Americans and the Russians, who had not been privy to the military plans and who felt that their military forces were being put to the test and possibly brought into nuclear conflict. In military disgrace, and with gold and dollar reserves rapidly draining away as foreigners withdrew their sterling deposits, the United Kingdom was forced to come to terms with US plans for restoring the convertibility of sterling, at least on current account transactions, as a condition for receiving support from the International Monetary Fund. The French proceeded to strengthen their European connection without further dealings with the United Kingdom by moving the European Coal and Steel Community into the next phase of economic integration, the European Economic Community. Meanwhile, however, British unemployment remained low and economic growth continued at its decorous pace. The last of the rationing controls on consumer food products had been lifted in 1954, and by 1959 the Conservative Prime Minister, Harold Macmillan, could honestly claim in his successful re-election campaign "You've never had it so good."

Opportunity keeps knocking: 1958–73

The next fifteen years, however, were destined to shake British confidence in its postwar strategy. The war-torn economies of Europe had started their rapid recovery from a much lower base than in the United Kingdom, so economic planners assumed that their pace of growth would slacken off as they regained the prewar levels of output and per capita income, perhaps falling to the British rates. Instead, the members of the EEC continued to grow rapidly, enjoying what came to be termed the "golden age" of economic growth until 1973. Meanwhile, British growth continued at its sedate pace of the 1950s. The result is shown clearly in figures 14.3 and 14.4. Both use the OECD's base of 2000 US dollars in their purchasing power parity exchange rate with a given country to compare the United Kingdom's level of gross domestic product and per capita income with that of Germany, France, and Italy for the period 1960 to 2005 (the figure for 2005 is the OECD's estimates made in the middle

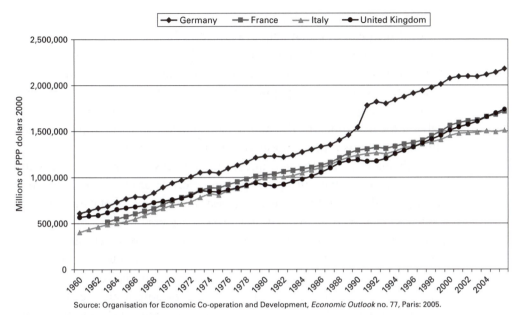

Source: Organisation for Economic Co-operation and Development, *Economic Outlook* no. 77, Paris: 2005.

Figure 14.3   GDP levels compared, 1960–2005

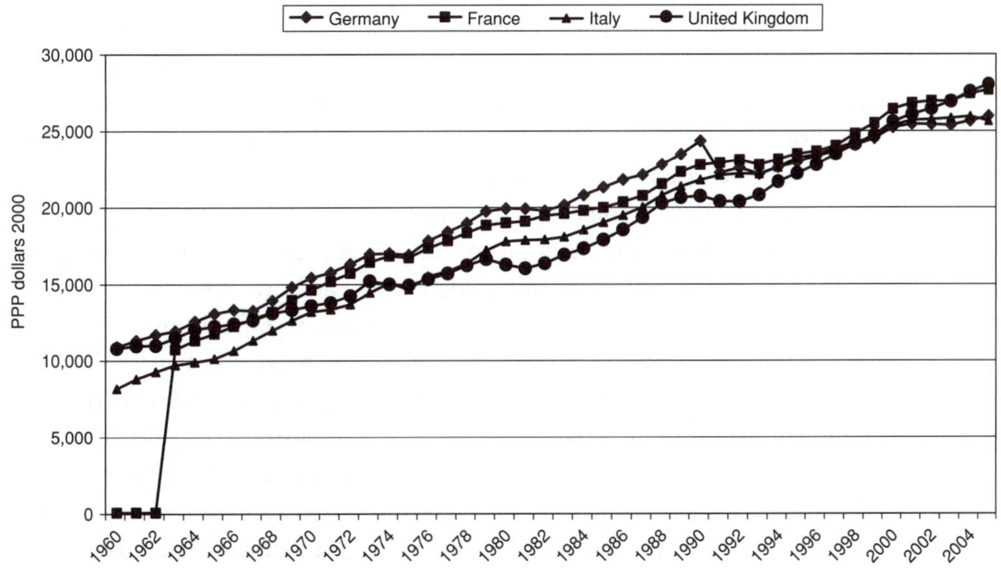

Source: Organisation for Economic Co-operation and Development, *Economic Outlook* no. 77, Paris: 2005.

Figure 14.4   GDP per capita compared, 1960–2005

of 2005, which was probably too optimistic for all four countries). In 1960 the United Kingdom's total output was already below that of West Germany, then it fell below that of France in 1970, and even that of Italy by 1979. The relative decline was even more dramatic in per capita terms, given the United Kingdom's faster growth in population. Barely behind West Germany in 1960, the United Kingdom's GDP per capita fell below France in 1966 and below Italy for the first time in 1977, and remained below all three from 1979 until after the breakup of the European Monetary System in 1992.

Much analysis has gone into uncovering the reasons for the United Kingdom's relative decline during the period before entering the EU. The first suspect was the relatively low level of investment relative to total output in the United Kingdom compared with the growth leaders on the Continent. This gave a very satisfactory explanation for the country's relatively slow growth during the 1950s and continued to be the favorite villain for British policy-makers through the 1960s, even as the close relationship between ratios of investment to output and the rate of growth of output among the OECD countries began to dissolve. Some even persisted with it during the 1970s, when it had disappeared completely.

The consensus in the most recent research is that the United Kingdom's rate of investment was not so much to blame as the low productivity of its investment. The low productivity of the new capital, in turn, has been attributed to the large proportion of it coming from the public sector, especially in housing and in the nationalized industries, which seemed more interested in maintaining large numbers of employees than in increasing productive efficiency. But, even in the private sector, new investment proved less productive than in West Germany or France. The conjecture here is that the fragmented structure of British labor unions and the ability of each small craft union to protect the jobs of its members by preserving out-of-date work rules prevented the new equipment from being used most efficiently. This made it difficult for even American or Japanese firms to achieve the same levels of productivity with their new plants built in the United Kingdom that they were able to reach in their home country. Economic historians have also drawn attention to the likelihood that investment in human capital in the United Kingdom was misdirected.[3] Lacking the intensive government- and business-supported apprenticeship programs of West Germany and the northern European countries, the United Kingdom could not match the productivity of their labor in specialized, small-scale production. Lacking the business training programs that supply skilled managers to US corporations, the United Kingdom could not match the productivity of American and Japanese firms in mass production.

Recognizing the power of export-led growth in the cases of both West Germany and Italy, the United Kingdom took the initiative in founding the European Free Trade Association to widen the European market for its own export industries. This combined the United Kingdom's traditional trading partners – Ireland, Portugal, Denmark, Norway, and Sweden – with the neutral countries in central Europe, Austria and Switzerland. A loose combination of countries, with three neutrals and four members of NATO, EFTA had no ambitions for political integration arising from economic integration. Rather, each country agreed to remove its tariffs on industrial imports from any of the other member countries. But each maintained its own tariff schedule against imports from other countries. US policy-makers were displeased at this obvious rebuff of multilateral trade relations by thirteen of the sixteen countries it had introduced to the advantages of multilateral clearing in the European Payments Union, following on from the Marshall Plan. They had to be content with the restoration of convertibility of each country's currency based on fixed exchange rates, which by itself allowed the multilateral clearing of trade imbalances regardless of the differences in trade barriers. Through another round of negotiations on tariff levels in the GATT, called the Dillon Round, the United States was able to extract the commitment by the members of each trade grouping that the average of their new tariff against the rest of the world would be no higher than the original average tariff. The hope remained, then, that reducing some of the tariff barriers within Europe would increase trade and lead to further tariff reductions as the advantages of more liberal trade became apparent.

Looking at the map, the seven countries formed an outer ring around the inner six countries constituting the EEC. All thirteen countries continued to be members of the Organisation for European Economic Cooperation, the European organization for administering the Marshall Plan funds, and then the European Payments Union. This organization had little of its original functions left to justify its existence, but the United States was now left out of all European economic policy discussions in addition. In 1960 the OEEC was formally dissolved and replaced by the OECD, the Organisation for Economic Co-operation and Development, made up of the sixteen European members of the OEEC plus the United States and Canada. It remains the main international organization for policy discussions among the rich industrial nations of the world, some of which may lead to policy coordination. More likely, such discussions may lead to some degree of policy convergence as alternative policies to counter similar problems are compared regularly and systematically. In this context, the British could keep closely informed of the increasingly obvious success of the EEC participants and the relatively lackluster performance of their own economy and that of their EFTA partners. Not only had the EEC countries caught up with the United Kingdom, as anticipated in the 1950s, they were now moving steadily past.

Concern about the relatively slow pace of British growth had already started to influence British policy-makers in the late 1950s, especially after the Suez debacle. In addition to the "fine tuning" of the demand side of the economy in the short run through fiscal policy, the Conservative government made an explicit effort at improving the long-run supply-side performance of the economy as well. Until the early 1960s, however, these efforts were limited to more vigorous action against the restrictive marketing practices that had become endemic in the United Kingdom since the rationalization movements in British industry in the 1930s. The Restrictive Practices Court (RPC), set up in 1956, managed to eliminate overt price-fixing arrangements throughout UK industry. Instead of leading to price competition that might have forced increases in productivity, however, it appears that the RPC simply encouraged the development of other means of market control. For example, trade associations were very effective in disseminating information on the market shares of firms, which could be used to monitor informal agreements. A second form of supply-side encouragement came in the form of government finance to achieve higher levels of research and development expenditures than in West Germany, France, or Italy. However, these were mostly for very expensive military projects with nuclear energy and supersonic aviation, which did nothing for industrial productivity.

Impressed by the evident French success in stimulating rapid industrialization, the Conservatives initiated a British version of "indicative planning" by setting up the National Economic Development Council (NEDC) in 1962. Lacking even the access to government-directed finance that the Commissariat du Plan enjoyed in France, however, the NEDC was unable to put any force behind its recommendations as to how to raise the rate of economic growth. In fact, the first "plan" proposed by the NEDC, in 1963, calling for a target of 4% annual rates of growth over the next three years, was quickly followed by a deflationary budget in 1964. This showed clearly that Conservative economic policy was still more focused on demand management to maintain the fixed exchange rate of the pound. Moreover, as the achievement of this goal seemed to require keeping down the pressure of rising wages on the rate of price inflation, the indicative planning efforts of the NEDC were accompanied by calls for a stronger "incomes policy." The idea was that increases in wages might be held down but the share of wages in national income could remain the same by agreeing that non-wage incomes would not rise any more rapidly. The TUC naturally objected that, while union contracts could enforce the wages part of the incomes policy, there was no comparable mechanism for keeping other incomes under control. Moreover, they wanted to increase the share of wages, not just keep it constant.

In 1964 the Labour Party, headed by Harold Wilson, came back to power, determined to make economic planning a success and, like the Gaullist regime in France, raise real wages as part of the social dividend from achieving higher rates of growth. Figure 14.1 shows how badly Labour failed, as growth rates, while positive, fell off and unemployment edged up. The basic problems that had confronted the Conservative government remained unsolved by the increased vigor of the Labour government. On the macroeconomic level, the problem was an increasingly overvalued exchange rate due to a fixed rate for sterling and higher rates of inflation in the United Kingdom than in its major trading partners.[4] This steadily reduced the market share for the United Kingdom's exports while increasing imports, so that the resulting adverse balance of payments again became the primary policy issue. On the microeconomic level, wage bargains struck with the TUC had to be offset with increased entitlements or increased power for the individual unions. In the short run, this raised expectations in the financial markets of future inflation, inducing speculative movements out of sterling. In the longer run, this reduced incentives to raise labor productivity by the reorganization of shop-floor practices much less than by increasing capital stock. In November 1967 the pound was at last devalued against the dollar, from $2.80 to $2.40.

The delay in devaluation was due to a dangerous combination of pride, presumption, and pragmatism. The pride lay in maintaining the role of the pound sterling as a reserve currency for the remaining countries staying in the sterling area, now reduced by the withdrawal of India and Argentina, but still including the former African colonies, Hong Kong, Malaysia, and Australia. As long as these countries and colonies maintained their deposits the United Kingdom had a credible claim to maintaining a major role within the IMF, second only to that of the United States. If official holders of sterling thought it would be devalued, however, it was feared the deposits would be withdrawn quickly. Such a run on sterling also concerned the Americans, whose gold stock was now less than the sum of dollars held by foreign central banks. Because a run on sterling might have created a spillover run on the dollar as well, US support for the pound was often forthcoming.

Moreover, there was a presumption among British economists and politicians that monetary policy would have little or no effect on the economy, even if it were freed of the constraint to keep the exchange rate fixed. The Radcliffe Commission was set up in 1959 to examine the British financial system and to assess the benefits of adopting West-German- or Italian-style monetary policy. It reported that the complex British system of specialized banks, other financial intermediaries, and sophisticated capital markets made it impossible for the Bank of England to control domestic credit expansion in the way that the Bundesbank or the Banca d'Italia was able to do.

Finally, the pragmatism lay in the realization that devaluation would immediately raise the overhang of the remaining sterling balances, while any advantage in increasing exports or decreasing imports would take one to two years to be realized. As it happened, the devaluation regained export competitiveness for the United Kingdom very quickly, and the United States and IMF provided overwhelming credit lines to the United Kingdom to defend the pound at the new parity, so no adverse consequences occurred on the capital account. The dangers of inflation breaking out with the devaluation were forestalled successfully by imposing wage and price freezes across the board at first, and only gradually relaxing them to allow wage increases in line with rises in the cost of living and in productivity. Pride was maintained, while the presumption was undermined, and pragmatists appreciated the value of capital controls.

Decolonization continued to completion as Britain withdrew its forces first from east of Suez and then from Cyprus and Malta. (Gibraltar remained the last British base in the Mediterranean, much to the continued chagrin of the Spanish.) This helped reduce British military spending to more sustainable levels, a consideration that became increasingly important as the costs of the welfare state, set up immediately after the war, now began to mount and mount. It also cast the United Kingdom clearly as a junior partner of the United States in the Western alliance, which did not bother the Labour government particularly when it came back into power in 1964. But dealing with the United States as supplicant during the successive balance of payments crises became increasingly expensive, especially as the expenses of the Vietnam War began to take their toll on the US balance of payments. One way to offset the diminished role of sterling as an official reserve asset for foreign central banks was to encourage the development of the eurodollar market in London. This helped restore the leading role of London bankers in the finance of international trade, even if most of that trade worldwide was now invoiced in dollars rather than in sterling. Eurodollars were simply deposits of dollars made in non-US banks and kept on account as dollars. The advantage to depositors was that the accounts were free from the restrictions placed by the US authorities on US bank practices, such as interest rate ceilings and withholding taxes on interest to be paid overseas. The eurodollar market developed rapidly in London after 1964. The other offset, pursued by both Labour in 1967 and Conservative governments from 1971 on, was to open up the European Economic Community market to British exporters, while subjecting British labor unions and management to healthy competition from the Continent.

The negotiations with the EEC were protracted and at times seem destined to failure, as the United Kingdom seemed determine to hold onto the advantages of the sterling area as it saw them while France was determined to maintain the methods of operation that had been developed within the EEC. Eventual compromise was reached by the United Kingdom extracting a commitment from the EEC to broaden its eligibility requirements for backward regions to receive Community aid, so that regions with low per capita incomes as a result of an industry becoming uncompetitive and declining would be eligible for assistance in addition to regions with low per capita incomes as a result of having no industrial base. This would bring EEC aid, it was thought, into declining industrial regions in the north of England, especially Lancashire, and into southern Scotland and south Wales. The hope was that enough regional subsidies would be forthcoming to offset what clearly would be net outpayments to the rest of the Community for food imports. These would now bear a high variable levy if imports continued from the sterling area and the United States or a high price if they came increasingly from within the Community. Other member states could see that they might also have regions that could become eligible for aid under the new, broadened criteria, and so the British proposals were accepted.

The other concession of sorts that the United Kingdom extracted was to broaden the membership of the African, Caribbean, and Pacific countries, so that the poorest of the sterling area countries and colonies could continue to enjoy preferred access to the British market and now to the rest of the European market in addition. New Zealand, however, didn't qualify as a low-income country, so final concessions were extracted to allow continued imports of New Zealand butter and lamb for the five-year transition period allowed for full compliance with the Common Agricultural Policy. The Common External Tariff, however, had to be imposed around the British market within four years. As it turned out, commitments of EEC resources to the price support system of the CAP were allowed to expand over the next decade, which limited the possibility for expanding regional aid, much less foreign aid, to the less developed countries now included in the ACP countries. All these concerns, however, were put aside over the next decade as much more pressing problems confronted the United Kingdom and the other members of the EEC than the distribution among them of the EEC's modest resources.

A shocking period: 1974–85

The negotiations for entry into the Common Market coincided with the end of the fixed rate regime of the Bretton Woods era, which was terminated by the United States in August 1971 when President Richard Nixon ordered the Federal Reserve System to stop selling gold to foreign central banks, especially those in France and West Germany. At home, the Conservative government of Edward Heath was under constant challenge from the labor unions, the strikes of which always seemed to bring a new round of pay increases. Drawing on the lessons of the 1967 devaluation, the United Kingdom let the pound float in 1972, assuming that it would fall relative to the dollar and to the European currencies and so stimulate exports. It did fall, but exports did not rise, while prices and wages did. To keep imports from rising too rapidly, the Heath government tried its hand at an incomes policy. The unions agreed to keep wage demands moderate so as not to push up prices, but only on condition that if prices did start rising rapidly they would be free to catch up. The threshold chosen was 7%; a rise in the retail price index greater than that would trigger a wave of wage increases greater than 7% by an amount equal to the shortfall of wages behind prices that had accumulated to that point. The effect was that the United Kingdom entered the Common Market in 1973 pursuing much the same line of policy as Italy at the time, providing accommodative financing by the central bank to allow nominal wages to rise as much as the price level. As in the Italian case, this made the United Kingdom very vulnerable to the first oil shock, and made the shock of entering the Continental system even harder.

The first-round effect was the same as in the other countries: a sudden, sharp rise in both unemployment and inflation. In the British case, however, the inflationary shock was exacerbated by the Heath government's income policy, because the threshold of 7% was quickly exceeded. The Labour government that came to power in March 1974, thanks to the support of the labor unions, naturally supported the catchup wage increases that followed. Given the continued indifference of both Labour and Conservative governments to any thought of controlling the growth of the money supply, these wage increases were readily financed by the banking sector, supported by the Bank of England's policy of keeping interest rates low. So the rise in inflation rates for the United Kingdom far exceeded that in the rest of western Europe, reaching a high of 27% in 1975. Fiscal policy was also lax, as first Heath and then Labour after the first election in 1974 had weak positions in Parliament, so they kept spending high and taxes steady. Accommodative monetary policy combined with loose fiscal policy in this case did nothing for unemployment rates, which also rose. The excessive inflation rates forced the floating pound to slide even further relative to both the US dollar and the European currencies. This encouraged speculative attacks on the pound, forcing it lower still. IMF assistance was limited in the amount it could offer and even then would be conditional on the United Kingdom's adopting an anti-inflationary policy.

Even though the United Kingdom was formally a member of the EEC at this point, the conditions of entry had factored in four- to five-year transition periods for switching fully to the Common Agricultural Policy or to the Common External Tariff. The shocks of adjustment to the Continental way of doing things were not yet a factor, but it was clear they would only make economic conditions worse in the short run. Consequently, Labour held a referendum in 1975 asking British voters whether they approved of the United Kingdom remaining in the European Economic Community on the terms negotiated by the Conservative government. Two-thirds approved. So the remaining way out of the oil shock quandary for the Labour government was to stake everything on developing the North Sea's oil-producing potential as quickly as possible. To make this pay off, however, required that oil prices remain at least as high as the OPEC cartel had raised them; the costs of exploiting offshore wells in one of the stormiest seas in the world were enormous. Consequently, the United Kingdom's interests with respect to dealing with the OPEC cartel were directly counter to those of the European oil importers.

By the end of 1976 the costs of importing the construction materials for North Sea oil facilities had increased the pressure on the balance of payments and the value of the pound to the point that IMF assistance was required. The conditions, as foreseen and already anticipated by the British government, were to impose a more anti-inflationary budget but also to remove exchange controls on capital account transactions. This meant freeing up the blocked sterling balances that remained from the end of World War II. As anticipated, they were rapidly withdrawn. Fortunately, North Sea gas exports began to appear in 1977, and oil exports in 1978. These helped reduce the deficit on the current account that might otherwise have occurred, but deficits still existed. Nevertheless, the pound stabilized, and even began to strengthen on the basis of strong capital imports.

The cause of these gyrations in the exchange rate of the pound remains an interesting issue for economists. A favorite explanation is that investors anticipated the higher interest rates and future export earnings from North Sea oil, which in fact did occur in 1979–81. But economic historians emphasize that the root causes of these phenomena – the second oil shock in 1979 and the Volcker shock in 1980 – could hardly have been anticipated in 1977.[5] A more plausible explanation is that removing restrictions on foreigners' deposits in the British financial system made the London capital market that much more attractive as a place for OPEC countries to deposit their excess profits. The eurodollar market was a natural focal point for this activity. The British government helped by putting a dollar guarantee on their new bonds. Even though denominated in sterling, their higher interest rates made them an attractive alternative to US government bonds. Whatever the cause, the pound strengthened and official reserves began to rise once again in the late 1970s.

With the external pressure off the government, the labor unions now struck for catchup pay increases. Resistance to these demands led to the fall of the Labour government and the election in May 1979 of a Conservative government led by Margaret Thatcher. Thatcher's term as Prime Minister was extended by two successive elections, in 1983 and 1987, until the end of 1990, when internal Conservative Party opposition to her domination of proceedings forced her to step down. These eleven and a half years of power made her the longest-serving Prime Minister in British history since Lord Liverpool, after the Napoleonic Wars. But her place in history will be determined less by the length of her term than by the depth of the changes in British society wrought by her economic policy. Her determination was to remove government regulation and interference as much as possible from the decision-making considerations by British producers and consumers so that markets for goods and services, capital and labor could function more efficiently. Toward this end, the first step was to get inflation under control by restricting the growth of the money supply. Later steps required denationalizing the nationalized industries and introducing privatization and market incentives into as much of the public sector as possible.

The beginning of the Thatcher era was shocking, to say the least, and not at all auspicious for the future of the government. Unemployment rose sharply, soon hitting the then unimaginably high figure of 2 million out of work, and then moving on to put a full 3 million on the dole. The growth rate of the economy was actually negative for two successive years, 1980 and 1981.

Inflation rose to nearly a record high in 1980. Even the pound began to decline relative to the dollar again in 1981. All the indicators of British macroeconomic performance that had obsessed governments from 1945 on deteriorated in the first two years of the Thatcher era. Nevertheless, her economic policy remained committed to reducing inflation by controlling the rate of growth of the money supply. True, her economists dithered over how to measure the money supply, and the announced targets were regularly exceeded. But, bad as things were, they seemed no worse than the travails being endured at the same time by the rest of western Europe. North Sea oil was now in full production and contributing larger and larger amounts to the current account.

By 1982 the worst was over for the United Kingdom, and recovery began to show up in renewed rates of growth, while inflation seemed to stay under control. No progress was made in terms of reducing unemployment, which continued to rise, but in comparison with the continued slow growth in the rest of western Europe the British did not look so bad, and they certainly were not doing as badly as they had become accustomed to doing in relation to France and West Germany. The success of British forces in the Falklands/Malvinas War of 1982 renewed British pride and no doubt helped re-elect Thatcher and the Conservative government in 1983. Without this kind of extra-economic boost to Thatcher's popularity it is quite possible that she would have been defeated, even if she had postponed holding the next general election to the end of a full five-year term, in 1984. Even then the effects of her reforms would not have had time to show up in increased rates of productivity and rising rates of growth. It was precisely this long lag time required for institutional changes to take effect coupled with the requirement to have new elections at least every five years that had inhibited previous Conservative Prime Ministers from initiating fundamental reforms. It also explains why the Thatcher reforms have not been speedily imitated by other industrial democracies.

After Thatcher's re-election came the Trade Union Act in October 1983, which was intended to break the power of trade union leaders by requiring them to subject their decisions on strikes or political contributions to direct vote by the union membership. The coal miners struck in 1984 to test the resolve of the Thatcher government and to rally other unions to their support. They failed on both counts, although the battle lasted for a year. The failure of the miners' strike meant that henceforth much of the ability of British labor unions in general to limit the reorganization of work practices and the effective use of labor-saving technology was dissipated. As British investment rates rose over the rest of the 1980s, so did the total factor productivity of

British manufacturing. Overall, the United Kingdom stopped falling behind the rest of western Europe and actually began catching up with France and West Germany, as figures 14.3 and 14.4 show.

This supply-side effect of Thatcher's economic policy was reinforced by a commitment to privatizing as much of the nationalized industries and the public sector as possible, starting in 1984. Although this could not be done systematically or quickly, given the entrenchments of at least forty years, eventually gas and electricity were privatized, then waterworks, as well as coal and steel, aviation, and telecommunications. In most cases, the revenues from the sale of the enterprises were used to reduce the government debt or income taxes, while expenditures in the future were no longer burdened by the need to subsidize inefficient and overstaffed operations. Unemployment rose as a result, but customers and taxpayers were satisfied with the results on the whole. Of course, objections were raised that regulators were allowing the prices charged by the utilities to rise too much to benefit the new shareholders and penalize the customers, or, conversely, that prices were being kept too low to benefit customers at the expense of shareholders. As privatization was usually carried out by giving the customers preferred purchase rights to the shares, however, the customers and the shareholders tended to be the same people. Consequently, losses suffered in one role were offset on average by gains in the other. Overall, improvements in the quality of the infrastructure encouraged private industry to increase its productivity further.

Thatcher's policy with respect to the EEC was also controversial. She fought incessantly with the other heads of government at the semi-annual meetings of the European Council over most initiatives being proposed. Eventually she won a sizable rebate from the Community in recognition of the United Kingdom's substantial net payment into the Community's coffers despite its having a lower per capita income than some of the net recipients (see chapter 4 for a discussion of the British rebate in the EU budget). In return, she allowed the Commission to expand in size by allowing each new member to have at least one commissioner. But she was also one of the prime movers in promoting the single market initiative in 1985, as it was consistent with her overall philosophy of reducing the amount of government regulations and the imposition of additional transactions costs on the operations of markets. When the momentum from the single market initiative was carried on by the Commission to the Delors Plan, which eventually culminated in the Maastricht Treaty of 1993, she raised stern objections. Both the common currency and the additional responsibilities that would be given to the EEC's supranational authority in foreign and social policy were anathema to her vision of revitalizing the British economy by freeing its markets of excessive government regulation and interference.

Only part of the European Union: 1986–2006

The renewed vitality of the UK economy in the early 1980s was achieved while the United Kingdom remained out of the European Monetary System. Initially, this made sense, because the United Kingdom had become a net oil exporter by the end of 1978. Since oil was invoiced in dollars, it would be to the United Kingdom's advantage to see the dollar strengthen relative to the pound, because then the oil earnings in dollars would have more purchasing power for extinguishing British liabilities denominated in pounds sterling. The interests of West Germany, France, and Italy as large net oil importers were exactly opposite. As it turned out, the combination of the second oil shock and the Volcker shock greatly improved the United Kingdom's situation with respect to the balance of payments, as reserves accumulated rapidly. The exchange rate, after strengthening relative to the dollar in 1978–80 as expected from the second oil shock, then weakened in common with the rest of the western European currencies during the Volcker shock of the early 1980s, even as the export surpluses continued from North Sea oil. When the third oil shock occurred in early 1986, however, the price of oil fell sharply and the British balance of trade began to weaken. Initially, however, the pound strengthened relative to the dollar even as it weakened relative to the deutsche mark and the currencies of the rest of the EMS countries. As part of the US-led effort to stabilize exchange rates in the late 1980s, the pound stabilized with respect to both the dollar and the deutsche mark. By 1990, as the balance of trade began to improve again, the United Kingdom seemed to be prepared to try anything to keep inflation from cropping up again. This finally led Thatcher to agree to commit the pound sterling to a fixed parity with the deutsche mark and the rest of the participating currencies in the Exchange Rate Mechanism of the EMS. If this move had convinced foreign investors that Italy had a credible commitment to stable prices, surely it would convince them of the United Kingdom's commitment! However, like Italy, the United Kingdom was now fully vulnerable to the economic shock caused by German reunification.

As a result, like Italy, the United Kingdom was forced to leave the Exchange Rate Mechanism and the EMS in September 1992. On the positive side, however, again like Italy, the United Kingdom's sharp devaluation of the pound sterling relative to the currencies of its primary trading partners in the EU created an export-led recovery and a resumption of higher growth rates than in France and Germany. The exit of the United Kingdom from the EMS occurred as the discussions over the ratification of the Maastricht Treaty were preoccupying western Europe. John Major, who had brought the United Kingdom into the EMS in October 1990 as the Chancellor of the Exchequer under Thatcher, was now her successor as Prime Minister. Reluctant to damage relations with the EU in the way that Thatcher had enjoyed doing, he argued for the British Parliament to ratify the treaty. To make the treaty more palatable to the Conservative Party, Major had negotiated an agreement that the United Kingdom could opt out of the Social Chapter of the treaty. This part of the treaty would have required the United Kingdom to harmonize its labor union legislation with that of the rest of the EU. Moreover, by withdrawing from the EMS in 1992 before ratification of the treaty, he was holding open the options for the United Kingdom of whether and when to rejoin the EMS as it progressed toward the treaty's objective of European Monetary Union.

Parliament approved, narrowly, and Major won re-election in 1992, again narrowly. In the meantime, British unemployment rates began to fall once again as the growth rate of the economy picked up. From an economic point of view, the British had the best of the economic worlds available to members: full access to the markets of the fifteen-member European Union for its exports, investors, and workforce, but, thanks to floating relative to the deutsche mark, avoiding the economic costs from the shock of German reunification. For foreign firms seeking access to the enlarged single market and the possible extension of it into central and east Europe in the near future, this meant that the United Kingdom was the preferred location for setting up distribution and manufacturing centers. So the United Kingdom became the fortunate recipient of increased foreign direct investment as well as being able to maintain its attractiveness for foreign portfolio investment in British securities. As the elections of 1997 came into view, both parties seemed content to continue this state of affairs as long as possible.

As demonstrated in figures 14.3 and 14.4, the Thatcher reforms helped the British economy during the 1980s start to catch up again with the other major economies of the EU, until the German reunification shock after 1990. By being in the EMS just when the full effect of the German reunification shock hit the European economies the United Kingdom once again managed to suffer from bad timing, exactly as it had first joined the EEC immediately

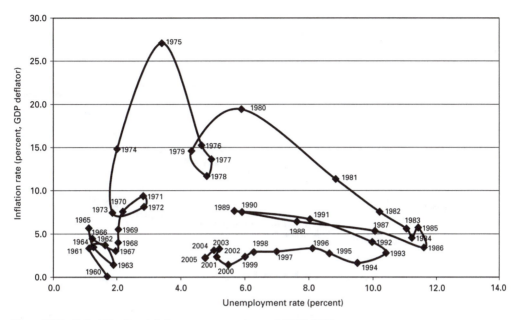

Figure 14.5 United Kingdom: inflation versus unemployment, 1960–2005

prior to the first oil shock hitting all industrialized economies. In retrospect, however, the United Kingdom's humiliating exit from the EMS in September 1992 turned around British fortunes. Ever since then British GDP has risen relative to the other three major economies in western Europe, and British per capita income actually became the highest of the four in 2005. Even the Labour government that took power in 1997 did not undo the Thatcher reforms, say by renationalizing any of the companies that she had privatized. Moreover, the monetary policy followed by the Bank of England, with its new-found independence, has kept UK inflation within range of the eurozone inflation rates.

The exceptional performance of the UK economy during its resurgence from 1992 to 2005 shows up most clearly in its labor market. Figure 14.5 highlights that the famous "Phillips Curve," which owed its origin to the evident tradeoff between inflation and unemployment rates in the historical experience of the United Kingdom, disappeared after the Thatcher reforms took full effect. Unemployment at first was very sensitive to reductions in the inflation rate during the 1980s, and continued to respond excessively to the minor reductions in inflation rates needed at the beginning of the 1990s to keep the pound sterling exchange rate fixed with the appreciating deutsche mark. Since 1993, however, the United Kingdom has managed to keep domestic inflation quite

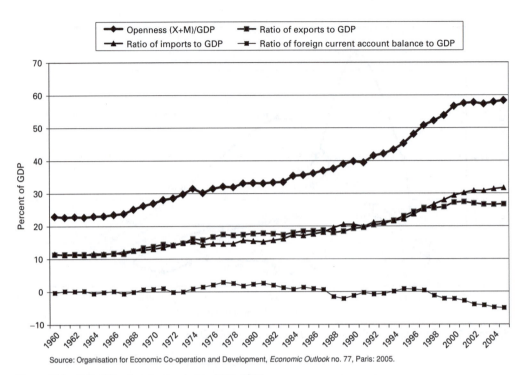

Source: Organisation for Economic Co-operation and Development, *Economic Outlook* no. 77, Paris: 2005.

Figure 14.6   United Kingdom: foreign sector, 1960–2005

stable while reducing unemployment to much lower levels than in Germany or France. The British experience, in short, vindicates the argument of the European Central Bank that Germany and France need labor market reforms to reduce their unemployment rates rather than higher inflation.

Conclusion

Today, as for most of its history, the United Kingdom is not really sure if it is better to be part of Europe or to be separate from Europe. Clearly, now that it is part of the European economy to a much greater extent than since the seventeenth century, it is better off economically. But the United Kingdom may not be clearly better off politically if it supports the Franco-German architectural design for the Continent in the twenty-first century. This dilemma between support for the economic goals and resistance to the political ambitions of France and Germany came out clearly in the United Kingdom's internal conflict over joining the European Monetary Union. There the economic gains seem clear but minor, whereas the political gains, or losses, are not at all clear but may be major. The question remains, however: if the British exceptionalism in economic institutions continues to work better for its economy, why do Germany and France continue to resist adopting the Thatcher economic reforms and continue to disparage the Anglo-American model of market economies?

Some of the answer may lie in the difference in the foreign trade patterns of the United Kingdom, shown in figure 14.6. Recall as well that the relative importance of the EU-25 for UK foreign trade (57%) is less than for either Germany (65%) or France (67%). But the crucial difference lies in the relative importance of the growth of exports in the respective economies. The United Kingdom's economic success, starting in the 1980s and interrupted only by the brief experience with the European Monetary System at the beginning of the 1990s, did not depend on export-led growth. Indeed, as the importance of foreign trade has leveled off for the United Kingdom since 2000, it has begun to run larger import deficits – which would be anathema to France and Germany. Thanks to a flexible exchange rate with the eurozone, the UK economy can now adjust to these trade deficits with a depreciation of the pound, if the deficits cannot be financed otherwise. As has turned out consistently since the Thatcher reforms took hold, however, the United Kingdom's trade deficits are easily financed by continued imports of capital, much as has been the case with the US economy since the Reagan reforms there at the beginning of the 1980s. As a result, the pound/euro exchange rate has held rather steady despite the rising import deficits on the current account.

NOTES

1. Leslie Pressnell, *External Economic Policy since the War*, vol. I, *The Post-War Financial Settlement*, London: HMSO, 1987, p. 413.
2. The Volcker shock refers to the decision in 1980 by Paul Volcker, head of the Federal Reserve System in the US, to focus on restricting the growth of the US money supply to the exclusion of other monetary goals. The result was a sudden skyrocketing of US interest rates, which both strengthened the dollar on foreign exchanges (increasing the effect of the second oil shock on oil-importing countries) and plunged the US economy into a sharp, if short, recession.
3. Steve Broadberry, "Technological leadership and productivity leadership in manufacturing since the industrial revolution: implications for the convergence thesis," *Economic Journal* 104, 1994, pp. 291–302.
4. The real exchange rate between any two countries is calculated by deflating each currency by the price index in that country. To find the real price of the pound sterling in terms of deutsche marks, for example, one should divide the "real" deutsche mark, DM/P_{DM}, by the

real pound, $£/P_{UK}$. Rearranging, one multiplies the fixed nominal exchange rate, DM/£, by the ratio of price indexes, P_{UK}/P_{DM}. Therefore, if the price level in the United Kingdom rises relative to that in West Germany, the real exchange rate of the former has risen, making its exports less competitive compared with those of the latter.

5. James Foreman-Peck, "Trade and the balance of payments," in Nicholas Crafts and Nicholas Woodward, eds., *The British Economy since 1945*, Oxford: Clarendon Press, 1991, pp. 141–79.

15 Italy: political reform versus economic reform

Introduction

Since the German reunification shock in 1990 Italy has been more concerned about changes in its political system than in maintaining its leading role in the development of the European Union. As a consequence, when the lira was attacked by foreign exchange speculation in September 1992 Italy withdrew from the European Monetary System and allowed the lira to float. The substantial devaluation that resulted helped renew Italy's exports, especially to its trading partners in the EU, producing a much more satisfactory economic performance, especially in the industrial north, than in Germany and France – until Italy rejoined the EMS at the end of 1996. Since then, however, Italy has been plagued by sluggish growth and continued high rates of unemployment, which have made political reforms more difficult. Coalitions led either by Romano Prodi, Prime Minister when Italy returned to the EMS in 1996, or by Silvio Berlusconi, Prime Minister briefly in 1994 and then again from 2001 to 2006, have differed in their approaches to both political and economic reforms.

The main economic problem facing Italy is the cost of servicing its huge public debt, which reached the equivalent of 122.7% of its gross domestic product by the end of 1994 and was estimated at around 120% in 2005. While the Italian government has run substantial surpluses in its primary government budget since 1992, the high interest charges on the existing stock of debt means that the overall budget continues to run in substantial deficit, well over the 3% guideline set by the Maastricht Treaty and the limit set by the Stability and Growth Pact.

Political differences between the coalitions led by Prodi and Berlusconi continue to thwart various initiatives designed to reduce the government deficit. In the fall of 1996 Prodi introduced a stringent budget designed to bring the

Table 15.1 Italy: basic facts

Area	301,230 km^2	7.6% of EU-25
Population (July 2005 estimate)	58,103,033	12.7% of EU-25
GDP (2004 estimate, PPP)	$1,609 billion	13.8% of EU-25
Per capita income (PPP)	$27,700	103.0% of EU-25 average
Openness ([X+M]/GDP)	58.2%	60% with EU-25
Birth rate (per 1,000)	8.89	Death rate (per 1,000) 10.30

Sources: Central Intelligence Agency, *World Factbook, 2005*, available at http://www.cia.gov/cia/publications/factbook; Statistical Office of the European Communities, *Europe in Figures: Eurostat Yearbook 2005*, Brussels: 2005.

Italian deficit under 3% GDP by January 1, 1998. He also proclaimed his intention to bring Italy into the European Monetary Union with the first group of entrants in 1999. Toward this end, he managed to put the Italian lira back into the Exchange Rate Mechanism of the European Monetary System at a very favorable exchange rate compared to the level in 1992 (see chapter 5). As a result, Italy joined the euro in the first group in 1999, and ever since has enjoyed low inflation but suffered slow growth and continued high unemployment (see figure 15.1).

Perhaps as a consequence of the reduced rates of growth and continued high unemployment, Prodi's Olive Tree coalition failed to withstand the Forza Italia coalition reconstituted by Silvio Berlusconi, who became Prime Minister again in the election of 2001. Eventually Berlusconi's government managed to put through a reduction in future pension obligations for government employees, but put off its effective date to 2008. The potential benefits of reduced pension obligations on this score, however, were largely offset by the government's willingness to absorb pension obligations from state-owned enterprises when they were privatized. A constitutional reform designed to strengthen the powers of the Prime Minister in the future was narrowly passed by the Italian legislature in 2005, but the opposition party has threatened a popular referendum to nullify it before it becomes effective. These political uncertainties have a long history in Italy, as illustrated by Berlusconi's second term, which started in 2001 and lasted till mid-2006, making him the longest-serving Italian Prime Minister since the end of World War II.

Italy, for all its ancient ruins and vestiges of Roman glory, is one of the newest nation states in Europe. Unification of the entire peninsula under one democratic government was not achieved until 1861. The longest-lived government since then has been the Fascist regime of Benito Mussolini, lasting from 1922 until his overthrow and execution in 1944. Much of the Fascist economic legacy remains in Italy, in the form of the massive state holding companies. The largest is the Istituto per la Ricostruzione Industriale (IRI), which includes as its subsidiaries not only manufacturing companies in the basic industries but also the national shipping company (Finmare), the national airline (Alitalia), the telephone company (Telecom Italia), the toll roads, and major banks. Comparable in influence is the Ente Nazionale Idrocarburi (ENI), which in addition to holding the monopoly on petroleum has extended its operations into petrochemicals and electricity.

It was obviously imperative to break up and privatize these holding companies, first, to improve their competitiveness and efficiency and, second, to reduce the drain on state finances, both by ending the requirement to subsidize them and by giving the government one-time reductions in its stock of debt. Over time, the state holding companies had gradually stagnated, becoming overstaffed and uncompetitive as political pressures forced them to provide opportunities for political patronage while remaining largely protected from economic pressures to perform efficiently.

The first tranche of 14.7% of ENI was sold to the public in 1995. Over the next two and half years three additional tranches of shares, amounting to 63% of the capital stock, were sold to the public. The €21 billion obtained was the largest amount received by any European government for privatization at that time. Part of ENI's success was due to its offering employees first chance at the shares. As the values rose with each successive offer, participation by employees rose as well, from 40% for the first offer to 70% for the fourth offer, in 1998. An additional 5% of the capital stock was sold to institutional investors in 2001, which reduced the government's share to just over 30%.

The privatization of the diversified holdings of IRI, by contrast, has not proceeded as easily. Most of IRI's holdings accumulated during the troubled 1970s were politically motivated bailouts, a process that continued in the 1980s, especially when Romano Prodi was its chairman, from 1982 to 1989. After Italy had been forced out of the EMS in September 1992, however, it was clear that the Italian government could no longer subsidize the numerous enterprises encompassed by IRI. At least 12% of the government's deficit was due to covering the losses of IRI. The enterprise was incorporated in 1992, which forced it to reduce its ratio of debt to equity under Italian civil law to 0.89:1 from the previous level of 13:1. The EU Commission also required Italy to withdraw state subsidies. Prodi returned as chairman, this time to preside over the painful process of gradual privatizing the various enterprises, piece by piece. Finally, in June 2000, IRI was liquidated. By then, its former companies made up 40% of the market capitalization of stocks traded on the Milan Stock Exchange. As of the end of 2006 the main outstanding enterprise that was once part of IRI that remains to be privatized is the state-owned (63.5%) airline, Alitalia.

Despite its recent difficulties, Italy was one of the first western European economies to experience export-led growth after World War II. Its medium-sized manufacturing firms, predominantly located in the north, have maintained export competitiveness in consumer goods. Its high-fashion goods for both men and women are well known, but its exports also include furniture, kitchen appliances, and upscale linens. Its success gradually transformed Italy from a source of migrant labor for the rest of western Europe in the 1950s to a net immigration country by the end of the 1970s. Despite being heavily dependent on imports for fuel and most raw materials, Italy has managed to record a net current account surplus for most of its postwar history. The surplus has been due to varying combinations of expanding exports, emigrants' remittances, and tourist expenditures.

The export success of Italy is even more remarkable for the generally inflationary environment created by its loose monetary policy, which lasted from the 1960s to rejoining the EMS in 1996. Recurrent bouts of inflation occurred as the deficit spending of the central government had to be accommodated by the Banca d'Italia, which until the 1990s was under the formal control of the Minister of Finance. It has to be said, however, that the recurring deficits did manage to maintain the Christian Democrat Party as the majority partner in most of the coalition governments formed until 1993. Despite the frequent changes of governing coalitions, Italy's underlying power structure was remarkably stable until the early 1990s. Then, evidence of pervasive corruption produced by crusading prosecutors determined to uproot the control of the Mafia in the south of Italy led to a widespread consensus that political reform was required. A series of reforming governments has ensued, dominated by central bankers (Carlo Ciampi, the governor of the Banca d'Italia, was chosen as the first caretaker Prime Minister, and Lamberto Dini, his successor, also became a caretaker Prime Minister), a successful businessman and proponent of free-market policies (Silvio Berlusconi, owner of several television networks and the leading soccer team in Italy), and even an economics professor (Romano Prodi). The prevalence of economically knowledgeable men as political leaders in the 1990s is striking, and indicates the high priority placed on economic reform. Moreover, the scandal in 2005 over the role of the Banca d'Italia in preventing a Dutch bank from buying out a leading Italian bank led to the resignation of Antonio Fazio as governor of the Banca d'Italia.

A striking feature of Italy's postwar economic arrangements has been the persistent efforts to improve the economic level of the south of Italy, the Mezzogiorno, as the region south of Rome is called. Since 1951 the Cassa per il Mezzogiorno has spent an average of 0.7% of Italy's measured GDP on a variety of development projects, intended to raise the standard of living of the southern Italians closer to that of the northern Italians. By the end of the 1980s, although per capita income had risen substantially in the south, it was still only 55% of the northern level – exactly as it had been in 1950, when the Cassa was formed. Moreover, it was clear that the financing of this effort came basically from the more prosperous north in the form of higher tax revenues and increased issues of government debt, which were held mainly in the north. Finally, it appeared that the south had become structurally dependent on state transfers, which were used to reinforce the patron–client relations that formed the basis of the Mafia's power. The two endemic problems of the Italian economy – the rising indebtedness of the central government and the persistent backwardness of the Mezzogiorno – were mutually aggravating.

That this situation could persist until the 1992 political reforms cannot be explained solely by political intransigence. A favorite explanation provided by economists is the rise and pervasiveness of the informal economy in Italy. Tax avoidance, evasion, and outright corruption are seen as part of the Italian national genius. Estimates of the importance of the informal, or unregistered and therefore unmeasured, economy range as high as 25 to 30% of the measured gross domestic product – a ratio far higher than in any of the northern EU economies. The economic incentives are clear for both northerners and southerners. The northerners wish to avoid paying taxes for which they see no comparable benefit in public services; the southerners wish to avoid appearing more prosperous and losing their entitlements to government transfers. Ironically, if the informal economy is included in measures of Italy's GDP, the government deficit is reduced considerably, and so Italian economists have argued they are close to meeting the Maastricht criterion of a deficit of under 3% of GDP!

The importance of the informal economy also, however, helps explain the political acceptance of the reform of the *scala mobile* in August 1992. The *scala mobile* indexed wages to the rise in the cost of living. As rising wages were a major cause of future rises in the cost of living, this system locked Italy into an inflationary process that was incompatible with maintaining a fixed exchange rate with the deutsche mark. So the rate was first frozen, and then amended so that it rose less than the cost of living, by the amount that labor productivity increased. By 1996 this had worked well to keep wage inflation down, but workers were becoming upset that actual inflation kept outstripping the estimated inflation rates used to calculate wage adjustments.

Moreover, years of political patronage for government employees and employees of the state holding companies had resulted in huge pension obligations. Not only did these imply further increases in the government's budget problems if they were not refinanced somehow, they also impeded the privatization of state enterprises, the pension obligations of which would presumably be sold with them if the state was to get any advantage at all. The pension problem for Italy, in common with all advanced industrial countries, is bound to become worse as the population ages. Beginning in the 1990s Italy's rate of natural population increase turned negative, with more people dying each year than being born.

In view of all these problems, Italy's main concern with EU policy is to maintain its preferred access to the internal market and to use the external pressures of EU directives on conditions for monetary union, competitiveness, and agricultural reform to push through much-needed economic reforms against domestic political resistance. The resistance of the central bank governor, Antonio Fazio, to allowing an Italian bank to be taken over by either a Dutch or Spanish bank in 2005 was in direct violation of EU directives about allowing competition of financial services within the single market. Despite the independence of the Banca d'Italia from the Italian government, the EU directives on financial services and competition enabled the Italian government to force Fazio's resignation. Modernizing Italy's financial sector and allowing foreign capital to enter on favorable terms is important if the remaining economic reforms are to succeed.

Macroeconomic policy indicators: 1960–2005

Figure 15.1 shows the performance of the Italian economy since 1960 in terms of growth rates of GDP, inflation rates, and unemployment rates. Until 1971 Italy was one of the star performers in the high-growth league of continental Europe. Unemployment rates, while high by French and West German standards, were stable and concentrated in the Mezzogiorno, which was seen as economically backward. Beginning in the late 1960s, however, wage pressures built up in northern Italy, leading to serious strikes and to wage inflation, which was accommodated by the Banca d'Italia. Hit heavily by the two oil shocks in the 1970s, Italy managed reasonable rates of growth only at the expense of very high inflation rates. Even these, however, failed to protect it

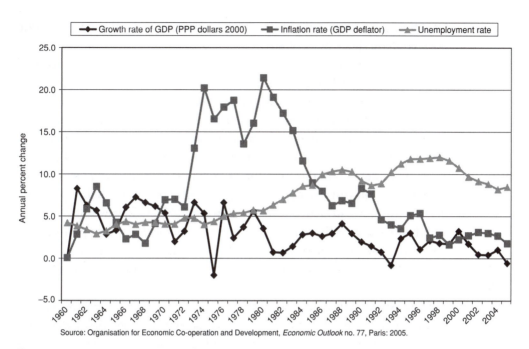

Source: Organisation for Economic Co-operation and Development, *Economic Outlook* no. 77, Paris: 2005.

Figure 15.1   Italy: policy results, 1960–2005

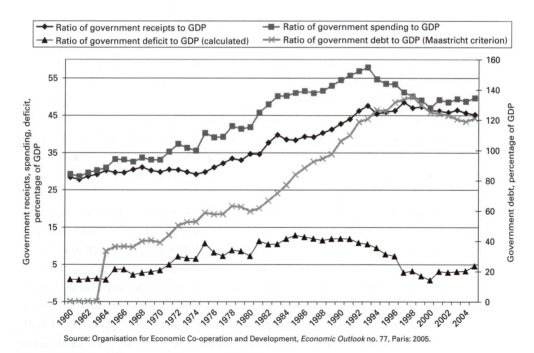

Source: Organisation for Economic Co-operation and Development, *Economic Outlook* no. 77, Paris: 2005.

Figure 15.2   Italy: government performance, 1960–2005

from the decline in growth rates and rise in unemployment that occurred with the second oil shock of 1979/80.

The 1980s, until the German reunification shock of 1990, saw reduced inflation rates and higher unemployment rates, with growth stabilizing at reasonable rates. The downward course in inflation rates was interrupted for a couple of years, partly because of a surge of capital imports, beginning early in 1990, when Italy tightened its commitment to the EMS by narrowing its exchange rate band to +/− 2.25% from the previous +/− 6% it had pledged since 1978. Removing this amount of exchange rate risk while still paying high interest rates on its large stock of government debt made Italian portfolio investments very attractive to other Europeans, including wealthy Italians, who had been investing their export profits abroad for years (part of their tax evasion genius). Nevertheless, Italian growth kept declining as import demand from its EU customers fell off in response to the German reunification shock.

The crisis for Italy culminated in September 1992, when its efforts to maintain its central par rate with the strong franc and deutsche mark exhausted its reserves of foreign exchange. Jointly with the United Kingdom, Italy abandoned the EMS and let the lira float to its equilibrium level in the foreign exchange markets. The financial uncertainty, combined with the political uncertainty as more and more Italian politicians were indicted on charges of corruption, actually resulted in negative GDP growth in 1993. But, from then on, the competitive advantages regained by Italian manufacturers as a result of the devalued lira led to sustained growth rates of GDP. While nowhere close to the economic miracle rates of the 1960s, they were enviably higher than the levels achieved by Germany and France. Nevertheless, unemployment rates remained high, as expanding firms found it much safer to hire additional labor in the informal market than to incur the heavy liabilities of fixed wages, heavy social security contributions, and dismissal restrictions for labor hired in the formal market.

After rejoining the EMS at the end of 1996 and participating as one of the founding members of the common currency starting in 1999, Italy's economy has suffered declining rates of growth and sustained high rates of unemployment. Meanwhile, the demands on the government of paying out pensions and unemployment benefits have forced both deficit and debt ratios higher, as shown in figure 15.2. Berlusconi's initiatives in 2004 to decrease tax rates in an effort to stimulate the economy encountered opposition, given the return to deficits. Likewise, his proposals to reduce the constraints on firms from dismissing employees were defeated, for fear that they would simply increase the burden of unemployment benefits to the government. And his proposals to decrease pension payouts have been watered down and delayed to 2008. It is no wonder, given the political constraints on his economic proposals, that Berlusconi has been one of the strongest critics of the restrictive monetary policy of the European Central Bank. Even his arch-rival, Romano Prodi, condemned the Stability and Growth Pact's limit of 3% on government deficits while he was President of the European Commission.

Because France and Germany are Italy's biggest customers, there has been a natural tendency for Italy to associate itself with any initiative the two major powers agree upon for the future course of the EU. Italy's internal divisions between north and south, however, epitomize the contrast between the interests of the poor countries on the periphery of the EU, which benefit from the diversion of cohesion and structural funds toward them, and the interests of the rich countries in the heart of the EU, which must pay for these transfers. If the Northern League political party, which wishes to undo the 1861 unification of Italy, were to succeed in dividing Italy into two countries, for example, the rich north would have 122% of the average per capita income of the EU and would be by far the wealthiest country in the EU. By contrast, the poor south would have less than 70% of the average per capita income of the EU-15 and would be as poor as Ireland, Greece, Portugal, and Spain on average – and would be entitled to at least one-quarter of the cohesion funds. If the rest of the EU were to take the lessons of Italy's history to heart, however, they would seek to limit as quickly and firmly as possible the use of cohesion funds as an instrument of political assimilation, much less as a means of economic development. The more recent example of Germany's failure to bring East Germany up to the per capita income levels of West Germany, combined with Italy's experience, helps account for the restrictions placed on EU redistribution funds in the budget proposed for 2006–2013.

From bilateralism to multilateralism: 1945–63

Italy emerged from World War II in much the same condition as West Germany, in that its distribution network and consumer production facilities were devastated by wartime destruction and overburdened by the return of refugees and demobilized soldiers. As a result, its per capita income was perhaps half that before the war, and some estimates put it as low as the 1900 level. Also like West Germany, its producer goods facilities, especially in engineering products and transport equipment, had been greatly expanded during the war by the Fascist regime. Even with the destruction imposed by bombing and demolition by the warring armies, the total capital stock available was probably only 8% less than in 1938, while in the engineering sector it may have been as much as 50% greater, even allowing for wartime losses.[1] The basis for postwar industrial expansion was thus similar to West Germany's: a modern industrial plant available for conversion to consumer goods once it could be staffed and provisioned, and markets had been opened up. Unlike West Germany, however, it was not permanently divided by the Allied powers, although the country had been physically divided during the last two years of the war. The reunification of the country took place immediately, rather than forty-five years later, as it did in Germany. This required immediate attention to "making both ends meet," in the felicitous phrase of Ferruccio Parri, the Prime Minister in 1945. In retrospect, it might have been better for Italian long-run growth prospects to have delayed dealing with the backward part of the country, as in the German case.

Another major difference from West Germany was that there was no currency reform in Italy. The currency continued to be the prewar lira, and Italy joined the International Monetary Fund with its exchange rate pegged at 100 lira to the dollar. This was a substantial devaluation from its prewar value of 19 to the dollar, but it still did not take sufficient account of the tremendous increase of currency issued during the war. Not only the Fascist government of Mussolini, during the active participation of Italy in the war, but also the revolutionary government during the civil war that followed his fall from power relied primarily on seigniorage, the creation of new money, to finance their military expenditures. This practice continued after the war as the peacetime governments confronted the need to re-establish national unity and create legitimacy for the new republic. One estimate suggests that the Italian money supply had increased fifteen-fold in the seven years from 1938 to 1945. Most of this increase came in the form of notes, which rose from 57% of the total to over 70%.[2] In the next two years the money supply increased at even faster rates, as prices were liberalized and commercial banks began to expand their loan operations, which leveraged up the increase in note issue into even larger increases in deposits. The official rate of the lira was raised from 100 to 225 to the dollar at the end of 1946, reflecting the rapid inflation that had taken place.

In May 1947 a new government headed by the Christian Democrat Alcide de Gasperi came to power. De Gasperi immediately made the governor of the Banca d'Italia, Luigi Einaudi, his Deputy Prime Minister and Budget Minister. In this position, Einaudi was able to enact legislation that permitted the central bank to exercise control both over the emission of new money and the banking sector's ability to expand deposits. The key was to impose effective reserve requirements on the banks for the first time. By September 1947 Einaudi had increased these to 25% of deposits. Henceforth, the government could continue to run deficits (which it did relentlessly), but instead of financing them by issuing notes it could now finance them by issuing short-term debt. Banks could count this as part of their reserves, and typically preferred holding government debt to notes because the debt earned them interest, usually at high rates. So most of the government's new debt was sold to banks rather than to the public.

Banks continued to expand their loans on the basis of their increased reserves, but now at a much reduced rate, because 25% of any deposits created had to be backed by legal reserves in addition to the cash reserves they kept on hand to meet fluctuations in withdrawals. This "Italian monetary arithmetic" allowed the government to continue deficit spending, and both the central bank and the banking sector to expand the money supply, while keeping inflation at modest rates and stabilizing the exchange rate of the lira. This had been devalued by Einaudi in August 1947 to 350 lira to the dollar. In September 1949, when a general devaluation of European currencies occurred, he devalued the lira again to 625 to the dollar. There it remained until the problems of the 1960s.

In trade developments, Italy quickly found it had a comparative advantage with the rest of western Europe in engineering products and transport equipment, as well as chemicals and clothing. By 1961 production of these had all expanded dramatically, creating an export-led growth miracle for Italy. This was directed mainly toward western Europe (60%), and especially toward its partners in the EEC after 1958 (30%). Export earnings helped finance the growth of imports as well, composed mainly of food and raw materials at first, and then fuel in increasing importance during the 1960s. Despite clear evidence of export-led growth, however, Italy routinely ran a deficit on trade in goods and services. This was more than covered, typically, by growing tourism expenditures and, especially, emigrants' remittances. For the rest of western Europe, in these early years, Italy's true comparative advantage was in tourist sites and migrant labor. The returns from these "invisibles" on the current account led to a remarkable increase in Italy's foreign reserves. From barely $26 million at the end of 1947, when Einaudi's reforms began to take hold, they had expanded to $4.6 billion at the end of 1961.[3]

The Marshall Plan played an important role in focusing Italian policymakers' attention on critical investment programs and in strengthening the economic liberalism of the early Italian governments. De Gasperi had been disappointed in early 1947 when he went to the United States in person to seek aid specifically for Italy. It was on his return in May that he shook up his Cabinet by replacing left-wing ministers with more conservative types, bringing in Einaudi as Budget Minister and Deputy Premier among others. Marshall's speech came the next month, and Italy was an eager participant in the resulting European Recovery Plan. In response to the American request for specific plans for using the grants, the Saraceno Plan was devised between the summers of 1947 and 1948. It focused on productive investment in heavy industry and infrastructure, much like the Monnet Plan in France. The intent was to position Italy for competing effectively in the forthcoming liberalization of European markets. It specifically anticipated restricting the growth of consumption. While the plan had even less force behind it than the Monnet Plan in France, a comparison of its projections to 1952 and the results actually achieved by the end of the Marshall Plan indicates that its goals were realized to a surprising extent. The only major shortfall was for rail freight, but this was due to the unexpectedly large increase in freight transport by road.[4] Much of the Marshall Plan aid went directly to finance the capital projects of Italy's huge state holding companies, the IRI for iron and steel production, as well as a huge range of machinery from household appliances to heavy equipment, and ENI for hydroelectric power plants and oil refineries. Both were viewed with suspicion by American advisors at the time, but each became a huge, vertically integrated, conglomerate. Only in the 1990s did steps begin to privatize parts of each.

The comparative advantage of Italy in providing migrant labor for the rest of western Europe was corroborated by large unemployment, especially in the south. This became an increasing concern first of American advisors, who encouraged public works projects along the lines of the Tennessee Valley Authority for creating jobs. Moreover, a series of peasant revolts broke out due to the excess labor force in agriculture. Over 40% of the total Italian labor force was in the agricultural sector at the end of World War II. The peasant revolts aimed first at land reform, the breaking up of the large estates that prevailed in particular in southern Italy. Their demands were met by setting up "reform zones," within which the least utilized land might be confiscated for redistribution to peasants. Most such redistributions occurred in the south, and despite the unattractive nature of the confiscated land they did lead to an increase in the area farmed by peasant-owners. The other solution to underemployment in rural and southern Italy, of course, was migration to the cities in northern Italy, especially in the triangle formed by Genoa, Turin, and Milan. However, despite the rise of manufacturing output in the booming export sectors, very few new jobs were created in the manufacturing sector. Part of the explanation was the capital-intensive nature of the most successful firms. Part was the growing strength of labor unions in the north, which prevented easy access to their high-paying, skilled-labor jobs. And the remaining part was to the restrictions on labor mobility that had been imposed by the Fascist regime before the war. The last such Act, passed in 1939, forbade anyone of working age to move from his or her locality to another within Italy without a written employment contract from the new location. It was not repealed until 1961, although it had been increasingly ignored during the postwar years.[5]

The resolution of the unemployment/land distribution dilemma was confided to the Cassa per il Mezzogiorno, founded in August 1950. From the beginning, its efforts to close the gap in per capita incomes between the south and north of Italy had been failures. But each failure led to more funding, either on the grounds that the initial projects had not been large enough to generate self-sustaining development, or that they had been misdirected and different projects were required. The first projects focused on improvements to the worthless land being redistributed to discontented peasants. This meant irrigation projects and roads and lucrative contracts for manufacturing and construction firms in the north. Re-evaluating the lack of progress in closing the income differential, the Cassa shifted its priorities toward large-scale industrial projects. Again, these had an immediate effect on stimulating expansion in the manufacturing sector for capital goods in the already dynamic north. The end result was to encourage continued outmigration from the south, both abroad and to the north. In this way, the unemployment problem was gradually eliminated. In 1963 the unemployment rate dropped to its lowest level in the twentieth century (see figure 15.1), a level it seems unlikely to reach again.

In sum, the first sixteen years of the Italian miracle (1947–63) can be explained by an unusually favorable set of circumstances that happened to combine at this time. First and foremost was the political commitment of the Italian government toward export promotion and a firm attachment to the rest of western Europe. Under de Gasperi and then Einaudi, the Italian government embraced Marshall Plan aid and joined the International Monetary Fund in 1947, while taking steps to stabilize the exchange rate of the lira and to make it fully convertible for foreign trade within the confines of the European Payments Union. Italy was also an original member of the North Atlantic Treaty Organization (NATO), despite being nowhere close to the Atlantic, and quickly joined the European Coal and Steel Community in 1953, despite being left out of the original negotiations that determined its institutional design. These commitments culminated with the Treaty of Rome, signed in 1957 to set up the European Economic Community.

The second favorable circumstance was the enormous supply of labor in rural Italy, which helped provide cheap, productive labor to the construction and manufacturing sectors in Italy, as well as to much of the rest of western Europe, especially France and Germany. The third factor was the ready supply of financing available to Italian industry from the plowback of profits or from the government-directed banking sector. The high rates of investment by both private and public firms were matched by high rates of saving. These were motivated, as in the rest of war-torn Europe, by the desire of individuals to rebuild as quickly as possible a secure stock of assets to replace what had been lost during the Depression, the war, the disruption of the postwar settlements, or in the process of migrating. A liberal economic environment, an elastic labor supply, and high rates of saving and investment combined to allow Italy to catch up quickly with the levels of technical advance available in the United States and the more advanced industrial countries in western Europe.

From emigration to immigration: 1963–73

The policy variables traced out in figure 15.1 do not show any particular break in pattern after 1963. Some important changes did occur in the political sphere, however, which were to lay the basis for increasing problems in the future. The center-right coalition that had guided Italy out of postwar depression into the "golden age" of economic growth was replaced by a center-left coalition that was more responsive to the social needs of transplanted workers and the aging population. The new Republic of Italy formed after the war had deliberately built in numerous checks on the power of government bureaucracy to control the economy and society, so as to avoid the recurrence of Fascism. But the governing politicians quickly found that they had to establish legitimacy the "old-fashioned way," namely by granting favors to constituents and building up a base of patronage. As labor became scarce for Italy's expanding economy, labor unions were able to exercise more influence over wages and working conditions. Firms responded by investing more in labor-saving capital and reducing the rate of increase in employment. Government responded by investing more in public works projects designed to increase employment. Growth continued as a result, but inflation began to rise, and under the surface tensions were increasing as southern migrants tried to assimilate in the north and returning migrants from abroad tried to re-establish themselves.

Tensions led to the "hot autumn" of 1969, the delayed counterpart of the "events of May" that had disrupted the economy and political system of France the year before. Strikes, which had been increasing in number and severity over the course of the 1960s, now became general and essentially closed down the Italian economy for a while. The government responded by strengthening the role of the unions in industry and the public sector even further. An essential part was indexing wages to the cost of living index more closely and more widely than before. The *scala mobile*, thus amended, was a key factor in accelerating inflation when the first oil shock hit the Italian economy at the end of 1973. The pension schemes were also altered to widen their coverage and to index their outpayments less to the previous earnings of the retiree and more to the general rise in the cost of living and in the average wage level. This was to prove an increasing burden on the financial resources of the state. As in the case of France, a general rise in wages was agreed on, and labor unions were given more power over work rules. Finally, the level of unemployment benefits was increased to 100% of the worker's previous earnings and the duration of eligibility was increased.

This latter concession opened a Pandora's box. Not only were laid-off workers now less likely to search hard for new jobs, since they could maintain their standard of living without the nuisance of actually working for an income, but unions could press for higher wages knowing that the resulting layoffs would make their members no worse off. Firms then were willing to accede to demands for higher wages, knowing they could lay off more workers without facing union resistance. Faced with the duty of paying higher contributions to unemployment insurance and eventually faced with restrictions imposed by the government on firing workers, however, the firms became increasingly reluctant to hire new workers. So both firms and unions conspired to make the government pay higher levels of unemployment benefits to ever-larger numbers of unemployed.

The rise of the informal economy in this period led to the de facto division of Italy into three major regions – the north, the south, and the center. Each began to identify itself separately from the rest of Italy, much as Italians had traditionally identified first with their family, then with their village, and then with the rest of the world, quite overlooking the role of the Italian nation state in their lives. The ruling political coalitions in the government, despite the rapid change of Cabinets that began in this period, were remarkably stable in their composition. They always consisted of the Christian Democrat Party and its current leader at the heart of the coalition, with temporary, uneasy alliances made with just enough parties in Parliament to reach a bare majority. This meant that any small party could defect and create another change in Cabinet if it thought it would benefit some way. The upshot of this system of proportional representation in Parliament meant that even the political parties found it in their interests to conspire against the nation state!

The overall stability in the leadership of the government that resulted, however, meant that no new political initiatives were forthcoming to deal with Italy's changed role in the world and its changed economic structure. Such changes as did occur merely strengthened the existing organizations – the labor unions, the huge public sector combines, the Cassa per il Mezzogiorno, and even the Mafia. The result was an increasingly rigid structure unable to withstand the shocks that faced all of Europe in the 1970s.

Financing the oil shocks: 1974–85

The weaknesses of the government that had been deliberately built into the constitution of the Italian republic prevented it from defending itself from the combined assault on its resources by workers, firms, and politicians. The consequence was ever-larger government deficits and a mounting stock of debt to be serviced. Figure 15.2 shows clearly what happened. The first oil shock shifted this inflationary mechanism that had been constructed in 1969 into high gear. Italy suffered the highest and most persistent rates of inflation of any western European country through the two oil shocks of the 1970s. The depressed economies of the rest of Europe meant rising unemployment there as well, so more Italian workers returned home. Italy, like France, was faced with "stagflation," which it had managed to create for itself by its own policies. The stock of government debt, which had already been high at 30% of GDP in the mid-1960s, rose to over 50% by 1982.

Individuals responded by moving into the "informal economy," which meant that not only did they avoid paying income taxes, a time-honored Italian tradition made possible by weak government, but they also avoided reporting their employment, so they could continue to draw unemployment benefits, pensions, and disability pay. Moreover, the small and medium-sized firms hiring them could avoid paying social security contributions, which added at least 40% to the cost of formal labor, and actually offer the workers higher direct wages as a result. Now both workers and employers found it beneficial to conspire against the state to enlarge the informal, unrecorded part of the Italian economy.

In the midst of this increasing dysfunctionality of the state, one step was taken that held out the promise of eventual recuperation. This was the determination of the Banca d'Italia to join the European Monetary System and commit Italy to maintaining a fixed exchange rate with respect to the strong, stable currencies among its primary trading partners. In one sense, the Banca d'Italia was joining the general conspiracy against the weak government, allying itself with the powerful and independent Bundesbank to resist the pressure placed on it by national politicians to increase the money supply and ease the controls on domestic credit. But, in a more important sense, it was reaffirming the original commitment of Italy to European integration. Even though it had the highest margins of fluctuation for its central par rate with the ECU, 6% in place of the normal 2.5%, Italy was now on track to restoring the stable lira that had characterized the years of the economic miracle. Moreover, it was assuring its primary trading partners that it would not be engaged in competitive, advantage-seeking devaluations. The evident success of West Germany in weathering the first oil shock by appreciating its currency against the dollar was an incentive for initiating a strong currency policy, but an even stronger incentive was the unwillingness of the Bundesbank to continue supporting the lira without such a commitment by the Banca d'Italia and the Italian government. Previous loans to Italy to help it meet payments for imported oil had led to a return flood of the deutsche marks to business accounts in West Germany, making the Bundesbank uneasy about this temporary loss of control over West German money supply. Still, the Italian commitment to the EMS was a major step to take.

More than any other western European country, Italy was dependent on imported oil as the primary source of energy for its now industrial economy. In common with the bilateral deals that West Germany was striking with Iran and France with Iraq and Algeria, Italy turned to Libya as a prime source for assured supplies of vital fuel. It also made overtures to the Soviet Union for tapping into that country's vast reservoirs of natural gas and petroleum, and attempted a series of countertrade arrangements – such as Fiat factories for fuel at fixed prices. Threatened by renewed rural unrest, Italy was reluctant to see Greece, much less Spain and Portugal, enter into the Common Agricultural Policy and compete with its farmers in the south. Having seen employment opportunities in the rest of the Common Market taken up by foreign guest workers imported into West Germany from Turkey and Yugoslavia and into France from Portugal and Spain, Italy could no longer rely on its EEC partners to absorb its labor surplus. In view of all these forces tending to reduce Italy's reliance on mutual support from the other member states of the EEC, its commitment to enter the European Monetary System when it began operation in 1979 is all the more striking.

Of course, this made Italy, like France, all the less capable of meeting the second oil shock in 1979 and the subsequent Volcker shock (see chapter 5), except by further government spending and enlarged deficits. From an already high ratio of government debt to GDP of over 50% in 1982, the ratio quickly rose to over 100% by the end of the 1980s. Unemployment nevertheless rose even more sharply, as the rate of inflation was brought down close to Community levels. With rising unemployment and increased rates of retirement came permanent demands on central government spending for unemployment benefits and pensions. The early 1980s saw Italy's real GDP growth staggering at its lowest rates since 1947. No wonder, then, that Italy welcomed the single market initiative and the promise of expanded markets for Italian goods, which had proven their attractiveness to the rest of the world in previous decades.

In and out of the EMS: 1986–2006

In common with the rest of the EEC, Italy enjoyed renewed strong rates of growth in the mid-1980s and was able to continue bringing down the rate of inflation. Only a couple of devaluations were necessary for the lira within the EMS. As all the European currencies devalued against the US dollar in the early 1980s, Italy was able to increase its exports outside western Europe. Moreover, the collapse in the price of oil after 1985 helped Italy more than the rest of western Europe due to its greater dependence on imported oil. Unemployment nonetheless remained high, and even began increasing again by 1986. The government's deficits continued. However, thanks to its commitment to the European Monetary System, the Italian government found that the market for its debt had been greatly enlarged. Now that Italian bonds, with their high rates of interest paid in lira, could also be expected to pay these rates in francs or deutsche marks, they became an attractive asset for investors in the rest of western Europe. Italian monetary arithmetic, first discovered with the financial repression imposed on Italian banks by Einaudi in 1947 and then amplified by the appeal of high-yield, very liquid financial assets to the Italian public, now received another boost from entry into a fixed exchange rate regime with its wealthier trading partners in western Europe.

The access to a wider market for Italian financial assets was taken advantage of by Italian support for the removal of capital controls as an extension of the single market. One of the four freedoms was the movement of capital. Initially, this led to a boom in the Milan Stock Exchange. Italian banks were forced to compete with foreign banks and with mutual funds for their deposits for the first time in their history. Mutual funds sprang up to direct household savings into Italian equities, and foreign banks and investment firms set up shop in Milan to gain access to these high-yielding, exchange-rate-riskless assets for their customers. Italy helped the process by renouncing the 6% fluctuation bands in 1989, reducing them to the 2.5% used by everyone else. Immediately, an influx of fresh capital occurred, pasting the lira against the upper intervention band. This success, as much as anything, helped persuade first Spain and then even the United Kingdom to join the EMS in 1990. Unfortunately, it also encouraged the Italian government to continue its deficits and the building up of its mountain of overhanging debt.

As a result, Italy, now committed to close parity with the deutsche mark in foreign exchange markets and stripped of its previous defenses, which relied on capital controls and limited competition within the financial sector, was more vulnerable than any other western European country to the German reunification shock that occurred in late 1990 (see chapter 12). Foreign capital that had found the high interest rates of Italian bonds attractive now found the rising interest rates in Germany even more attractive. Moreover, excess savings available for investment in Italian bonds by the rest of western Europe were now diminished. Foreign capital that had flowed in quickly began to flow out just as rapidly. The mounting pressure on Italian foreign reserves culminated in September 1992, when Italy was forced to withdraw from the European Monetary System and let the lira float. It promptly fell sharply, and only slowly begun to rise back toward its previous levels. In 1996 re-entry into the EMS was negotiated, with the new exchange rate of the lira to the ECU of 1906.48, compared to its original rate of 1148.15. This amounted to a devaluation of the Italian currency of two-thirds over the twenty years preceding the adoption of the euro in 1999.

As figure 15.1 shows, the devalued lira allowed Italian growth rates to rise again, led by increased exports, shown in figure 15.4 below. The rate of inflation continued to be low, while unemployment began to fall again after an initial increase. The favorable experience of Italy on withdrawal from the EMS, in common with that of the United Kingdom (chapter 14), which withdrew or was ejected at the same time, should have shaken Italian confidence in the continued value of following the lead of France and Germany toward deeper and deeper modes of economic integration. In the end, it did not, primarily because Italy was now more preoccupied with reforming the weak, corrupt, and now dysfunctional political system it had created at the end of World War II. The determination of independent prosecutors to root out the influence of the Mafia in the south led to revelations of political corruption in the north as well, and eventually to a revulsion against the entire political establishment.

The primary budget of Italy – that is, the part that excludes payment of interest on the outstanding stock of accumulated debt – continues to be in surplus. Meanwhile, the continued low rates of inflation and reductions in budget deficits have led to a fall in the rates of interest on government debt. Any fall in interest rates, in turn, reduces significantly the amount of spending on debt service that is required, as older debt issues with high interest rates can be paid off by issuing new debt with the lower interest rates. Prodi was confident that, if the foreign exchange markets gave increasing credibility to the Italian commitment to the European Monetary Union, interest rates would continue to fall. The combined effects of falling debt service and a primary budget surplus could lead quickly to an overall surplus. That would begin a downward trend in the stock of government debt, which could satisfy the Maastricht criterion that satisfactory progress should be under way to reduce the proportion of debt to gross domestic product to under 60%. Figure 15.2 shows that his optimism was justified in the short run, but political reality has stymied further progress since 2001.

Another factor that should accelerate the fall in the deficit and the debt ratio is the continued rise in the measured level of Italian GDP. This results from two factors. First, and more important initially, is an attempt to include in the official statistics some estimate of the size of the informal sector, which is presumed to be larger than in any other member country in the EU. Second, as tax reforms are made and regulations on the hiring and firing practices of firms are rationalized, more economic activity should become evident in the formal sector. But all this depends on the continued commitment of Italian governments to economic reform along the lines shown to be effective in the American and British cases during the 1980s. Figure 15.3 shows that, under the 2001–2006 Berlusconi administration, significant reductions in the unemployment rate have occurred while low rates of inflation have been maintained, in common with the rest of the eurozone countries. Unemployment, however, remains high, in common with the experience of Germany and France – and for much the same reasons: political reluctance to make the structural reforms in labor markets that encourage firms to hire new workers. The British example, described in the previous chapter, has been emulated successfully by several of the smaller European Union countries, which are dealt with in the next chapter.

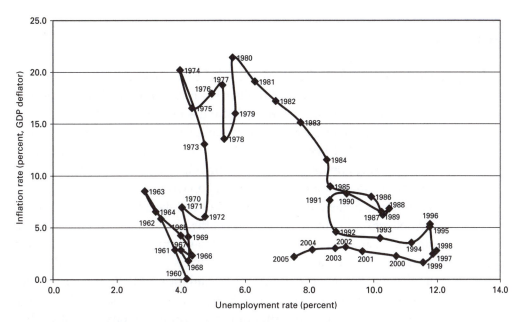

Figure 15.3 Italy: inflation versus unemployment, 1960–2005

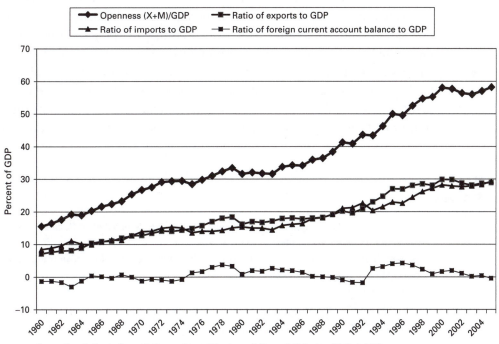

Source: Organisation for Economic Co-operation and Development, *Economic Outlook* no. 77, Paris: 2005.

Figure 15.4 Italy: foreign sector, 1960–2005

Conclusion

Italy's commitment to the development of a Europe integrated economically and cooperating peacefully politically remains undiminished despite the travails, both economic and political, that it has undergone in the past decade. Despite opting out of the European Monetary System in 1992 and remaining out until the end of 1996, it affirmed its desire to remain on the "fast track" of European integration by being in the first wave of entrants to the European Monetary Union, promoted by France and Germany. In common with the core countries of the European Union, Italy has signed the Schengen Accord, which obliges it to enforce at its borders the same controls on immigration from central and eastern Europe that Germany imposes and on immigration from North Africa that France imposes. This is consistent with its desire to limit the influx of refugees from Albania, and the former Yugoslavia as well.

Italy has a split personality in its European identity, just as it has a deep split between the north and south internally in its national identity. While the major powers of Germany and France insist on projecting forward into the twenty-first century their common vision of Europe, formed in the 1950s, while the United Kingdom remains on the sidelines, as diffident and dubious now as it was about this vision in the 1950s, Italy may well play a decisive role in determining Europe's future. In re-examining its own constitutional structure and experimenting with different routes toward dismantling the remains of its Fascist economic institutions, Italy may well work out realistic and pragmatic procedures that will be useful for the accession countries making their transitions from socialist economic structures to market capitalist institutions.

NOTES

1. Vera Zamagni, *The Economic History of Italy, 1860–1990: Recovery after Decline*, Oxford: Clarendon Press, 1993, p. 321.
2. George Hildebrand, *Growth and Structure in the Economy of Modern Italy*, Cambridge, MA: Harvard University Press, 1965, pp. 16–17.
3. Ibid., p. 79, note 2.
4. Zamagni, p. 328, note 1.
5. Ibid., p. 312, note 27.

16   The small open countries: free trade or customs union?

Introduction

The "basic facts" summarized below in table 16.1 demonstrate the economic similarities of these five small, rich, open economies. Three of them were at the heart of the drive toward economic unity that began in western Europe after World War II. Belgium and Luxembourg had already formed an economic union with a common currency in 1921, the Belgium–Luxembourg Economic Union, which was renewed in 1945 after the end of Nazi occupation. In 1947 the Netherlands signed a customs union agreement with the BLEU to form Benelux, the precursor of the European Economic Community's customs union, formed ten years later.

Meanwhile, Austria was incorporated into the Third Reich with the *Anschluss* of 1938, where it remained until the end of World War II. Until 1958 Austria was divided into four occupation zones by the Allied powers, with Vienna ruled by each on a rotating basis. Only in 1955 was a state treaty signed with the Allied powers that enabled Austria to re-emerge as a sovereign nation state. The condition written into the Austrian constitution that Austria maintain permanent neutrality, however, was essential to gain the approval of the Soviet Union. The desire of Austria to join the economic upswing of western Europe led to its joining the European Free Trade Association, even though its major trading partner continued to be West Germany. Soviet pressure against Austria joining the European Economic Community kept Austria from applying formally until after the Soviet regime had collapsed, in 1991. By 1995 Austria was a member of the EU and an immediate participant in the European Monetary System, as it had informally tied its national currency, the schilling, to the deutsche mark for many years.

Switzerland is the outlier among these five countries, as the oldest sovereign state among them. Indeed, its origins as a sovereign state date back to 1291.

Table 16.1 Small open countries: basic facts

Area	(kilometers^2)	of EU-25
Austria	83,870	2.1%
Belgium	30,528	0.8%
Luxembourg	2586	0.1%
Netherlands	41,526	1.0%
Switzerland	41,290	1.0%
Population	(July 2005 estimate)	of EU-25
Austria	8,184,691	1.8%
Belgium	10,364,388	2.3%
Luxembourg	468,571	0.1%
Netherlands	16,407,491	3.6%
Switzerland	7,489,370	1.6%
GDP	(2004 estimate, PPP)	of EU-25
Austria	$255.9 billion	2.2%
Belgium	$316.2 billion	2.7%
Luxembourg	$27.3 billion	0.2%
Netherlands	$481.1 billion	4.1%
Switzerland	$251.9 billion	2.2%
Per capita income	(PPP)	of EU-25 average
Austria	$31,300	116.4%
Belgium	$30,600	113.8%
Luxembourg	$58,900	219.0%
Netherlands	$29,500	109.7%
Switzerland	$33,800	125.7%
Openness	([X+M]/GDP)	with EU-25
Austria	105.2%	77%
Belgium	182.9%	75%
Luxembourg	284.4%	82%
Netherlands	142.7%	68%
Switzerland	92.4%	60% (estimate)
Vital statistics (per 1,000)	Birth rate	Death rate
Austria	8.81	9.70
Belgium	10.48	10.22
Luxembourg	12.06	8.41
Netherlands	11.14	8.68
Switzerland	9.77	8.48

Sources: Central Intelligence Agency, *World Factbook, 2005*, available at http://www.cia.gov/cia/publications/factbook; Statistical Office of the European Communities, *Europe in Figures: Eurostat Yearbook 2005*, Brussels: 2005.

NB: Switzerland, although not a member of the EU, is here presented as though it is, for comparison purposes.

Divided into twenty-six separate cantons that speak four different languages (German, French, Italian, and Romansch), Switzerland's unique political structure could be a model for a peaceful Europe, if Europe were surrounded by easily defended mountain ranges. Maintaining strict neutrality among the constantly warring states of the Continent ever since has proved economically beneficial to the Swiss Confederation. Surrounded by fascist states in World War II, Switzerland managed to keep its independence through a combination of accommodation to Nazi economic demands and mobilization of its armed forces. After the war Switzerland served as the headquarters for the remaining specialized agencies of the defunct League of Nations as well as for the Bank for International Settlements, which served as the clearing house for the European Payments Union (discussed in chapter 2). But it has retained its neutrality firmly, joining the United Nations formally only in 2002. Popular referendums have consistently resulted in rejecting closer associations with the European Union, or even the European Economic Area. Nevertheless, Switzerland's economy should be analyzed in comparison to the other four countries already in the European Union. Like the others, it is small, rich, and open and concentrates its trade with the European Union, especially with the German economy.

Figure 16.1 compares the progress of GDP per capita in these five countries. Clearly, the recent expansion of the EU has been very favorable to Luxembourg, as the expansion of highly paid officials in the EU has increased its per capita income far above the other countries in western Europe, or in the world. More interesting is the leveling off of Switzerland's per capita income, which suggests that its political isolation from surrounding Europe is no longer paying off for it in economic terms, as it has for most of the preceding centuries. Austria's late entrance to the EU, by contrast, has benefited it considerably especially with the recent expansion of EU membership into central and eastern Europe. Overall, the comparison of per capita incomes suggests that it did not make much difference to these countries economically whether they belonged to the European Union or not until the late 1980s. After 1992, however, there are persistent divergences in per capita income.

Free trade (Austria and Switzerland) versus customs union (Benelux)

Austria

Austria's desire to join the EU was long-standing; only its treaty commitment to remain militarily neutral prevented it from applying for membership in the

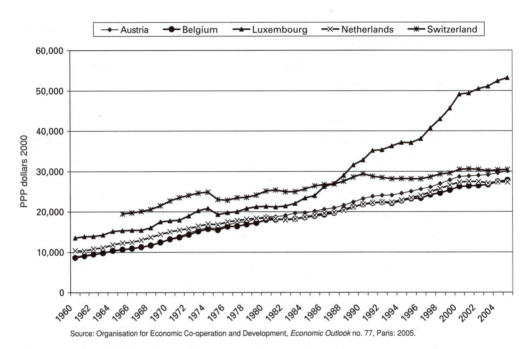

Source: Organisation for Economic Co-operation and Development, *Economic Outlook* no. 77, Paris: 2005.

Figure 16.1   GDP per capita compared, 1960–2005

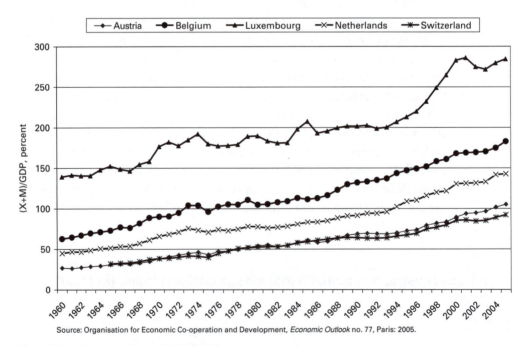

Source: Organisation for Economic Co-operation and Development, *Economic Outlook* no. 77, Paris: 2005.

Figure 16.2   Openness compared, 1960–2005

1960s. Benefiting from Marshall Plan aid and the clearing arrangements of the European Payments Union, not to mention the restoration of its traditionally close trading ties with both West Germany and Italy, Austria was one of the economic miracle countries of the 1950s. Growth slowed in the 1960s as it felt the disadvantage of being excluded from the customs union that included its two largest trading partners. But, along with the other members of EFTA, it received mutual tariff elimination on industrial products with the EEC in 1972, which revitalized its export trade.

The end of the Bretton Woods era forced Austria, along with all the western European countries, to make a strategic decision on the proper exchange rate policy to follow. Luckily, as it turned out, it decided to peg the Austrian schilling to the deutsche mark, but only after the mark had revalued relative to the dollar and all the other European currencies by 10% in 1969. Thereafter, the deutsche mark and the schilling were inseparable, to the extent that Austria immediately joined the Exchange Rate Mechanism of the EMS upon its membership in the EU. It may be noted, however, that, following West German monetary reform in 1948, the schilling had depreciated sharply against the deutsche mark through the early 1950s. In 1945 1 schilling equaled 1 deutsche mark; from 1969 the rate was set at 7 schillings to 1 deutsche mark.

Austria met the oil shocks of the 1970s initially by an expansionary fiscal policy, despite the decision to peg its currency to the strengthening deutsche mark. Predictably, this combination of strong monetary and weak fiscal policy led to severe balance of payments deficits. The docility of Austrian labor unions combined with the commitment of Austria's nationalized industries to maintain employment helped keep down both inflation and unemployment relative to much of western Europe. For the second oil shock, in 1979, Austria decided to maintain the peg to the deutsche mark and forgo expansionary monetary or fiscal policy. Instead, emphasis was placed on the gradual liberalization of labor and commodity markets, and some partial privatization to increase the efficiency of the state enterprises. Nevertheless, its growth pattern from 1979 until 1995, when it joined the EU formally, was very similar to that of Germany, thanks to the exchange rate policy.

Since 1995, however, Austria's per capita income and degree of openness have both increased, unlike the situation for unified Germany (discussed in chapter 12). Vienna's geographical position, as much as its historic ties – dating back centuries – with central and eastern Europe, has made it a center of finance for industry and trade in the accession countries. Its manufacturing exports are still tied to Germany's capital goods industries, so exports have grown with the rebound of Germany's exports. Further, a more conservative government since the election of 2000 has reduced income taxes and future pension obligations while initiating several privatizations of nationalized enterprises. Even the post office appears to be on schedule for privatization, with the success of measures taken to reduce its subsidies and make it profitable. In short, while benefiting from access to the customs union since 1995, Austria's economic success since has owed more to its distinctive domestic economic policies: lowering taxes and decreasing future pension liabilities.

Switzerland

Switzerland, now the "white hole" in the center of the map of the EU, has prized its independence and sovereignty since the Middle Ages. Relying on the EU for over one-half of its exports and two-thirds of its imports, it has resisted joining the EU, or any other international organization, in order to preserve the advantages of neutrality within a frequently war-torn Europe. Only after the collapse of Soviet hegemony in eastern Europe did Switzerland join even the United Nations and the IMF, although it had had observer status from the beginning of those two international organizations. In 1992 its government applied for membership in the EU, along with the other members of EFTA (save for Iceland and Liechtenstein). In 1993, however, its electorate voted against joining even the European Economic Area. With that, the Swiss government withdrew, for the time being, its application. Maintaining its sovereignty may help it to preserve its alpine beauty against the pollution of EU truck traffic, keep exceptionally high subsidies to its dairy industry, and maintain control over the number of foreign (mostly Italian) workers in its service sector. But, being landlocked and completely dependent on imports for petroleum supplies, Switzerland has to maintain open economic relations with the EU, which now surrounds it.

A series of bilateral negotiations between the federal government of Switzerland and the EU Commission therefore began in 1993, which culminated in agreements covering the seven areas of most concern to the Swiss economy: the free movement of persons, the elimination of technical barriers to trade, public procurement markets, civil aviation, overland transport, agriculture, and research. The agreements were signed on June 21, 1999, in Luxembourg and approved by the Swiss people in a referendum in May 2000. They came into force on June 1, 2002. Since 1999 a second series of bilateral negotiations have been ongoing, with Switzerland trying to expand access to the EU market for its industries, especially in pharmaceuticals, food processing, and electricity, and the EU trying to constrain, if not eliminate, Switzerland's traditional role as a refuge for flight capital from European tax authorities. In 2003 Switzerland signed accords with the EU in which Switzerland agreed to withhold taxes amounting to 35% of interest earned by EU nationals on Swiss savings accounts and to remit three-quarters of the proceeds to EU governments. In this way, the Swiss government gained tax revenue that the Swiss electorate would never have conceded while also preserving the secrecy of Swiss bank accounts, so as to preserve Switzerland's role as one of the world's financial centers. Even so, it is doubtful that Switzerland would have acceded to EU demands had it not been for the furor created by the claims of families of Holocaust victims on the Swiss bank accounts they had established before World War II.

In 1934 Switzerland passed a banking law permitting anonymous bank accounts to be established. Until 1938, when Switzerland incorporated Nazi racial classifications into its restrictions on migration, the banking law facilitated the flight capital of non-Aryans, especially Jews, from Nazi Germany to Switzerland as a safe haven. In 1942 Switzerland closed its borders completely, facilitating Hitler's fanatical goal of eliminating non-Aryan elements from the German homeland. The accounts previously established by victims of the Holocaust, therefore, remained dormant and untapped, as the original owners perished and their heirs had no record of the accounts. Switzerland managed to ignore these accounts while continuing to act as a safe haven for flight capital through the Cold War. By 1995, however, the issues of reclaiming property seized by the Nazis in eastern Germany, as well as in the central and eastern European countries under Nazi occupation during World War II, became very important. International attention turned to Switzerland and Swiss bank accounts. Eventually a restitution fund of $1.25 billion was established by Swiss banks, and the names of 2,700 account holders believed to have perished during World War II have been published so that surviving heirs may make claims against the fund (see http://www.swissbankclaims.com/index.asp for details and links to the various reports by the Volcker Commission and the Bergier Commission). Since September 11, 2001, moreover, the Swiss government has cooperated with the United States and the European Union in taking steps against money laundering. Anonymity for Swiss bank account holders is no longer guaranteed to criminal or terrorist individuals and organizations.

In December 2005 further progress in the bilateral agreements occurred when Switzerland became part of the Schengen Accord, allowing the free movement of individuals from the EU through Switzerland. Switzerland also became part of the Dublin agreement at the same time, which enables Switzerland to refuse access to refugees if they have been rejected by any EU country.

Gradually, Swiss citizens may realize the advantages of full EU membership, which are already apparent to Swiss political and business leaders.

Belgium

Belgium arose as a separate, independent country only in 1830, after a brief period of being combined with the Kingdom of the Netherlands and a long history as the Austrian Netherlands. Created almost accidentally by great power agreement after a revolt against Dutch rule, Belgium has been at the center of European conflicts and compromises since the Battle of Waterloo. Devastated in both World War I and II as German armies launched their offensives against France through Belgian territory, Belgians have more cause than most Europeans to create institutions that will resolve Franco-German relations peacefully. The continual construction of new buildings for the EU in the European quarter of Brussels reflects Belgium's commitment to increasing the political capability of the European Union.

The success of the port of Antwerp reflects the economic benefits that Belgium has derived from the European Union. It is once again prospering as the major port, along with Rotterdam in the Netherlands, for ocean-going trade with northern Europe. Until the energy crisis of the 1970s Belgian coal fields created the basis for heavy industry and metal processing, as they had ever since the Middle Ages. Metals were imported from all over the world to be processed in Belgian factories, including copper, lead, and zinc from its former colony in Africa, the Belgian Congo (now known as the Democratic Republic of Congo and previously as Zaire), as well as iron ore from Luxembourg and Lorraine, and tin from Saxony and Malaysia. Since the 1960s, however, Belgium, like Luxembourg, has had to expand its service sector to find employment for workers made redundant by the contraction of its industrial sector. Unlike Luxembourg, it has not been able to keep down unemployment rates.

Moreover, divided between Flemish-speaking Flanders in the north and French-speaking Wallonia in the south, Belgium has its own internal conflicts to manage. In its transition to a service economy after its manufacturing base became uncompetitive during the 1970s, both regions have felt abused. Initially, this led to repeated bursts of inflation as the competing claims of the Flemish and Walloons were settled by expanding the money supply and increasing the government debt. By the 1990s Belgium had the highest ratio of government debt to GDP in the European Union, 134% in 1995.

After committing to the European Monetary System seriously in 1983, however, the internal conflicts could no longer be settled by accommodative finance. As early as 1975 regional parliaments were established, and by 1993 fiscal power had largely devolved to them. Despite its high debt to GDP ratio, still among the highest in western Europe, at 99.7% in 2005, Belgium was in the first group of countries to adopt the euro as its currency in 1999. The role of Brussels remains confused – it seems to have become the capital of its own country in name only, while it has become the capital of the European Union in every respect but name. The difficulties of governing a conflicted country while being forced to maintain a restrictive monetary and fiscal policy are daunting, especially when its major trading partners are stagnating. While the economic pain of cooperating with France and Germany is great at present, Belgians have only to look at their many military cemeteries and war memorials to realize the need to persevere.

Since entering the eurozone, both the Flemish and the Walloon regions have focused on the problem of continuing high unemployment rates, compounded by the low participation rates of the working-age population in the labor force. Only 60% of the Belgium population aged fifteen to sixty-four is employed or looking for employment, compared to the EU average of 70%. To confront this problem, the more conservative government elected in 2003 attempted to increase the number of jobs by encouraging firms to hire workers in various categories. For example, employer contributions to social security funds were reduced for both younger and older workers coming close to retirement age. Further, older workers were encouraged to stay employed longer than age fifty-five by a gradual raising of the age at which they become eligible for full pension benefits. Nevertheless, unemployment rates remain high, basically because employers in Belgium are still constrained from firing unsatisfactory workers once they have been hired. The contrasting experience in solving unemployment issues in the neighboring Netherlands shows how Belgium could meet its employment goals if it could mobilize the political will to enact Dutch-style reforms.

The Netherlands

The Netherlands may be known to tourists for wooden shoes, rounds of cheese, windmills, and tulips, but to economic historians it is known as the world's first modern economy, to demographers as the most densely populated country in the world, and to economists as, once again, one of the richest economies in Europe. At the end of World War II the great port of Rotterdam, where the Netherlands has for centuries controlled entry of the world's goods to the entire hinterland of the Rhine river drainage, was completely flattened, save for one windmill that was left as a landmark to guide successive waves of Allied bombers. Taking advantage of Marshall Plan aid and the logistical demands of Allied forces in Occupied Germany, the Netherlands constructed a much-enlarged and improved port facility. German economic expansion ever since has led to Dutch prosperity, not only through the perfection of its entrepôt (trans-shipment) role but also through the development of modern chemical plants and high-technology industry with preferred transport access to the markets of Europe and the world.

The oil shocks were a mixed affair for the Netherlands. The oil embargo imposed by the Arab members of OPEC in October 1973 hit the refineries and petrochemical plants of the Dutch earliest and most severely. But it also provoked the Dutch government finally to exploit the large natural gas deposits that lay in shallow, readily accessible areas under the Dutch portion of the North Sea. This opportunity, long deferred for fear of displacing coal miners, was taken up so rapidly that wages rose sharply in the now booming petroleum sector. As a small country with a relatively homogeneous population and a democratic government committed to communal welfare, the Netherlands could not prevent the high wages in the leading sector from leading to higher wages in the rest of the economy as well. Such high wages in sectors in which demand was not rising made Dutch products and services increasingly uncompetitive. In the short run, then, Dutch wage policy eroded the advantages of a strong currency that the West German economy was experiencing. British economists coined the term "Dutch disease" to describe this phenomenon, partly to discredit it before it infected the UK economy of the late 1970s. Dutch economists, however, have noted that the symptoms of the disease seemed more evident in the United Kingdom than in the Netherlands.

From the second oil shock until the labor market reforms in the mid-1990s the Dutch economy followed very much the pattern experienced by the West German economy. In particular, its monetary policy of maintaining a fixed exchange rate with the deutsche mark meant that it experienced fully the German economic experience with the reunification shock of the early 1990s. While the Netherlands adopted the common European currency in 1999 and accepted the restrictive monetary policy of the European Central Bank, it made important reforms in the labor market – reforms that enabled it to break away from the high unemployment rates that remained in Belgium, Italy, France, and Germany.

Figure 16.3 highlights the dramatic effects of the reforms. Not only did the overall unemployment rate fall continuously for several years but the participation rate of the Dutch population in the labor force rose as well.

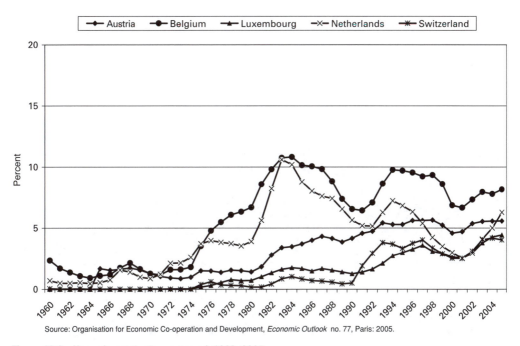

Source: Organisation for Economic Co-operation and Development, *Economic Outlook* no. 77, Paris: 2005.

Figure 16.3   Unemployment rates compared, 1960–2005

From two-thirds of the fifteen to sixty-four age group participating in the Dutch labor force in 1989, just before the German reunification shock of 1990, by 2005 nearly 80% were in the labor force, well above the EU average of 70%. The rise in participation rates has been especially marked for Dutch women, whose participation rates previously had been among the lowest in the EU. One reform limited access to unemployment benefits by reducing the time that benefits were paid at levels tied to the previous wage and requiring regular searches for employment by recipients. This "stick" policy, however, was supplemented by a "carrot" policy, which encouraged part-time work by women. Employers could hire temporary workers for less than full-time employment and pay less than full social security taxes on them. The rise in temporary employment accounted for most of the increase in participation rates overall and especially for women.

The rise in unemployment rates that began in 2002, however, highlighted the limitations to the Dutch reforms. The increase in the importance of temporary workers led to legislation protecting those workers, as well as permanent workers, from dismissal by their employers. Overall, then, the level of employee protection in the Netherlands was above the OECD average, although still below that in Belgium, Italy, France, or Germany. Restricting the hours of

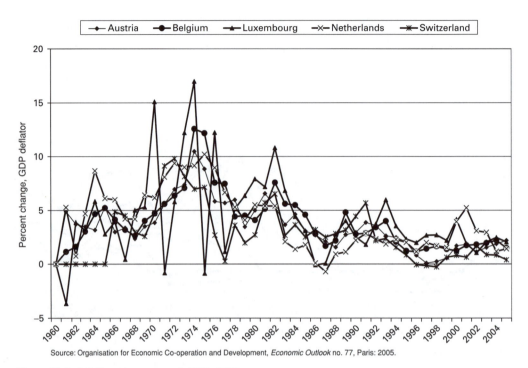

Source: Organisation for Economic Co-operation and Development, *Economic Outlook* no. 77, Paris: 2005.

Figure 16.4 Inflation rates compared, 1960–2005

temporary workers also meant that the average hours worked per year by the Dutch labor force were the lowest of all OECD countries in 2003. As a consequence, the slowdown in economic activity in 2002 for the eurozone as a whole led to a decrease in labor productivity and a loss of export competitiveness. The combined effects led to an increase in unemployment rates, once again approaching those in neighboring Belgium. Clearly, labor market reforms that allow a reallocation of labor in response to economic shocks require extensive changes in European Union institutions – changes that take time to be accepted by the public and take time to become effective in reducing unemployment permanently.

As figure 16.4 demonstrates, none of these small rich open economies can resort to temporary inflation measures to deal with unemployment problems, the Netherlands least of all, with its long-standing commitment to fixed exchange rates with Germany. Even Switzerland, although not bound by the eurozone's monetary policy, has persisted in maintaining the lowest inflation rates in western Europe since the reunification shock in Germany. Along with Luxembourg, it has also maintained the lowest unemployment rates in western Europe. The reason for this exceptional performance, however, is the very high proportion of foreign, usually seasonal, workers in both small countries. The foreign workers, largely Spanish in Switzerland and Portuguese in Luxembourg, take the brunt of fluctuations in employment opportunities, maintaining high rates of employment for the domestic labor force.

Luxembourg

Luxembourg is too hilly and rocky to think of being self-sufficient in agriculture, which makes up a smaller share of its GDP (1.7% in 1992) than in any other country in Europe other than the United Kingdom and Germany. When the oil shocks of the 1970s made its steel industry uncompetitive Luxembourg began to develop a large services sector, especially in finance. This trend continued into the 1990s, with the displaced workers from the steel industry moving into services, especially government. Luxembourg has also benefited enormously from the expenditures of the European Union on its facilities and staff located in the country. Luxembourg continues to profit from the expansion of European Union activities, especially with the enlargement of 2004.

Nearly 40% of Luxembourg's population, however, are foreigners, and 60% of those are Portuguese nationals. Integrating this substantial stock of permanent migrants into Luxembourg society remains a challenge for the government. Allowing dual nationality is one possibility, which the government hopes can be introduced before 2009, to give the foreign population a much stronger voice in Luxembourg's economic policy. As unemployment rises to higher than usual levels even for Luxembourg, the continuation of wage indexation is under attack. Belgium is the only other country still practicing this form of automatic inflation. For both countries, the restraint of monetary expansion by the European Central Bank means that wage indexation inexorably leads to higher rates of unemployment. Even Luxembourg's advantage as a financial center is undermined by the EU requirement that foreigners' savings accounts be taxed, with the majority of the revenues remitted to the EU country. Luxembourg's government gains some revenue from this requirement, which it supplemented by levying the same 10% withholding tax on savings by Luxembourg citizens.

Conclusion

All five of these small countries surrounding Germany were affected by World War II in different ways, which determined their responses to the reconstruction of Europe afterwards. Switzerland, steadfastly clinging to its independence and neutrality, managed to benefit as well from the role of its financial sector as a safe haven for the assets of refugees and as a money laundering center for Nazi operations. Throughout the Cold War period it maintained both its neutrality and its business model for its prosperous financial sector. Since 1995 the furor over the assets held in dormant accounts in Swiss financial institutions by victims of World War II has led Switzerland to re-evaluate its role in Europe and in the global economy. Switzerland discovered that, while long-standing neutrality keeps a country from making enemies, it does not help a country make friends either. One may expect to see the continued integration of the Swiss economy and institutions into the European Union as Swiss citizens see the advantages of neutrality progressively overwhelmed by the disadvantages.

Austria had no choice but to facilitate Nazi aggression during World War II, as it was incorporated into the Third Reich after 1938. With the end of the Cold War and the breakup of the Soviet Union, Austria had no difficulty in joining the EU in 1995 while preserving its neutrality, as mandated in its 1955 constitution. Ever since, Austria has been one of the most enthusiastic members of the European Union, joining the euro in the first group of members and approving the proposed EU constitution in 2005. But the country's long history outside the EU while maintaining strong economic relations with Germany means that Austria has specific reservations about accepting EU regulations. Austria's obsession with organic agriculture, an outcome of its heavily subsidized agriculture, for example, keeps Austria from accepting GMO products even when they have received approval from the European Commission. Its insistence on neutrality also undermines efforts by France and Belgium to create a unified military capacity for the EU.

The three small countries occupied by Nazi Germany during World War II have been at the forefront of initiatives to create the European Union – at least until the overwhelming rejection of the EU constitution by the Dutch electorate in the 2005 referendum. The joint success of the Benelux trio during the golden age of economic growth owed a great deal to their openness to trade with the resurgent West German economy. The oil shocks of the 1970s, however, led each of the three to seek separate solutions to the common problem, much as we saw earlier was the case for their large trading partners – France, West Germany, and Italy. The revival of growth in the 1980s due to the Single European Act and the fall in oil prices seemed to lock each of the three into the policies pursued to confront the previous rises in oil prices. Consequently, the German reunification shock posed separate challenges even as all three joined in the completion of the European Monetary Union by 1999.

The institutional changes required to confront the challenges of continued shocks from the forces of globalization are obvious to all three. By the end of 2005 only the Netherlands had taken serious steps to implement the necessary labor market reforms, while Belgium and Luxembourg remained committed to wage indexation and the nationwide negotiation of union contracts. Even the Netherlands paused in the process of labor market reforms to increase the annual hours of work for its part-time workers. Once again, all five countries look to the German economy for their economic policy.

17 The Scandinavian union: or separate ways?

Introduction

We deal in this chapter with the five member states that currently comprise the Nordic Council: Denmark, Finland, Iceland, Norway, and Sweden. Especially interesting is the sharply different policies of each major Nordic country with respect to the European common currency. Denmark consistently refuses to adopt the euro, even though it has been a member of the European Union the longest. Its central bank keeps the exchange rate of the Danish krone within narrow limits as part of the European Monetary System II, however. Sweden also manages to keep the exchange rate of its currency, the Swedish krona, in line with both the Danish krone and the euro, but refuses to join the European Monetary System, thanks to popular rejection of the idea of joining the euro in the referendum of September 2003. Both Norway and Iceland eschew the euro, the EMS, and the European Union. Nevertheless, these two outsiders have the highest rates of adoption of single market directives, better than any of the EMU members (see chapter 7). That leaves only Finland as a member of the European Union and the European Monetary Union using the euro as its currency. Figure 17.1, however, demonstrates that the exchange rates of all five have moved very much together since the creation of the common European currency. Since the creation of the euro in 1999, moreover, even Iceland's much-weakened currency has moved in parallel with the other Nordic currencies.

It is remarkable that, despite their different approaches to the formal institutions that make up the European Union, politically and economically the Nordic countries present a common front to the eurozone. The differences among the countries have deep historical routes. The Scandinavian countries are Denmark, Norway, and Sweden, and they did form a Scandinavian Union in the fifteenth century. Ever since, however, they have gone their separate ways

Table 17.1 Scandinavia: basic facts

Area	(kilometers²)	of EU-25
Denmark	43,094	1.1%
Finland	338,145	8.5%
Iceland	103,000	2.6%
Norway	324,220	8.2%
Sweden	449,964	11.3%
Population	(July 2005 estimate)	of EU-25
Denmark	5,432,335	1.2%
Finland	5,223,442	1.1%
Iceland	296,737	0.1%
Norway	4,593,041	1.0%
Sweden	9,001,774	2.0%
GDP	(2004 estimate, PPP)	of EU-25
Denmark	$174.4 billion	1.5%
Finland	$151.2 billion	1.3%
Iceland	$9.373 billion	0.1%
Norway	$183.0 billion	1.6%
Sweden	$255.4 billion	2.2%
Per capita income	(PPP)	of EU-25 average
Denmark	$32,200	119.7%
Finland	$29,000	107.8%
Iceland	$31,900	118.6%
Norway	$40,000	148.7%
Sweden	$28,400	105.6%
Openness	([X+M]/GDP)	with EU-25
Denmark	95.0%	72%
Finland	79.1%	64%
Iceland	89.1%	61%
Norway	70.4%	78%
Sweden	95.1%	65%
Vital statistics (per 1,000)	Birth rate	Death rate
Denmark	11.36	10.43
Finland	10.50	9.79
Iceland	13.73	6.68
Norway	11.67	9.45
Sweden	10.36	10.36

Sources: Central Intelligence Agency, *World Factbook, 2005*, available at http://www.cia.gov/cia/publications/factbook; Statistical Office of the European Communities, *Europe in Figures: Eurostat Yearbook 2005*, Brussels: 2005.

NB: Iceland and Norway, although not members of the EU, are here presented as though they are, for comparison purposes.

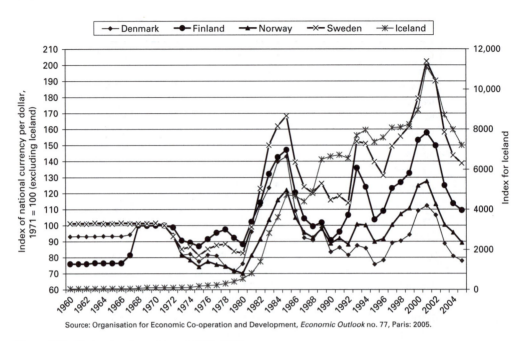

Source: Organisation for Economic Co-operation and Development, *Economic Outlook* no. 77, Paris: 2005.

Figure 17.1 Exchange rates compared, 1960–2005

in state formation while maintaining cooperation in matters of mutual concern through a variety of innovative institutional arrangements. The formal political union of Denmark and Sweden in the seventeenth century did not last long as the two monarchies pursued separate paths toward state building in the modern period.[1] During the height of the classical gold standard, 1878–1914, all three countries adopted the gold standard and maintained a formal currency union. Norway then split from Sweden at the beginning of the twentieth century, as did Greenland from Denmark. Iceland was separated from Denmark by force at the outset of World War II and declared its independence in 1944. Finland remained a separate country throughout.

During World War II Denmark and Norway were occupied by Nazi Germany, Sweden retained its neutrality while supplying the German *Wehrmacht's* need for steel products, Finland, having only recently achieved independence from the Soviet Union, was reoccupied by Russian forces, and Iceland served as an Allied airbase to protect transatlantic convoys from German submarines. Despite their different experiences during World War II, the five Nordic countries formed the Nordic Council (http://www.norden.org) after the war and have maintained regular contacts and informal agreements ever since. Their relationships with each other have actually strengthened over time despite the quite different relationship each country has had with the European Union. The collapse of the Soviet Union helped greatly in this regard, as it led to the creation in 1995 of the Council of Baltic Sea States (CBSS), consisting of the five Nordic countries, the three newly independent Baltic states of Estonia, Latvia, and Lithuania, plus Russia, Poland, and Germany, and the United Kingdom and United States as observers.

The differences among the Nordic countries in adopting EU institutional arrangements make their economic experiences especially interesting. Denmark maintained its strong economic relations with the rest of the Nordic Council after joining the European Economic Community in 1973. Even then, it was clear that Denmark's motivation for joining the Common Market was to maintain access to the market of the United Kingdom rather than a desire to cooperate with the Benelux countries in dealing with a resurgent West Germany. Norway's political leadership also wished to join the EEC with Denmark, for much the same reasons. Both Denmark and Norway had become founding members of NATO when it began in 1948 and both had strong economic relationships with both the United Kingdom and the United States. In 1973, as later in 1994, however, the Norwegian electorate voted (narrowly) against joining the European Economic Community formally.

Finland was in no position to join either NATO or a Nordic defense community, given the menacing presence of the Soviet Union along 1,000 kilometers of its border. Sweden's leaders worried that Swedish membership of NATO would also jeopardize the tenuous independence of Finland, so they maintained neutrality while supporting a strong military in a defensive mode. In the tensions of the Cold War, neither Finland nor Sweden felt that membership in the EEC would be consistent with their military neutrality. As in the case of Austria, however, the end of the Cold War at the beginning of the 1990s meant that both could enter the European Union, which they did in 1995, along with Austria.

While legally part of Denmark at the beginning of World War II, Iceland was quickly occupied by American and British forces and became an important base to provide air cover for transatlantic convoys. Iceland declared its independence from Denmark in 1944 and has remained independent ever since. Benefiting from Marshall Plan aid to modernize its fishing fleet after the war, Iceland has retained a privileged position for its vital fishing industry ever since, first fending off British fishing boats that came within its 200-mile offshore limit, and then refusing to be bound by the EU's Common Fishery Policy. Like Norway, however, Iceland has had to come to terms with the

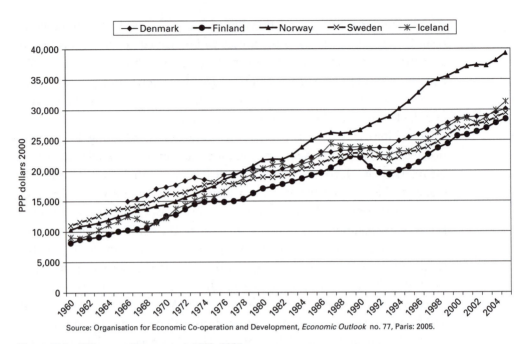

Source: Organisation for Economic Co-operation and Development, *Economic Outlook* no. 77, Paris: 2005.

Figure 17.2 GDP per capita compared, 1960–2005

single market directives of the EU and its Common Fishery Policy in order to maintain access to the EU market for its fish catch.

Figure 17.2 shows clearly how closely knit these five countries are economically despite their different relationships with the institutions of the European Union. Only since the oil shocks of the 1970s and the exploitation of its offshore oil deposits in the North Sea has Norway's per capita income exceeded that of the other four Nordic countries. The relative economic success of the Norwegians also explains their reluctance to join more formally the institutions of the European Union. The intensity of their trade with the members of the European Union, however, also explains why Norway and Iceland both agreed to contribute funds toward the common effort of the European Union to help the new accession countries in central and east Europe adopt EU institutions. They are also committed to the Millennium Project, spearheaded by the EU, which means increasing their contributions to development aid for the African, Caribbean, and Pacific countries.

All five countries, as one would expect given their relatively small size and relatively high levels of per capita income, have had high levels of openness to international trade as well. The experience of Denmark is noteworthy, in that joining the EEC in 1973 did little to increase its openness, which did

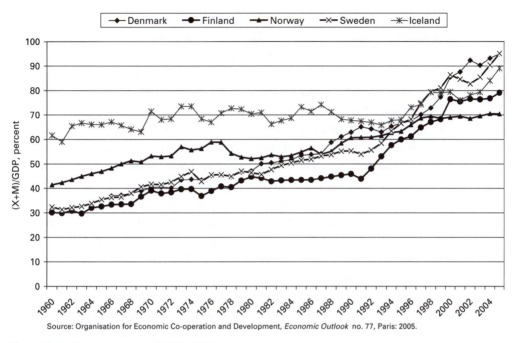

Source: Organisation for Economic Co-operation and Development, *Economic Outlook* no. 77, Paris: 2005.

Figure 17.3 Openness compared, 1960–2005

not begin to rise sharply until the reunification shock in Germany and the collapse of the Soviet Union. Finland suffered in the first years of the 1990s, the victim of the combined effect of the slowdown in the German economy and the collapse of its countertrade agreements with the Soviet Union. During the remainder of the 1990s, however, its eagerness to join the European Union and the common currency boosted its openness to its highest levels. Norway, the economic fortunes of which are so closely linked to the market for oil, has leveled off in terms of openness since 1998. Differences among the five in terms of openness, therefore, cannot be explained by the differences in their institutional arrangements with respect to the European Union.

Separate paths toward a common outcome

Denmark

Denmark, like the Netherlands and northern Belgium, has a historic tradition as an entrepôt economy due to its location at the entrance to the Baltic Sea. The Danish Sound for centuries was the source of rich tolls for

Danish rulers, until British naval power enforced freedom of the seas in the nineteenth century. Even then, the entrepôt role continued until the German empire took most of Schleswig-Holstein and built the Kiel Canal to link the North Sea directly with the Baltic through all-German territory. Building on a prosperous, well-educated agricultural population, Denmark became an industrialized economy based on export-oriented food processing at the end of the nineteenth century. It was not until the trade restrictions of the 1930s, which limited Denmark's access to manufactured imports and at the same time reduced its markets for exports of processed foodstuffs, that Denmark began to develop its industrial base. Serious industrialization, however, did not begin until the 1960s. Then, rapid structural change caused social stresses, which were eased by extending and deepening the social welfare services provided by the state, at the cost of rising public debt. When the oil shocks of the 1970s created large deficits in Denmark's foreign account, foreign indebtedness rose as well. Various incomes policy and price control schemes were attempted by the Social Democrat government and it even joined the European Monetary System in 1978. The second oil shock demonstrated finally the futility of these demand management approaches to supply-side problems. Unemployment and government spending both rose again while the economy stagnated.

Since September 1982 a Conservative-led government has progressively reduced government expenditures, raised taxes, and suspended wage indexation. Gradually Denmark's competitiveness improved, until it actually ran an export surplus in 1990. An interesting aspect of the renewed export boom was the increasing importance of trade with Germany and the decreasing importance of trade with the United Kingdom, despite its presence in the expanded Common Market after 1973. Due credit for the eventual surplus in 1990 must therefore be given to the increase in imports to the former East Germany that arose for Denmark's benefit from the reunification of Germany. Despite the obvious benefits they derive from participation in the single market and linking their currency to the deutsche mark, the Danish people rejected the Maastricht Treaty in the first referendum held on it in May 1992. Eventually, after a massive publicity campaign and specific reservations that exempted Denmark from the necessity of participation in European Monetary Union, the treaty was ratified by the Danish parliament (*Folketing*).

Since the popular rejection of the treaty, and later of joining the euro in the referendum of September 2000, the Danish government has nevertheless set monetary policy in line with that of the European Central Bank. The exchange rate of the Danish krone with the euro is kept within even narrower bounds than in the first Exchange Rate Mechanism, while interest rates are maintained in lock step with those set by the ECB. Unlike the major countries actually in the euro, however, Denmark has been able to keep its government deficit within the Maastricht limits, even running an occasional surplus. Moreover, it has done this while gradually reducing its unemployment rate to among the lowest levels within the EU.

The Danish government has been able to do this by standard labor market reforms, described above in the case of the Netherlands – namely restricting the generosity and duration of unemployment benefits while encouraging the rise of temporary employment possibilities. Reductions in taxation on labor incomes have also encouraged Danes to enter, and to remain longer in, the labor force. From the mid-1970s onward participation rates began to rise, from just under 75% of the working-age population to over 80% by 1990, where it has leveled off. While agriculture and manufacturing continue to lose jobs, the construction, finance, and services sectors generally continue to expand employment. The resulting high level of labor force participation allows the Danes to continue the financing of their typically generous welfare provisions for medical care and retirement pensions. The success of the government in continuing to run mild surpluses, in flat contradiction to the experience of the major euro countries, also allowed the interest rate on government bonds to fall below that of German government bonds by 2005. The Danish success story, however, is not unique among the Nordic five.

Finland

After World War II Finland managed to maintain an uneasy independence from the Soviet Union, basically by providing the Soviets with whatever raw materials and access to Finnish waters they wanted and by making sufficient military preparations as to make the Soviets pay a very high price in blood for any attempted takeover. Not only did Finland make it a point to pay off its war debt to the United States after – long after – World War I, it also paid off a huge reparations demand after World War II to the Soviets by 1952. This helped force industrialization to occur and made the Soviet Union the major market for Finnish trade, even as its trade with western Europe expanded in the 1960s. Imports of fuel from the Soviet Union were vital for Finnish industry, since 90% of its oil, 50% of its electricity, and all its natural gas came from there. Finland joined the OECD in 1972, but, unlike the rest of the OECD countries, managed to weather the oil shocks relatively well, thanks to its barter arrangements with the Soviet Union.

The collapse of the Soviet empire in 1989/90, however, brought all these economic advantages for Finland to an end. Beginning in January 1991 the Soviets imposed market-related prices for its deliveries of energy to Finland, which created a major balance of payments deficit for Finland and cut off its major export market as well. Finland plunged into a deep recession. Tying its fortunes to those of the EU at that time proved not to be successful, and Finland had to devalue sharply its currency, the markka, in 1992. Nevertheless, the Finnish population was the most enthusiastic of the populations voting on membership in the EU, and trade has rapidly grown with its western neighbors, especially Sweden and Norway.

After joining the EU formally in 1995, and the euro in 1999, Finland's economy has rebounded, driven by exports to new markets in the West. Credit for this turnaround of fortune, however, is due mostly to the domestic dynamic of one firm, Nokia. Starting as one of a number of small regional telephone companies within Finland at the end of the nineteenth century, Nokia became a major producer of cables after World War I. After World War II it found a large, steady consumer for its products in the Soviet Union, which allowed it to become one of the largest firms in Finland. When the oil shocks of the 1970s made it clear that Nokia should not rely so heavily on the Soviet market it began to diversify into a wide range of products, including forestry equipment, telephone equipment, and electronic control devices for industry. Even before the final collapse of the Soviet market Nokia was looking for a core industry to focus on. With the adoption of a standard GSM[2] technology for mobile phones in the European Union, Nokia decided to shift its large-scale production expertise into this new market. Joining the EU and locking in its production costs to the same currency as the bulk of its sales revenues obviously helped make the new business of mass manufacturing mobile phones a success. But the strategic key to Nokia's success was the ability to make major decisions independent of government policy or concerns and to implement them quickly and effectively with private finance, mainly by selling off its other assets.

While Finland has gradually brought down its unemployment rate to below the rest of the eurozone, levels remain above those of its Nordic neighbors. Moreover, the participation rate of the working-age population in the labor force remains relatively low as well – 72 to 74%, compared to over 80% in Denmark. Government debt rose sharply in response to the combined shocks of German reunification and Soviet collapse, which made entry into the euro-zone much more attractive for Finland compared to its Nordic neighbors. The low interest rates on Finnish debt after joining the euro helped the government run surpluses for several years and reduce the ratio of debt to GDP safely below the 60% level.

Iceland

Iceland's aid from the Marshall Plan amounted to the equivalent of 5% of its annual prewar GDP in its first year of operation and was devoted mainly to machinery and equipment. This was used to improve mechanization in both its farming and fishing sectors, although the fishing fleet had already more than doubled in size in the two years after the war. Improved productivity in its traditional export areas (99% of Iceland's exports were agricultural products in 1951)[3] helped Iceland regain export earnings to cover its essential imports of manufactured goods and fuels. The governments of Iceland and Norway were initially more concerned with regaining a sense of national identity than with maintaining a military establishment. Iceland, Norway, and Switzerland all depended on trade with western Europe, however, and they were eager to cooperate with the rest of Europe in any efforts to expand trade. The increasing hostility of the Soviet bloc toward trade with the West confirmed their need to participate in the OEEC. Indeed, by 1949, when NATO was formed, both Iceland and Norway were charter members. Iceland after its independence found it had preferred access to a common pool resource, the rich fishing grounds off its shores. Lying next to the main route for Soviet submarines and supply ships to enter the North Atlantic from their bases in the White Sea conferred a double advantage. The Americans spent large sums of money building and maintaining an airbase at Keflavik to monitor Soviet shipping movements, while the Soviets set up barter arrangements with Iceland, trading fuel for fish, to supply their fleets. At one point in the mid-1950s American military spending accounted for one-fifth of Iceland's national income! Exports of fish kept growing to the entire OEEC market and kept Iceland's tiny economy growing at the same high rates enjoyed in its export markets. In common with Norway and Switzerland, Iceland's small, open economy shared in the benefits of increased trade taking place with a rapidly growing western European economy.

When the EEC was formed, however, Iceland remained apart from both it and the EFTA alternative. Part of the motivation was to insist on its independence from Denmark, which was one of the charter members. In addition, however, it had begun a fishing dispute with both Germany and the United Kingdom, which ruled out any amicable association with either the EEC or EFTA at the time. This led eventually to common acceptance of the twelve-mile limit off a country's coast as the exclusive fishing grounds for any country's fishing fleet, but at the time it disrupted Iceland's fishing activity, leading to large deficits for both the government and the balance of payments. A new government came to power in October 1959, led by the Independence Party, having won the election on the grounds that it would put both the economy and the government budget on a sounder basis.

Toward this end, two devaluations of the króna followed in short order: from $1.00 = 16.286 kr in February 1960 to $1.00 = 38.00 kr, and then in August 1961 to $1.00 = 57.00 kr. A 300% devaluation was adequate to restore Iceland's competitiveness for its main export – frozen fish. At the same time, the new government insisted on exclusive fishing rights for the Icelandic fleet within twelve miles of Iceland's shores. After some skirmishes with British war-ships, agreement was reached with the United Kingdom and Germany that this would become effective within three years. In the meantime, other fishing boats, mainly British, could approach within six miles of Iceland. Fish exports resumed their growth, the Icelandic fleet expanded, but the fish population stock failed to grow. By 1968 there was a serious shortfall in the fish catch, which produced a sharp fall in Iceland's GDP as well (see figure 17.2). This forced Iceland to reconsider its outsider status from the European markets. It reached an agreement in December 1969 with the other members of EFTA to join that organisation, which it did in March 1970. In 1972 it signed a trade agreement with the EEC, which eliminated tariffs on about 70% of Iceland's exports, mainly fresh and frozen fish. Beyond entering into the spirit of mul-tilateral trade liberalization more than a decade later than the rest of Europe, Iceland's policy responses were the same as ten years earlier. First a devalua-tion, this time to $1.00 = 88.00 kr, and then an attempt to expand its exclusive fishing rights from twelve to fifty miles offshore. This provoked a more serious confrontation with UK warships, which were called in to protect British fishing boats trawling between twelve and fifty miles offshore. The confrontation also led to a further devaluation of the króna against the dollar, in December 1972, to $1.00 = 97.25 kr. The final period of golden growth for Iceland thus began and ended with devaluations and successful attempts to expand the country's exclusive fishing grounds. Having depleted the supply of herring in the first fifteen years following independence, Iceland's fishermen proceeded to deplete the supply of cod in the next fifteen years. Maintaining a Scandinavian-style welfare state in an economy for which the national income is dependent on each year's fish catch, however, makes it impossible to stabilize government budgets. Sporadic eruptions of volcanoes do not help matters either.

When the Bretton Woods system of fixed exchange rates collapsed in 1971, Iceland had devalued at first as part of the adjustment necessary to continue

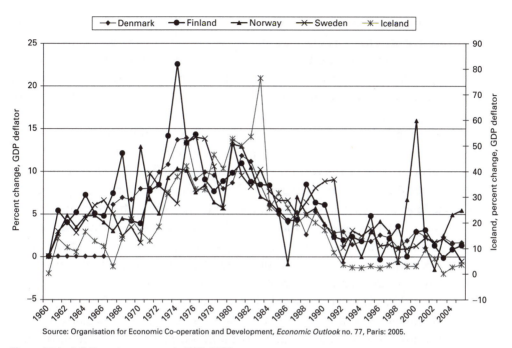

Source: Organisation for Economic Co-operation and Development, *Economic Outlook* no. 77, Paris: 2005.

Figure 17.4 Inflation rates compared, 1960–2005

high rates of government spending and contain domestic inflation. But, as fish harvests rose with settlement of the Cod War, as it was labeled by the British press, and prices began to soar for Iceland's fish thanks to much greater access to the EEC market, its currency began to appreciate relative to the dollar. Further, as the Soviet Union was its primary supplier for petroleum and did not price according to OPEC standards but instead on the basis of long-term countertrade agreements, Iceland was relatively insulated from the price shocks. So Iceland confronted the first oil shock with an appreciating currency. As a small, open economy, however, it was still subject to the income shocks in its trading partners. Countering the decline in export earnings and employment by increased subsidies to the agricultural and fishing sectors, the government kept increasing its deficits and financing them with increased money supply. This led to raging inflation, as shown in figure 17.4; Iceland's experience with inflation during the oil shocks of the 1970s was by far the most erratic among the Nordic five.

Nevertheless, the government achieved its primary objective; unemployment rates remained low throughout the turbulent 1970s. By 1979, however, it had to take recourse yet again to the policy action that had brought Iceland through the crises of the late 1950s and the late 1960s. This time, it claimed an exclusive fishing zone for its fleet within 200 miles offshore! By 1983 Iceland's fishing fleet, having exhausted the stocks of herring in the 1950s and cod in the 1960s, was now proceeding to deplete Atlantic salmon. This kept growth rates up in the mid-1980s, counter to the typical European experience. Iceland's fish catch dropped off again at the end of the 1980s, however, as a consequence of the constant overfishing.

Iceland's response, predictable by now, was to send its fishing boats into hitherto sacrosanct waters, this time those around Svalbard Island. This frozen bit of territory well above the Arctic Circle had been made an international zone by the Treaty of Paris in 1920, which placed it under Norwegian protection. Iceland claimed that, since Denmark was a signatory to the treaty and Iceland was part of Denmark at the time, it had access to the international waters around Svalbard and their still undepleted fishing grounds. Norway, in its role as protector of the territory (and of its own fishing fleet), disagreed, having made Svalbard part of its reserved fishing grounds at the beginning of the 1980s. (Svalbard is roughly 1,000 miles from either Oslo or Reykjavik.) No doubt this will be resolved to Iceland's advantage as the smaller country, because Norway would not like to see the EU's fishing fleets become involved in the settlement of the dispute. By 2005 Iceland's deep-sea fish catch remained its major source of export earnings due to its preferred access to the EU and European Economic Area (EEA) market. Cod and herring were equally important in the total allowable catch (TAC) allotted to Iceland under the Common Fisheries Policy.

In facing the challenges of the 1990s, Iceland had the advantage of stable long-term political leadership, which directed Iceland's economy toward the energy and tourism sectors with increasing success. The exploitation of Iceland's thermal energy sources combined with the attraction of rising prices for aluminum led to large-scale investment projects in eastern Iceland. Given the small size of the Iceland economy, the influx of large-scale foreign investment to complete the power and aluminum plants had a major impact. Wages rose, housing prices climbed, and inflation seemed to get beyond the control of the central bank. The exchange rate of the Iceland króna rose even as the central bank increased its purchases of dollars on the foreign exchange markets. Meanwhile, Icelandic enterprises took advantage of the influx of foreign capital to expand the numbers of airlines and consumer marketing chains. Unemployment remained low as a result.

The collapse of the Soviet Union at the beginning of the 1990s led to the creation in 1995 of the Council of Baltic Sea States. Iceland's leading role in the CBSS gives it even closer contacts with, and influence on, the rest of the European Union since the accession of the Baltic states and Poland in 2004. Of all the Nordic states, then, Iceland has created the most innovative range of institutional responses, both internationally and domestically, to the development of the European Union, even as it remains the most peripheral country geographically.

Norway

Norway was occupied by the Nazis early in World War II to provide German submarines and airplanes a secure flank from which to harass Allied convoys. Wartime destruction was severe in terms of loss of population, bombing of port installations, and German destruction of housing and infrastructure in the initial invasion and final withdrawal from northern Norway. But Norwegian aluminum production was vital to the German war effort, so extensive construction of hydroelectric facilities, aluminum plants, and mines as well as the related infrastructure for transport and communication took place. Aid to Norway, amounting to nearly 6% of its prewar national income, went partly to importing machinery and equipment, and especially for building up its merchant marine. Although Norway's substantial foreign reserves at the end of the war derived mostly from the shipping services its state shipping line, Nortraship, had provided to the Allies during the war, over one-half of its shipping had been lost during the war. A substantial part of US aid was used to import foodstuffs from the United States, as Norway, like the United Kingdom, continued food rationing and price controls well after the war. Price controls were not lifted on food until 1952, but rationing and price control on automobiles lasted until 1960.[4]

On three separate occasions, 1961, 1972, and 1994, Norway applied for membership in the EU. It was rejected the first time, along with the United Kingdom, and the last two times it was the Norwegian electorate that narrowly rejected joining. Despite the desire of the government and the business community to join the EU, the resistance of the electorate means that Norway is not likely to apply again for some time, although it remains a member of the European Economic Area with Iceland. Norway's abundant oil supplies have enabled it to sustain a high rate of growth despite maintaining an even more elaborate social welfare system than its Nordic neighbors, Denmark and Sweden. Moreover, it has exploited its excellent fjord harbors and cheap hydroelectric power at the head of the harbors to create a prosperous manufacturing industry. It had second thoughts about being out of the EU in the late 1980s, but this was due more to the drop in oil revenues than to fears of losing access to the EU market. The political decision to opt out of the EU, first in the 1970s and then in the 1990s, has had no adverse economic consequences for Norway, and is not likely to so long as its export industries have access to the EU market and the price of oil remains firm, especially since 2002.

In the first oil shock, which followed Norway's second decision to opt out of the European Union, Norway followed an easy money policy, which facilitated construction of its North Sea oil platforms, but also depreciated the krone in terms of the dollar. This was a sensible strategy for a country that rapidly became a net exporter of oil, which was priced in dollars. Norway's export earnings, therefore, were enhanced by the devaluation of its currency. By the time of the third oil shock in the mid-1980s, however, Norway's monetary policy, and its inflation rates, had converged to typical European values. At the beginning of the 1990s Norway tried, in common with other European Economic Area countries, to peg the krone to the ECU to show good faith in negotiating tariff-free access to the EU countries. All the EEA countries abandoned that effort in 1992 just as the United Kingdom and Italy were forced out of the EMS. Norway's currency had to devalue; only Switzerland revalued. As a result, Norway's export earnings were enhanced thereafter, even before the price of oil rose again after 2001. By 2005 they had reached record levels, in terms both of dollar amounts and of proportion of GDP.

Norway's access to North Sea oil has allowed it to finance a costly welfare state, encompassing not only high wages in the public sector, including education and health services, but also high prices for agricultural and dairy products produced domestically. Whenever oil revenues expand, as they have since 2001, pressures build to reallocate them toward current consumption, both public and private. Hence, a center-right coalition government voted narrowly into office in 2001 could make only marginal structural reforms in the Norwegian labor market, including reduced unemployment benefits for state employees and allowance for the use of overtime hours and temporary employees by private employers. In the election in autumn 2005, however, a left-center coalition was elected on campaign promises to undo these reforms and even to imitate the failed French policy of restricting the length of the working week. The Norwegian case highlights, this time for a small, relatively homogeneous country, the political difficulty that governments encounter when trying to make structural reforms in labor markets. The Norwegian unemployment rate, while rising before the oil boom began in 2003, remains low relative to the EU-25 level, and low even by comparison with the other Nordic countries.

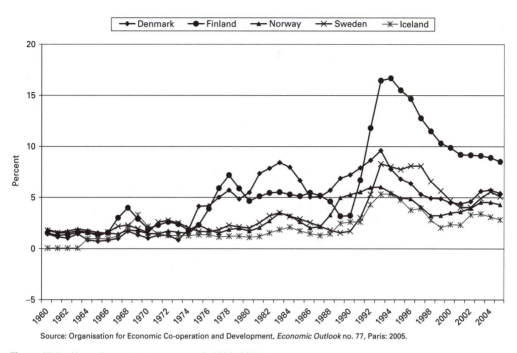

Source: Organisation for Economic Co-operation and Development, *Economic Outlook* no. 77, Paris: 2005.

Figure 17.5   Unemployment rates compared, 1960–2005

Sweden

Despite Sweden's neutral status during World War II, it benefited from Marshall Plan aid and the restoration of the traditionally strong trade ties with West Germany after the war. Justifiably proud of the success of its welfare state, established in the 1930s as a "middle way" between capitalism and socialism, it perfected the redistributive mechanisms of its society while enjoying high growth rates in the 1950s and 1960s. It ensured the continuation of Swedish-style socialism with political reforms in 1970, which provided shorter terms of office and a single-chamber parliament elected by proportional representation. Unfortunately, the rigidity of the institutions for redistribution made it very difficult for Sweden to find a suitable response to the successive oil shocks. Like Austria, it tried to peg its currency, the krona, to that of its major trading partner. Unfortunately, it chose the European basket currency, the ECU, rather than the deutsche mark. As a result, it experienced more of the oil shock in terms of dollar prices than either Austria or West Germany.

Moreover, the Swedish government provided increased employment opportunities directly, rather than through state enterprises as with Austria. Giving public employees strong unions with rights to strike then made it impossible to impose the efficiency-enhancing reforms that were possible in Austria. Worse, it actually nationalized companies in the hardest-hit sectors such as steel and shipbuilding, increasing the burden of subsidies for the state. A mounting crisis showed up as wages continued to grow rapidly in response to wage procedures, which effectively institutionalized the "Dutch disease" in Sweden. As in the Netherlands in the 1970s, wage increases won by the most productive workers in Sweden, typically in the export-oriented multinational firms, were the standard for wage adjustments for the rest of the labor force, especially in the growing public sector. As wages rose, labor productivity grew more and more slowly, even more slowly than in the EEC, probably because the high interest rates needed in Sweden to keep the krona in line with the ECU raised the cost of the capital required to modernize Swedish industry. By 1991 Swedish per capita income had fallen from third place among the OECD countries to fourteenth. At this time, Sweden had the largest public sector of any country in western Europe, equivalent to 60% of GDP and employing one-third of the labor force.

In 1992 the conservative-oriented government of Karl Bildt began privatization and tax reform and reduced welfare entitlements, as well as formally announcing that the krona would be linked to the ECU again after several devaluations in the 1980s. The exchange rate crisis of 1992 that took the United Kingdom and Italy out of the formal Exchange Rate Mechanism also took Sweden and Finland out of their informal commitment to it. Despite joining the EU in 1995, Sweden has still (2006) not committed itself even to start the process of joining the eurozone by locking its exchange rate with the euro in the ERM. For Bildt's troubles, which also included negotiating terms for Sweden's entry into the EU, his government was voted out of power in 1994. Entry into the EU was still approved, narrowly, by the electorate, but the dismantling of the rigid redistributive mechanisms of the state sector was put on hold for the time being.

The new Prime Minister, Goran Persson, continued the tight monetary and fiscal policy initiated by Bildt. At the end of 1996 Sweden announced its intention to join the ERM and participate in the common currency of the EMU starting in 1999, despite increased grumbling at the weakening of welfare benefits. As the government began to tighten its expenditures on health, pension, and unemployment benefits in order to meet the Maastricht criteria on government deficits and debt ratios, however, public opinion turned further against the EMU and the government backed off, even while proclaiming its support for the EU and eventual membership in the eurozone. Re-elected narrowly in 2002, as unemployment had started falling and the economic

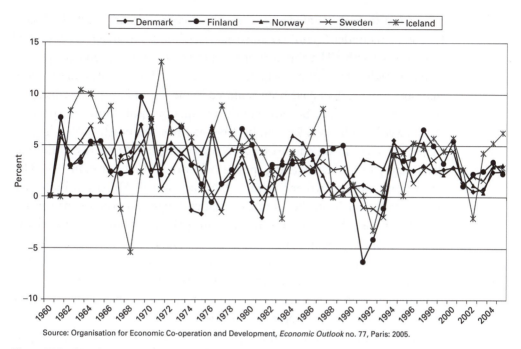

Source: Organisation for Economic Co-operation and Development, *Economic Outlook* no. 77, Paris: 2005.

Figure 17.6 Growth rates compared, 1960–2005

growth rate had picked up again, the Persson government revived the idea and held a referendum in September 2003. The Swedish voters turned down the proposal, much as the Danish voters had three years earlier. The relative prosperity of the Swedish economy at the time, at least compared to France, Germany, and Italy, also helped undermine the government's arguments in favor of joining. With the continued rise in the price of oil afterwards, however, growth slackened and unemployment began to rise again – but, instead of turning public opinion in favor of the euro, the sluggish economic performance turned public opinion against the Persson administration, which lost the general election held in September 2006.

Nevertheless, the economic record of Sweden under ten years of socialist government compares favorably with the rest of the Nordic countries, and with the Swedish economy's previous ten years, when it managed to record large deficits, slow growth, and rising unemployment. Figure 17.6 compares the real GDP growth rates (always in 2000 PPP dollars) of the five Nordic countries.

The relative success of the Swedish economy under these adverse conditions shows how it is possible, after all, for an elaborate welfare state to meet the political demands of the electorate in an advanced democracy. The right mix of institutions in an advanced industrial economy can supply the transfer payments under Scandinavian socialism without endangering continued economic growth.[5] The key to Sweden's success has been the encouragement of much higher rates of participation in the labor force by its citizens, both male and female, than have been achieved in the rest of Europe. Swedish participation rates in the labor force of the population aged fifteen to sixty-four have never been below 75% and by 1990 had reached nearly 85%. The participation rates of women are especially high compared to the rest of Europe, consistently just four percentage points below that of men (e.g. in 1991 84% of men and 80% of women were in the labor force). Moreover, both men and women remain in the labor force much longer on average than in the rest of Europe, which increases the amount paid into pension plans relative to the amount drawn out. Finally, as observed everywhere in advanced industrial economies, increased participation rates for women in the labor force, especially at younger ages, decreases total fertility and ultimately reduces the dependency ratio in the economy. (Note in table 17.1 that Sweden has the lowest birth rate of all the Nordic countries.)

When Sweden had the presidency of the European Union in the first part of 2003 it initiated an EU-wide study of how to increase participation rates elsewhere in the Union, especially for women and for older men and women. Much of the "structural reforms" in European labor markets since then has been directed toward emulating the Swedish success in these two dimensions, as well as in reducing the risks to employers of hiring new employees who may not work out. By reducing income taxes on wages and increasing the length of working time required for full pension rights, the Swedish government was able to encourage both Swedish men and women to stay in the labor force longer. This helped restore economic growth and the government budget by the end of the 1990s. Sadly, while the Persson administration was able to tweak the costs somewhat of the Swedish welfare state in the late 1990s, by 2005 it had lost public support for making further structural reforms along the lines that had proved successful in Denmark and the Netherlands. Even the Swedish model has its limits in gaining popular support, it appears.

Conclusion

With the expansion of the EU in 2004 to include the Baltic states, the northern tier of European countries provides an interesting array of institutional responses to the economic challenges of the twenty-first century. In technology, all five have advanced rapidly into the new age of information communications technology (ICT), with Finland's Nokia taking the lead at first, but provoking an effective response by Sweden's Ericsson. In labor market reforms Sweden has achieved participation rates that are the envy of the rest of Europe, but it has difficulty in implementing other reforms to facilitate occupational mobility, as in Denmark or Finland. Norway and Iceland show that government dependence on exploiting a natural resource need not lead to authoritarian rule or confiscatory taxation. Their concerns over fishing rights and location-specific energy sources have limited their enthusiasm for international institutions that require ceding important elements of economic sovereignty. In sum, all five show the possibilities of "free-riding" on effective economic institutions by making reciprocal agreements bilaterally with the European Union and with each other. The first example given in this chapter, the interesting convergence of the exchange rate movements of the five currencies with respect to the dollar since the introduction of the euro in 1999, shows the possibilities for individual countries to copy effective economic institutions, even if they do not adopt them formally. The next chapter compares the contrasting experiences of the four countries making up the southern periphery of the European Union, but it also concludes with the same lessons about the adoption of effective institutions.

NOTES

1. See the interesting analysis in Tim Knudsen and Bo Rothstein, "State building in Scandinavia," *Comparative Politics* 26 (2), 1994, pp. 203–20.
2. Global System for Mobile, a digital European cellular standard, based on TDMA (time division multiple access) technology, specifically developed to provide system compatibility across country boundaries. This compatible network enables GSM cellular users to use a single cellular phone throughout Europe, most of Asia, and parts of North and South America and have every call billed to one account. Countries have been rapidly building GSM networks, resulting in over 160 million fully working subscribers in over 125 countries.
3. Alan Milward, *The Reconstruction of Western Europe, 1945–51*, London: Metheun, 1983, p. 441.
4. Fritz Hodne, *The Norwegian Economy, 1920–1980*, New York: St. Martin's Press, 1983, pp. 144–5.
5. See Peter Lindert, *Growing Public: Social Spending and Economic Growth since the Eighteenth Century*, 2 vols., New York: Cambridge University Press, 2004, especially his analysis of the success of the Swedish welfare state.

18 The latecomers: lessons in preparation

Introduction

The four countries analyzed in this chapter have valuable lessons to share with the ten accession countries of 2004. Each of them entered the EU when it was very poor relative to the existing membership; each had to make sweeping changes in domestic institutions to be accepted into the EU; and each has become much better off economically over time, but in quite different ways. Their separate routes toward eventual prosperity and accommodation with the institutions of the EU provide useful insights for subsequent entrants, which are analyzed in chapter 19. Figure 18.1 shows that the course of each latecomer was erratic, to say the least.

Despite their common exclusion from the original make-up of the European Economic Community, all four countries experienced rapid rates of GDP expansion during the golden age of economic growth, from 1960 to 1973. Ireland stood out, however, with the slowest-growing economy among the four. Its per capita income declined from the level of Spain to that of Portugal before it joined the EEC, along with the United Kingdom and Denmark, in 1973. Thereafter, Ireland's growth performance improved, but it did not regain its leadership among the four until the mid-1990s. This was the result of a marked acceleration in its growth rates in the late 1980s, the result not of improved adaptation to the EU's *acquis communautaire* but, rather, of a radical change in domestic economic policy. Ireland's switch to a low level of income tax and flexible labor market regulations has raised hackles among the largest economies in the eurozone, all the more because it is being imitated by a number of the accession countries that joined the EU in 2004.

Greece joined in 1980, and managed to have the weakest growth of all four countries thereafter, until it too changed domestic policies in 2000 in order to join the eurozone. The change in monetary policy has led to a sharp revival

Table 18.1 Latecomers: basic facts

Area	(kilometers²)	of EU-25
Greece	131,940	3.3%
Ireland	70,280	1.8%
Portugal	92,391	2.3%
Spain	504,782	12.7%
Population	(July 2005 estimate)	of EU-25
Greece	10,668,354	2.3%
Ireland	4,015,676	0.9%
Portugal	10,566,212	2.3%
Spain	40,341,462	8.8%
GDP	(2004 estimate, PPP)	of EU-25
Greece	$226.4 billion	1.9%
Ireland	$126.4 billion	1.1%
Portugal	$188.7 billion	1.6%
Spain	$937.6 billion	8.0%
Per capita income	(PPP)	of EU-25 average
Greece	$21,300	79.2%
Ireland	$31,900	118.6%
Portugal	$17,900	66.5%
Spain	$23,300	86.6%
Openness	([X+M]/GDP)	with EU-25
Greece	57.2%	56%
Ireland	190.2%	62%
Portugal	89.0%	78%
Spain	69.5%	71%
Vital statistics (per 1,000)	Birth rate	Death rate
Greece	9.72	10.15
Ireland	14.47	7.85
Portugal	10.82	10.43
Spain	10.10	9.63

Sources: Central Intelligence Agency, *World Factbook, 2005*, available at http://www.cia.gov/cia /publications/factbook; Statistical Office of the European Communities, *Europe in Figures: Eurostat Yearbook 2005*, Brussels: 2005.

in Greek growth rates, leading to lower reliance on EU structural and agricultural support funds. In both the Irish and Greek cases, their initial reliance on the redistribution mechanisms of the EU's agricultural and regional policies actually reduced the governments' incentives to make radical changes in economic policy. Ireland and Greece, therefore, stand out as clear examples of the problem that economists label as "moral hazard": unconditional relief

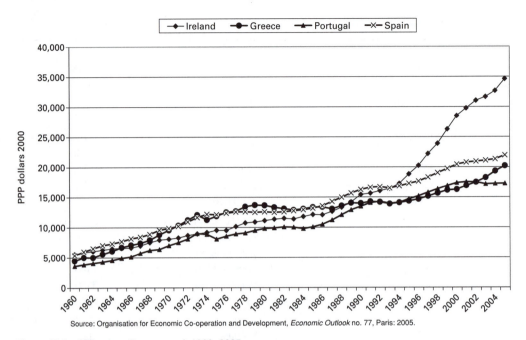

Source: Organisation for Economic Co-operation and Development, *Economic Outlook* no. 77, Paris: 2005.

Figure 18.1   GDP per capita compared, 1960–2005

to a poor country can keep it poor indefinitely by enabling it to maintain its dysfunctional economic policies. In both cases, it was the shock to the government of being excluded from the European Monetary System that created, finally, the incentives to make radical changes in domestic economy policies. Ireland's shock came in 1992, when it was forced to devalue sharply to stay in the new Exchange Rate Mechanism. Greece's shock came in 1999, when it was excluded from the first round of countries to join the euro while fellow latecomers Portugal and Spain reaped the advantages stemming from lower interest rates and increased foreign investment.

The contrasting examples of Portugal and Spain reinforce the lesson regarding the danger that the EU's redistributive finance mechanisms tend to create moral hazard problems. Both Portugal and Spain were deliberately excluded from membership in the EU until well after the fall of their respective authoritarian dictatorships in the mid-1970s. Not until 1986 were they finally allowed to enter, well after both had proved the endurance of their democratic regimes by repeated elections without military coups or revolutions. In the meantime, both had managed to survive the oil shocks of the 1970s, and – unlike Ireland and Greece, when those two entered the EU – both Portugal and Spain enjoyed renewed growth after 1986. Since that time, even though both were in the first group of countries to adopt the euro in 1999 and have had their monetary policy set by the European Central Bank ever since, their experience has diverged again. Due to differences in domestic policies, especially marked in the labor markets, Spanish growth has recovered while Portugal is once again slipping to the bottom rank among the four latecomer countries.

The experience of these four countries, therefore, has set the stage for the EU's attitude toward the accession countries, especially those under communist rule in central and eastern Europe. The redistribution of agricultural and regional support to the accession countries is strictly limited, with emphasis on technical training and legal guarantees for foreign investments instead. The accession countries, observing the recent history of their predecessors joining the EU, have also realized that their domestic policies are the key to eventual economic success, not reliance on the EU or imitation of any particular country in the EU. The recent Irish success with attracting foreign direct investment by exceptionally favorable tax and regulatory terms for foreign companies, however, has generated a number of attempts at imitation.

Ireland

Ireland's traumatic relationship with the United Kingdom has dominated its economic, as well as its political, life for centuries. That relationship will continue to be traumatic so long as the island is separated into Northern Ireland, part of the United Kingdom since the Act of Union in 1800, and the Republic of Ireland, separated from the United Kingdom in 1921. Political separation in the 1920s did not lead to economic success for the Republic, however, due to autarkic policies designed to cut trade links with Britain and develop home industry. These policies were first imposed by the United Kingdom in the 1920s as a means of obtaining compensation for property taken by the new Irish state. But Irish nationalists eagerly embraced these same policies in the 1930s as a means of eliminating dependence on British manufactures. Ireland remained neutral throughout World War II, so while it received little damage it also received little Marshall Plan aid. Not until 1957 did Ireland join the World Bank and the International Monetary Fund, the twin pillars of the Bretton Woods system set up by the United States and the United Kingdom. And it took another ten years for it to sign on to the General Agreement on Tariffs and Trade, the third pillar of the postwar international economic system. By this time, however, Irish trade was expanding rapidly, especially with the United Kingdom, and economic growth was finally being achieved. So it was essential for Ireland to join the EEC when the United Kingdom's third application for membership was finally accepted in 1973.

However, there were no oil or natural gas deposits off the coasts of Ireland, so the British strategy for coping with the first oil shock was never considered. Also in contrast to the United Kingdom, Ireland benefited greatly from its membership in the EEC. The EEC's agricultural price supports were extravagantly high for Irish farmers, who comprised a much larger part of the backward Irish economy than their British counterparts. Further, the increasingly generous disbursements of regional aid helped improve hitherto neglected highways and other infrastructure throughout the island. It was not unreasonable for Ireland to join the European Monetary System in 1978 even while the United Kingdom opted out. In the long run this has proved a wise decision, but in the short run the Irish punt appreciated against the British pound along with the rest of the EMS currencies. For Ireland, this meant a loss of a large part of the British market for its exports at a time when the potential market for its exports on the Continent was stagnant, due to the deep recession afflicting industrial western Europe. Ireland was therefore especially hard hit during the second oil shock. The expansionary demand policies pursued by the Irish government only made inflation worse, and necessitated readjustments of the Irish central rate within the exchange rate grid of the EMS. Government debt soared as a percentage of GDP, and unemployment rates were among the highest in western Europe.

From the mid-1980s on Irish governments cut spending while maintaining faith with the EMS and the tight monetary policy of the Bundesbank. As a result, unemployment remained high, emigration increased, and governments changed much more frequently. By the mid-1990s, however, the cumulative effects of deregulation, reduced interest rates, and foreign investor confidence in the stability of the Irish punt relative to the deutsche mark encouraged rising investment. This led to resumed economic growth, rising per capita incomes, and a rapid fall in both government deficits and stocks of debt as a percentage of GDP. Thanks to the large stock of government debt outstanding by 1992, a sharp fall in the interest rate demanded by investors in Irish bonds meant a sharp reduction in government expenditures on debt service. This reduced the deficit, and surpluses throughout the 1990s reduced the stock of debt as well. Moreover, as private investment increased, the largest part of which is foreign-financed, Irish workers are now encouraged to stay in Ireland instead of migrating elsewhere. Even those who have sought jobs elsewhere in the EU are induced to return and to meet the demand for new construction and service workers; immigrants are arriving from central and east Europe as well.

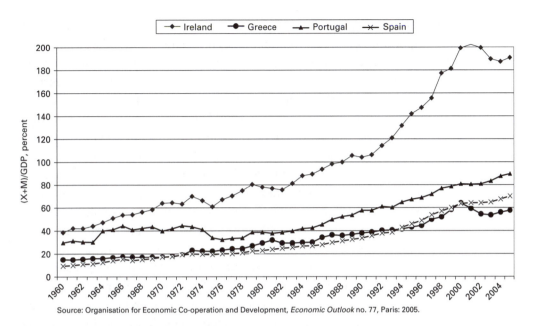

Source: Organisation for Economic Co-operation and Development, *Economic Outlook* no. 77, Paris: 2005.

Figure 18.2   Openness compared, 1960–2005

Ireland for centuries has created a culture sympathetic to net emigration; in the twenty-first century it has to deal with the social and cultural adjustments needed for a country experiencing net immigration.

The Irish success story was touted in the 1990s as an example of how restrictive fiscal policy can be expansionary, essentially by crowding in private investment as interest rates fall with the reduction of government debt. But it helps greatly to be a small country with a large part of its debt held by foreigners in countries with floating exchange rates, such as the United Kingdom and the United States, and it helps also to have an internationally mobile labor force when things are going well. The dependence of Ireland's industry on multinational firms that are exploring investment opportunities the world over also raises the concern that the Irish investment boom is too dependent on the generosity of strangers.[1] The investment can stop when the multinational firms decide to expand instead in central and eastern Europe, or in Asia. Even cheaper labor is accessible now in those countries and equally friendly government taxes and regulations may possibly exist, at least in the new EU members.

Figure 18.2 shows clearly that the Irish success has been associated with a dramatic rise in openness; a rise that came to a halt in 2001, although it had not yet been reversed by 2005. Economists always note, however, that gross *national* product has not grown to the same extent as gross *domestic* product. Given the importance of foreign multinationals in Ireland, which take advantage of the very low taxes on corporate income by putting as much of their revenue as possible in their Irish branches and subsidiaries, a large part of the income generated by domestic production in Ireland goes to foreign corporations. Our measure of openness, therefore, would be even more dramatic if we took GNP as the base instead of GDP. The halt in the rise of openness in 2001, however, was also associated with a fall in GDP growth to more sustainable rates – albeit rates that were still enviable for other eurozone economies.

Moreover, Irish inflation rates, which were much higher than the average eurozone rates in 2000–2003, have subsequently actually fallen below the eurozone average (see figure 18.3), just as Irish per capita income has risen above the eurozone average.[2] Finally, Irish unemployment rates remain the lowest in the EU, while the government continues to enjoy budget surpluses and the lowest ratio of government debt to GDP in the Union. This contrasts sharply with the experience of the next low-income country to enter the EU: Greece. Among the four countries considered here, however, Greece was the last to join the euro and to impose a tight money policy on its economy.

Greece

Greece was the next peripheral member state to join the EU, entering in 1980. Its ancient history, unique culture, and, above all, strategic location at the eastern end of the Mediterranean and southern outlet of the Black Sea have made its political history increasingly turbulent. At the beginning of the nineteenth century western Europe took serious notice of Greece's attempts to break away from the rule of the Ottoman Empire and aided its war for independence, begun in 1821. Ever since, Greece has gradually expanded its territory, usually by conquest, but always with the consent of the great powers in Europe at the time. At the end of World War II both British troops and Greek resistance forces, led by the Communists (ELAS), could take credit for the final departure of German troops, in October 1944. Armed conflict then broke out between the British troops and the ELAS forces, with the United Kingdom prevailing and restoring the prewar constitutional monarchy. Unable to continue meeting the expense of the defense of Greece by 1947, the United Kingdom asked for US support. This led to the Truman Doctrine, which in turn initiated the long-term American strategy of lending military support if necessary to ensure that communists did not take control of governments in western Europe. In this perspective, Marshall Plan aid was the necessary economic support to enable non-communist governments to establish their postwar legitimacy after being in exile during Nazi occupation.

Even with the rapid rebuilding of damaged infrastructure, especially the Corinth Canal and the various port facilities, Greece's political system remained in turmoil. The monarchy proved increasingly unpopular with the population, which led to the rise of socialist parties in the legislature. This led to either the king or a military junta disbanding the elected government, which in turn provoked even more determined opposition from the population. While the rest of Europe was enjoying the golden age of 1950–73, Greece was wracked with political disputes and excessive military expenditures. Between the repressive regulations of economic life imposed by the military or monarch when in power and the excessive expenditures on social subsidies instituted by the socialists when they were in power, Greece managed reasonable rates of growth, but accompanied by increased income inequality. Finally, the ruling military junta from 1967 to 1973 was discredited by its failure to incorporate Cyprus into Greece, a failure so abysmal that it led to the Turkish occupation of the northern part of the island, from 1974 to the present.

Since 1974, however, Greece has become a parliamentary democracy. Its economic policies were similar to those of Ireland (described above) in trying to achieve import substitution industrialization and relative self-sufficiency, and they were equally ineffective. Now with a democratic government, however, Greece was eligible once again to be considered for membership in the EEC, which would give it access to the resources of the much richer countries in western Europe. From the perspective of the EEC, the motivation for admitting Greece in 1980 was to lend it the economic support of democratic Europe and to discourage any thought of a resumption of military rule. Unfortunately for the economic development of Greece over the next two decades, its political elite responded in much the same fashion as described earlier for southern Italy. The generous subsidies and agricultural protection provided by the European Economic Community were directed by the socialist governments as political favors inside Greece rather than being used as incentives to promote economic growth and efficiency. If Ireland's record is disappointing because it did not do better than the richer countries in the EU until the 1990s, Greece's record until 2000 was truly dismal, because it did not even manage to keep pace. Only in 1996 was there the promise of implementing sounder economic policies that might begin the resurgence of growth that has occurred in other countries whenever they imitate the successful economic policies employed in the rest of the EU.

While Greece benefited from the increased disbursement of Cohesion Funds set up after the admission of Austria, Finland, and Sweden in 1995, its agricultural sector faced a new challenge in responding to the reform of the Common Agricultural Policy in 1992. True, Greek farmers prospered from receiving subsidies in the form of price supports now instead of the income supplements they had received previously. And Greek specialties in olives and Mediterranean fruits and vegetables continued to have an excellent market in the EU. But Greece was unable to continue to import cheap animal products from its traditional sources of supply in the Mediterranean, on account of the EU's quantitative restrictions on imports of meat from Third World countries. The increased prices of meat and food products now imported from the EU members were sufficient to shift Greece's agricultural trade with the EU from a net surplus before entry to a net deficit afterwards. They continued to have a deficit in agricultural trade with their traditional trade partners, so, from having a comparative advantage in agriculture, they now appeared to have a comparative disadvantage. This anomaly, of course, was really the result of the radically changed price structure of agricultural products created for Greece by its entry into the EU. (Something similar has occurred for the transition economies of central and east Europe during the first decade of their trade with the EU.) Worse, the improved economic situation for Greek farmers as they shifted production into the grain products most heavily subsidized under the CAP retarded the structural changes in the Greek economy needed to generate productivity increases and economic growth.

Socialist-inspired policies, approved by the electorate in election after election, sustained employment, however, in state-owned or state-subsidized industries. Greece emerged, along with Spain, as a country with persistently high rates of unemployment, the combined result of restrictions on private firms dismissing employees (which meant that they resisted hiring new employees in the first place) and generous unemployment benefits. The Greek government financed the benefits by an expansive monetary policy on the part of the central bank, which was very much under the control of the central government. The result was a consistent pattern of inflation far in excess of other EU countries, which kept Greece out of the Exchange Rate Mechanism, even though the drachma had to be included as part of the European Currency Unit used for accounting purposes in distributing EU funds.

As shown in figure 18.3, the Greek rate of inflation was the highest among these four poorer countries at the height of the two shocks of the 1970s. Only Portugal vied with it for excessive rates of inflation in response to the supply-side shocks that hit all European countries in the decade from 1974 to 1984. But

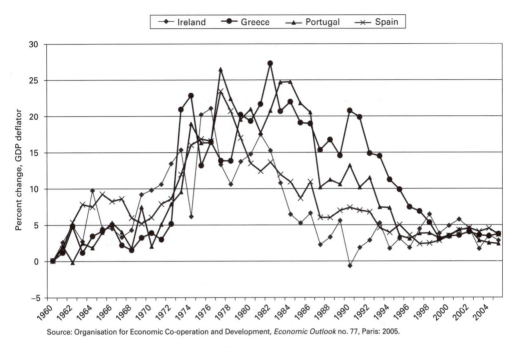

Source: Organisation for Economic Co-operation and Development, *Economic Outlook* no. 77, Paris: 2005.

Figure 18.3   Inflation rates compared, 1960–2005

Portugal's commitment to the European Monetary System in 1992 brought its inflation down to the rates of the rest of EMS countries by 1996, while Greece remained out until the end of 1999. From 2000 on, however, Greek inflation finally matched the low rates of the rest of Mediterranean Europe, to the benefit of its private economy and to the government's payment of interest to bondholders.

Unemployment, as explained above, did not respond fully to the improved economic climate for the private sector, due to continued restrictions on the labor market. Given the lack of structural reforms in the labor market as of 2006, the Greek economy does show a continued tradeoff between unemployment and inflation rates (see figure 18.4). The problem is that the privatization of state-owned enterprises results in labor redundancies, which increases unemployment. The proceeds gained by the government can be used to lower the level of government debt, which helps reduce debt service even further than the substantial decline created by the fall in interest rates on new government debt as a result of joining the eurozone. How long the fall in debt service can continue, however, depends on whether the government can reduce future expenditures on rising unemployment benefits and early pension payments provided to the workers laid off during privatization. In this respect, it is instructive to look at the case of Portugal, which entered the European

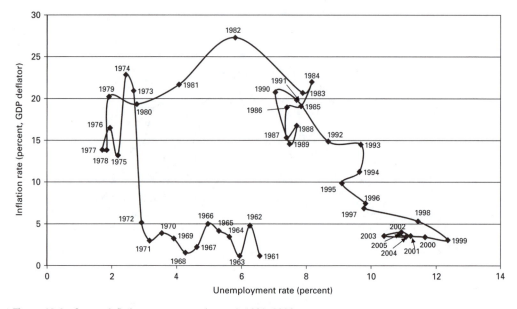

Figure 18.4   Greece: inflation versus unemployment, 1961–2005

Monetary System eight years earlier than Greece, and managed to do so by extensive privatization without making labor market reforms, much as in the case of Greece. The result there has been a gradual rise in unemployment and continued pressure on state finances.

Portugal

Portugal, the smaller Iberian cousin of Spain, had a very similar economic and political history in the twentieth century, usually anticipating events in Spain by a few years. Portugal's experience with a republic began in 1910, which was overthrown by a military junta in 1926, but without much internal strife. In 1928 an economics professor, Antonio de Oliveira Salazar, began forty years of authoritarian rule. Eschewing any connection to the dominant European ideologies of capitalism, communism, socialism, or fascism, Salazar promulgated "Lusitanian integralism," which in practice looked like Portuguese fascism to the rest of the world. This meant it had an Atlantic, not European, orientation, but nonetheless maintained an autarkic economic policy with extensive regulation of the economy and preferential political favors extended to the regime's supporters. The policy worked well for Portugal compared with the rest of Europe through the 1930s and 1940s. The 1950s, however, demonstrated the cumulative disadvantages of autarky compared with the economic miracles taking place in the rest of Europe. Even Spain was doing better, thanks to American aid.

Portugal, a participant from the start in the OEEC and Marshall Plan aid, joined the British-initiated European Free Trade Association in 1960. Trade expanded rapidly with the EFTA members, but fell with its overseas possessions. In the early 1960s revolts in its African colonies of Angola, Mozambique, and Guinea-Bissau led to increasing expenditures by Portugal for the development of its African resources, even as there were increases in inflows of foreign direct investment to the home country from the United States and Portugal's trading partners in EFTA. Tourism receipts also increased, as well as emigrant remittances, to cover a growing trade deficit. Emigration was so important, stimulated both by higher wages in northern Europe and the threat of military service in Africa, that Portugal actually lost population during its growth spurt from 1960 to 1973. In 1968 Salazar stepped down in favor of a hand-picked successor, Marcello Caetano. Caetano tried to liberalize the economy but was increasingly frustrated by political resistance and sharply divided opinion within the ruling class over the appropriate change of strategy for the country. Finally, in 1974, a military coup led by younger officers ousted Caetano, brought about a withdrawal from the African colonies, and initiated attempts to integrate Portugal more closely with western Europe.

To do this on the EEC's terms, however, representative democratic institutions had to be instituted and legitimated, which they had been by 1977, when Portugal applied for membership, ahead of Spain. Like Spain, Portugal suffered political upheaval at the same time as it endured the twin oil shocks of the 1970s. But, also like Spain, Portugal benefited from the return of large numbers of its emigrant workers, bringing their accumulated savings back from abroad. In addition, nearly 1 million ex-colonials returned to the home country, bringing with them their human and financial capital as well. These capital infusions, plus the advantage of no longer spending large sums abroad to maintain military control of the colonies, helped Portugal weather the oil shocks better than would have been possible otherwise.

Moreover, the EEC greeted the application of Portugal very favorably, recognizing the importance of economic advance for stabilizing its infant democratic institutions. Tariffs against Portuguese manufactures were dropped quickly, while Portugal was allowed to lower its tariffs gradually over a ten-year period. Extensive financial aid was also extended, starting in October 1975. The advantages of the trade arrangements for Portugal quickly elicited

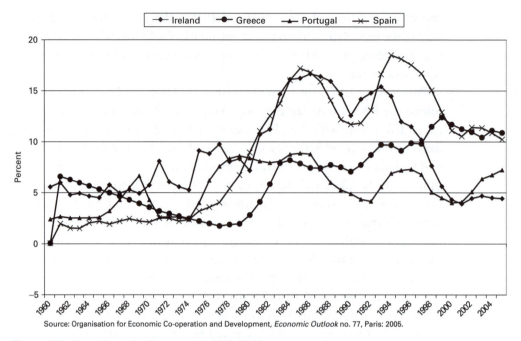

Source: Organisation for Economic Co-operation and Development, *Economic Outlook* no. 77, Paris: 2005.

Figure 18.5   Unemployment rates compared, 1960–2005

renewed foreign direct investment, to take advantage of its newly plentiful labor supply as well as its market access to all of western Europe. This was further encouraged when Portugal entered the EEC, in 1986.

The one encumbrance to rapid economic growth arising from the fall of the Salazar–Caetano dictatorship was the widespread nationalization of basic industrial and financial firms in the initial stages of the revolution. When foreign investment tailed off in the late 1980s the subsidies required to maintain employment levels in the state enterprises led to inflationary pressures, less investor confidence, and a marked slowdown in growth rates. At that stage of economic evolution it appeared that Portugal began learning lessons from Spain, rather than the reverse, as had been the case earlier. For example, Portugal entered the Exchange Rate Mechanism of the EMS only in April 1992, over two years after Spain. The result after that was increasing convergence in the economic performance of the two countries – Portugal's inflation rate fell toward the low Spanish rates while its unemployment rate rose towards that of Spain.

In common with Spain, however, the liberalization of Portuguese economic institutions under the Caetano administration's authoritarian control helped prepare Portugal to take advantage of membership in the European Union when it finally joined. Trade expanded rapidly, especially toward the EU, as one would expect in the case of a new member of a customs union. Especially noteworthy in Portugal's case, however, was the increase in trade with Spain as the mutual tariffs and trade restrictions between the two Iberian countries were dismantled as part of their assimilation of EU institutions.

As in the case of Ireland and Spain, industrialization by invitation led to an initial surge of foreign direct investment, also attracted by the opportunity to take advantage of low wages and the privatization of state-owned enterprises. Unlike Ireland and Spain, however, Portugal could not sustain the influx of foreign investment, despite the attraction of stable prices and cheap labor. Two factors were due to policy failures by Portugal: (1) the continued protection of workers from dismissal, especially in state-owned enterprises, which still dominated public utilities and manufacturing; and (2) the relative backwardness of the education level of the Portuguese population, especially in comparison to Ireland and Spain. The third factor was beyond the control of Portuguese policy-makers: (3) the geographic location of the country made the markets of the EU less accessible than from Spain, not to mention from most of the accession countries of 2004.

Portugal benefited greatly from the disbursement of EU structural funds when it joined, using them primarily to finance improvements in its infrastructure. The express highway system expanded from only 240 kilometers in 1987 to over 1,000 by 2004, and the telephone system increased its coverage by 70% during the 1990s compared to the OECD average of a 25% increase. To overcome its geographical separation from the EU markets, Portugal also initiated the construction of a high-speed rail link from Lisbon to Madrid. In addition, the government began plans to construct a much larger international airport to serve Lisbon, as well as to make smaller existing airports available to low-cost airlines. The structure of the Portuguese economy changed dramatically in response to the combination of EU subsidies and government initiatives. The construction and services sectors, especially, rose in relative importance, both in their share of total output (from 47.7% in 1980 to 69.0% in 2000) and employment (from 53.6% in 1980 to 65.4% in 2001). Meanwhile, agriculture's share of the Portuguese labor force, which had fallen from 48.8% in 1953 to 19.2% in 1980, leveled off at slightly over 12% after the country joined the Common Agricultural Policy fully in the 1990s. The continued rise in the share of services thereafter was attributable to a decline in the shares of manufacturing and construction in employment.

Such rapid and thoroughgoing structural change in the economy, naturally enough, created political tensions. Helping to meet the requirements of the European Monetary System in 1992, a more conservative government was elected, to continue the process of privatization in order to bring state finances under control. Further efforts to raise taxes by increasing value added tax to 19%, well above the EU average, and to reduce loopholes in the collection of income taxes led to increased dissatisfaction on the part of the electorate, however, and an avowedly socialist government was elected at the beginning of 2005. Even the new government, however, was under pressure from the EU to bring the budget deficit under control by reducing expenditures and raising taxes. The government responded by raising VAT again, to 21%, increasing the eligibility age for the retirement of public employees from sixty to sixty-five, decreasing unemployment benefits, and capping pay increases for teachers and nurses. The new government quickly lost public favor, leading to the election of a conservative politician, Anibal Cavaco Silva, as President in January 2006, based on his success in taking Portugal into the EMS while he was Prime Minister, from 1985 to 1995. Meanwhile, the EU's laxer interpretation of the Stability and Growth Pact, which started in 2005, gave the government, still with a socialist Prime Minister, a three-year grace period in which to bring its deficit back under the 3% of GDP limit. Portugal's experience of twenty years of membership in the EU highlights for other countries the continuing difficulties of coping with structural changes in the economy while confronting the different institutional requirements of the European Union.

Spain

The Iberian countries, Spain and Portugal, in contrast to Greece, were politically quiescent (i.e. repressed by fascist dictatorships) for the first thirty years after World War II. They had both been neutral during the war, albeit Portugal was favored with Marshall Plan aid while Spain was not. For strategic reasons (access to the southern Atlantic from the Azores to Brazil) and domestic political considerations (long-standing mercantile relations with the United Kingdom and the United States), Portugal had tilted to the Allies. Spain, on the other hand, had inclined toward the Nazis; General Franco and his Falange party had prevailed in the Spanish Civil War of the 1930s only thanks to military aid and advice provided by Nazi Germany and Fascist Italy. Both countries, however, pursued autarkic economic policies as a counterpart to their political isolation from the rest of Europe after the Allied victory in World War II. Portugal's policies were more successful than Spain's, probably because its economic sphere was much broader. Portugal retained control of its resource-rich colonies in Africa (Angola on the west and Mozambique on the east) and its entrepôt outposts in India (Goa) and China (Macao) until the early 1970s, and also maintained intensive trade relations with Brazil. Spain, however, had been stripped of its last overseas colonies following the Spanish-American War of 1898, and both Mexico and Argentina, natural trading partners for Spain, were at this time as equally committed as Spain toward achieving a self-sufficient economy.

In the initial years of postwar reconstruction in Europe Spain found that it could open trade with the rest of western Europe, as it did not require scarce dollars in exchange for exports of citrus, nuts, and wine to the Marshall Plan and European Payments Union countries. While ostracized politically by the rest of Europe, Spain managed to re-establish economic relations with western Europe, first through expanding bilateral trade with France, Italy, and the United Kingdom, and then indirectly through greater trade with the United States – and all this while being excluded from the Marshall Plan and later the European Payments Union.[3] Cut off from the reconstruction efforts under way in the rest of Europe, the economy stagnated during the late 1940s. A great deal of effort was made to achieve self-sufficiency in wheat production, so as to minimize Spain's need for foreign exchange. Increasingly complicated sets of multiple exchange rates were imposed on top of ad hoc import and export quotas. These were intended to cope with the lack of foreign exchange and the difficulty of earning any within the new international system of trade and finance surrounding it in Europe. Inevitably, they simply reinforced Spain's autarky and political isolation while thwarting any possibility of sustained economic growth. Nonetheless, with US support, Spain began to change policy starting in 1953, when American military aid began to arrive.

Fernando Guirao (1998) has argued persuasively, however, that, even in this period of economic travail, Spain found that its dominant trade partners were the member countries of the OEEC. Even though all of them joined in ostracizing the Franco regime politically, France, Italy, and the United Kingdom all found it beneficial to import Mediterranean foodstuffs and strategic raw materials from a nearby country that could not demand dollars in exchange but, instead, had to be content with blocked currencies or countertrade. Although Argentina did provide an important share of Spain's imports, especially of grain and beef, its role was fleeting and essentially gone by 1950, even when rapprochement between Argentine President Perón and Franco was at its peak. US trade picked up after the accord in 1953, when American military aid began to arrive in exchange for access to air- and naval bases in Spain.

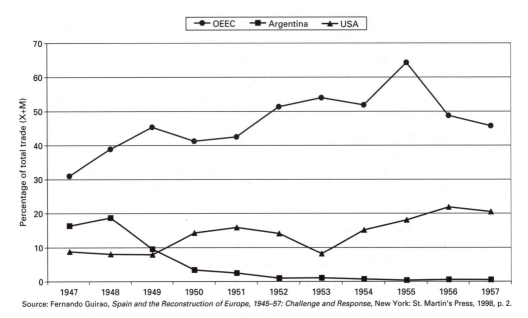

Source: Fernando Guirao, *Spain and the Reconstruction of Europe, 1945–57: Challenge and Response*, New York: St. Martin's Press, 1998, p. 2.

Figure 18.6   Spain's pattern of trade, 1947–57

Some improvement did occur in the Spanish economy in the early 1950s, but it seems to be mostly because of the arrival of American aid. This may have sustained Franco's autarkic policy a bit longer, much as American military bases in Greece provided extended support for that dictatorship. However, just as in Greece, American aid fell off in the late 1950s to lower levels. Meanwhile, Spanish attempts to industrialize, under strict direction from the central government, led to increasing foreign trade deficits. These placed growing pressures on the central bank's reserves, which constrained the country's entire economic strategy. The government reacted with an impressive turnabout in economic policy in 1959. This was aimed at opening up the economy to the rest of Europe, by reducing barriers to trade, migration, and capital movements, while strengthening the political power of the regime by maintaining strict controls over the tax system, the labor market, and the financial sector.

Spanish political stability depended on making economic progress, and this had to be accomplished by increasing economic relations with western Europe. Excluded deliberately from both the EEC and EFTA when they were formed at the expiration of the European Payments Union in 1958, Spain devised its unique response: the development of the *apertura* policy in Spain in 1959 and its acceptance into the OECD in 1960, the successor international organization to the OEEC. From 1960 on Spain shared in the general "golden age" of economic growth experienced by the OECD countries generally, while enduring the political and social tensions created by rapid structural change. Industrialization led to a rapid decline in the labor force employed in the agricultural sector and in the population living in rural areas. Then, the death of Franco in 1975 meant that Spain endured wrenching political change at the same time as it was trying to cope with the first oil shock, which was creating economic havoc through the industrialized world.

Franco's death enabled the joint development of a constitutional monarchy and parliamentary democracy. Franco had laid plans to restore the successor to the Bourbon dynasty, Juan Carlos I, to the Spanish throne after his death. Meanwhile, the Spanish political and intellectual elite, in exile since the end of the Civil War in 1939, returned in order to ensure that a parliamentary democracy would begin functioning. The peaceful and symbiotic relationship between the two forms of government, which exists in most other countries in Europe, was sealed by the dramatic action of the King in February 1981. On national television he donned full uniform, marched alone into the Cortes (the legislative assembly), where rebellious soldiers were holding the legislature hostage at gunpoint, and ordered the rebels to lay down their arms – a classic act of Spanish heroism that established simultaneously the legitimacy of the monarchy and the parliament.

The oil shocks and the political uncertainty of the transition period from 1974 through 1981 had devastated the industrial base that had arisen during the economic miracle period. Its key elements – iron and steel, shipbuilding, and cement – were all energy-intensive, so they were especially hard hit by the oil shocks. The political uncertainty made it difficult for strong remedial action to be taken, such as freeing energy prices to force a reallocation of resources. Nevertheless, overall economic growth was sustained by the prosperity of agriculture and the rise in commodity prices, the growth of the service sector, and the return of not just exiles but Spanish workers from abroad. The returning migrants brought with them heavy inflows of repatriated capital, financial as well as human. This helped finance the import deficits created by the oil shocks. Ironically, and unexpectedly, the oil shocks and the political shocks of the late 1970s were to some degree offsetting for Spain.

Industrial growth resumed in the 1980s as the political situation stabilized with a socialist government in power. Nevertheless, the high rate of unemployment that had arisen during the previous decade remained implacable, staying at the highest level in the European Economic Community. Due to political resistance from France and Italy, Spain's entry into the EEC was delayed until 1986, and even then the terms were unusually harsh. Full access to the

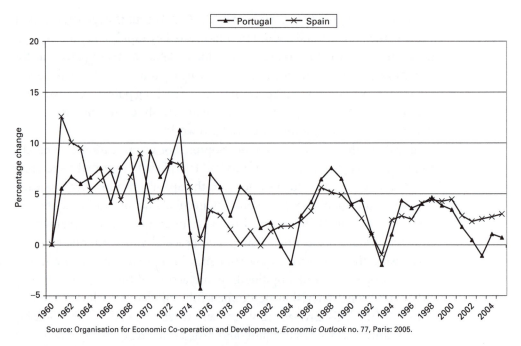

Source: Organisation for Economic Co-operation and Development, *Economic Outlook* no. 77, Paris: 2005.

Figure 18.7   Growth rates compared, 1960–2005

Common Market would be granted only after seven years and participation in the Common Agricultural Policy for all of Spanish agriculture was phased in over a ten-year period. Only gradually has Spain been able to disentangle itself from the web of restrictive regulations that bound up its economy for the benefit of Franco's dictatorship. In retrospect, the intermittent spurts of growth and structural change since 1960 have derived more from state-directed and -controlled initiatives than from an embrace of competitive markets. Figure 18.7 enables a comparison to be made between the fits and starts of growth by Portugal and Spain over the entire period of export-led growth for both countries, 1960 to 2005. By the beginning of the twenty-first century Spain's continued progress toward liberalization was drawing it ahead of its Iberian neighbor.

Spain's earliest growth spurt, in contrast to that in Portugal, was directed more toward the manufacturing and services sectors. Investment rates rose along with the expansion of trade, but more of the increased investment went into the expanding export sectors and less into housing stock. The new technology embodied in Spain's capital formation meant that nearly 60% of its growth in output came from improved productivity rather than just more capital and labor. The structural transformation of the Spanish economy as a result was the most striking among the four countries. Agricultural employ-ment fell from over 40% of the labor force to under 25%. Two million workers left agriculture in the ten years from 1961 to 1970. This provided a poten-tially elastic supply of labor for the expanding industrial, construction, and urban services sectors as well as a steady stream of migrant workers to France, Switzerland, and Belgium. Relatively little of the labor, however, went into manufacturing, due to the regime's maintenance of restrictive controls on the industrial labor force. As a result of government policy, then, most of the increase in industrial output was due to expanded capital stock and greatly increased productivity.

Emigrants' remittances grew, as did export earnings from labor- and natural-resource-intensive products, which helped boost imports rapidly while keeping the current account close to balance, although trade deficits did appear more frequently at the end of the period. Meanwhile, inflation was kept under relatively good control, largely because of IMF conditions imposed in the devaluation of the peseta in 1967. At this time, it was changed to 70 pesetas to the dollar from the 60 that had been settled on in 1959, when exchange controls were lifted and multiple exchange rates eliminated. The government's budget also went from a chronic deficit to being, more often than not, balanced. By 1973 enough progress had been made in the foreign sector and in the fiscal situation of the central government for the Bank of Spain to be given full authority, for the first time, over managing the foreign reserves of the country. Thus, well before the European Union countries had formed the European Monetary System with the intention of securing the de facto independence of their central banks from government control, Spain had already established the institutional basis for a stable currency.

The background conditions for Spain's extremely high unemployment lev-els in the 1980s, which rose to over 17% by 1985, began at the end of the Franco regime, when the first steps were taken to install a social welfare system along corporatist lines. When labor unions had been outlawed under Franco, employers were constrained by the state to provide the security of employment and benefits that otherwise might be obtained through collective bargaining. In the years following Franco's death the rigidities that Falangist regulations had created in Spanish labor markets were maintained even as European-style labor movements were gradually allowed to emerge. In 1977 freedom of association was recognized under the Decree on Labor Relations. This decree allowed the right to strike and collective bargaining, while also permitting the dismissal of individuals and groups of employees if enterprises needed to adjust to economic conditions. Trade unions had to organize at a national, or at least regional, level, as the new laws limited their effectiveness at the enterprise level. Anything that would allow more flexibility in labor markets was therefore opposed by labor unions as they sought to establish themselves on European models. Unemployment rose to the highest levels in western Europe as a result.

Spain and Portugal finally became full members of the EEC in 1986. Spain, with a population nearly double that of the other three periphery countries combined, and not much below that of the major four countries in the EEC, was able to exercise effective leadership in coalescing the four countries as a political bloc within the Community. As a result, they were increasingly able to extract development assistance from the rest of the member countries, all much richer and more advanced. The share of the EEC budget allocated to structural funds increased even as the share devoted to agricultural subsidies decreased, in response to the overall budgetary pressures on the EEC. The net effect was to change the basis for supporting the heavily agricultural members of the EEC from price supports to income supplements and development projects.

This strategy culminated when the "poor four" were able to extract contributions toward a Cohesion Fund from the European Free Trade Association countries as their price for agreeing to the European Economic Area agreement between the EU and EFTA. All the remaining EFTA countries were wealthier than the average for EU countries, so their participation in the single market widened the gap between rich and poor countries. The Cohesion Fund is intended solely for disbursal among the poor periphery, and is now part of the *acquis communautaire* of the EU. Given the small size of the EU budget, however, it is doubtful how effective this redistribution will be in maintaining (or regaining) economic convergence among the EU members. Moreover, Italy's experience of subsidizing the Mezzogiorno for half a century with no convergence in per capita incomes indicates that this kind of regional development policy is not a sensible long-run strategy.

Of the four countries that are currently receiving the bulk of the regional funds disbursed by the EU, Spain stands out as having the smallest amount relative to the size of its economy as measured by its gross domestic product (table 18.2). Until the most recent budget period, 2000–2006, when the Irish economy had emerged from the ranks of low per capita countries into one with an above-average per capita income, Spain consistently drew the smallest proportion of Structural and Cohesion Fund amounts from the EU relative to either its gross domestic product or its gross fixed capital formation (GFCF). True, Spain received much larger absolute amounts of funds due to the much

Table 18.2 Payments to and receipts from the European Union

Country	% GDP paid 1986–8	% GDP paid 1989–93	% GDP paid 1994–7	% GDP received 1986–8	% GDP received 1989–93	% GDP received 1994–7	% GDP net 1986–8	% GDP net 1989–93	% GDP net 1994–7
Ireland	1.2	1.2	1.3	5.4	6.5	5.2	4.2	5.3	3.9
Greece	0.9	1.0	1.2	3.7	5.2	5.3	2.8	4.2	4.1
Portugal	0.9	1.1	1.3	1.9	3.4	4.3	1.0	2.3	3.0
Spain	0.9	1.1	1.0	1.1	1.6	2.3	0.2	0.5	1.3

Source: Carmela Martín, *The Spanish Economy in the New Europe*, trans. Philip Hill and Sarah Nicholson, New York: St. Martin's Press, 2000, p. 215.

larger size of its population relative to the other three peripheral economies, but it also appears to have used the funds it received more efficiently than either Greece or Portugal.

Spanish agriculture stagnated until the industrialization program under Franco's *apertura* policy came into force. By 1960 agricultural output had already fallen to less than 25% of the Spanish economy, but from that point on the decline was steady, falling to 10% by 1975 and the death of Franco, and then to just over 6% by 1986 and Spain's entry into the European Economic Community. Since that time the agricultural sector has continued to decline in relative importance, falling to under 4% of GDP by 2000. In response to EEC membership Spanish agriculture changed the composition of its production, toward fewer cereals and more livestock, as well as toward higher-value food products such as wine, fruits, and vegetables. All in all, the fears of Italian and French competitors that membership of the Common Agricultural Policy would be exploited by Spanish producers at their expense have not been realized, thanks to the long preparation period during which the modernization of Spanish agriculture has been taking place, beginning in the early 1950s.

In common with the other three late entrants from the periphery of western Europe, Spain experienced a continued rise in the importance of foreign trade overall, as well as a marked change in orientation toward the other members of the EU customs union. Analyzing the trade patterns more closely, one finds that Spain has consistently run a trade surplus with the rest of the EU, while running consistent trade deficits with the oil-exporting countries, in common with most of western Europe. Overall, however, Spain ran a trade deficit of substantial proportions in the first few years after joining the EU, attributed in part to capital imports from the rest of western Europe to take advantage of relatively cheap labor in Spain. Upon closer examination, however, it appears

Table 18.3 Economic effects of the Structural and Cohesion Funds

% GDP	Ireland	Greece	Portugal	Spain
1989–93	2.5	2.6	3.0	0.7
1994–9	1.9	3.0	3.3	1.5
2000–2006	0.6	2.8	2.9	1.3
% GFCF				
1989–93	15.0	11.8	12.4	2.9
1994–9	9.6	14.6	14.2	6.7
2000–2006	2.6	12.3	11.4	5.5

Source: European Commission, *Unity, Solidarity, Diversity for Europe, Its People and Its Territory: Second Report on Economic and Social Cohesion,* Brussels: 2001, p. 122.

that the capital imports needed to finance the substantial trade deficit came from outside the EU, mainly the United States and Japan. Also interesting is the trade surplus that Spain gradually built up with Latin America, which in this case seems clearly related to the capital exports to Latin America that Spain began to make in the 1990s.

The other aspect of openness, of course, is the movement of people across frontiers that used to require passport controls and labor restrictions. Spanish guest workers were an important part of the foreign labor force in France and Switzerland during the 1960s, but mostly returned during the restrictions on guest worker programs that became universal in western Europe after the oil shocks of the 1970s. Spanish fertility rates became the lowest in western Europe over the course of the 1990s, so that Spain had become a country of net immigration by the beginning of the twenty-first century. Nevertheless, emigrant remittances remained an important part of Spanish foreign exchange earnings, and Spanish remittances home still exceeded remittances out of Spain by its foreign workers. Spanish workers abroad earned higher incomes than the foreign workers earned in Spain. The main lesson from Spain's experience in the EU, for both the EU and the current accession countries to realize, is that entry into the customs union has a much greater impact than entry into the common labor market. Trade, in the Spanish case, clearly substituted for migration, perhaps because by the time Spain entered the EU it had already made the major structural shift in population from rural to urban areas that accompanies industrialization and modernization. With that shift came not only higher incomes within the Spanish economy but also lower fertility rates and greater incentives to stay in Spain, with its expanding employment opportunities.

Internal political problems continue to plague the Spanish government. ETA (Basque nationalist) terrorists foment domestic political tension, which might be alleviated eventually within the larger political context of the EU. Spain, like the other three countries, benefits from tourism and emigrant remittances, relatively cheap labor, and the ability to induce further foreign direct investment if the correct policies are pursued. It remains nervous, however, about its reduced political influence within the EU as expansion continues into eastern and central Europe, and engineered a commitment from the EU that its regional funds would not be reduced before the end of 2006. To date, the Spanish economy has prospered while enjoying the benefits of EU membership, but these benefits have not stemmed so much from the grants received from the richer countries as from the legitimacy that EU directives and regulations continue to give to Spanish legislation and policies. These policies began working their way into the consciousness of the Spanish government even as early as the 1950s, when Spain was politically excluded from all the institutions that were laying the groundwork for the eventual success of the European Union economies. The process stretched over three decades at least, and is not yet complete. It is only very recently, under the center-right government of José Aznar that was in power from 1996 to 2004, that Spain began serious progress in deregulation and privatization, increasingly seen as vital to economic growth. While Spain's gas and electricity markets were fully liberalized in January 2003, prices are tightly regulated for the next ten years and expected to rise (at up to 2% a year) rather than fall, despite being among the highest in Europe already.

Conclusion

As the GDP per capita figures in figure 18.1 at the start of this chapter show, three of the four "periphery" economies are still relatively poor compared with the rest of the European Union member states. The exception is Ireland, thanks to its extraordinary growth in the late 1990s and the unique success of its "industrialization by invitation" policy. Greece and Portugal are still below 80% of the average EU per capita income despite the fact that average was lowered substantially by the addition of the ten accession states in 2004. Their common poverty has brought them together as a voting bloc within the EU, which has enabled them to obtain an increasing share of the EU budget in the form of regional development funds and, since 1995, Cohesion Funds largely financed by contributions from the richest member states. Their history of progress (or lack of it, in the case of Greece) since joining the EU, however, has shown that their poverty can be attributed in large part to poor economic policies. Membership in the EU has helped them re-evaluate their economic strategies, so that a consensus development program may be developing among them. By radically changing policies, Ireland has seen a dramatic rise in its per capita income, from close to 50% when it started to 90% of the EU-15 average and 120% of the EU-25 average in 2005. By not changing policies, in contrast, Greece saw its per capita income remain at 50% of the EU's average until very recently, when it, too, joined the common currency in 2000 after finally implementing the necessary monetary reforms. The experience of Ireland and Greece holds out a large measure of hope for policy-makers in other less developed countries, that selecting the right policy mix can make a difference.

The experience of Spain and Portugal also underscores the importance of domestic policy changes whether a country is a member of the European Union or not. Prior to entering the EU in 1986 Spain had already begun to make important changes in its economic policies, starting as early as 1959. Even under the authoritarian political regime of Franco steps were being taken toward opening the Spanish economy to European competition and expanding trade relations with the rest of the world. This meant that, when Spain did enter the EU, the new requirements of the single market and, eventually, the common currency policy simply reinforced the legitimacy of these structural changes. By contrast, Portugal clung to autarkic policies until after the death of Salazar. Moreover, even after the loss of its overseas empire in the mid-1970s, Portugal's socialist government used its access to EU funds to retain political power while protecting Portuguese capital and labor from external competition. Eventually, the election of a center-right government enabled Portugal to start making structural reforms, which facilitated economic growth, much as in the case of Greece.

The electoral defeats of center-right governments in both Portugal and Spain in 2004/2005, however, underscores the political risks of rapid deregulation and privatization when undertaken under adverse economic conditions. Perhaps the transition economies of central and eastern Europe can apply some of the lessons learned by these earlier arrivals in the EU. The next chapter takes up the economic experiences of the accession countries as they make their transition from autarkic, authoritarian, and centrally planned economies to market-driven capitalist economies within the framework of EU institutions.

NOTES

1. See Fred Gottheil, "Ireland: what's Celtic about the Celtic Tiger?," *Quarterly Review of Economics and Finance* 43 (5), 2003, pp. 720–37.
2. More about this phenomenon in chapter 19, when the Balassa–Samuelson effect under fixed exchange rate regimes is discussed.
3. See Fernando Guirao, *Spain and the Reconstruction of Europe, 1945–57: Challenge and Response*, New York: St. Martin's Press, 1998.

19   The newcomers: building institutions

Introduction

The ten accession countries that entered the European Union in 2004 represent the greatest challenge yet for the development of the EU's political and economic institutions. Their economic diversity is obvious from the "basic facts" presented in table 19.1. The accession countries' range of sizes alone makes it difficult for the European Union to have a uniform policy toward each. The difficulty of formulating policy toward them is compounded by the dispersion of their per capita incomes as well. To elicit economic policy lessons from their experiences to date, we must divide them up according to their economic history and their geographic location. Accordingly, we analyze the five central and eastern European countries (CEE-5) as a group: the Czech Republic, Hungary, Poland, the Slovak Republic, and Slovenia.

These five are also the first countries to make the transition from failed centrally planned economies under Soviet (or Yugoslav, in the case of Slovenia) domination to a reasonably successful form of market capitalism very much modeled on the continental European members of the European Union. By most economic criteria, as well as most political criteria, all five countries have completed their transition. Most economic activity is now in the private sector; most prices have been liberalized so that markets can allocate resources according to consumer demand; governments restrict themselves to the regulation of market activity under a consistent rule of law; and subsequent elections have replaced governments several times without resort to military coups or violent revolution.

Nonetheless, from the viewpoint of the European Union, their transition is not yet complete. Only gradually will each country be allowed to participate fully in the redistribution of funds under the EU budget to agriculture and regional development projects, or in the free movement of labor under the

Table 19.1 Newcomers: basic facts

Area	(kilometers²)	of EU-25
Cyprus	9,250	0.2%
Czech Republic	78,866	2.0%
Estonia	45,226	1.1%
Hungary	93,030	2.3%
Latvia	64,589	1.6%
Lithuania	65,200	1.6%
Malta	316	0.0%
Poland	312,685	7.9%
Slovak Republic	48,845	1.2%
Slovenia	20,273	0.5%
Population	*(July 2005 estimate)*	*of EU-25*
Cyprus	780,133	0.2%
Czech Republic	10,241,138	2.2%
Estonia	1,332,893	0.3%
Hungary	10,006,835	2.2%
Latvia	2,290,237	0.5%
Lithuania	3,596,617	0.8%
Malta	398,534	0.1%
Poland	38,635,144	8.5%
Slovak Republic	5,431,363	1.2%
Slovenia	2,011,070	0.4%
GDP	*(2004 estimate, PPP)*	*of EU-25*
Cyprus	$14.5 billion	0.1%
Czech Republic	$172.2 billion	1.5%
Estonia	$19.2 billion	0.2%
Hungary	$149.3 billion	1.3%
Latvia	$26.5 billion	0.2%
Lithuania	$45.2 billion	0.4%
Malta	$7.2 billion	0.1%
Poland	$463.0 billion	4.9%
Slovak Republic	$78.9 billion	0.7%
Slovenia	$39.4 billion	0.3%
Per capita income	*(PPP)*	*of EU-25 average*
Cyprus	$20,300	75.5%
Czech Republic	$16,800	62.5%
Estonia	$14,300	53.2%
Hungary	$14,900	55.4%
Latvia	$11,500	42.8%
Lithuania	$12,500	46.5%
Malta	$18,200	67.7%
Poland	$12,000	44.6%
Slovak Republic	$14,500	53.9%
Slovenia	$19,600	72.9%

(cont.)

Table 19.1 (*cont.*)

Openness	([X+M]/GDP)	with EU-25
Cyprus	92.7%	60%
Czech Republic	221.4%	78%
Estonia	177.8%	72%
Hungary	197.2%	72%
Latvia	101.6%	77%
Lithuania	113.9%	59%
Malta	174.7%	60%
Poland	72.5%	74%
Slovak Republic	205.7%	80%
Slovenia	114.2%	71%
Vital statistics (per 1,000)	*Birth rate*	*Death rate*
Cyprus	12.57	7.64
Czech Republic	9.07	10.54
Estonia	9.91	13.21
Hungary	9.76	13.19
Latvia	9.04	13.70
Lithuania	8.62	10.92
Malta	10.17	8.00
Poland	10.78	10.01
Slovak Republic	10.62	9.43
Slovenia	8.95	10.22

Sources: Central Intelligence Agency, *World Factbook, 2005*, available at http://www.cia.gov/cia/publications/factbook; Statistical Office of the European Communities, *Europe in Figures: Eurostat Yearbook 2005*, Brussels: 2005.

Schengen Agreement. Most interesting at this point (2006) is the issue of when each will want to join the common currency and subject its monetary policy to the control of the European Central Bank. All have agreed that they will try to meet the entry requirements, which are still modeled on the now obsolete Maastricht criteria. But, as the examples of Denmark, Finland, and Sweden show, a member country still has the sovereign right to determine when it might enter. There is no formal mechanism to force a recalcitrant country to join against the wishes of its government.

If the five central and eastern European countries can be analyzed as a bloc of successful entrants to the European Union, the three Baltic states represent a remarkable success story, even if their levels of per capita income and small size would seem to put them at the bottom of the group. Of all the transition economies now in, or ever likely to enter, the European Union, only the Baltic states were actually part of the Soviet Union. This means that their previous bureaucracies, responsible for central planning and the administration of all economic activity, were Russian-speaking, and often Russian nationals. The challenge of developing a corps of public officials competent to administer the EU's *acquis communautaire* in the Baltic states was, therefore, the most daunting task facing the European Commission. To date, their levels of per capita income remain the lowest among the member states. They are fortunate that the Nordic Council (chapter 17) has taken a special interest in their economic future by including them as members of the Council of Baltic Sea States, which will complement the development initiatives of the European Union. Through this new institutional arrangement, even Iceland and Norway, although not members of the EU, can justify offering development aid and technical assistance to the three Baltic states.

Finally, we must acknowledge the presence of Cyprus and Malta, two Mediterranean island states that, unlike Iceland in the middle of the Atlantic Ocean, could no longer be free riders on the expansion of trade with and among the EU's Mediterranean countries. From the viewpoint of the European Union, the case for including them was clearly political, not economic. Given the shift in voting power to Germany and the accession states that trade primarily with Germany, it was sensible for the Mediterranean member states to welcome Cyprus and Malta as a bit of counterbalance to the increased weight of northern Europe within the enlarged EU. But both islands have significantly higher levels of economic development than the former transition economies, and their main concerns in the future will be political, rather than economic.

The central and eastern European five

Figure 19.1 is the standard representation of the transition experience of the economies under Soviet rule or domination as they collapsed at the end of 1989. Taking the absolute (and doubtlessly mismeasured) level of gross domestic product of each country in 1989 as 100, economists track the subsequent levels over the following period. All five saw an immediate collapse in measured GDP that lasted for several years. They varied then in timing their respective turnarounds, which began their rebound toward previous levels. The timing of each country's recovery from the initial "transition shock" also varied. Poland reached it first and the Czech Republic last (though some analysts argue, however, that this was due to Poland's initial level being lower than the Czech

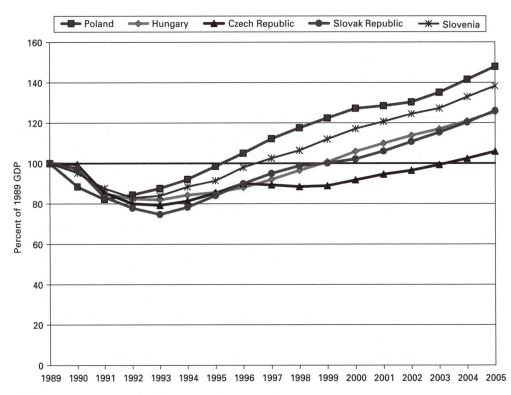

Figure 19.1   GDP in transition, CEE-5, 1989–2005

Republic's in 1990). Finally, each has had a different trajectory of growth since regaining the initial level of GDP.

Figure 19.1 highlights the diversity of transition experience over the period 1989–2005. Clearly, Poland was the first country to begin a turnaround, and the first to achieve the pre-existing levels of GDP, and it continues to outpace the other countries in levels of GDP. It set the standard in terms of setting a coherent set of policies for making the transition and executing them with relative success. Given the publicity attending the Polish experience and its willingness to take advice from Western experts, it is interesting that the other countries nevertheless tried other policies and other sequences of policies. The result of these national idiosyncrasies in transition policies is that economists now have a fascinating set of "natural experiments" to analyze and evaluate. The next country to begin a turnaround was Slovenia, and it was also the next country to achieve its previous level of GDP, taking seven and a half years compared to Poland's six. Ever since, Slovenia's GDP has ranged just below that of Poland. Hungary and the Slovak Republic followed far behind, and bringing up a distant rear has been the Czech Republic.

The Washington consensus

On the face of it, Poland's success argues for other countries to follow what it called its "big bang" policy, which was initiated almost immediately after the ending of Soviet domination, in 1990. Economic consultants from the IMF and World Bank, eager to help Poland make the transition as quickly as possible, agreed that Poland needed to implement policies that the IMF had found useful in dealing with authoritarian regimes in Latin America and, occasionally, in Africa. The "Washington consensus" was that Poland needed to stabilize the macroeconomic situation, privatize as much of the economy as possible, and liberalize markets from price and quantity regulations. None of these policies – *stabilization, privatization*, and *liberalization* – would achieve a successful transition by itself. All had to be implemented eventually, in order, for each to have the desired effect.

Stabilization meant that the government had to have a balanced budget and that the central bank had to maintain price stability through independent control of the money supply. Only then could private enterprise compete on a level playing field to attract capital and labor into more productive employment than in the public sector or in state-owned enterprises. In turn, state-owned enterprises had to be *privatized*, with guarantees of property rights so that owners would have the incentives to reallocate labor and capital more efficiently and to invest in new technology. Finally, only if the markets were *liberalized* from the price and quantity controls that were the heart of centrally planned economies could the new, privately owned firms have the right signals for allocating capital, labor, and technology most productively. The question remained: what was the best sequence for making these changes when all of them had to be introduced for the first time?

The answers varied from country to country, each depending on its domestic political environment, its previous trading contacts with the Western industrialized countries, its existing economic structure left from Soviet (or Serb) domination, and its need for Western assistance. Poland decided to implement all three reforms simultaneously – its so-called "big bang" policy. The political argument in favor of this was twofold: (1) no single interest group could be sure that it would lose more than it would gain when the final transition was accomplished so domestic political opposition to reforms was diffused and ineffective; and (2), given the heavy indebtedness of the Polish government to

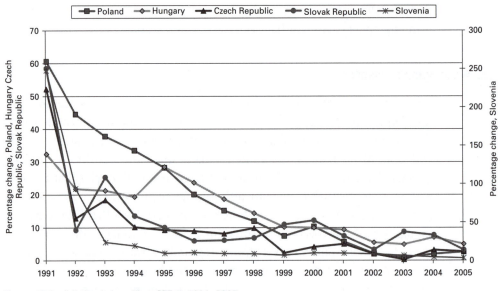

Figure 19.2 Inflation in transition, CEE-5, 1991–2005

Western governments and international banks, it needed IMF approval of its policies in order to secure debt relief. But Poland did moderate the process of privatization, reserving large state-owned enterprises on the basis that their employees could not be made unemployed suddenly, especially given the lack of revenues for the government. Foreign direct investment was allowed, but had to consist of at least $50,000 from any individual. Finally, the central bank helped moderate the impact of the shock to the Polish public by only gradually reducing the rate of inflation (see figure 19.2).

At the other extreme from Poland's big bang was the Czech Republic. Part of the problem there was the sharp differences between the economic structure of the Czech Republic and that of the Slovak Republic when both were under Soviet domination and combined into Czechoslovakia. Large-scale, heavy industry plants built on the Soviet model existed in Slovakia but not so much in the Czech Republic. Privatization was delayed by deliberations over the conflicting needs of the equitable privatization sought by the Czech half of the country and the maintenance of employment in the large military production plants sought by the Slovaks. Only when the two agreed to separate into separate countries, in 1992, did privatization begin. Both then proceeded with the liberalization of prices, followed by macroeconomic stabilization, and serious privatization began only after three years. Then the Czech Republic delayed further by developing a two-stage voucher system, designed so that all Czech citizens would have an equal chance at gaining in the increased efficiency of privatized firms. With their vouchers based on their previous income, Czechs could invest their vouchers in any of several competing investment funds. The investment funds, in turn, would use the vouchers they collected to bid for various state enterprises. The problem, it turned out, lay in the difficulties of forcing the investment funds to make a go of the enterprises they had bought and produce satisfactory returns for their investors, rather than selling off the assets and absconding with the proceeds.

Hungary and Slovenia followed intermediate courses. Hungary had already begun some price liberalization before 1990, which it continued, but its first priority was the privatization of large state enterprises, and it actively solicited foreign investors. The gradual reform of state finances was financed by the proceeds of privatization. Slovenia privatized some major manufacturing firms, but then delayed proceeding with privatizing telecommunications, insurance, and banks until after entry into the EU. Further progress in privatization in both countries now comes under the scrutiny of the European Commission's subsidy surveillance responsibility.

To date, none of the five has been able to bring back to reasonable levels the unemployment that resulted from the transition shock. Again, experiences varied, as shown in figure 19.3. The variations reflect the differences in the speed and severity of the transition undertaken in each case, not the problems of continued high unemployment that exist in many of the euro-zone countries. The pattern of unemployment in each case during the first eight to nine years of transition moves inversely to the initial decline in total output and then the gradual recovery of output four to five years into the transition. Thereafter, a second transition appears to have occurred, as market forces vied with government changes in labor market regulation to increase the recorded levels of unemployment. The numbers for Poland, Hungary, the Czech Republic and the Slovak Republic are comparable throughout, and conform to the OECD standards of classifying unemployment. The numbers for Slovenia, by contrast, vary widely between the Slovenian government figures, the EU adjusted figures, or the CIA estimates. The problems of dealing with the large-scale industrial plants in Poland and the Slovak Republic appear to have finally come home to roost in the rise in recorded unemployment rates in both countries, as each tries to make headway toward privatizing large-scale state enterprises. Only Hungary, with its emphasis on joint ventures so as to encourage foreign direct investment, has managed to make continued progress in reducing unemployment levels.

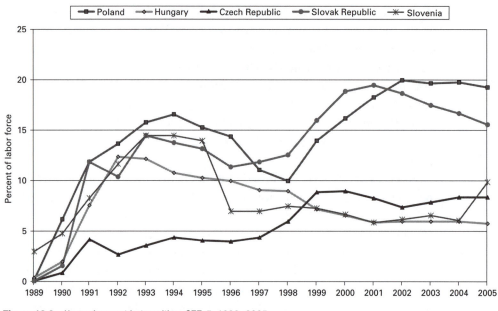

Figure 19.3 Unemployment in transition, CEE-5, 1989–2005

According to a World Bank study issued in 2005, a possible explanation for the second transition problem of the five central European countries may be the relative difficulty of doing business in each country. Surveying the regulatory apparatus of 155 countries and then comparing the ranking of each country according to per capita income with its ranking according to the regulatory ease of doing business, the World Bank found a very high correlation: 0.77. The five central European countries, however, had a substantially higher ranking in terms of per capita income than in terms of regulatory ease. Their average per capita income rank was 34/155, ease of doing business 49/155, and simple regulatory complexity 73/155. The transposition of EU regulations on top of the existing regulations left over from the bureaucratic apparatus of central planning has not helped, and may have hindered, the process of creating a legal and regulatory environment to support a market economy. The cumbersome nature of the EU's *acquis communautaire* for new enterprise comes out in the World Bank's finding that the EU's average rank in per capita income is much higher (15) than its rank in the ease of doing business (30) or simple regulation (47). Complete transposition of the EU's *acquis* may not be the solution after all for these countries, although it was one of the conditions laid down by the EU in the Copenhagen criteria for the transition countries to become members of the EU.

The Copenhagen criteria

By sharp contrast with the Washington consensus criteria for the transition economies, which focused on the economic characteristics of a successful market economy, the European Union set out a more comprehensive set of criteria for the transition economies if they were to become full members of the European Union. The "Copenhagen criteria" were laid out at the European Council meeting of heads of government in Copenhagen at the end of 1993. By this time, it was clear that all the central and eastern European countries desired to join the European Union as quickly as possible. It was also clear that they were not content with the association agreements that the EU had signed with each individual country. In keeping with the practice of the EU to exercise strong bargaining power on behalf of the interests of its constituent states in trade agreements, the EU's association agreements limited access to its market by imposing quotas on the quantity of goods that could be imported duty-free. Agricultural products, of course, were subject to restrictions based on health and safety requirements as well as the variable levy to bring prices up to CAP support levels. By the end of 1993 the EU leaders recognized that the transition economies would have to become members of the EU eventually. To ensure that their entry would not be too disruptive to the institutions already created and in the process of being created at the time, the EU specified very restrictive criteria. (The euro was just starting the process of replacing the legacy currencies and negotiations were just concluding on accepting Austria, Finland, Sweden, and Norway.) The candidate countries had to meet the EU's standards in the functioning of their political institutions, the competitiveness of their economic firms, and the capacity of their administrative organs to implement the EU's directives and regulations.

Politically, each country had to show that it had a functioning democracy, with universal voter franchise, secret ballots, fair elections, the rule of law, and the protection of human rights. Under the latter heading, equal rights for women and protection for minorities (however defined – by religion, language, ethnicity, or race) were required. Capital punishment for any crime also had to be abolished.

Economically, each country had to show that its firms were capable of competing with the products and services that would be allowed free access to their markets. In other words, the EU wanted to avoid taking on the responsibility of subsidizing uncompetitive industries or rebuilding the infrastructure of a backward economy. Needless to say, the example of the costs of dealing with

East Germany after its sudden absorption into West Germany in 1990 was very much on the minds of the EU leaders.

Administratively, each country had to show that it could transpose and administer the laws, directives, and regulations of the EU – the *acquis communautaire*. In other words, the existing framework and practices of the EU were not to be watered down, much less altered, for the benefit of the candidate countries. The elements of the *acquis* were further broken out into thirty separate chapters, and each chapter was evaluated individually for each candidate country annually. The lessons learned from the past experiences with allowing Ireland and Greece in rapidly without extensive tutelage were clearly responsible for this criterion.

The Copenhagen criteria appeared at the time to be efforts to delay or even obstruct the entry of several, if not most, of the candidate countries. Indeed, initially they were separated explicitly into Tier 1, Tier 2, and beyond categories. It was not until the 2003 Copenhagen summit of EU leaders that ten of the candidates were accepted, with only Bulgaria, Romania, and Turkey excluded. In retrospect, however, the ten years of tutelage and preparation of institutions in the candidate countries by the European Commission were a welcome remedy to the deficiencies of the programs imposed on transition economies by the Washington consensus. The reason seems clear: whatever the shortcomings or outright failings of the EU's economic policies in general, the institutions required to make a modern market economy operate successfully have been developed in the context of implementing the EU's economic policies.

The Washington consensus programs of stabilization, privatization, and liberalization simply omitted institution building initially. Unfortunate experiences with IMF reform programs in South America, Africa, and especially in Russia eventually persuaded the World Bank and IMF officials that at least one institutional change was needed – namely independent central banks, to enforce effective stabilization programs. The EU's vision of institutional requirements, of course, goes far beyond independent central banks to putting monetary policy completely out of the hands of national governments, as well as creating regulatory mechanisms to protect the operation of competitive markets. As of 2004 a "great divide" had arisen among the transition economies, with some countries exceeding their previous levels of output and continuing to grow while other countries had simply stalled or even regressed. The countries acceding to the European Union (and assimilating their common institutions) were clearly on the path to convergence with the market economies of the OECD, while the countries simply negotiating with the IMF and World Bank over the conditionality of various loan programs were failing

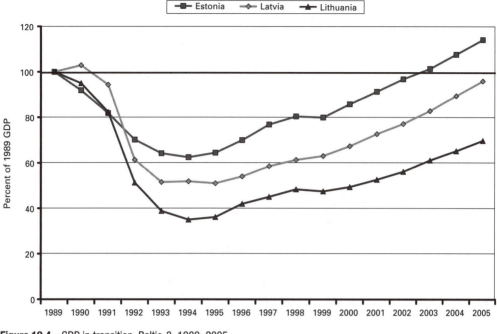

Figure 19.4   GDP in transition, Baltic-3, 1989–2005

to make progress. Institutions matter, and the process of building them and making them operate effectively requires time and constant attention. The most remarkable success stories for the EU's exercise in institution building in transition economies has been in the Baltic states.

The Baltic states

The standard transition graph for the three Baltic states of Estonia, Latvia, and Lithuania highlights the extreme difficulties that these three states went through while trying to establish once again their independence from the Soviet Union. For all three, the initial shock was more severe than for the central and eastern European five, mainly because they were much more dependent upon the Russian economy for the viability of their industrial base. Further, their turnaround to recovery was delayed two years beyond that for the central European transition economies. Finally, the combination of financial crises in Asia in mid-1997 and then in Russia in late 1998 staggered the recovery path for all three of these small former Soviet states.

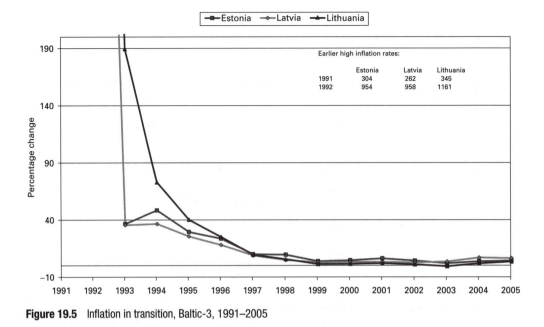

Figure 19.5   Inflation in transition, Baltic-3, 1991–2005

Since 1999, however, all three have begun to experience rapid economic growth, as a result of a combination of institutional reforms in the financial sector, the adoption of EU-compatible laws for foreign companies, and the eventual recovery of the Russian economy as well as the continued prosperity of their Scandinavian neighbors. The primary institutional reform of interest to economists has been the adoption of a currency board in place of the former state monopoly bank in all three Baltic states, albeit at different times and with different results, as shown in figure 19.5.

Estonia was the first to abandon the Russian ruble and establish its own currency, the kroon (EEK), in June 1992, the same as its prewar currency. The currency board set up to issue the new currency exchanged it at the rate of EEK8 to DM1. Estonia could maintain this rate because its currency board issued kroons only in exchange for gold or foreign exchange that was convertible into deutsche marks. Moreover, it began its initial issue based on a large amount of gold reclaimed from western European central banks into which the Bank of Estonia had moved its reserves when World War II broke out. Finally, Estonia deliberately undervalued the kroon at EEK8 to DM1 in order to promote exports to the West. (Recall that the western European countries all tried to overvalue their currencies after World War II to increase their imports!) Given that the nominal exchange rate cannot be altered, the real exchange rate can only rise as a result of Estonia running higher rates of inflation than in the eurozone. This does tend to happen despite the existence of the currency board. We discuss the reasons for this below.

Latvia was the second country to drop the ruble as the domestic medium of exchange. First it introduced a transition currency, called the Latvia ruble (rublis), in May 1992, which it pegged initially to the Russian ruble. Given Russia's highly inflationary monetary policy at the time, Latvia was quickly flooded with rapidly depreciating Russian rubles. So the Latvian rublis was allowed to float, made legal tender, and rapidly strengthened relative to the Russian ruble until the national currency, the lat (also the name of the prewar currency), was introduced in May 1993. Latvia chose to regulate the supply of currency with an independent central bank, initially headed by a strongly anti-inflationary governor, rather than using a currency board. Part of the reason was that it did not have nearly as much gold to be repatriated, so some other means of building up foreign reserves was required. A strong central bank able to maintain high interest rates to attract foreign reserves and committed to fixed targets for the supply of money it will create can have the same restrictive effect on the supply of money as a currency board. In addition, it can take proactive steps to increase the supply of foreign reserves, which a currency board cannot.

Finally, like Estonia, Latvia tried to keep its currency undervalued. This policy was formalized in February 1994 when it de facto pegged the lat to the Special Drawing Right (SDR) of the IMF at 0.8 lat to SDR1. This is a basket currency similar to the ECU, but with the dollar, yen, and several other non-European currencies weighted in. As with the Estonian kroon, the Latvian lat was undervalued at this rate, but it was maintained until Latvia switched to pegging to the euro in 1999, just in time to take advantage of the depreciation of the euro relative to the SDR and the dollar.

Lithuania was the last country to stabilize its currency and to bring infla-tion under control. It had a weak central bank that had to accommodate the financing demands of a strong government. Lithuania did not break with the Russian ruble until October 1992, when it introduced the talonas as a tran-sition currency, which was allowed to float in the foreign exchange markets. By summer 1993 Lithuania had regained 5.8 tons of gold from Western banks in which it had been placed at the outbreak of World War II, and had accu-mulated another $200 million of hard currency reserves. It then introduced the litas (again, the same name as the interwar currency) and tried to peg it to the dollar, undervaluing it deliberately. The weak central bank, however, had little control over the money supply and the litas quickly appreciated, but in terms of the nominal exchange rate rather than in terms of more rapid rates of inflation. In April 1994 Lithuania finally caught on to the advantages of the institutional innovations of its neighbors and introduced a currency board modeled on Estonia's successful example. It pegged the litas to the dollar, which had been depreciating against both the deutsche mark and the Special Drawing Right, at four litas to $1.00.

Pegging one's currency to that of one's major trading partners is a sensible policy for a small, open economy, as discussed in chapter 5. Unfortunately, a sensible monetary policy, even when combined with a sound fiscal policy, as it has been in the Baltic states, is not sufficient for a smooth transition from plan to market. All three states were hit by serious bank failures: first Estonia in 1993, and then Latvia in 1995 and Lithuania at the end of that year. Estonia let the shareholders and depositors bear the full brunt of the losses for its failed banks. Contrary to fears that this might lead to a systemic shock drying up all sources of credit in the country, this "let the weak fail" policy actually reassured depositors in those banks that remained open. While Estonia's transition was delayed, its recovery soon outstripped that of either Latvia or Lithuania. At the other extreme, Lithuania seemed committed to bailing out its failed banks, at least to some extent. The continued uncertainties over the degree of fraud among its banks and the extent of bad loans outstanding prolonged Lithuania's drop in GDP.

By the time these monetary reforms and financial recoveries began to take effect, all three began serious efforts to adopt the *acquis communautaire* of the EU and become full-fledged members. In the process, all three have enjoyed substantial rates of foreign direct investment, which have more than offset the increased prices of imports of energy from Russia. The process of privatizing manufacturing firms proceeded rapidly at first, but then stalled when it came to state-owned utilities such as telecommunications, port facilities, and elec-tricity. The financial sector, however, has been largely privatized and benefits from the strong presence of Western banks.

As in the case of the central European transition economies, the unem-ployment rates in the Baltic states first rose sharply, then gradually fell until the financial crisis shocks of the late 1990s hit. Since 2000, however, all three have reduced their unemployment rates successfully. The reasons, however, are not to be found in the kind of labor market reforms that reduced unem-ployment rates in the success stories of Ireland, the United Kingdom, and the Netherlands discussed in earlier chapters. Those reforms basically made it easier for employers to fire unsatisfactory workers, thereby encouraging

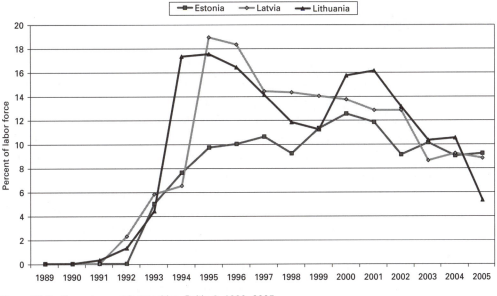

Figure 19.6   Unemployment in transition, Baltic-3, 1989–2005

expanding firms to hire more freely in the first place. In the case of all the transition economies, firing unproductive workers from previously state-owned and large-scale enterprises increases the pension obligations of the state to the previous employees. Given the excess of death rates over birth rates in all three Baltic states (see table 19.1), the pension obligations of the governments are only going to increase over time with the rapid aging of the population.

Instead, all three Baltic states have led the rest of the accession states in making the conditions for doing business easier, thereby encouraging continued inflows of foreign direct investment. The World Bank study cited above ranks all three Baltic states well above their level of per capita income in terms of the ease of doing business. Employment, therefore, keeps rising in the services sector and in new manufacturing areas, which arise in response to expanding markets in the West. As a consequence, unemployment rates remain low in the urban areas where new investment and service industries are concentrated, while long-term unemployment remains high in the rural areas and around the former Soviet-era industrial plants. In the long run, however, the continued emigration of younger and more skilled workers to the employment opportunities in the Scandinavian countries, Ireland, and the United Kingdom will certainly require major changes in pension funds for the remaining populations.

Cyprus and Malta

Malta said goodbye to a long-standing British naval base in 1979 and began to pursue a policy of neutrality, which it enshrined in its constitution in 1987. Like Austria, Malta did not feel that its neutral status prohibited it from joining the EU after the collapse of the Soviet Union. In July 1990 it applied for membership in the EU. The general election in 1996, however, led to a withdrawal of its application as the opposition party, the Malta Labour Party, came to power. On the economic side, however, Malta continued to abolish tariffs and to enjoy tariff-free access to the EU. Its foreign trade, both for exports and imports, consists mostly of machinery and transport equipment as well as manufactures and semi-manufactures. Both exports and imports are mainly with Italy, with Germany and the United Kingdom a distant second and third place in importance. Since 1989 the central bank has pegged its currency, the Maltese lira, to a basket of currencies made up of the dollar, the pound sterling, and the ECU. The economy has shown strong growth since the mid-1980s, which continued into the mid-1990s despite an appreciation of the Maltese lira against the Italian lira.

Cyprus signed an Association Agreement with the EU in 1973, which was intended to lead to a full customs union over a period of ten years. But the division of the island the next year postponed this indefinitely. Again, in May 1987, another agreement was signed for a customs union, this time to be achieved in two stages, the first one lasting ten years and the second for four or five years. In 1990 the Republic of Cyprus applied for full membership, introduced a value added tax, and pegged the Cyprus pound to the ECU. The European Commission approved the entry of Cyprus, subject only to concern over determining the future of the Turkish-occupied part of the island. Despite the continued division of Cyprus, however, the Republic of Cyprus joined the EU with the others in 2004.

Since the mid-1980s the Cyprus economy has enjoyed rates of growth well above the EU average. However, keeping the Cyprus pound pegged to the appreciating ECU gradually slowed growth in the 1990s. The trade patterns are strongly oriented to the EU, which takes 40% of its exports, mainly light manufactures, and provides over 50% of its imports, mostly intermediate inputs for manufacturing, but also capital and consumer goods. The Arab countries of the Middle East are an import-export market as well, but account for less than 5% of imports. In recent years the Republic of Cyprus has tried to replace Lebanon as a regional financial center. Toward this end it has increasingly deregulated the financial sector so as to allow interest rates to vary and to permit capital movements in and out of the country. Entrepreneurs from the states of the former Soviet Union are among the first wave of foreign businesses to respond to this initiative. As a result of the influx of foreign capital in response to these initiatives, the Cyprus pound has tended to strengthen even relative to the ECU. This has dampened somewhat the traditional sources of export earnings, especially tourism.

The ambition of Greek Cyprus to join the EU, however, led to the adoption of EU rules on the regulation of the financial sector, especially on the reporting of interest earnings by investors from EU countries. After September 11, 2001, the EU also tightened up rules on monitoring large transfers of funds in an effort to curb money laundering activities by drug smugglers and terrorist organizations. For both Cyprus and Malta, therefore, political motives for joining the EU clearly outweighed economic motives. In the case of Cyprus, membership in the EU gave it a stronger bargaining hand in negotiating the terms of any reunification of the island. The possibility of Cyprus now being in a position to block the accession of Turkey to the EU led to pressure by Turkey to get the Turkish Cypriots to agree to the UN proposal for the terms of reunification in a referendum held in 2005. The Greek Cypriots then voted against the proposal, apparently in the belief that they now had a much stronger bargaining position and could extract stronger concessions from both Turkey and Turkish Cyprus in the future. Both Malta and Cyprus have confronted increasing pressures from illegal immigrants and refugees from countries outside the EU, so membership gives both small islands a voice in forming a general EU policy on immigration and refugees, while giving both access to the resources of the EU for returning or relocating refugees.

Conforming to the *acquis communautaire* of the EU in the years preceding membership, however, proved less than beneficial to both of these small economies. Unlike the case of the transition economics, both islands were already small open economies, dependent upon foreign trade, and both had already made special trade arrangements with the EU. Consequently, neither country reaped the benefits of trade expansion that aided the transition economies in the years preceding accession. Neither country is eligible for structural funds, given their relatively high levels of per capita income. Moreover, by accepting the high prices of agricultural goods under the CAP the real income of both populations will be hurt. By overvaluing their currencies relative to the euro, however, the cost of food imports from the EU can be reduced for both countries. Both Cyprus and Malta decided to join the Exchange Rate Mechanism II in May 2005 in order to prepare for adopting the euro by the end of 2007. Clearly, the motivations of the two small islands in joining the euro are different in substance from those of the three small Baltic countries. This raises the general question of whether and when each accession country should join the euro.

The next transition: adopting the euro

All ten accession countries agreed in their respective treaties of accession to adopt the euro as their national currency as soon as feasible. All are subject to the approval of the European Commission, which maintains the Maastricht criteria for determining if a country is ready to join the common currency. Despite the changes in the Exchange Rate Mechanism after 1993 (increasing the band width of exchange rate fluctuations from +/− 2.5% to +/− 15%) and in the Stability and Growth Pact after 2004 (allowing government deficits to exceed the equivalent of 3% of GDP under special circumstances deemed to enhance European unity), the Maastricht criteria are still applied to the accession countries. Adherence to the ERM II for two years with fluctuations typically kept within +/− 2.5% is expected, along with low inflation rates kept within one and a half percentage points of the average of the lowest three rates in the eurozone and interest rates within two percentage points of the average of the lowest three rates. Keeping government deficits under 3% of GDP and the stock of general government debt to GDP under 60% are still criteria, despite the repeated violation of both criteria by current members of the eurozone.

As of 2004 there was little doubt that all ten accession countries could meet these criteria in a timely fashion and adopt the euro as their national currencies by 2007. Indeed, the three Baltic states immediately joined the ERM II to signal their eagerness to adopt the euro as soon as possible, with Slovenia signing up in June 2004. A year later both Cyprus and Malta joined up. The remaining four countries in central Europe delayed, however, with the Czech Republic explicitly delaying until 2008 or possibly later.

Only Cyprus and Malta breached the 60% limit on debt/GDP set by the Maastricht Treaty, as well as the 3% limit on the deficit/GDP ratio. Poland and Hungary also fell short on the deficit criterion. As noted in chapter 5 on the economics of the euro, the governments of these four countries have good reasons to join the eurozone to take advantage of the low interest rates on government debt that all member countries in the eurozone enjoy. These are not good reasons, of course, for the European Central Bank

Table 19.2 Comparison of accession countries with Maastricht criteria, 2004

Country	ERM II	Inflation, HICP (%)	Long-term interest rate (%)	Deficit/GDP (%)	Debt/GDP (%)
Cyprus	May 2005	2.1	5.2	−5.2	72.6
Czech Republic		1.8	4.7	−5.0	37.0
Estonia	May 2004	2.0		+0.3	4.8
Hungary		6.5	8.1	−5.5	59.9
Latvia	May 2004	4.9	5.0	−2.0	14.7
Lithuania	May 2004	−0.2	4.7	−2.6	21.4
Malta	May 2005	2.6	4.7	−5.2	73.8
Poland		2.5	6.9	−5.6	47.2
Slovak Republic		8.4	5.1	−3.9	44.5
Slovenia	June 2004	4.1	5.2	−2.3	30.8
Reference value		2.4	6.4	−3	60

Source: European Central Bank, *Convergence Report 2004*, Frankfurt: 2005.

to accept them as new members, which is why Cyprus and Malta, at least, joined the Exchange Rate Mechanism, version II, early on to try to show their new commitment to monetary stability. The Baltic states, with their currency board arrangements already geared to the euro, have no problems with the exchange rate commitment, and in 2004 only Estonia and Lithuania among the ten accession countries met all five Maastricht criteria. Hungary, Malta, and Poland had the greatest difficulties. It is not clear from the Maastricht criteria why the Czech and Slovak Republics have opted not to join the ERM II, as their government deficits were their only failing points. There are, however, good reasons for their recalcitrance, as well as that of Poland and Hungary.

The Balassa–Samuelson effect

As the Bretton Woods system began to take full effect in 1958 with fixed exchange rates and full convertibility on current account among the western European countries and the United States and Canada, two economists independently noted that less developed countries might not benefit as much from the system as these more advanced countries. Bela Balassa[1] and Paul Samuelson[2] pointed out, that once less developed countries committed to a fixed exchange rate with more advanced trading partners and opened up trade relations, their domestic price levels tended to rise more rapidly than the price levels in the more advanced countries. The result, unfortunately for the poorer countries, was that their real exchange rate (RER to economists) would continue to appreciate, making their export products less competitive and import substitutes more competitive.

We noted above that Ireland, Portugal, and Spain all had higher inflation rates than the rest of the eurozone when they first joined the euro. Only after Ireland's per capita income had risen above the EU-15 average did its inflation rate drop below the average for the eurozone. The explanation for the Balassa–Samuelson effect is that poor countries are poor mainly because they do not trade very much with the rest of the world, but that also means that their price levels are low relative to the rest of the world. The consequence of not trading much is that their agricultural and manufacturing sectors, protected from competition, become less productive relative to more advanced countries, and wage incomes are correspondingly lower. Much of the economy's output becomes non-tradable, therefore. Trade barriers protect their jobs in manufacturing and agriculture while most services are inherently non-tradable. The general level of consumer prices will also be low, the result of low money wages throughout the economy.

Once trade opens up with the more advanced countries of the world, however, the prices of tradable goods in the less developed countries tend to rise very quickly toward the common world price. They are clearly doing that already in the accession countries, given the removal of the previous trade barriers that prevented trade between east and west Europe. As wages rise in the now tradable sectors of the developing economy in response to the gains from trade, the wages in the non-tradable sectors of the developing economy rise as well, raising the general price level. The more rapidly their trade expands relative to their trading partners the more rapidly their price level rises as well relative to their more advanced trading partners.

If the developing countries are also forced to maintain a fixed nominal exchange rate with their more advanced trading partners, their RER will continue to appreciate as long as their domestic inflation rates are higher than those in the more advanced economies. That, of course, is exactly the scenario that confronts the low-income accession countries, which is why they are well advised to delay joining the eurozone until their price levels are close to those in the rest of the EU. As of 2003, while the prices of tradable goods in the accession countries were moving close to those in the EU-15, the general level of consumer prices in the central and east European accession states was much lower. Table 19.3 compares the consumer price levels and the per capita gross

Table 19.3 Comparison of prices and productivity in accession
countries with euro-12 average, 2003

Country	Consumer price level, % of euro-12	Per capita GDP, % of euro-12
Cyprus	91	77
Czech Republic	54	66
Estonia	60	46
Hungary	56	57
Latvia	54	39
Lithuania	52	43
Malta	70	68
Poland	51	43
Slovak Republic	49	49
Slovenia	75	72

Source: Statistical Office of the European Communities, *Europe in
Figures: Eurostat Yearbook 2005*, Brussels: 2005.

domestic products in the accession countries as of 2003 with the average of
the twelve countries then in the eurozone.

Despite the clear evidence in table 19.3 that the accession countries should
not jeopardize their future economic development by joining the fixed
exchange rate regime of the eurozone for some time to come, economists
have failed to find much evidence of the Balassa–Samuelson effect among the
accession countries before 2004. The reason lies, one suspects, in the relative
flexibility of most accession countries' exchange rates with the euro before
2004. Figure 19.7a demonstrates that only the Czech Republic really stabilized
and even strengthened its currency relative to the euro before accession. Not
surprisingly, the Czech Republic is also the central European country where
the Balassa–Samuelson effect seems most prevalent.

The course of the exchange rates of the accession countries' currencies with
respect to the euro from January 1996 through December 2005, combined with
the figures on the comparative inflation rates in the accession countries and the
eurozone, demonstrate the problems of the second transition, the transition
to the euro. Although inflation rates in the transition economies were falling
through the 1990s, they remained above those in the EU. Consequently, even
though the nominal exchange rates with respect to the euro were falling, the real
exchange rates were not falling as rapidly. Since the formal adoption of the euro
and serious commitments by the accession countries to tie their currencies
to the euro since January 1999, inflation rates have remained above the EU

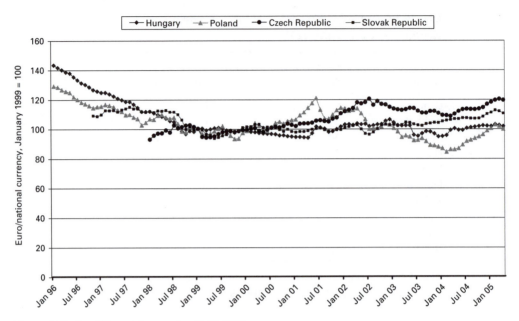

Figure 19.7a Euro/Višegrad-4 currencies, 1996–2005

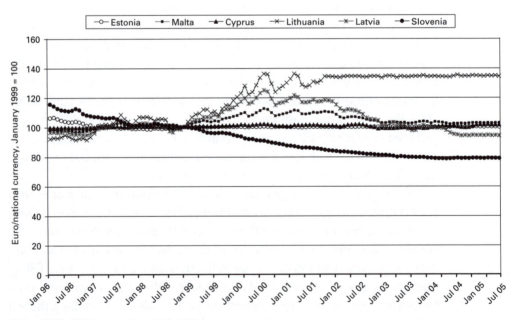

Figure 19.7b ERM II currencies, 1996–2005

average even while nominal exchange rates have stabilized, again leading to appreciation in RERs. After accession became a certainty nominal exchange rates even tended to rise, exacerbating the rise in real exchange rates.

The consequences of the rise in RERs have not shown up in any meaningful way, as the current account deficits have been covered by increased capital imports to finance the establishment of new manufacturing and service firms. Figures 19.8a and 19.8b show the corresponding current account balances (annual rather than monthly) for the eight accession countries that are also transition economies. Most have been running current account deficits since the transition began, which is economically desirable in their situation because the current account deficits imply capital account imports to finance the deficits. If the capital imports are not sufficient to cover the current account deficits, either the level of international reserves or the exchange rate must fall. Reviewing the previous graphs of the exchange rates, it is obvious that, for the CEE-5 countries, the initial stages of the transition with very high inflation rates led to falling nominal exchange rates. With the reduction in inflation rates, the exchange rates have stabilized and in a few cases even begun to appreciate. Nevertheless, the current account deficits continued, implying that, with the promise of accession to the EU, capital imports continued. The question remains whether a commitment to adopt the euro will encourage continued capital imports, or whether the Balassa–Samuelson effect, which leads to a rise in real exchange rates for transition economies, will dominate.

In the case of the CEE-5, it appears that the Balassa–Samuelson effect was taking effect for the Czech Republic and Slovenia with their accession to the EU. For the Baltic states, by contrast, the previous adherence to fixed exchange rates with respect to the euro may have created a Balassa–Samuelson effect at the time of the euro's formal adoption in 1999, but the property rights enforcements and financial sector reforms required for accession to the EU have more than offset the effects of appreciating real exchange rates. Thus, the adoption of the euro is a less important issue in general for the accession countries than the encouragement they can offer to foreign investment in general. Low corporate income tax rates (imitating the success of Ireland in the 1990s), the encouragement of joint ventures with the guarantee of free movement for capital (imitating the success of Hungary), flexible labor market regulations (imitating the success of the United Kingdom), and government investment in transportation and communication infrastructure are all factors that weigh in the decision by companies, both domestic and foreign, to continue investing in an economy.

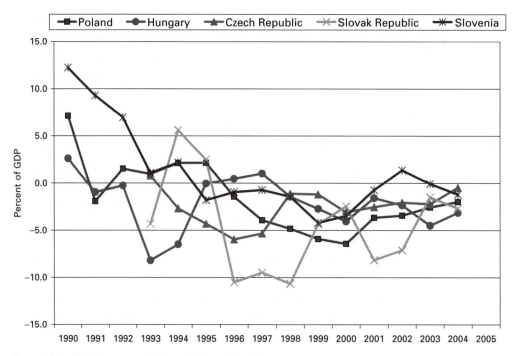

Figure 19.8a Current account balances, CEE-5, 1990–2005

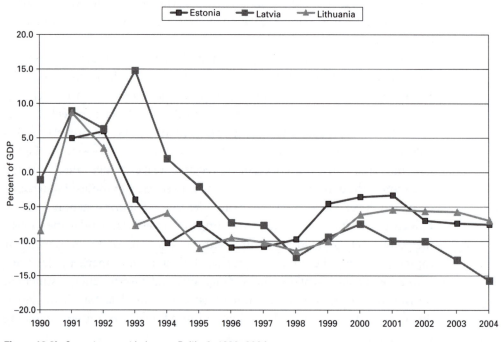

Figure 19.8b Current account balances, Baltic-3, 1990–2004

Conclusion

The lessons of previous expansions of the European Union made the incumbent members reluctant to extend the same privileges and subsidies to the much poorer and less prepared countries that clamored to enter after the collapse of the Soviet Union. By insisting that the candidate countries demonstrate their capacity to participate in the European Union's institutions without burdening the budget with excessive demands for agricultural support and regional aid, the EU actually helped them to cross the divide from dysfunctional centrally planned economies to functioning market economies more rapidly than previous poor candidate countries. The contrast between the Washington consensus principles of stabilization, privatization, and liberalization and the Copenhagen criteria of political, economic, and administrative institution building shows the importance of institution building before implementing desirable economic policies. To date, the Washington consensus and Copenhagen criteria have proved to be excellent complements, rather than alternative paths, to economic success. It remains to be seen how the continued experiments of the accession countries to catch up with the richer incumbent countries will affect the future economic policies and institutions of the European Union. More daunting challenges lie ahead in the form of the next group of candidate countries, which we consider in the next chapter.

NOTES

1. Bela Balassa, "The purchasing power parity doctrine: a reappraisal," *Journal of Political Economy* 72 (6), 1964, pp. 584–96.
2. Paul A. Samuelson, "Theoretical notes on trade problems," *Review of Economics and Statistics* 46 (2), 1964, pp. 145–54.

The future members: customs union as substitute or stage one for the EU

Introduction

The European Commission seriously considered the possibility of including Bulgaria and Romania in the clutch of accession countries that joined in 2004, but concluded that they were not yet capable of meeting the requirements of full membership. As late as 2006 concerns remained about the level of corruption in both governments and their delays in passing new laws to conform with EU legislation. Both countries count on joining in 2007, however. A major issue also arose over the potential candidacy of Turkey, long an applicant, and eventually awarded special status as a member of the customs union. Despite the formidable challenges to the EU posed by including Turkey, which are evident from table 20.1, the EU agreed to enter serious negotiations with Turkey as a candidate country starting in 2005. At the same time, two of the former Yugoslav republics, Croatia and Macedonia, were elevated to candidate status. This means that the Commission will issue formal reports annually that assess the level of conformity of these countries to the thirty-five or thirty-eight chapters of EU legislation they are required to enact and then enforce. Finally, the bitter and bloody breakup of the former Yugoslavia has left the EU with the perennial problem of the Balkans.

The "Balkans problem" arose in the fifteenth century, when a fragmented Europe confronted an expansionist Ottoman Empire, confounded Europeans throughout the eighteenth and nineteenth centuries, led directly to World War I, and resurfaced with the ethnic cleansings of the 1990s. These bloody affairs arose when the artificial state of Yugoslavia, created as a federation of Croats, Serbs, and Slovenes after World War I and recreated as a socialist federal republic after World War II, fell apart in the 1990s. The conflicts were especially devastating in Bosnia-Herzegovina and the Kosovo province of Serbia. As a result, Albania, Bosnia-Herzegovina, and Serbia and Montenegro

Table 20.1 Future members: basic facts

Area	(kilometers²)	of EU-25
Albania	28,748	0.7%
Bosnia-Herzegovina	51,129	1.3%
Bulgaria	110,910	2.8%
Croatia	56,542	1.4%
Macedonia	25,333	0.6%
Romania	237,500	6.0%
Serbia and Montenegro	102,350	2.6%
Turkey	780,580	19.6%
Population	*(July 2005 estimate)*	*of EU-25*
Albania	3,563,112	0.8%
Bosnia-Herzegovina	4,025,476	0.9%
Bulgaria	7,450,349	1.6%
Croatia	4,495,904	1.0%
Macedonia	2,045,262	0.4%
Romania	22,329,977	4.9%
Serbia and Montenegro	10,829,175	2.4%
Turkey	69,660,559	15.2%
GDP	*(2004 estimate, PPP)*	*of EU-25*
Albania	$18.15 billion	0.2%
Bosnia-Herzegovina	$28.3 billion	0.2%
Bulgaria	$67.0 billion	0.6%
Croatia	$53.3 billion	0.5%
Macedonia	$15.6 billion	0.1%
Romania	$186.4 billion	1.6%
Serbia and Montenegro	$28.4 billion	0.2%
Turkey	$551.6 billion	4.7%
Per capita income	*(PPP)*	*of EU-25 average*
Albania	$4,900	18.2%
Bosnia-Herzegovina	$6,800	25.3%
Bulgaria	$9,000	33.5%
Croatia	$11,600	43.1%
Macedonia	$7,400	27.5%
Romania	$8,300	30.9%
Serbia and Montenegro	$2,600	9.7%
Turkey	$7,900	29.4%
Openness	*([X+M]/GDP)*	*with EU-25*
Albania	63.2%	n.a.
Bosnia-Herzegovina	87.0%	n.a.
Bulgaria	127.1%	51%
Croatia	103.9%	67%

(*cont.*)

Table 20.1 (*cont.*)

Macedonia	92.0%	58%
Romania	79.9%	71%
Serbia and Montenegro	n.a.	n.a.
Turkey	58.0%	51%
Vital statistics (per 1,000)	*Birth rate*	*Death rate*
Albania	15.08	5.12
Bosnia-Herzegovina	12.49	8.44
Bulgaria	9.66	14.26
Croatia	9.57	11.38
Macedonia	12.00	8.73
Romania	10.70	11.74
Serbia and Montenegro	12.12	10.49
Turkey	16.83	5.96

Sources: Central Intelligence Agency, *World Factbook, 2005*, available at http://www.cia.gov/cia/publications/factbook; Statistical Office of the European Communities, *Europe in Figures: Eurostat Yearbook 2005*, Brussels: 2005.

are subject to international scrutiny coordinated and overseen by the European Commission. The prospect of eventual membership in the European Union is extended to these countries in the hope that their governments will respond positively and peacefully in the way that the Baltic states and central European countries have to date. In this chapter, we consider in turn the cases of Bulgaria and Romania as the most advanced accession countries, the pivotal case of Turkey, and then the remains of the Yugoslav state – Croatia and Macedonia on the one hand, and Albania and Serbia and Montenegro on the other hand.

The acceding countries (Bulgaria and Romania)

Figures 20.1 to 20.3 show clearly the relative lack of progress made by these two eastern European countries in the transition process up to 2005. After fifteen years of economic experimentation in both countries, neither has really shown that it is capable of sustained catchup with the rest of Europe, or even with the previous accession countries.

By the time the other transition economies were entering the EU formally Bulgaria and Romania had barely recovered the 1989 level of GDP, the last year of central planning. Figures 20.2a and 20.2b indicate the scale of their

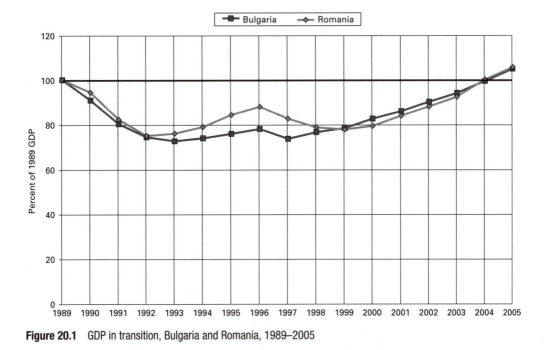

Figure 20.1 GDP in transition, Bulgaria and Romania, 1989–2005

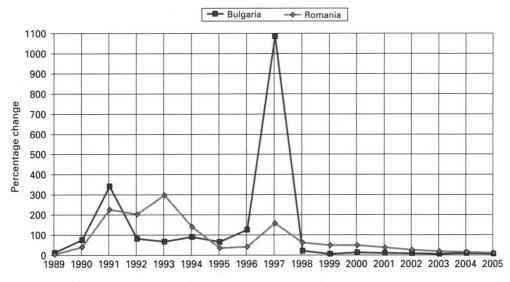

Figure 20.2a Inflation in transition, Bulgaria and Romania, pre-1998 scale, 1989–2005

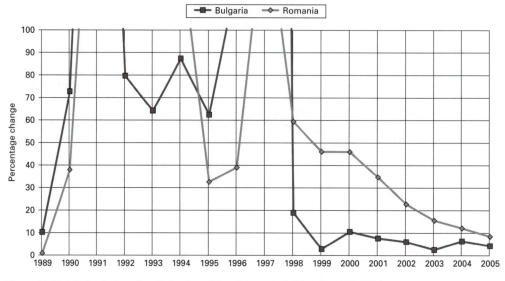

Figure 20.2b Inflation in transition, Bulgaria and Romania, post-1998 scale, 1989–2005

problems by the extraordinarily high rates of inflation through the early, most disruptive period of the 1990s. Bulgaria finally adopted a currency board in 1998 to bring inflation under control (the stabilization element of the Washington consensus, as explained in chapter 19). Bulgaria's relative success in combating inflation is shown in figure 20.2b, which cuts off at inflation rates over 100% annually. Since 1998 Bulgaria's inflation problems have ended, but figure 20.3 shows that the consequence was a sharp increase in unemployment rates, leading to political hesitation in maintaining the pace of economic reform.

Dominated by the ex-Communists and uncertain over its orientation as well as its transition strategy, Bulgaria has floundered in the meshes of its planned economy. Its plan was among the last instituted in the eastern bloc and it may be the last to disappear. In common with the Baltic states, Bulgaria's plan, starting in the 1970s, focused on building up a strong, specialized industrial base and providing labor released from the agriculture sector by collectivizing farms. Up to the mid-1980s Bulgaria was one of the success stories of Soviet-style economic development, as its industrial output soared and urbanization took off. In common with the rest of the Soviet bloc, however, output leveled off in the late 1980s, leading up to the final collapse in 1989.

Unlike the other countries, Bulgaria had no public consensus on how to proceed out of the plan. Restoring property rights to the previous smallholders in agriculture after the collapse of communism proved time-consuming, to say the least. Given the uncertainty over access to the land, agricultural output

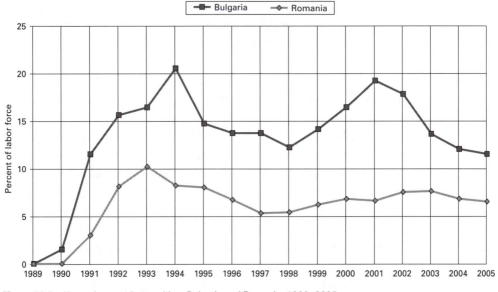

Figure 20.3   Unemployment in transition, Bulgaria and Romania, 1989–2005

dropped. Worse, similar disputes occurred in the industrial sector, further delaying privatization. In fact, only by the end of 1995 had Bulgaria finally settled on a privatization scheme, which was a blend of the Czech two-stage and the Russian one-stage coupon disbursements and subsequent auctions. But it was dubious how well this would be carried out, given past internal disputes. Indeed, by the summer of 1996 the Bulgarian lev had depreciated once again by one-half.

The immediate source of the problems was that the central bank tried to bail out the failed Vitosha Bank for Agricultural Credit and then became involved as well with the First Private Bank, the largest private bank in the country. A weak central bank, apparently more interested in bailing out overextended banks than in regulating them, was both cause and effect of Bulgaria's lack of political will for undertaking the transition. The collapse of the government that followed in 1997 led to the replacement of the central bank with a currency board. Imitating the successful examples of the Baltic states in dealing with financial crises exacerbated by accommodative finance from a weak central bank, Bulgaria's currency board issued the new lev only in exchange for an equivalent amount of, first, deutsche marks then, later, euros.

The result has been dramatic: inflation has dropped within Maastricht criteria and the promise of fixed exchange rates has led to an increase in foreign direct investment. The subsequent freeing of capital controls in 2004 led to a further increase in foreign investment, and the upsurge, partly speculative, helped finance a widening current account deficit. Nevertheless, the IMF warned Bulgaria about the size of this deficit given that one condition of its outstanding loan to Bulgaria is progress toward stabilization, which includes reducing the current account deficit. Bulgaria, however, needs continued foreign direct investment to bring in the latest technology to its manufacturing and distribution sectors and to continue reducing the overall rate of unemployment.

Romania applied for membership in 1995 shortly after its Europe Agreement with the EU had come into force (February 1995). The trade terms of the Europe Agreement had already taken effect in May 1993, and it was that year that Romania's GDP began to recover, albeit accompanied by a fresh spurt in inflation. Although a half of Romania's exports and imports were with the EU by 1994, its foreign trade overall did not grow as rapidly as in the other transition countries. Part of this was due to historical legacy, part to the slow pace of transition.

Communist control of Romania began in 1947, but Soviet troops were expelled from the country in 1959. The unique characteristics of Romania began with the assumption of power in 1965 by Nicolae Ceauşescu. This egomaniac and dictator managed to pursue a Soviet-style development strategy that was more Soviet than the Soviets'. Not only did he insist on building up an industrial base consisting of very large-scale plants but he also attempted to achieve self-sufficiency, even avoiding trade with the rest of the Soviet bloc as much as possible. His idiosyncratic economic policy was tolerated by the Soviets, since the army was kept relatively weak and Romanians paid the full price for their fuel imports from Russia. Ceauşescu pursued ties with the West, mainly to obtain technical assistance and capital goods for his industrial policy. The policy was enforced by his personal security force, but any gains from it were captured by Ceauşescu's family.

Economic growth stagnated in the 1980s, especially by comparison with Bulgaria. By 1989 the average Romanian was the worst off among all the central and east Europeans. Romania's economic policy under communism was notable for the high degree of centralized control over the plan, its emphasis on heavy industry, and the persistence with which it was pursued, continuing long after other countries, including the Soviet Union, had altered their strategies.

As a consequence, the collapse of the regime was the most violent within the eastern bloc. Ceauşescu and his family fled for their lives in December 1989, were caught, summarily tried, and promptly executed. The disaffected communist leaders assumed power, renaming their party the National Salvation Front (NSF). Elections were held in 1990, which the NSF won, and economic reforms began to get under way in March/April 1991. These included establishing a weak central bank and signing a deal with the IMF for stabilization loans conditioned on fiscal reforms and devaluation of the national currency, the leu. Fresh elections were held in fall 1992, based on the constitution adopted in November 1991. Again, the NSF dominated. As with the case of Lithuania discussed above, the relative stability of political control has slowed down the movement to a market economy.

Romania's transition process has been more gradual than in the other countries, mainly because of the slow pace of privatization. This only began to get under way in October 1995, with a two-stage process similar to that successfully demonstrated earlier by the Czech Republic. Vouchers were issued to the public at nominal prices, and then could be used to purchase shares in various mutual funds authorized to bid on state enterprises put up for auction. The expansion in output, which began in 1993 and has continued since, has been unusual in that the most rapid increases have not been in services, as in the other transition economies, but in consumer goods. This reflects the relatively miserable consumption standards endured by the Romanian people under Ceaușescu's rule. But it also reflects the changeover in Romania's industrial base from heavy manufacturing to light manufacturing, which is directed toward satisfying pent-up domestic demands rather than finding export markets in the surrounding region.

Romania was the first transition economy to apply for membership in NATO and offered peacekeeping troops for Bosnia-Herzegovina. One of the legacies of Ceaușescu's craze for monumental construction projects is the Danube–Black Sea–Rhine Canal. This provides a secure, cheap transportation route for oil produced in the Caspian Sea fields and shipped to the Black Sea to be carried into the heart of the European Union. Moreover, this would reduce the pressure on the EU to admit Turkey in order to maintain access to the Black Sea through the Bosporus. Romania's location is its best asset to date and the strongest argument for its accession to the EU.

Nevertheless, Romania is confronted with the same problems as Bulgaria as far as the IMF and the EU are concerned. Excessive corruption in the government and the judiciary discourage the mobilization of domestic savings to finance investment in the economy. Disputes have arisen over the pace and extent of privatization of state enterprises. By 2005 the Romanian central bank had decided to tighten monetary policy by targeting the inflation rate. This change in policy, combined with the elimination of capital controls in line with EU requirements for accession, led to a further surge in foreign investment and helped continue financing a large current account deficit. The

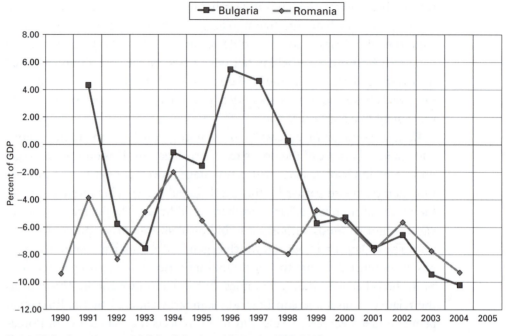

Figure 20.4 Current account deficits, Bulgaria and Romania, 1990–2005

rise in foreign reserves and the strengthening of the exchange rate of the leu, however, indicate that the current account deficit was driven more by foreign demand than excessive domestic demand. The economic indicators, then, were positive for both countries to enter the EU on schedule, even if the institutions required by the EU and the IMF were not yet in place.

Turkey

As of 2006 Turkey was enjoying a remarkable recovery from a disastrous financial and economic crisis in 2000 and 2001, and engaged in full-blown negotiations with the EU for eventual membership. Ironically, the 2000 crisis, just as Turkey became a full participant in the customs union of the EU, demonstrated that membership in the customs union is not the critical ingredient for European economic success either. Fortunately, the crisis shook both the EU and the government of Turkey into taking seriously the institutional reforms that had been laid down by the EU for the central and eastern European transition economies. Implementing those structural reforms, which by 2000 had led to the successful transitions discussed in the previous chapter, proved equally beneficial in the case of Turkey. The case of Turkey is especially instructive because of the length of time it has taken to make the reforms, even after a brief period of success with similar reforms in the early 1980s. Turkey's economic experience since World War II helps us understand the difficulties that arise in making subsequent institutional reforms after one set of reforms have outlived their original usefulness.

After World War II and participation in the Marshall Plan aid and European Payments Union programs, Turkey nevertheless maintained its basic strategy of import substitution that had proven successful in the 1930s and 1940s. The ruling Democrat Party built up an agrarian power base by expanding the agricultural sector, both in terms of the acreage under cultivation and the number of smallholders engaged. This simply emphasized and completed a policy begun earlier with the Land Distribution Law of 1946. During the first period of redistribution, between 1947 and 1954, the government put approximately 3 million acres of farmland and common pastures into cultivation by 142,000 rural families. Many of them were refugees from Bulgaria. In the next five years another 5 million acres were brought into cultivation from public lands. The construction of roads and electrification in the new farming areas accounted for much of the capital formation in the economy, in addition to the intensive mechanization that took place. The number of tractors increased from about 1,000 in 1946 to nearly 42,000 in 1960. Although this was a dramatic increase, it was far less than the number of new farm households, which meant that most smallholders still had to content themselves with the traditional oxen.

The rapid growth that persisted was financed by continued deficits both on the government's account and on the foreign account. Unlike the other participants in the European Payments Union, however, Turkey began to reverse its liberalization of foreign trade by 1954. From then until the military takeover in 1960 it engaged in an increasing variety of import restrictions, export subsidies, and exchange controls, quite in opposition to the removal of quantitative restrictions and the move toward the full current account convertibility of currencies that was taking place in western Europe. The foreign exchange crisis caused by Turkey's inability to follow the other countries into convertibility in 1958 led to a stabilization program under IMF guidance beginning in August 1958. The IMF insisted then, as it would in nearly all future IMF programs, that Turkey devalue the lira. The recalcitrance of the Turkish government, however, stretched out the process for nearly three years, by altering first the exchange rate on imports and then the rate for exports. Finally, in August 1960, the official price of a US dollar was increased from TL2.80 to TL9.00, a devaluation of over 300%.

The military government in power from 1960 to 1961 also imposed draconian reductions in government spending. This terminated the first phase of Turkish growth. Expansion of the cultivated area ceased, although nearly 40% of the rapidly growing labor force continued to be in the agricultural sector. Improvements in mechanization dropped off sharply. The emphasis turned toward investment in state economic enterprises, but since these were primarily capital-intensive projects they created few employment opportunities. While the Democrat government had passed a good deal of progressive social legislation, providing pension plans for government employees and improved health care, it never enacted unemployment insurance. The solution for unemployment by workers displaced from agriculture thus became migration abroad.

In the next phase of the golden age of growth, from 1960 to 1973, Turkey continued to remain outside both European sets of arrangements to expand trade. It was not immune, however, to economic developments in Europe. The restoration of democratic government in 1962 led to a change in economic policy, but the change was to improve the rationality of the import substitution strategy by adopting national plans similar to those that seemed to be so successful in Europe. Attributing the successes of France and the Netherlands to the implementation of their successive five-year plans, Turkey invited the distinguished Dutch economist Jan Tinbergen (who shared the first Nobel Prize in Economics with Ragnar Frisch of Norway) to help design comparable plans for Turkey. The resumption of high rates of growth in the 1960s, then, in Turkey as in the other countries of Europe, was based on the same strategies that had begun in the 1950s, but they were now implemented with greater confidence and care.

Turkey's planned economic development produced typically high growth rates for GDP, averaging over 5.5% in the period from 1960 to 1973. Unfortunately, more and more of its investment, still very low as a proportion of GDP at under 18%, was directed to white elephants: 50% of investment had to be in the public sector, and much of the remainder in the private sector was directed to ancillary firms of the large state enterprises. Moreover, population continued to grow rapidly, the rate averaging over 2.5% annually in the 1960–73 period. This was by far the highest rate of population growth in the OECD at the time. Given its very low level of per capita income at the outset, therefore, it should have seen much higher rates of growth of per capita income. A large part of the explanation for this unsatisfactory performance must lie in the failure to move labor out of the agricultural sector and into industry or urban employment. Nearly three-quarters of Turkey's labor force was in agriculture as late as 1960, and even after the first oil shock 54% was still in agriculture as late as 1977.[1]

If Turkish development plans could not absorb the growing labor force, European industry could use it. Over these fourteen years millions of Turkish male workers went to western Europe, mainly to West Germany. Intended as temporary guest workers, the most able became long-term residents of Germany as their firms hired them permanently. Earning far higher wages than was possible in their home country, these men remitted large sums in total back to Turkey. Guest worker remittances covered at times up to one-third of Turkey's imports and were far more important than the total of foreign aid or investment credits provided by the OECD countries. This period of laggard development ended, however, when a military-backed government once again assumed power between 1971 and 1973.

This government had to remedy the accumulated problems created by foreign and government account deficits. It also put on hold any thought of Turkey enjoying closer economic relations with the EEC. The previous democratic governments had applied for membership as early as July 1959, and received associate member status at the end of 1964. The intention on both sides was that Turkey would eventually have full membership, much as the Association Agreements with east and central European countries in the 1990s led to their accession in 2004.

With the first oil shock in 1973 Turkey continued its import substitution policy, but now it had to protect its state economic enterprise employees from a fall in real wages. This policy increased further the traditional government deficit. Meanwhile, the country had to meet a vastly increased import bill for fuel while losing a large part of the emigrants' remittances, as Turkish workers were sent home as rapidly as possible by their host countries. By the middle of 1974 all the bilateral agreements for the use of temporary labor in the EEC ended, reducing the inflow of remittances to Turkey from its workers abroad.

Typically, the government responded by spending more money. From 1974 on it was clearly public sector spending that drove the Turkish rates of inflation ever higher, culminating in hyperinflation when the second oil shock hit in 1979/80.[2] Despite the spending, unemployment continued to rise along with inflation. Finally, the government had to accept terms set by the IMF in 1978 to obtain relief on its balance of payments deficit. Both debt service and import payments had risen while emigrants' remittances had dropped off sharply and the excessive inflation rates worked to overprice Turkish exports. The IMF insisted the government reduce spending mainly by cutting subsidies to state enterprises, devalue the lira sharply (once again), and move toward

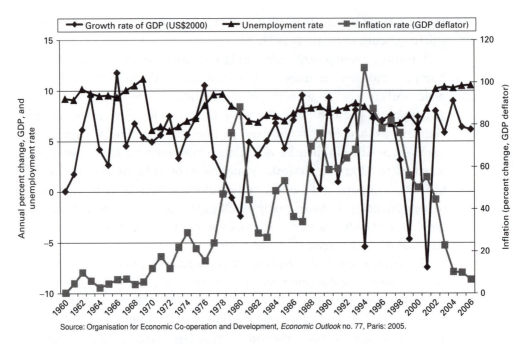

Source: Organisation for Economic Co-operation and Development, *Economic Outlook* no. 77, Paris: 2005.

Figure 20.5   Turkey: policy results, 1960–2005

export promotion while lifting quantity restrictions on imports – in short, the Washington consensus without institutional reforms.

The immediate result was a sharp decline in Turkish GDP, adverse balance of payments, and, with continuing rapid population growth, a drastic drop in per capita income. The government fell, but the caretaker military government that assumed temporary power for the period from 1980 to 1983 continued the draconian policies mandated by the IMF. Maintaining the course toward export promotion and letting production respond to market signals, Turkey saw a turnaround in its economic fortunes by 1981. Recovery continued into the mid-1980s. Figure 20.5 shows the course of Turkey's growth rates of GDP, inflation, and unemployment rates over the entire period from 1960 to 2005. The 1980s and the years after 2001 stand out as successful episodes within a generally disheartening pattern of repeated crises, shown in the spikes of inflation.

The architect of the remarkable turnaround in the 1980s was Turgut Özal. As a staff economist at the IMF in the 1970s, he was very familiar with IMF practice and with the logic of the standard IMF stabilization programs. Put in charge of implementing the measures by the coalition government elected at the end of 1979, he instituted the radical reform program that was put into effect in January 1980. The military takeover followed in September, but Özal was kept in charge of the economy. A new constitution was enacted in 1982, and in a general election held on the basis of the new constitution Özal was elected as Prime Minister in the restored civilian government, a position he held until he became President of Turkey in 1989. He died in office in 1993.

Özal's export promotion policy certainly proved successful on its own terms. Exports expanded rapidly as a share of Turkey's GDP, which resumed growth rates in the neighborhood of 5% per annum. Structural change began to increase overall productivity again as more of the labor force moved out of agriculture into manufacturing. Manufacturing's share of GDP rose, as it should in a country that is developing successfully. Closer examination of Turkey's export performance, however, raises some interesting questions. The destination of Turkey's rising exports was not the rich industrial countries of the West so much as the newly rich OPEC countries in the Middle East. In 1970 developed countries took 75% of Turkey's exports and less developed countries only 10%. By 1984 developed countries took only slightly more than 50% while the less developed countries' share had risen to over 40%.[3]

Looking in more detail at this counterintuitive change in the pattern of exports shows that much of the increase took place to two countries in partic-ular, Iran and Iraq. These two major oil exporters were at war with each other throughout the initial period of Turkey's liberalization. Moreover, much of the expansion in exports to the Middle East was in food products, not man-ufactures. On the import side, Turkey increased its share of raw materials, including fuel, which may indicate one way that Iran and Iraq were financ-ing their war against each other. While export promotion obviously had the desired effects at the macroeconomic level, it is more doubtful that it had the desired effects at the microeconomic level of stimulating technological change and productivity, as well as of transferring resources from agriculture to man-ufacturing. Figure 20.6 demonstrates that Turkey could not sustain its initial attempt at export-led growth after Özal's death.

With both economic growth and democratic government restored in the mid-1980s, Turkey welcomed the single market initiative. In fact, its contin-ued civilian rule and continued move toward successful trade liberalization renewed Turkish optimism that its long-standing application to join the EU might finally be accepted. The only positive response that Turkey received, however, was to renew negotiations in 1994 for Turkey to join the customs union of the European Union. Such an agreement had been signed in Ankara, however, in 1973, over twenty years earlier. The unanticipated effects of the oil shock of 1973 on the EEC economies was the primary reason that the customs union was put on hold at that time. Over the following twenty years

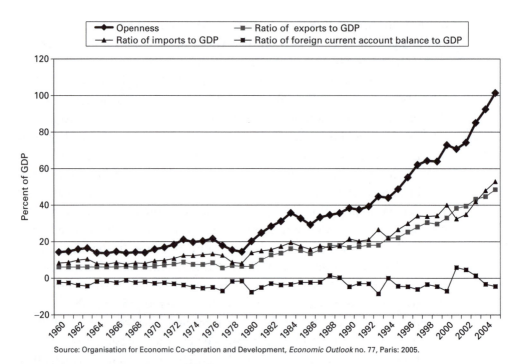

Source: Organisation for Economic Co-operation and Development, *Economic Outlook* no. 77, Paris: 2005.

Figure 20.6   Turkey: foreign sector, 1960–2005

various incidents further delayed its implementation – the Turkish invasion of Cyprus in 1974, its military regimes from 1980 to 1983, and the EU membership of Greece, hostile to Turkish membership. Even in the original version, tariffs were to fall to EU levels only very gradually, one set over twelve years and another over twenty-two years. Özal's initiative when he was President of Turkey led to the final breakthrough in negotiations. He promised that Turkey would not object to Cyprus entering the EU if the customs union agreement proceeded. In return, Greece lifted its veto on the customs union agreement going forward, although it delayed until the end of 1996 lifting its veto on granting "financial cooperation" to Turkey to compensate for its loss in customs revenues.

The customs union agreement, which took full effect at the beginning of 1996, implies that Turkey has the same low external tariff on manufactured goods with the rest of the world as the EU. This would be a necessary step toward eventual membership in any event, and Malta and Cyprus were included in the customs union as well before their respective accessions. In Turkey's case, however, the customs union could well be a substitute for membership. Full membership would imply the right of Turkish workers to seek employment anywhere in the EU, and that is not attractive to any of the current members. They are all agreed that it is much better to substitute trade flows for migration pressures. This means encouraging German and Swiss manufacturers to set up plants in Turkey and export their products back to the EU instead of importing Turkish workers to their plants in western Europe.

The implication of substituting "trade for migration" in this manner, of course, is that Turkey should receive large inflows of foreign direct investment (recall the case of West German investment in East Germany after 1990). Indeed, figure 20.6 shows that such investment did occur after 1996, helped along by conditional loans from the IMF. The conditions, similar to those of sixteen earlier IMF programs dealing with Turkey, required Turkey to devalue, maintain a government primary surplus (exclusive of interest payments on the stock of outstanding government debt), and begin various structural reforms in agriculture, pensions, and taxes. The influx of foreign investment that came on the heels of the $4 billion from the IMF, however, undercut the incentives in Turkey to sustain such reforms.

By the end of 2000 the failure of the Turkish government to continue privatization, or any of the various structural reforms recommended by the IMF, combined with liquidity concerns on the part of European banks, led to these banks withdrawing their loans. Figures 20.5 and 20.6 show the severity of the financial crisis that ensued. This time, even the voters in Turkey demonstrated that "enough was enough" by changing government once again. The moderate Islamist party Justice and Development (AKP), led by Recep Tayyip Erdogan, came to power. Erdogan promised to meet the Copenhagen criteria for membership in the EU and petition again for Turkey's candidacy to be accepted by the European Commission. Formal negotiations, in fact, began in October 2005, shortly after the IMF renewed its loan for three years in May 2005.

The terms of the IMF loan, reflecting the revised Washington consensus, required the Turkish government to continue privatization, increase the surplus in the government's budget by eliminating soft financing for state-owned enterprises, and impose stricter regulations on the banking sector. While the EU's human rights requirements for Turkey under the Copenhagen criteria, discussed in the preceding chapter, have drawn the most publicity, the formal establishment of the independence of the central bank in line with EU requirements has had dramatic effects in taming inflation. The introduction of the "new Turkish lira" in 2005 signaled the change in monetary policy. In common with the experience of Bulgaria and Romania, when capital controls were lifted and central bank independence from government borrowing requirements established, Turkey's exchange rate has strengthened and foreign reserves increased despite a large continuing current account deficit.

The combination of EU institutional and administration reforms with IMF monetary and fiscal conditionality for its loans seems to be working well in the candidate countries of Bulgaria, Romania, and now Turkey. What about the former Yugolav republics of Croatia and Macedonia?

Croatia and Macedonia

In 2004 Croatia was recommended for candidacy to membership in the EU by the Commission, but formal talks did not begin until October 2005. Shortly thereafter, Macedonia (formally, the Former Yugoslav Republic of Macedonia) was also recommended for candidacy. These were the first positive steps taken by the EU to hold out the promise of eventual membership to these now fractured elements of the one-time republic of Yugoslavia. In light of the lessons learned from the process of enlargement that culminated in 2004, the EU has made some changes in its procedures for accession. On the part of aspiring countries, changes have also been made in light of the experiments made by the various accession countries.

On the EU's side, the extensive investigation into a potential member country's qualifications for meeting the Copenhagen criteria has been broadened further. For example, Macedonia, in making its formal application to the EU in February 2005, turned in no fewer than 14,000 pages to respond to the Commission's inquiries. Moreover, the Commission has increased the number of "chapters" that have to be examined and approved under the heading of administrative capacity from thirty-one to thirty-five, breaking down the financial and agricultural chapters into several parts. Finally, the lag between the formal recommendation of candidacy by the Commission and the start of formal negotiations has been extended. The likelihood is that negotiations will continue for much longer than previously, with the EU granting fewer transition arrangements or temporary derogations.

On the side of the potential candidates, the experience of the successful applicants from the Baltic states and central and eastern Europe makes them more willing to accept both the necessity of enacting and enforcing the legislation required by the EU and to take on the structural reforms required by the IMF. The governments in both Croatia and Macedonia have standing agreements with the IMF under which the central banks maintain tight monetary policies to maintain fixed exchange rates with the euro. The result in both cases is low rates of inflation compared to the rest of the Balkans, but slightly higher than rates in the less advanced countries of the eurozone. This is due to the exceptionally high rates of increase in the prices of services in both countries as wages rise in the tradables sectors – the Balassa–Samuelson effect, as described in the previous chapter. Commitment to a fixed exchange rate with the euro, of course, amplifies the Balassa–Samuelson effect, and the resulting appreciation in the real exchange rate helps account for the relatively sluggish expansion of exports in both countries. Meanwhile, the central government in both countries is committed to relatively balanced budgets, neither one having recourse to loans from its central bank and neither one having established international creditworthiness for its government debt.

The willingness of both countries to take on simultaneously the requirements of the Washington consensus and the Copenhagen criteria is encouraging. Consequently, even Albania, Bosnia-Herzegovina, and Serbia and Montenegro are encouraged to consider applying for membership. If the EU succeeds in this effort to assimilate the Balkan states into the rest of Europe, it will have moved well beyond its original vision of solving the problems left over from World War II that created the division of Europe. Indeed, by incorporating the Balkan states into the European Union, the EU will have made a major step in solving a problem left over from World War I!

NOTES

1. Bent Hansen, *The Political Economy of Poverty, Equity, and Growth: Egypt and Turkey*, New York: Oxford University Press (in conjunction with the World Bank), 1991, p. 358.
2. Ibid., p. 372, note 9.
3. Ibid., p. 394.

Suggestions for further reading

Keeping up with the expansion of the European Union's range of activities in economic policies and the policy responses by the various European countries over time is a daunting challenge. Fortunately, an increased range of resources are available for instructors and students, especially on the World Wide Web. For the European Union, the website http://europa.eu.int/index_en.htm provides a gateway into all the activities of the European Commission, often with full reports and statistics available for downloading. Monthly reports on the eurozone countries as well as research reports on particular monetary and financial issues are available at the website of the European Central Bank, http://www.ecb.int/home/html/index.en.html. For all the European countries, the OECD provides useful overviews on policy issues that compare European policies with those in North America, Japan, South Korea, and Australia and New Zealand: http://www.oecd.org/home/. Especially useful are their studies on agricultural policy and regulatory reform. Libraries with subscriptions to Source OECD provide their patrons with downloadable reports and statistical series, including regular "Country reports" on each member country, as well as the biannual OECD *Economic Outlook*, which covers current policy issues for all the OECD countries, individually and as a group.

A broader, more comparative and global perspective is offered in the IMF's biannual *World Economic Outlook*, also available for viewing on the IMF's website: http://www.imf.org. For more readable discussions of current policy issues with a stronger emphasis on domestic political issues, the Economist Intelligence Unit provides frequent country reports, which are also available for downloading from libraries that subscribe to their online service. Students should be encouraged as well to subscribe to or read regularly the *Economist* magazine and the *Financial Times* newspaper, both of which have worldwide subscription services. Academic journals give frequent coverage to relevant issues, but the *Journal of Common Market Studies* focuses on specific European Union issues from a political science perspective, while the *European Economic Review* is the preferred outlet for more technical work by economists.

In addition to the sources cited in the various chapters, readers desiring deeper background or more detail on particular aspects of the European Union have a wide range of materials available.

Part I: The economics of the European Union

Chapter 1

The EU's website http://europa.eu.int/comm/budget/index_en.htm gives the latest details on the ongoing budget negotiations. In recent years the expenditures and revenues have been broken down by member state, acknowledging the need for individual governments to justify their presence in the EU to their electorate. Daniel Strasser, *The Finances of Europe: The Budgetary and Financial Law of the European Communities*, European Commission, Brussels: 1992, gives the historical background that led to the British rebate in the 1980s and the seven-year perspective. Helen Wallace, William Wallace, and Mark A. Pollack, eds., *Policy-Making in the European Union*, 5th edn., Oxford and New York: Oxford University Press, 2005, go into detail on the way the EU's institutions operate in practice, while the European Commission, *How the European Union Works: A Citizen's Guide to the EU Institutions*, Luxembourg: Office for Official Publications of the European Communities, c.2003, explains how they should work. John Peterson and Michael Shackleton, *The Institutions of the European Union*, 3rd edn., Oxford and New York: Oxford University Press, 2002, explain how they do work.

Desmond Dinan, *Europe Recast: A History of European Union*, Boulder, CO: Lynne Rienner, 2004, describes the political forces that have led to "ever closer union" over time and then the massive enlargement to include central and eastern Europe in 2004. His *Encyclopedia of the European Union*, Boulder, CO: Lynne Rienner, 2000, is a useful reference guide to the increasingly complicated structure of the EU. Maria Green Cowles and Desmond Dinan, *Developments in the European Union 2*, Basingstoke and New York: Palgrave Macmillan, 2004, is a continuation of a series designed to keep teachers and students up to date with political developments.

Chapter 2

Historical treatments vary from Alan Milward's *The European Rescue of the Nation-State*, Berkeley: University of California Press, 1992, and his earlier *The Reconstruction of Western Europe, 1945–1951*, Berkeley: University of California Press, 1984, to John Gillingham's *Coal, Steel, and the Rebirth of Europe, 1945–1955*, Cambridge: Cambridge University Press, 1991. Barry Eichengreen, ed., *Europe's Post-War Recovery*, Cambridge and New York: Cambridge University Press, 1995, puts the European initiatives in a broader, American-led, perspective. Francis H. Heller and John R. Gillingham, eds., *The United States and the Integration of Europe: Legacies of the Postwar Era*, New York: St. Martin's Press, 1996, contrast the European and American motives and initiatives that culminated in the creation, eventually, of the European Union.

Chapter 3

The theoretical basis for customs union analysis dates back to J. E. Meade, *The Theory of Customs Unions*, Amsterdam: North-Holland, 1968. More recent treatments include any international trade textbook, but see in particular Dean A. DeRosa, *Regional Integration Arrangements: Static Economic Theory, Quantitative Findings, and Policy Guidelines*, Washington, DC: World Bank, Development Research Group, Trade, 1998. Empirical analysis originated with Bela Balassa, ed., *European Economic Integration*, Amsterdam: North-Holland and New York: Elsevier, 1975. Updates on trade patterns are provided for the European Union annually by Eurostat, in the publication *Europe in Figures: Eurostat Yearbook* – which can be compared with the *Direction of Trade* issued annually by the IMF. Trade issues are dealt with in the WTO's annual *Trade Policy Review* of the European Union and the major member countries. The US Trade Representative reports annually to Congress its *National Trade Estimate of Foreign Trade Barriers*, which includes substantial sections on the European Union.

In riposte, the European Union now issues regularly its estimates of barriers to foreign trade in the United States. Specific details on the EU's customs unions are updated regularly at http://europa.eu.int/comm/taxation_customs/customs/index_en.htm.

Chapter 4

Again, the Europa website provides the latest information on the Common Agricultural Policy at http://europa.eu.int/comm/agriculture/index_en.htm. For comparison with other countries, the OECD's annual publication *Agricultural Policies in OECD Countries* is useful, as are the reports on the progress of the latest trade negotiations by the WTO. An early study by the IMF, *The Common Agricultural Policy of the European Community*, Occasional Paper no. 62, Washington, DC: International Monetary Fund, 1988, provides useful, brief background. The US Department of Agriculture's Economic Research Service offers regular reports and studies that offer useful background on the effects of the CAP on US agriculture and world trade, available at www.ers.usda.gov.

Chapter 5

A huge amount has been written on the euro, but the best textbook treatment remains that by Paul de Grauwe, *Economics of Monetary Union*, 5th edn., New York: Oxford University Press, 2002, which covers more of the theory using a Keynesian rather than a monetarist approach. See also V. Clausen, *Asymmetric Monetary Transmission in Europe*, Berlin, Heidelberg, and New York: Springer Verlag, 2001; João Loureiro, *Monetary Policy in the European Monetary System: A Critical Appraisal*, Berlin, Heidelberg, and New York: Springer Verlag, 1996; and Iannis A. Mourmouras and Michael G. Arghyrou, *Monetary Policy at the European Periphery*, Berlin, Heidelberg, and New York: Springer Verlag, 2000, for more detailed studies. Earlier studies leading up to the euro include:

Euromoney, September 1996;
European Economy 54, December 1993;
International Monetary Fund, *World Economic Outlook*, Washington, DC: October 1998;
Kindleberger, Charles, *A Financial History of Western Europe*, 2nd edn., New York: Oxford University Press, 1993;
Neal, Larry, and Daniel Barbezat, *The Economics of the European Union and the Economies of Europe*, New York: Oxford University Press, 1998;
Roger, Scott, *The Management of Foreign Exchange Reserves*, Economic Paper no. 38, Basle: Bank for International Settlements, 1993; and
Ungerer, Horst, *The European Monetary System: The Experience, 1979–82*, Washington, DC: International Monetary Fund, 1983.

Chapter 6

The European Central Bank issues monthly and annual reports on monetary and price developments within the eurozone, all downloadable from its website: http:// www.ecb.int/home/

html/index.en.html. The EMU – Monitor issues an independent appraisal of the effects of the ECB's monetary policy regularly, available from the Zentrum für Europäische Integrations-forschung's website: http://www.zei.de/download/zei_emu.

Chapter 7

The Single Market Scoreboard, available annually at the website http://europa. eu.int/comm/internal_market/score/index_en.htm, is useful for tracking the progress of the single market, as well as the new issues that keep arising as the Commission continues to enlarge its competency in the area of competition. The initial study by the Commission was G. Nerb, *The Completion of the Internal Market: A Survey of European Industry's Perception of the Likely Effects*, Brussels: Directorate-General for Economic and Financial Affairs, 1988.

Chapter 8

The progress of the Schengen Agreement can be followed at http://europa.eu.int/scadplus/leg/en/lvb/l33020.htm under the heading of "Summaries of European Legislation," as well as a scoreboard on individual member countries' progress in providing free movement for workers within the European Union. Overall views of immigration patterns and policies can be followed in the annual SOPEMI reports from the OECD, *International Migration Trends*. The OECD's annual report on *Labour Force Statistics* is also valuable for tracking trends in labor force participation rates by age and gender for each OECD country. An overview of the challenges of labor market reforms for the leading OECD countries is Horst Siebert, ed., *Structural Change and Labor Market Flexibility: Experience in Selected OECD Economies*, Tübingen: Mohr, 1997.

Chapter 9

The European Commission issues regular reports on competition policy, available at http://europa.eu.int/comm/competition/index_en.html, and on enterprise and industry at http://europa.eu.int/comm/enterprise/index_en.htm. It is useful to follow up the implementation of the recommendations of the Lamfalussy Report, the Committee of Wise Men, *Final Report of the Committee of Wise Men on the Regulation of European Securities Markets*, Brussels: 2001, on either of the Commission's websites above. The European Central Bank issues Occasional Papers on its website, http://www.ecb.int/pub/scientific/ops/date/html/index.en.html, that deal with Europe's financial markets in general, such as that by Heiko Schmeidel and Andreas Schönenberger, *Integration of Financial Market Infrastructures in the Euro Area*, Occasional Paper no. 33, Frankfurt: 2005. Readers are well advised to check the latest developments on the various securities exchanges – the London Stock Exchange (http://www.londonstockexchange.com/en-gb/), EuroNext (http://www.euronext.com), and the Frankfurt Stock Exchange (http://deutsche-boerse.com) – as well as the financial press in general. In addition to *The Economist* and the *Financial Times*, the magazine *Euromoney* has excellent, focused coverage of Europe's capital markets.

Chapter 10

The Commission publishes regular reports on the results of its regional policy results to date, publishing its second report, *Unity, Solidarity, Diversity for Europe, Its People and Its Territory: Second Report on Economic and Social Cohesion*, in 2001 before issuing its first report in 2002, *First Progress Report on Economic and Social Cohesion*! The website is http://europa.eu.int/comm/regional_policy/index_en.htm. The European Parliament's Committee of the Regions also publishes its regular reports, such as *Territorial Cohesion in Europe*, Luxembourg: 2003. Bernand Funck and Lodovico Pizzati, eds., *European Integration, Regional Policy, and Growth*, Washington, DC: World Bank, 2003, provide an overview of the challenges of the EU's regional policy with respect to both "old" and "new" Europe. See also James A. Caporaso, *The European Union: Dilemmas of Regional Integration*, Boulder, CO: Westview Press, 2000.

The extension of the EU's redistribution policies to the developing world before the breakup of the Soviet Union is covered by Enzo R. Grilli, *The European Community and the Developing Countries*, New York and Cambridge: Cambridge University Press, 1993. Jaime de Melo and Arvind Panagariya, eds., *New Dimensions in Regional Integration*, New York and Cambridge: Cambridge University Press, 1993, provide an overview of regional trade arrangements in imitation of the obvious success of the European Union.

Chapter 11

The number of books on the European Union as the other economic superpower continues to proliferate. A skeptical view of its accomplishments is found in John Gillingham, *European Integration, 1950–2003: Superstate or New Market Economy?*, Cambridge: Cambridge University Press, 2001. A much rosier perspective is Jeremy Rifkin, *The European Dream; How Europe's Vision of the Future is Quietly Eclipsing the American Dream*, New York: Penguin Books, 2004. A quantitative analysis of the growth of the European economies since the end of World War II and its sources is Bart van Ark and Nicholas Crafts, eds., *Quantitative Aspects of Post-War European Economic Growth*, Cambridge: Cambridge University Press, 1996. Excellent country studies for most of the western European economies, as well as western Europe as a whole, are in Nicholas Crafts and Gianni Toniolo, eds., *Economic Growth in Europe since 1945*, Cambridge: Cambridge University Press, 1996. A briefer set of studies that includes the Višegrad four in eastern Europe is Bernard Foley, ed., *European Economies since the Second World War*, New York: St. Martin's Press, 1998. Other recent studies focusing on the challenges of an enlarged European Union and its changing relationship with the United States include:

Calleo, David P., *Rethinking Europe's Future*, Princeton, NJ: Princeton University Press, c.2001;

Cameron, Fraser, ed., *The Future of Europe: Integration and Enlargement*, London and New York: Routledge, 2004;

Kagan, Robert, *Of Paradise and Power: America and Europe in the New World Order*, New York: Alfred A. Knopf (distributed by Random House), 2003;

Lindberg, Tod, ed., *Beyond Paradise and Power: Europe, America, and the Future of a Troubled Partnership*, New York: Routledge, 2005;

Majone, Giandomenico, *Dilemmas of European Integration: The Ambiguities and Pitfalls of Integration by Stealth*, Oxford: Oxford University Press, 2005;

Sapir, André, *An Agenda for a Growing Europe: The Sapir Report*, Oxford and New York: Oxford University Press, 2004; and

Tsoukalis, Loukas, *What Kind of Europe?*, Oxford and New York: Oxford University Press, 2003.

Part II: The economies of Europe

Chapter 12 – Germany

Horst Siebert, *The German Economy: Beyond the Social Market*, Princeton, NJ: Princeton University Press, c.2005, is authoritative. Earlier analyses of the much-studied German economy, both West and East, are:

Abelshauser, Werner, *Wirtschaftsgeschichte der Bundesrepublik Deutschland 1945–1980*, Frankfurt: Suhrkamp, 1983;

Berger, Helga, and Albrecht Ritschl, "Germany and the political economy of the Marshall Plan, 1947–52: a re-revisionist view," in Barry Eichengreen, ed., *Europe's Post-War Recovery*, Cambridge: Cambridge University Press, 1995;

Carlin, Wendy. "West German growth and institutions, 1945–90," in Nicholas Crafts and Gianni Toniolo, eds., *Economic Growth in Europe since 1945*, Cambridge: Cambridge University Press, 1996;

Economist Intelligence Unit, *Country Report: Germany*, London: semi-annual "Main reports," updated monthly;

Giersch, Herbert, Karl-Heinz Paqué, and Holger Schmieding, eds., *The Fading Miracle: Four Decades of Market Economy in Germany*, Cambridge: Cambridge University Press, 1992;

Hardach, Karl, *The Political Economy of Germany in the Twentieth Century*, Berkeley: University of California Press, 1980;

Kramer, Alan, *The West German Economy, 1945–1955*, German Studies Series, New York: Berg, 1991;

Lipschitz, Leslie, and Donogh McDonald, eds., *German Unification: Economic Issues*, Occasional Paper no. 75, International Monetary Fund, Washington, DC: 1990;

Ritschl, Albrecht O., "An exercise in futility: East German economic growth and decline, 1945–89," in Nicholas Crafts and Gianni Toniolo, eds., *Economic Growth in Europe since 1945*. Cambridge: Cambridge University Press, 1996; and

Wallich, Henry C., *The Mainsprings of the German Revival*, New Haven, CT: Yale University Press, 1955.

Chapter 13 – France

The latest analysis of France's difficulties in coming to grips with the enlargement of the EU and globalization in general is Timothy B. Smith, *France in Crisis: Welfare, Inequality, and Globalization since 1980*, Cambridge and New York: Cambridge University Press, 2004. Other useful references are:

Adams, William J., *Restructuring the French Economy*, Washington, DC: Brookings Institution, 1989;

Carré, Jean-Jacques, Paul Dubois, and Edmond Malinvaud, *La Croissance française: un essai d'analyse économique causale de l'après-guerre*, Paris: Le Seuil, 1972;

Divisia, François, René Pupin, and René Roy, *A la recherche du franc perdu*, Paris: Société d'Editions Hommes et Mondes, 1995;

Economist Intelligence Unit, *Country Report: France*, London: "Main reports" semi-annually, updates monthly;

James, Harold, *International Monetary Cooperation since Bretton Woods*, New York: Oxford University Press in conjunction with the International Monetary Fund, 1996;

Machin, Howard, and Vincent Wright, eds., *Economic Policy and Policy-Making under the Mitterrand Presidency, 1981–84*, New York: St. Martin's Press, 1985;

Resnick, Stephen A., and Edwin M. Truman, "An empirical examination of bilateral trade flows in western Europe," in Bela Balassa, ed., *European Economic Integration*, Amsterdam: North-Holland, 1975;

Saint-Paul, Gilles, "Economic reconstruction in France: 1945–1958," in R. Dornbusch, R. Layard, and W. Nolling, eds., *Post-War Economic Reconstruction: Possible Lessons for Eastern Europe*, Cambridge, MA: MIT Press, 1993;

Saint-Paul, Gilles, "France: real and monetary aspects of French exchange rate policy under the Fourth Republic," in Barry Eichengreen, ed., *Europe's Post-War Recovery*, Cambridge: Cambridge University Press, 1995;

Sautter, Christian, "France," in Andrea Boltho, ed., *The European Economy: Growth and Crisis*, Oxford: Oxford University Press, 1982; and

Sicsic, Pierre, and Charles Wyplosz, "France, 1945–92," in Nicholas Crafts and Gianni Toniolo, eds., *Economic Growth in Europe since 1945*, Cambridge: Cambridge University Press, 1996.

Chapter 14 – United Kingdom

Despite the relatively good performance of the British economy compared to the continental European countries, memories of the nineteenth-century pre-eminence seem to pervade analyses to the present. See, for example, Paul Johnson and Roderick Floud, eds., *The Cambridge Economic History of Modern Britain*, vol. III, *Structural Change and Growth, 1939–2000*, Cambridge and New York: Cambridge University Press, 2004, and Peter Clarke and Clive Trebilcock, eds., *Understanding Decline: Perceptions and Realities of British Economic Performance*, Cambridge and New York: Cambridge University Press, 1997. Other works of interest include:

Alford, B. W. E., *British Economic Performance, 1945–1975*, Cambridge: Cambridge University Press, 1993;

Bean, Charles, and Nicholas Crafts, "British economic growth since 1945: relative economic decline . . . and renaissance?," in Nicholas Crafts and Gianni Toniolo, eds., *Economic Growth in Europe since 1945*, Cambridge: Cambridge University Press, 1996;

Britton, A. J. C., *Macroeconomic Policy in Britain 1974–1987*, Cambridge: Cambridge University Press, 1991;

Broadberry, Steve, "Technological leadership and productivity leadership in manufacturing since the industrial revolution: implications for the convergence thesis," *Economic Journal* 104, 1994, pp. 291–302;

Buxton, Tony, Paul Chapman, and Paul Temple, eds., *Britain's Economic Performance*, London: Routledge, 1994;

Crafts, Nicholas, "'You've never had it so good?': British economy policy and performance, 1945–60," in Barry Eichengreen, ed., *Europe's Post-War Recovery*, Cambridge: Cambridge University Press, 1995;

Crafts, Nicholas, and Nicholas Woodward, eds., *The British Economy since 1945*, Oxford: Clarendon Press, 1991;

Economist Intelligence Unit, *Country Report: Britain*, London: "Main reports" annually, monthly updates;

Eltis, Walter, *Britain, Europe and EMU*, New York: St. Martin's Press, 2000;

Floud, Roderick, and Donald N. McCloskey, eds., *The Economic History of Britain since 1700*, vol. III, *1939–1992*, 2nd edn., Cambridge: Cambridge University Press, 1994;

Northcott, Jim, *The Future of Britain and Europe*, London: Policy Studies Institute, 1995; and

Pressnell, Leslie, *External Economic Policy since the War*, vol. I, *The Post-War Financial Settlement*, London: HMSO, 1987.

Chapter 15 – Italy

The problems of corruption and regionalism continue to plague Italian economic policy-makers, as recounted in Carlo Tullio-Altan, *La nostra Italia: clientelismo, trasformismo e ribellismo dall'unità al 2000*, Milan: EGEA (Università Bocconi), 2000, for those who read Italian. English-language sources include:

Böhm, Bernhard, and Lionello F. Punzo, eds., *Economic Performance: A Look at Austria and Italy*, Heidelberg: Physica-Verlag, 1994;

Donata, Pierpaolo, "Social welfare and social service in Italy since 1950," in Roger Girod, Patrick de Laubier, and Alan Gladstone, eds., *Social Policy in Western Europe and the USA, 1950–1980: An Assessment*, New York: St. Martin's Press, 1985;

Economist Intelligence Unit, *Country Report: Italy*, London: "Main reports" annually, monthly updates;

Hildebrand, George, *Growth and Structure in the Economy of Modern Italy*, Cambridge, MA: Harvard University Press, 1965;

Kostoris, Fiorella Padoa Schioppa, *Italy, the Sheltered Economy*, Oxford: Clarendon Press, 1993;

Locke, Richard M., *Remaking the Italian Economy*, Ithaca, NY: Cornell University Press, 1995;

Podbielski, Gisele, *Italy: Development and Crisis in the Post-War Economy*, London: Oxford University Press, 1974;

Rey, Guido, "Italy," in Andrea Boltho, ed., *The European Economy, Growth and Crisis*, Oxford: Oxford University Press, 1982;

Rossi, Nicola, and Gianni Toniolo, "Italy," in Nicholas Crafts and Gianni Toniolo, eds., *Economic Growth in Europe since 1945*, Cambridge: Cambridge University Press, 1996; and

Zamagni, Vera, *The Economic History of Italy, 1860–1990: Recovery after Decline*, Oxford: Clarendon Press, 1993.

Chapter 16 – Small open countries

Most treatments of these countries place them in the larger European or OECD context, but specialized treatments include:

Böhm, Bernhard, and Lionello F. Punzo, eds., *Economic Performance: A Look at Austria and Italy*, Heidelberg: Physica-Verlag, 1994;

Cassiers, Isabelle, "'Belgian miracle' to slow growth: the impact of the Marshall Plan and the European Payments Union," in Barry Eichengreen, ed., *Europe's Post-War Recovery*, Cambridge: Cambridge University Press, 1995;

Cassiers, Isabelle, Philippe De Villé, and Peter M. Solar, "Economic growth in postwar Belgium," in Nicholas Crafts and Gianni Toniolo, eds., *Economic Growth in Europe since 1945*, Cambridge: Cambridge University Press, 1996;

de Vries, Johan, *The Netherlands Economy in the Twentieth Century*, Assen: Van Gorcum and Co., 1978;

Economist Intelligence Unit, *Country Reports*, London: "Main reports" annually, updates quarterly;

Lambelet, Jean-Christian, *L'Economie suisse*, Paris: Economica, 1993;

Mommen, André, *The Belgian Economy in the Twentieth Century*, London: Routledge, 1994;

Organisation for Economic Co-operation and Development, *Economic Survey of the Netherlands, 2005*, Paris: 2005;

Organisation for Economic Co-operation and Development, *Regulatory Reform in the Netherlands*, Paris: 1999;

Schwock, René, *Switzerland and the European Common Market*, New York: Praeger, 1991;

Tschudi, Hans-Peter, "Swiss social policy since 1950," in Roger Girod, Patrick de Laubier, and Alan Gladstone, eds., *Social Policy in Western Europe and the USA, 1950–1980: An Assessment*, New York: St. Martin's Press, 1985;

Union Bank of Switzerland. *The Swiss Economy, 1946–1986. Data, Facts, Analyses.* Zurich: Union Bank of Switzerland, 1987; and

van Ark, Bart, Jakob de Haan, and Herman J. de Jong, "Characteristics of economic growth in the Netherlands during the postwar period," in Nicholas Crafts and Gianni Toniolo, eds., *Economic Growth in Europe since 1945*, Cambridge: Cambridge University Press, 1996.

Chapter 17 – Scandinavia

An interesting defense of Sweden's welfare state and the way it is financed is given by Peter Lindert, *Growing Public: Social Spending and Economic Growth since the Eighteenth Century*, Cambridge and New York: Cambridge University Press, 2004. Other useful background sources are:

Denmark

Johansen, Hans Christian, *The Danish Economy in the Twentieth Century*, New York: St. Martin's Press, c.1987;

Organisation for Economic Co-operation and Development, *Regulatory Reform in Denmark*, Paris: 2000;

Finland

Bordes-Marcilloux, Christian, *Three Assessments of Finland's Economic Crisis and Economic Policy*, Helsinki: Bank of Finland, 1993; and

Norway

Moses, Jonathon Wayne, *Open States in the Global Economy: The Political Economy of Small-State Macroeconomic Management*, New York: St. Martin's Press, 2000;

Sweden

Lindbeck, Assar, *Turning Sweden Around*, Cambridge, MA: MIT Press, 1994;

Magnusson, Lars, *An Economic History of Sweden*, London and New York: Routledge, 2000;

Miles, Lee, *Fusing with Europe? Sweden in the European Union*, Aldershot and Burlington, VT: Ashgate, c.2005;

Whyman, Philip, *Sweden and the "Third Way": A Macroeconomic Evaluation*, Aldershot and Burlington, VT: Ashgate, 2003;

Chapter 18 – Latecomers

A nice overview of the experiences of these four economies, which came into the European Union as relatively autarkic and backward economies, and the lessons their experiences hold for the countries of central and eastern Europe is found in the special issue (no. 5) of the *Quarterly Review of Economics and Finance*, volume 43, edited by Werner Baer and Larry Neal.

Ireland

Gottheil, Fred, "Ireland: what's Celtic about the Celtic Tiger?," *Quarterly Review of Economics and Finance* 43 (5), 2003, pp. 720–37.

Kennedy, Kieran A., and Brendan R. Dowling, *Economic Growth in Ireland: The Experience since 1947*, New York: Barnes and Noble, 1975.

Kennedy, Kieran A., Thomas Giblin, and Deirdre McHugh, *The Economic Development of Ireland in the Twentieth Century*, London: Routledge, 1988.

Organisation for Economic Co-operation and Development, *Regulatory Reform in Ireland*, Paris: 2001.

Ó Gráda, Cormac, and Kevin O'Rourke, "Irish economic growth, 1945–88," in Nicholas Crafts and Gianni Toniolo, eds., *Economic Growth in Europe since 1945*, Cambridge: Cambridge University Press, 1996.

O'Hagan, John. *The Economy of Ireland: Policy and Performance of a Small European Country*, New York: St. Martin's Press, 1995.

Greece

Freris, A. F., *The Greek Economy in the Twentieth Century*, London: Croom Helm, 1986.

Jouganatos, George A., *The Development of the Greek Economy, 1950–1991: An Historical, Empirical, and Econometric Analysis*, Westport, CT: Greenwood Press, 1992.

Oltheten, Elizabeth, George Pinteris, and Theodore Sougiannis, "Greece in the European Union: policy lessons from two decades of membership," *Quarterly Review of Economics and Finance* 43 (5), 2003, pp. 774–806.

Pagoulatos, George, *Greece's New Political Economy: State, Finance, and Growth from Postwar to EMU*, New York: Palgrave Macmillan, 2003.

Pirounakis, Nicholas G., *The Greek Economy: Past, Present and Future*, New York: St. Martin's Press, 1997.

Portugal

Baer, Werner, and Antonio Nogueira Leite, "The economy of Portugal within the European Union: 1990–2002," *Quarterly Review of Economics and Finance* 43 (5), 2003, pp. 738–54.

Baklanoff, Eric N., *The Economic Transformation of Spain and Portugal*, New York: Praeger, 1978.

Corkill, David, *The Portuguese Economy since 1974*, Edinburgh: Edinburgh University Press, c.1993.

das Neves, Cesar, and João Loureiro, "Portuguese postwar growth: a global approach," in Nicholas Crafts and Gianni Toniolo, eds., *Economic Growth in Europe since 1945*, Cambridge: Cambridge University Press, 1996.

Lains, Pedro, "Catching up to the European core: Portuguese economic growth, 1910–1990," *Explorations in Economic History* 40 (4), 2003, pp. 369–86.

Spain

Guirao, Fernando, *Spain and the Reconstruction of Europe, 1945–57: Challenge and Response*, New York: St. Martin's Press, 1998.

Harrison, Joseph, *The Spanish Economy from the Civil War to the European Community*, Cambridge: Cambridge University Press, 1995.

Lieberman, Sima, *Growth and Crisis in the Spanish Economy 1940–9*, London: Routledge, 1995.

Martín, Carmela, *The Spanish Economy in the New Europe*, trans. Philip Hill and Sarah Nicholson, New York: St. Martin's Press, 2000.

Neal, Larry, and Maria Concepcion Garcia-Iglesias, "The economy of Spain without and within the European Union: 1945–2002," *Quarterly Review of Economics and Finance* 43 (5), 2003, pp. 755–73.

Organisation for Economic Co-operation and Development, *Regulatory Reform in Spain*, Paris: 2000.

Prados de la Escosura, Leandro, and Jorgé C. Sans, "Growth and macroeconomic performance in Spain, 1939–93," in Nicholas Crafts and Gianni Toniolo, eds., *Economic Growth in Europe since 1945*, Cambridge: Cambridge University Press, 1996.

Salmon, Keith G., *The Modern Spanish Economy. Transformation and Integration into Europe*, London: Pinter, 1991.

Tamanes, Ramon, *The Spanish Economy: An Introduction*, New York: St. Martin's Press, 1986.

Tortella, Gabriel, *The Development of Modern Spain: An Economic History of the Nineteenth and Twentieth Centuries*, Cambridge, MA: Harvard University Press, 2000.

Chapter 19 – Newcomers

There are several journals now devoted to the issues of the transition economies, such as *Economics of Transition*, published by Blackwell and available online at www.blackwell-publishers.co.uk, and *Problems of Economic Transition*, published by M. E. Sharpe and available at www.mesharpe.com, as well as the regular reports by the European Bank of Reconstruction and Development with the title *Transition Report*, published annually but with regular *Transition Report Updates*, and analyses in the *EBRD Economic Review*. Background readings include Occasional Papers by IMF teams on individual countries and policy areas, as well as:

Blanchard, Olivier Jean, *The Economics of Post-Communist Transition*, Oxford: Clarendon Press, 1997;

Blanchard, Olivier Jean, Kenneth A. Froot, and Jeffrey D. Sachs, *The Transition in Eastern Europe*, vol. I, *Country Studies*, and vol. II, *Restructuring*, Chicago: University of Chicago Press (in conjunction with the National Bureau of Economic Research), 1994;

Cochrane, Nancy, and Ralph Seeley, *EU Enlargement: Implications for New Member Countries, the United States, and World Trade*, Outlook Report no.WRS040501, Washington, DC: Economic Research Service, US Department of Agriculture, 2004, available online at www.ers.usda.gov;

Lavigne, Marie, *The Economics of Transition from Socialist Economy to Market Economy*, New York: St. Martin's Press, 1995;

Organisation for Economic Co-operation and Development, *Migration Policies and EU Enlargement: The Case of Central and Eastern Europe*, Paris: 2001; and

Smith, Alan, *The Return to Europe: The Reintegration of Eastern Europe into the European Economy*, Basingstoke: Macmillan, 2000.

Chapter 20 – Future members

At http://europa.eu.int/comm/enlargement/index_en.htm, the European Commission maintains regular, in-depth reports on the current accession countries, the candidate countries, and even potential candidate countries. More background on the sources of economic problems and policy developments for the accession and candidate countries can be found in the sources mentioned for chapter 19, as well as:

Hansen, Bent, *The Political Economy of Poverty, Equity, and Growth: Egypt and Turkey*, New York: Oxford University Press (in conjunction with the World Bank), 1991;

Oni, Ziya, and James Riedel, *Economic Crises and Long-Term Growth in Turkey*, Comparative Macroeconomic Study, Washington, DC: World Bank, 1993;

Organisation for Economic Co-operation and Development, *Turkey: Crucial Support for Economic Recovery*, Review of Regulatory Reform, Paris: 2002; and

Turnock, David, *The Romanian Economy in the Twentieth Century*, London: Croom Helm, 1986.

Index